COMMON CORE MATHEMATICS

A Story of Ratios

Grade 8, Module 4: Linear Equations

consider the source

JB JOSSEY-BASS™

A Wiley Brand

Cover design by Chris Clary

Published by Jossey-Bass
A Wiley Brand
One Montgomery Street, Suite 1200, San Francisco, CA 94104-4594—www.josseybass.com

ISBN: 978-1-118-81104-7

Printed in the United States of America
FIRST EDITION
PB Printing   10 9 8 7 6 5 4 3 2 1

WELCOME

Dear Teacher,

Thank you for your interest in Common Core's curriculum in mathematics. Common Core is a non-profit organization based in Washington, DC dedicated to helping K-12 public schoolteachers use the power of high-quality content to improve instruction.[1] We are led by a board of master teachers, scholars, and current and former school, district, and state education leaders. Common Core has responded to the Common Core State Standards' (CCSS) call for "content-rich curriculum"[2] by creating new, CCSS-based curriculum materials in mathematics, English Language Arts, history, and (soon) the arts. All of our materials are written by teachers who are among the nation's foremost experts on the new standards.

In 2012 Common Core won three contracts from the New York State Education Department to create a PreKindergarten–12th grade mathematics curriculum for the teachers of that state, and to conduct associated professional development. The book you hold contains a portion of that work. In order to respond to demand in New York and elsewhere, modules of the curriculum will continue to be published, on a rolling basis, as they are completed. This curriculum is based on New York's version of the CCSS (the CCLS, or Common Core Learning Standards). Common Core will be releasing an enhanced version of the curriculum this summer on our website, commoncore.org. That version also will be published by Jossey-Bass, a Wiley brand.

Common Core's curriculum materials are not merely aligned to the new standards, they take the CCSS as their very foundation. Our work in math takes its shape from the expectations embedded in the new standards—including the instructional shifts and mathematical progressions, and the new expectations for student fluency, deep conceptual understanding, and application to real-life context. Similarly, our ELA and history curricula are deeply informed by the CCSS's new emphasis on close reading, increased use of informational text, and evidence-based writing.

Our curriculum is distinguished not only by its adherence to the CCSS. The math curriculum is based on a theory of teaching math that is proven to work. That theory posits that mathematical knowledge is most coherently and

---

1. Despite the coincidence of name, Common Core and the Common Core State Standards are not affiliated. Common Core was established in 2007, prior to the start of the Common Core State Standards Initiative, which was led by the National Governors Association and the Council for Chief State School Officers.

2. *Common Core State Standards for English Language Arts & Literacy in History/Social Studies, Science, and Technical Subjects* (Washington, DC: Common Core State Standards Initiative), 6.

effectively conveyed when it is taught in a sequence that follows the "story" of mathematics itself. This is why we call the elementary portion of this curriculum "A Story of Units," to be followed by "A Story of Ratios" in middle school, and "A Story of Functions" in high school. Mathematical concepts flow logically, from one to the next, in this curriculum. The sequencing has been joined with methods of instruction that have been proven to work, in this nation and abroad. These methods drive student understanding beyond process, to deep mastery of mathematical concepts. The goal of the curriculum is to produce students who are not merely literate, but fluent, in mathematics.

It is important to note that, as extensive as these curriculum materials are, they are not meant to be prescriptive. Rather, they are intended to provide a basis for teachers to hone their own craft through study, collaboration, training, and the application of their own expertise as professionals. At Common Core we believe deeply in the ability of teachers and in their central and irreplaceable role in shaping the classroom experience. We strive only to support and facilitate their important work.

The teachers and scholars who wrote these materials are listed beginning on the next page. Their deep knowledge of mathematics, of the CCSS, and of what works in classrooms defined this work in every respect. I would like to thank Louisiana State University professor of mathematics Scott Baldridge for the intellectual leadership he provides to this project. Teacher and trainer Jill Diniz, who is the lead writer for grades 6–12, has brought extraordinary intelligence and judgment to this work. Jill's ability to thrive in situations in which others would be lucky just to persevere, is uncommon.

Finally, this work owes a debt to project director Nell McAnelly that is so deep I'm confident it never can be repaid. Nell, who leads LSU's Gordon A. Cain Center for STEM Literacy, oversees all aspects of our work for NYSED. She has spent days, nights, weekends, and many cancelled vacations toiling in her efforts to make it possible for this talented group of teacher-writers to produce their best work against impossible deadlines. I'm confident that in the years to come Scott, Robin, and Nell will be among those who will deserve to be credited with putting math instruction in our nation back on track.

Thank you for taking an interest in our work. Please join us at www.commoncore.org.

Lynne Munson
President and Executive Director
Common Core
Washington, DC
October 25, 2013

Common Core's 6-12 Math Staff

Scott Baldridge, Lead Mathematician and Writer
Robin Ramos, Lead Writer, PreKindergarten–5
Ben McCarty, Mathematician

Nell McAnelly, Project Director
Tiah Alphonso, Associate Director
Jennifer Loftin, Associate Director
Catriona Anderson, Curriculum Manager, PreKindergarten–5
Jill Diniz, Lead Writer, 9-11 and Curriculum Manager

Sixth Grade

Erika Silva, Lead
Debby Grawn
Glenn Gebhard
Krysta Gibbs

Sixth and Seventh Grade

Anne Netter, Lead
Beau Bailey
Saki Milton
Hester Sutton
David Wright
Korinna Sanchez

Seventh Grade

Julie Wortmann, Lead
Joanne Choi
Lori Fanning
Bonnie Hart

Eighth Grade

Stefanie Hassan, Lead
Winnie Gilbert
Sunil Koswatta, Mathematician

Ninth Grade

Miki Alkire
Chris Bejar
Carlos Carrera
Melvin Damaolao
Joe Ferrantelli
Jenny Kim
Athena Leonardo

Rob Michelin
Noam Pillischer
Alex Sczesnak

Tenth Grade

Pia Mohsen, Lead
Bonnie Bergstresser
Ellen Fort
Terrie Poehl

Ninth, Tenth, and Eleventh Grade

Kevin Bluount
Wendy DenBesten
Abe Frankel
Thomas Gaffey
Kay Gleenblatt
Sheri Goings
Pam Goodner
Selena Oswalt
William Rorison
Chris Murcko
Surinder Sandhu
Pam Walker
Darrick Wood

Statistics

Henry Kranendonk, Lead
Michael Allwood
Gail Burrill
Beth Chance
Brian Kotz
Kathy Kritz
Patrick Hopsfensperger
Jerry Moren
Shannon Vinson

Document Management Team

Kristen Zimmerman

Advisors

Richard Askey
Roger Howe
James Madden
Roxy Peck
James Tanton

Table of Contents[1]

Linear Equations

---

[1] Each lesson is ONE day, and ONE day is considered a 45-minute period.

Grade 8 • Module 4

Linear Equations

OVERVIEW

In Module 4, students extend what they already know about unit rates and proportional relationships (**6.RP.A.2**, **7.RP.A.2**) to linear equations and their graphs. Students understand the connections between proportional relationships, lines, and linear equations in this module (**8.EE.B.5**, **8.EE.B.6**). Also in this module, students learn to apply the skills they acquired in Grades 6 and 7, with respect to symbolic notation and properties of equality (**6.EE.A.2**, **7.EE.A.1**, **7.EE.B.4**) to transcribe and solve equations in one variable and then in two variables.

In Topic A, students begin by transcribing written statements using symbolic notation. Then, students write linear and non-linear expressions leading to linear equations, which are solved using properties of equality (**8.EE.C.7b**). Students learn that not every linear equation has a solution. In doing so, students learn how to transform given equations into simpler forms until an equivalent equation results in a unique solution, no solution, or infinitely many solutions (**8.EE.C.7a**). Throughout Topic A students must write and solve linear equations in real-world and mathematical situations.

In Topic B, students work with constant speed, a concept learned in Grade 6 (**6.RP.A.3**), but this time with proportional relationships related to average speed and constant speed. These relationships are expressed as linear equations in two variables. Students find solutions to linear equations in two variables, organize them in a table, and plot the solutions on a coordinate plane (**8.EE.C.8a**). It is in Topic B that students begin to investigate the shape of a graph of a linear equation. Students predict that the graph of a linear equation is a line and select points on and off the line to verify their claim. Also in this topic is the standard form of a linear equation, $ax + by = c$, and when $a, b \neq 0$, a non-vertical line is produced. Further, when a or $b = 0$, then a vertical or horizontal line is produced.

In Topic C, students know that the slope of a line describes the rate of change of a line. Students first encounter slope by interpreting the unit rate of a graph (**8.EE.B.5**). In general, students learn that slope can be determined using any two distinct points on a line by relying on their understanding of properties of similar triangles from Module 3 (**8.EE.B.6**). Students verify this fact by checking the slope using several pairs of points and comparing their answers. In this topic, students derive $y = mx$ and $y = mx + b$ for linear equations by examining similar triangles. Students generate graphs of linear equations in two variables first by completing a table of solutions, then using information about slope and y-intercept. Once students are sure that every linear equation graphs as a line and that every line is the graph of a linear equation, students graph equations using information about x- and y-intercepts. Next, students learn some basic facts about lines and equations, such as why two lines with the same slope and a common point are the same line, how to write equations of lines given slope and a point, and how to write an equation given two points. With the concepts of slope and lines firmly in place, students compare two different proportional relationships

Module 4:	Linear Equations	
Date:	11/7/13	

3

represented by graphs, tables, equations, or descriptions. Finally, students learn that multiple forms of an equation can define the same line.

Simultaneous equations and their solutions are the focus of Topic D. Students begin by comparing the constant speed of two individuals to determine which has greater speed (**8.EE.C.8c**). Students graph simultaneous linear equations to find the point of intersection and then verify that the point of intersection is in fact a solution to each equation in the system (**8.EE.C.8a**). To motivate the need to solve systems algebraically, students graph systems of linear equations whose solutions do not have integer coordinates. Students use an estimation of the solution from the graph to verify their algebraic solution is correct. Students learn to solve systems of linear equations by substitution and elimination (**8.EE.C.8b**). Students understand that a system can have a unique solution, no solution, or infinitely many solutions, as they did with linear equations in one variable. Finally, students apply their knowledge of systems to solve problems in real-world contexts, including converting temperatures from Celsius to Fahrenheit.

Optional Topic E is an application of systems of linear equations (**8.EE.C.8b**). Specifically, a system that generates Pythagorean triples. First, students learn that a Pythagorean triple can be obtained by multiplying any known triple by a positive integer (**8.G.B.7**). Then, students are shown the Babylonian method for finding a triple that requires the understanding and use of a system of linear equations.

Focus Standards

Understand the connections between proportional relationships, lines, and linear equations.

8.EE.B.5   Graph proportional relationships, interpreting the unit rate as the slope of the graph. Compare two different proportional relationships represented in different ways. *For example, compare a distance-time graph to a distance-time equation to determine which of two moving objects has greater speed.*

8.EE.B.6   Use similar triangles to explain why the slope m is the same between any two distinct points on a non-vertical line in the coordinate plane; derive the equation $y = mx$ for a line through the origin and the equation $y = mx + b$ for a line intercepting the vertical axis at b.

Analyze and solve linear equations and pairs of simultaneous linear equations.

8.EE.C.7   Solve linear equations in one variable.

      a.   Give examples of linear equations in one variable with one solution, infinitely many solutions, or no solutions. Show which of these possibilities is the case by successively transforming the given equation into simpler forms, until an equivalent equation of the form $x = a$, $a = a$, or $a = b$ results (where a and b are different numbers).

      b.   Solve linear equations with rational number coefficients, including equations whose solutions require expanding expressions using the distributive property and collecting like terms.

Module 4:	Linear Equations
Date:	11/7/13

4

8.EE.C.8 Analyze and solve pairs of simultaneous linear equations.

    a. Understand that solutions to a system of two linear equations in two variables correspond to points of intersection of their graphs, because points of intersection satisfy both equations simultaneously.

    b. Solve systems of two linear equations in two variables algebraically, and estimate solutions by graphing the equations. Solve simple cases by inspection. *For example, 3x + 2y = 5 and 3x + 2y = 6 have no solution because 3x + 2y cannot simultaneously be 5 and 6.*

    c. Solve real-world and mathematical problems leading to two linear equations in two variables. *For example, given coordinates for two pairs of points, determine whether the line through the first pair of points intersects the line through the second pair.*

Foundational Standards

Understand ratio concepts and use ratio reasoning to solve problems.

6.RP.A.2 Understand the concept of a unit rate a/b associated with a ratio a:b with b ≠ 0, and use rate language in the context of a ratio relationship. *For example, "This recipe has a ratio of 3 cups of flour to 4 cups of sugar, so there is 3/4 cup of flour for each cup of sugar." "We paid $75 for 15 hamburgers, which is a rate of $5 per hamburger."*[2]

6.RP.A.3 Use ratio and rate reasoning to solve real-world and mathematical problems, e.g., by reasoning about tables of equivalent ratios, tape diagrams, double number line diagrams, or equations.

    a. Make tables of equivalent ratios relating quantities with whole-number measurements, find missing values in the tables, and plot the pairs of values on the coordinate plane. Use tables to compare ratios.

    b. Solve unit rate problems including those involving unit pricing and constant speed. *For example, if it took 7 hours to mow 4 lawns, then at that rate, how many lawns could be mowed in 35 hours? At what rate were lawns being mowed?*

Apply and extend previous understandings of arithmetic to algebraic expressions.

6.EE.A.2 Write, read, and evaluate expressions in which letters stand for numbers.

    a. Write expressions that record operations with numbers and letters standing for numbers. *For example, express the calculation "Subtract y from 5" as $5 - y$.*

    b. Identify parts of an expression using mathematical terms (sum, term, product, factor, quotient, coefficient); view one or more parts of an expression as a single entity. *For example, describe the expression $2(8 + 7)$ as a product of two factors; view $(8 + 7)$ as both a single entity and a sum of two terms.*

---

[2] Expectations for unit rates in this grade are limited to non-complex fractions.

c.   Evaluate expression at specific values of their variables. Include expressions that arise from formulas used in real-world problems. Perform arithmetic operations, including those involving whole-number exponents, in the conventional order when there are no parentheses to specify a particular order (Order of Operations). *For example, use the formulas $V = s^3$ and $A = 6s^2$ to find the volume and surface area of a cube with side length $s = \frac{1}{2}$.*

Analyze proportional relationships and use them to solve real-world and mathematical problems.

7.RP.A.2   Recognize and represent proportional relationships between quantities.

a.   Decide whether two quantities are in a proportional relationship, e.g., by testing for equivalent ratios in a table or graphing on a coordinate plane and observing whether the graph is a straight line through the origin.

b.   Identify the constant of proportionality (unit rate) in tables, graphs, equations, diagrams, and verbal descriptions of proportional relationships.

c.   Represent proportional relationships by equations. *For example, if total cost t is proportional to the number n of items purchased at a constant price p, the relationship between the total cost and the number of items can be expressed as $t = pn$.*

d.   Explain what a point (x, y) on the graph of a proportional relationship means in terms of the situation, with special attention to the points $(0, 0)$ and $(1, r)$ where r is the unit rate.

Use properties of operations to generate equivalent expressions.

7.EE.A.1   Apply properties of operations as strategies to add, subtract, factor and expand linear expressions with rational coefficients.

Solve real-life and mathematical problems using numerical and algebraic expressions and equations.

7.EE.B.4   Use variables to represent quantities in a real-world or mathematical problem, and construct simple equations and inequalities to solve problems by reasoning about the quantities.

a.   Solve word problems leading to equations of the form $px + q = r$ and $p(x + q) = r$, where p, q and r are specific rational numbers. Solve equations of these forms fluently. Compare an algebraic solution to an arithmetic solution, identifying the sequence of the operations used in each approach. *For example, the perimeter of a rectangle is 54 cm. Its length is 6 cm. What is its width?*

Focus Standards for Mathematical Practice

MP.1   **Make sense of problems and persevere in solving them.** Students analyze given constraints to make conjectures about the form and meaning of a solution to a given situation in one-variable and two-variable linear equations, as well as in simultaneous linear equations. Students are systematically guided to understand the meaning of a linear equation in one variable, the natural occurrence of linear equations in two variables with respect to proportional relationships, and the natural emergence of a system of two linear equations when looking at related, continuous proportional relationships.

MP.2   **Reason abstractly and quantitatively.** Students decontextualize and contextualize throughout the module as they represent situations symbolically and make sense of solutions within a context. Students use facts learned about rational numbers in previous grade levels to solve linear equations and systems of linear equations.

MP.3   **Construct viable arguments and critique the reasoning of others.** Students use assumptions, definitions, and previously established facts throughout the module as they solve linear equations. Students make conjectures about the graph of a linear equation being a line, then proceed to prove this claim. While solving linear equations, they learn that they must first assume that a solution exists, then proceed to solve the equation using properties of equality based on the assumption. Once a solution is found, students justify that it is in fact a solution to the given equation, thereby verifying their initial assumption. This process is repeated for systems of linear equations.

MP.4   **Model with mathematics.** Throughout the module, students represent real-world situations symbolically. Students identify important quantities from a context and represent their relationship in the form of an equation, table, and graph. Students analyze the various representations and draw conclusions and/or make predictions. Once a solution or prediction has been made, students reflect on whether the solution makes sense in the context presented. One example of this is when students determine how many buses are needed for a field trip. Students must interpret their fractional solution and make sense of it as it applies to the real world.

MP.7   **Look for and make use of structure.** Students use the structure of an equation to make sense of the information in the equation. For example, students write equations that represent the constant rate of motion for a person walking. In doing so, they interpret an equation like $y = \frac{3}{5}x$ as the total distance a person walks, y, in x amount of time at a rate of $\frac{3}{5}$. Students look for patterns or structure in tables and show that a rate is constant.

Terminology

New or Recently Introduced Terms

- **Slope** (Slope is a number that describes the "steepness" or "slant" of a line. It is the constant rate of change. Example: The slope, m, of the graph of line l below is $m = \frac{3}{7}$.)

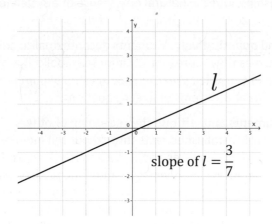

slope of $l = \dfrac{3}{7}$

- **System of Linear Equations** (A system of linear equations, also referred to as simultaneous linear equations, is the set of at least two linear equations. Example: $\begin{cases} x + y = 15 \\ 3x - 7y = -2 \end{cases}$ is a system of linear equations.)

- **Solution to a system of linear equations** (If an equation has two variables, then a solution is a pair of numbers from the domain of the variables that, when each number from the pair is substituted into all instances of its corresponding variable, makes the equation a true number sentence. Example: The solution to the system of linear equations $\begin{cases} x + y = 15 \\ 3x - 7y = -2 \end{cases}$ is the ordered pair $\left(\frac{103}{10}, \frac{47}{10}\right)$ because the ordered pair is a solution to each linear equation of the system and it is the point on the plane where the graphs of the two equations intersect.)

Familiar Terms and Symbols[3]

- Linear Expression
- Equation
- Unit rate
- Term

---

[3] These are terms and symbols students have seen previously.

Module 4:	Linear Equations
Date:	11/7/13

- Coefficient
- Like terms
- Variable
- Solution

Suggested Tools and Representations

- Scientific calculator
- Online graphing calculator (for example: https://www.desmos.com/calculator)
- Graph paper
- Straight-edge

Assessment Summary

Assessment Type	Administered	Format	Standards Addressed
Mid-Module Assessment Task	After Topic B	Constructed response with rubric	8.EE.C.7, 8.EE.B.5
End-of-Module Assessment Task	After Topic D	Constructed response with rubric	8.EE.B.5, 8.EE.B.6, 8.EE.C.7, 8.EE.C.8

Mathematics Curriculum

Topic A:

Writing and Solving Linear Equations

8.EE.C.7

Focus Standard:	8.EE.C.7	Solve linear equations in one variable.
		a. Give examples of linear equations in one variable with one solution, infinitely many solutions, or no solutions. Show which of these possibilities is the case by successively transforming the given equation into simpler forms, until an equivalent equation of the form $x = a$, $a = a$, or $a = b$ result (where a and b are different numbers).
		b. Solve linear equations with rational number coefficients, including equations whose solutions require expanding expressions using the distributive property and collecting like terms.
Instructional Days:	9	

Lesson 1: Writing Equations Using Symbols (P)[1]

Lesson 2: Linear and Non-Linear Expressions in x (P)

Lesson 3: Linear Equations in x (P)

Lesson 4: Solving a Linear Equation (P)

Lesson 5: Writing and Solving Linear Equations (P)

Lesson 6: Solutions of a Linear Equation (P)

Lesson 7: Classification of Solutions (S)

Lesson 8: Linear Equations in Disguise (P)

Lesson 9: An Application of Linear Equations (S)

In Lesson 1, students begin by transcribing written statements into symbolic language. Students learn that before they can write a symbolic statement, they must first define the symbols they intend to use. In Lesson 2, students learn the difference between linear expressions in x and non-linear expressions in x, a distinction that is necessary to know whether or not an equation can be solved (at this point). Also in Lesson 2 is a quick

---

[1] Lesson Structure Key: **P**-Problem Set Lesson, **M**-Modeling Cycle Lesson, **E**-Exploration Lesson, **S**-Socratic Lesson

review of terms related to linear equations, such as constant, term, and coefficient. In Lesson 3, students learn that a linear equation in x is a statement of equality between two linear expressions in x. Students also learn that an equation that contains a variable really a question: Is there a value of x that makes the linear equation true? In Lesson 4, students begin using properties of equality to rewrite linear expressions, specifically using the distributive property to "combine like terms." Further, students practice substituting numbers into equations to determine if a true number sentence is produced.

In Lesson 5, students practice the skills of the first few lessons in a geometric context. Students transcribe written statements about angles and triangles into symbolic language and use properties of equality to begin solving equations (**8.EE.C.7b**). More work on solving equations occurs in Lesson 6, where the equations are more complicated and require more steps to solve (**8.EE.C.7b**). It is in Lesson 6 that students learn that not every linear equation has a solution (**8.EE.C.7a**). This leads to Lesson 7, where students learn that linear equations either have a unique solution, no solution, or infinitely many solutions (**8.EE.C.7a**). In Lesson 8, students rewrite equations that are not obviously linear equations then solve them (**8.EE.C.7b**). In Lesson 9, students take another look at the Facebook problem from Module 1 in terms of linear equations (**8.EE.C.7a**).

| Topic A: | Writing and Solving Linear Equations |
| Date: | 11/7/13 |

Lesson 1: Writing Equations Using Symbols

Student Outcomes

- Students write mathematical statements using symbols to represent numbers.
- Students know that written statements can be written as more than one correct mathematical sentence.

Lesson Notes

The content of this lesson will continue to develop the skills and concepts presented in Grades 6 and 7. Specifically, this lesson builds on both 6.EE.B.7 (Solve real world and mathematical problems by writing and solving equations of the form $x + p = q$ and $px = q$), and 7.EE.B.4 (Solve word problems leading to equations of the form $px + q = r$ and $p(x + q) = r$.)

Classwork

Discussion (4 minutes)

Show students the text of a mathematical statement compared to the equation.

MP.2

The number 1,157 is the sum of the squares of two consecutive odd integers divided by the difference between the two consecutive odd integers.	$1{,}157 = \dfrac{x^2 + (x+2)^2}{(x+2) - x}$

Ask students to write or share aloud (a) how these two are related, (b) which representation they prefer, and (c) why. Then, continue with the discussion that follows.

- Using letters to represent numbers in mathematical statements was introduced by René Descartes in the 1600s. In that era, people used only words to describe mathematical statements. Use of letters, or symbols, to represent numbers not only brought clarity to mathematical statements, it also expanded the horizons of mathematics.

- The reason we want to learn how to write a mathematical statement using symbols is to save time and labor. Imagine having to write the sentence: "The number 1,157 is the sum of the squares of two consecutive odd integers divided by the difference between the two consecutive odd integers." Then, imagine having to write the subsequent sentences necessary to solve it; compare that to:

  Let x represent the first odd integer. Then,

  $$1{,}157 = \frac{x^2 + (x+2)^2}{(x+2) - x}$$

- Notice that x is just a number. That means the square of x is also a number, along with the square of the next odd integer and the difference between the numbers. This is a symbolic statement about numbers.

- Writing in symbols is simpler than writing in words, as long as everyone involved is clear about what the symbols mean. This lesson focuses on accurately transcribing written statements into mathematical symbols. When we write mathematical statements using letters, we say we are using symbolic language.

Lesson 1:	Writing Equations Using Symbols
Date:	11/7/13

- All of the "mathematical statements" in this lesson are equations. Recall that an equation is a statement of equality between two expressions. Developing equations from written statements forms an important basis for problem solving and is one of the most vital parts of algebra. Throughout this module, there will be work with written statements and symbolic language. Students work first with simple expressions, then with equations that gradually increase in complexity, and finally with systems of equations (more than one equation at a time).

Example 1 (3 minutes)

Throughout Example 1, have students write their thoughts on personal white boards or a similar tool and show you their transcription(s).

- We want to express the following statement using symbolic language: A whole number has the property that when the square of half the number is subtracted from five times the number, we get back the number itself.
- Do the first step, and hold up your white board.
  - *First, we define the variable. Let x be the whole number.*
- Using x to represent the whole number, write "the square of half the number."
  - $\left(\frac{x}{2}\right)^2$ or $\left(\frac{1}{2}x\right)^2$ or $\left(\frac{x^2}{4}\right)$ or $\left(\frac{1}{4}x^2\right)$

> **Scaffolding:**
> - Alternative written statement:
> - A whole number has the property that when half the number is added to 15, we get the number itself.
> - $\frac{1}{2}x + 15 = x$

Ask students to write their expression in more than one way. Then, have students share their expressions of "the square of half the number." Elicit the above responses from students (or provide them). Ask students why they are all correct.

- Write the entire statement: A whole number has the property that when the square of half the number is subtracted from five times the number, we get back the number itself.
  - $5x - \left(\frac{x}{2}\right)^2 = x$

Challenge students to write this equation in another form. Engage in a conversation about why they are both correct. For example, when a number is subtracted from itself, the difference is zero. For that reason, the equation above can be written as $5x - \left(\frac{x}{2}\right)^2 - x = 0$.

Example 2 (4 minutes)

Throughout Example 2, have students write their thoughts on personal white boards or a similar tool and show you their transcription(s).

- We want to express the following statement using symbolic language: Paulo has a certain amount of money. If he spends six dollars, then he has $\frac{1}{4}$ of the original amount left.
- What is the first thing that must be done before we express this situation using symbols?
  - *We need to define our variables; that is, we must decide what symbol to use and state what it is going to represent.*

> **Scaffolding:**
> You may need to remind students that we do not have to put the multiplication symbol between a number and a symbol. It is not wrong if we include it, but by convention (a common agreement), it is not necessary.

Lesson 1:   Writing Equations Using Symbols
Date: 11/7/13

13

- Suppose we decide to use the symbol x. We will let x be the amount of money Paulo had originally. How do we show Paulo's spending 6 dollars using symbols?

  - *To show that Paulo spent 6 dollars, we write: $x - 6$.*

- How do we express: "he has $\frac{1}{4}$ of the original amount"?

  - *We can express it as: $\frac{1}{4}x$.*

- Put the parts together to express: "Paulo has a certain amount of money. If he spends 6 dollars, then he has $\frac{1}{4}$ of the original amount left." Use x to represent the amount of money Paulo had originally.

  - $x - 6 = \frac{1}{4}x$.

Challenge students to write this equation in another form. Engage in a conversation about why they are both correct. For example, students may decide to show that the six dollars plus what he has left is equal to the amount of money he now has. In symbols: $x = \frac{1}{4}x + 6$.

Example 3 (8 minutes)

Throughout Example 3, have students write their thoughts on personal white boards or a similar tool and show you their transcription(s).

- We want to write the following statement using symbolic language: When a fraction of 57 is taken away from 57, what remains exceeds $\frac{2}{3}$ of 57 by 4.

- The first step is to clearly state what we want our symbol to represent. If we choose the letter x; then we would say: "Let x be the fraction of 57" because that is the number that is unknown to us in the written statement. It is acceptable to use any letter to represent the unknown number, but regardless of which letter we use to symbolize the unknown number, we must clearly state what it means. This is called defining our variables.

  > **Scaffolding:**
  > - Alternative written statement:
  > - When a number is taken away from 57, what remains is four more than 5 times the number.
  > - $57 - x = 5x + 4$

- The hardest part of transcription is figuring out exactly how to write the statement so that it is accurately represented in symbols. Begin with the first part of the statement: "When a fraction of 57 is taken away from 57"—how can we capture that information in symbols?

  - *Students should write: $57 - x$.*

- How do we write $\frac{2}{3}$ of 57?

  - *If we are trying to find $\frac{2}{3}$ of 57, then we multiply $\frac{2}{3} \cdot 57$.*

- Would it be accurate to write: $57 - x = \frac{2}{3} \cdot 57$?

  - *No, because we are told that "what remains exceeds $\frac{2}{3}$ of 57 by 4."*

  > **Scaffolding:**
  > If students have a hard time thinking about these transcriptions, give them something easier to think about. One number, say 10, exceeds another number, say 6, by 4. Is it accurate to represent this by:
  > $$10 - 4 = 6?$$
  > $$10 = 6 + 4?$$
  > $$10 - 6 = 4?$$

- Where does the 4 belong? "What remains exceeds $\frac{2}{3}$ of 57 by 4." Think about what the word *exceeds* means in the context of the problem. Specifically, which is bigger: $57 - x$ or $\frac{2}{3}$ of 57? How do you know?

  - *$57 - x$ is bigger because $57 - x$ exceeds $\frac{2}{3}$ of 57 by 4. That means that $57 - x$ is 4 more than $\frac{2}{3}$ of 57.*

- We know that $57 - x$ is bigger than $\frac{2}{3} \cdot 57$ by 4. What would make the two numbers equal?

  - *We either have to subtract 4 from $57 - x$, or add 4 to $\frac{2}{3} \cdot 57$ to make them equal.*

- Now, if x is the fraction of 57, then we could write $(57 - x) - 4 = \frac{2}{3} \cdot 57$, or $57 - x = \frac{2}{3} \cdot 57 + 4$. Which is correct?

  - *Both transcriptions are correct because both express the written statement accurately.*

- Consider this transcription: $(57 - x) - \frac{2}{3} \cdot 57 = 4$. Is it an accurate transcription of the information in the written statement?

  - *Yes, because $57 - x$ is bigger than $\frac{2}{3} \cdot 57$ by 4. That means that the difference between the two numbers is 4. If we subtract the smaller number from the bigger number, we have a difference of 4 and that is what this version of the transcription shows.*

Example 4 (4 minutes)

Throughout Example 4, have students write their thoughts on personal white boards or a similar tool and show you their transcription(s).

- We want to express the following statement using symbolic language: The sum of three consecutive integers is 372.

- Do the first step, and hold up your white board.

  - *Let x be the first integer.*

- If we let x represent the first integer, what do we need to do to get the next consecutive integer?

  - *If x is the first integer, we add 1 to x to get the next integer.*

- In symbols, the next integer would be $x + 1$. What do we need to do now to get the next consecutive integer?

  - *We need to add 1 to that integer, or $x + 1 + 1$; this is the same as $x + 2$.*

- Now express the statement: The sum of three consecutive integers is 372.

  - *$x + x + 1 + x + 2 = 372$.*

> **Scaffolding:**
>
> Explain that *consecutive* means one after the next. For example, 18, 19, and 20 are consecutive integers. Consider giving students a number and asking them what the next consecutive integer would be.

Students may also choose to rewrite the above equation as $3x + 3 = 372$. Transforming equations, such as this, will be a focus of the next few lessons when students begin to solve linear equations. Ask students why both equations are correct.

Example 5 (3 minutes)

Throughout Example 5, have students write their thoughts on personal white boards or a similar tool and show you their transcription(s).

- We want to express the following statement using symbolic language: The sum of three consecutive odd integers is 93.
- Do the first step, and hold up your white board.
  - *Let x be the first integer.*
- If we let x represent the first integer, what do we need to do to get the next consecutive odd integer?
  - *If x is the first integer, we add 2 to x to get the next odd integer.*
- In symbols, the next odd integer would be $x + 2$. What do we need to do now to get the next odd consecutive integer?
  - *We need to add 2 to that integer, or $x + 2 + 2$; this is the same as $x + 4$.*
- Now express the statement: The sum of three consecutive odd integers is 372.
  - *$x + x + 2 + x + 4 = 93$.*
- Represent the statement "The sum of three consecutive odd integers is 93" in another way. Be prepared to explain why both are correct.
  - *Answers will vary. Accept any correct answers and justifications. For example, students may write $(x + x + x) + 6 = 93$ and state that it is equivalent to the equation $x + x + 2 + x + 4 = 93$. Because the Associative and Commutative properties of addition were applied, those properties do not change the value of an expression.*

Scaffolding:

Consider giving kids an odd number, then asking them what the next consecutive odd number is. Then ask student what they need to add to go from the first number to the second number.

Exercises 1–5 (10 minutes)

Students complete Exercises 1–5 independently or in pairs.

Exercises 1–5

Write each of the following statements using symbolic language.

1. The sum of four consecutive even integers is -28.

   Let x be the first integer. Then, $x + x + 2 + x + 4 + x + 6 = -28$.

2. A number is four times larger than the square of half the number.

   Let x be the number. Then, $x = 4\left(\frac{x}{2}\right)^2$.

3. Steven has some money. If he spends *nine* dollars, then he will have $\frac{3}{5}$ of the amount he started with.

   Let x be the amount of money Steven started with. Then, $x - 9 = \frac{3}{5}x$.

---

4. The sum of a number squared and three less than twice the number is 129.

    Let x be the number. Then, $x^2 + 2x - 3 = 129$.

5. Miriam read a book with an unknown number of pages. The first week she read five less than $\frac{1}{3}$ of the pages. The second week she read 171 pages and finished the book. Write an equation that represents the total number of pages in the book.

    Let x be the total number of pages in the book. Then, $\frac{1}{3}x - 5 + 171 = x$.

Closing (4 minutes)

Summarize, or ask students to summarize, the main points from the lesson:

- We know how to write mathematical statements using symbolic language.
- Written mathematical statements can be represented as more than one correct symbolic statement.
- We must always begin writing a symbolic statement by defining our symbols (variables).
- Complicated statements should be broken into parts or attempted with simple numbers to make the representation in symbolic notation easier.

Lesson Summary

Begin all word problems by defining your variables. State clearly what you want each symbol to represent.

Written mathematical statements can be represented as more than one correct symbolic statement.

Break complicated problems into smaller parts or try working them with simpler numbers.

Exit Ticket (5 minutes)

Name _____   Date_____

Lesson 1: Writing Equations Using Symbols

Exit Ticket

Write each of the following statements using symbolic language.

1. When you square five times a number you get three more than the number.

2. Monica had some cookies. She gave seven to her sister. Then, she divided the remainder in half, and she still had five cookies.

Exit Ticket Sample Solutions

> **Write each of the following statements using symbolic language.**
>
> 1. When you square five times a number you get three more than the number.
>
>   *Let x be the number. Then, $(5x)^2 = x + 3$.*
>
> 2. Monica had some cookies. She gave seven to her sister. Then, she divided the remainder in half, and she still had five cookies.
>
>   *Let x be the original amount of cookies. Then, $\frac{1}{2}(x - 7) = 5$.*

Problem Set Sample Solutions

Students practice transcribing written statements into symbolic language.

> **Write each of the following statements using symbolic language.**
>
> 1. Bruce bought two books. One book costs four dollars more than three times the other. Together, the two books cost him $72.
>
>   *Let x be the cost of the less expensive book. Then, $x + 4 + 3x = 72$.*
>
> 2. Janet is three years older than her sister Julie. Janet's brother is eight years younger than their sister Julie. The sum of all of their ages is 55.
>
>   *Let x be Julie's age. Then, $x + 3 + x - 8 + x = 55$.*
>
> 3. The sum of three consecutive integers is $1,623$.
>
>   *Let x be the first integer. Then, $x + x + 1 + x + 2 = 1,623$.*
>
> 4. One number is six more than another number. The sum of their squares is 90.
>
>   *Let x be the smaller number. Then $x^2 + (x + 6)^2 = 90$.*
>
> 5. When you add 18 to $\frac{1}{4}$ of a number, you get the number itself.
>
>   *Let x be the number. Then, $\frac{1}{4}x + 18 = x$.*
>
> 6. When a fraction of 12 is taken away from 17, what remains exceeds one-third of seventeen by six.
>
>   *Let x be the fraction of 12. Then, $17 - x = \frac{1}{3} \cdot 17 + 6$.*
>
> 7. The sum of two consecutive even integers divided by four is 189.5.
>
>   *Let x be the first even integer. Then, $\frac{x + x + 2}{4} = 189.5$.*
>
> 8. Subtract seven more than twice a number from the square of one-third of the number to get zero.
>
>   *Let x be the number. Then, $\left(\frac{1}{3}x\right)^2 - (2x + 7) = 0$.*
>
> 9. The sum of three consecutive integers is 42. Let x be the middle of the three integers. Transcribe the statement accordingly.
>
> $x - 1 + x + x + 1 = 42$.

Lesson 1:   Writing Equations Using Symbols
Date: 11/7/13

Lesson 2: Linear and Non-Linear Expressions in x

Student Outcomes

- Students know the properties of linear and non-linear expressions in x.
- Students transcribe and identify expressions as linear or non-linear.

Classwork

Discussion (4 minutes)

- A symbolic statement in x with an equal sign is called an equation in x. The equal sign divides the equation into two parts, the left side and the right side. The two sides are called *expressions*.

- For sake of simplicity, we will only discuss expressions in x, but know that we can write expressions in any symbol.

- The following chart contains both linear and non-linear expressions in x. Sort them into two groups and be prepared to explain what is different about the two groups.

$5x + 3$	$-8x + \dfrac{7}{9} - 3$	$9 - x^2$
$4x^2 - 9$	$0.31x + 7 - 4.2x$	$\left(\dfrac{x}{2}\right)^3 + 1$
$11(x + 2)$	$-(6 - x) + 15 - 9x$	$7 + x^{-4} + 3x$

Linear expressions are noted in red in the table below.

$5x + 3$	$-8x + \dfrac{7}{9} - 3$	$9 - x^2$
$4x^2 - 9$	$0.31x + 7 - 4.2x$	$\left(\dfrac{x}{2}\right)^3 + 1$
$11(x + 2)$	$-(6 - x) + 15 - 9x$	$7 + x^{-4} + 3x$

MP.3

- Identify which equations you placed in each group. Explain your reasoning for grouping the equations.
  - *Equations that contained an exponent of x other than 1 were put into one group. The other equations were put into another group. That seemed to be the only difference between the types of equations given.*

- Linear expressions in x are a special type of expression. Linear expressions are expressions that are sums of constants and products of a constant and x raised to a power of 0, which simplifies to a value of 1. Non-linear expressions are also sums of constants and products of a constant and a power of x. However, non-linear expressions will have a power of x that is not equal to 1 or 0.

- The reason we want to be able to distinguish linear expressions from non-linear expressions is because we will soon be solving linear equations. Non-linear equations will be a set of equations you learn to solve in Algebra I, though we will begin to solve simple non-linear equations later this year (Module 7). We also want to be able to recognize linear equations in order to predict the shape of their graph, which is a concept we will learn more about later in this module.

Lesson 2:	Linear and Non-Linear Expressions in x	
Date:	11/7/13	

20

Example 1 (3 minutes)

- A linear expression in x is an expression where each term is either a constant, an x, or a product of a constant and x. For example, the expression $(57 - x)$ is a linear expression. However, the expression $2x^2 + 9x + 5$ is not a linear expression. Why is $2x^2 + 9x + 5$ not a linear expression in x?

  - *Students should say that $2x^2 + 9x + 5$ is not a linear expression because the terms of linear expressions must either be a constant, an x, or the product of a constant and x. The term $2x^2$ does not fit the definition of a linear expression in x.*

> *Scaffolding:*
> - Terms are any product of an integer power of x and a constant or just a constant.
> - Constants are fixed numbers.
> - When a term is the product of a constant(s) and a power of x, the constant is called a coefficient.

Example 2 (4 minutes)

- Let's examine the expression $4 + 3x^5$ more deeply. To begin, we want to identify the terms of the expression. How many terms are there, and what are they?

  - *There are two terms, 4 and $3x^5$.*

- How many terms are comprised of just constants, and what are they?

  - *There is one constant term, 4.*

- How many terms have coefficients, and what are they?

  - *There is one term with a coefficient, 3.*

- Is $4 + 3x^5$ a linear or non-linear expression in x? Why or why not?

  - *The expression $4 + 3x^5$ is a non-linear expression in x because it is the sum of a constant and the product of a constant and positive integer power of $x > 1$.*

Example 3 (4 minutes)

- How many terms does the expression $7x + 9 + 6 + 3x$ have? What are they?

  - *As is, this expression has 4 terms: $7x, 9, 6,$ and $3x$.*

- This expression can be transformed using some of our basic properties of numbers. For example, if we apply the Commutative Property of Addition, we can rearrange the terms from $7x + 9 + 6 + 3x$ to $7x + 3x + 9 + 6$. First, we can apply the Associative Property of Addition:

$$(7x + 3x) + (9 + 6)$$

  Next, we apply the Distributive Property:

$$(7 + 3)x + (9 + 6)$$

  Finally,

$$10x + 15$$

- How many terms with coefficients does the expression $10x + 15$ have? What are they?

  - *The expression has one term with a coefficient, $10x$. For this term, the coefficient is 10.*

- Is $10x + 15$ a linear or non-linear expression in x? Why or why not?

  - *The expression $10x + 15$ is a linear expression in x because it is the sum of constants and products that contain x to the 1st power.*

Lesson 2:	Linear and Non-Linear Expressions in x
Date:	11/7/13

21

Example 4 (2 minutes)

- How many terms does the expression $5 + 9x \cdot 7 + 2x^9$ have? What are they?
  - *The expression has three terms: 5, $9x \cdot 7$, and $2x^9$.*
- How many terms with coefficients does the expression $5 + 9x \cdot 7 + 2x^5$ have? What are they?
  - *The expression has two terms with coefficients: $63x$ and $2x^5$. The coefficients are 63 and 2.*
- Is $5 + 9x \cdot 7 + 2x^9$ a linear or non-linear expression in x? Why or why not?
  - *The expression $5 + 9x \cdot 7 + 2x^9$ is a non-linear expression in x because it is the sum of constants and products that contain x raised to a power that is greater than 1.*

Example 5 (2 minutes)

- Is $94 + x + 4x^{-6} - 2$ a linear or non-linear expression in x? Why or why not?
  - *Students may first say that it is not a linear nor non-linear expression in x because of the -2. Remind them that subtraction can be rewritten as a sum, i.e., $+ (-2)$; therefore, this expression does fit the definition of non-linear.*

Example 6 (2 minutes)

- Is the expression $x^1 + 9x - 4$ a linear expression in x?
  - *Yes, $x^1 + 9x - 4$ is a linear expression in x because x^1 is the same as x.*
- What powers of x are acceptable in the definition of a linear expression in x?
  - *Only the power of 1 is acceptable because x^1 is, by definition, just x.*

Exercises 1–12 (14 minutes)

Students complete Exercises 1–12 independently.

Exercises 1–12

Write each of the following statements in Exercises 1–12 as a mathematical expression. State whether or not the expression is linear or non-linear. If it is non-linear, then explain why.

1. The sum of a number and four times the number.

    Let x be a number; then, $x + 4x$ is a linear expression.

2. The product of five and a number.

    Let x be a number, then $5x$ is a linear expression.

3. Multiply six and the reciprocal of the quotient of a number and seven.

    Let x be a number, then $6 \cdot \dfrac{7}{x}$ is a non-linear expression. The number $\dfrac{7}{x} = 7 \cdot \dfrac{1}{x} = 7 \cdot x^{-1}$ is the reason it is not a linear expression. The exponent of the x is the reason it is not linear.

---

4. Twice a number subtracted from four times a number, added to 15.

   Let x be a number, then $15 + (4x - 2x)$ is a linear expression.

5. The square of the sum of six and a number.

   Let x be a number, then $(x + 6)^2$ is a non-linear expression. When you multiply $(x + 6)^2$, you get $x^2 + 12x + 36$. The x^2 is the reason it is not a linear expression.

6. The cube of a positive number divided by the square of the same positive number.

   Let x be a number, then $\dfrac{x^3}{x^2}$ is a non-linear expression. However, if you simplify the expression to just x, then it is linear.

7. The sum of four consecutive numbers.

   Let x be a number, then $x + x + 1 + x + 2 + x + 3$ is a linear expression.

8. Four subtracted from the reciprocal of a number.

   Let x be a number, then $\dfrac{1}{x} - 4$ is a non-linear expression. The term $\dfrac{1}{x}$ is the same as x^{-1}, which is why this expression is not linear. It is possible that a student may let x be the reciprocal of a number, $\dfrac{1}{x}$, which would make the expression linear.

9. Half of the product of a number multiplied by itself, three times.

   Let x be a number; then, $\dfrac{1}{2} \cdot x \cdot x \cdot x$ is not a linear expression. The term $\dfrac{1}{2} \cdot x \cdot x \cdot x$ is the same as $\dfrac{1}{2}x^3$, which is why this expression is not linear.

10. The sum that shows how many pages Maria read if she read 45 pages of a book yesterday and $\dfrac{2}{3}$ of the remaining pages today.

    Let x be the number of remaining pages of the book, then $45 + \dfrac{2}{3}x$ is a linear expression.

11. An admission fee of $10 plus an additional $2 per game.

    Let x be the number of games, then $10 + 2x$ is a linear expression.

12. Five more than four times a number, then twice that sum.

    Let x be the number, then $2(4x + 5)$ is a linear expression.

Closing (5 minutes)

Summarize, or ask students to summarize, the main points from the lesson:

- We have definitions for linear and non-linear expressions.
- We know how to use the definitions to identify expressions as linear or non-linear.
- We can write expressions that are linear and non-linear.

Lesson 2: Linear and Non-Linear Expressions in x
Date: 11/7/13

Lesson Summary

Linear expressions are sums of constants and products of constants and x raised to a power of 0 or 1. For example, $4 + 3x$, $7x + x - 15$, and $\frac{1}{2}x + 7 - 2$ are all linear expressions in x.

Non-linear expressions are also sums of constants and products of constants and a x raised to a power that is not 0 or 1. For example, $2x^2 - 9$, $-6x^{-3} + 8 + x$, and $\frac{1}{x} + 8$ are all non-linear expressions in x.

Exit Ticket (5 minutes)

	Lesson 2:	Linear and Non-Linear Expressions in x		Lesson 2 8•4
	Date:	11/7/13		24

Name _____   Date_____

Lesson 2: Linear and Non-Linear Expressions in x

Exit Ticket

Write each of the following statements as a mathematic expression. State whether the expression is a linear or non-linear expression in x.

1.   Seven subtracted from five times a number, then the difference added to nine times a number.

2.   Three times a number subtracted from the product of fifteen and the reciprocal of a number.

3.   Half of the sum of two and a number multiplied by itself three times.

Exit Ticket Sample Solutions

> **Write each of the following statements as a mathematic expression. State whether the expression is a linear or non-linear expression in** x**.**
>
> 1. Seven subtracted from five times a number, then the difference added to nine times a number.
>
>   *Let x be a number.* $(5x - 7) + 9x$.
>
>   *The expression is a linear expression.*
>
> 2. Three times a number subtracted from the product of fifteen and the reciprocal of a number.
>
>   *Let x be a number.* $15 \cdot \frac{1}{x} - 3x$.
>
>   *The expression is a non-linear expression.*
>
> 3. Half of the sum of two and a number multiplied by itself three times.
>
>   *Let x be a number.* $\frac{1}{2}(2 + x^3)$.
>
>   *The expression is a non-linear expression.*

Problem Set Sample Solutions

Students practice writing expressions and identifying them as linear or non-linear.

> **Write each of the following statements as a mathematic expression. State whether the expression is linear or non-linear. If it is non-linear, then explain why.**
>
> 1. A number decreased by three squared.
>
>   *Let x be a number, then $x - 3^2$ is a linear expression.*
>
> 2. The quotient of two and a number, subtracted from seventeen.
>
>   *Let x be a number, then $17 - \frac{2}{x}$ is a non-linear expression. The term $\frac{2}{x}$ is the same as $2 \cdot \frac{1}{x}$ and $\frac{1}{x} = x^{-1}$. That is why it is not a linear expression.*
>
> 3. The sum of thirteen and twice a number.
>
>   *Let x be a number, then $13 + 2x$ is a linear expression.*
>
> 4. 5.2 more than the product of seven and a number.
>
>   *Let x be a number, then $5.2 + 7x$ is a linear expression.*
>
> 5. The sum that represents tickets sold if 35 tickets were sold Monday, half of the remaining tickets were sold on Tuesday, and 14 tickets were sold on Wednesday.
>
>   *Let x be the remaining number of tickets, then $35 + \frac{1}{2}x + 14$ is a linear expression.*

| Lesson 2: | Linear and Non-Linear Expressions in x |
| Date: | 11/7/13 |

6.   The product of 19 and a number, subtracted from the reciprocal of the number cubed.

Let x be a number, then $\frac{1}{x^3} - 19x$ is a non-linear expression. The term $\frac{1}{x^3}$ is the same as x^{-3}. That is why it is not a linear expression.

7.   The product of 15 and number, multiplied by itself four times.

Let x be a number, then $(15x)^4$ is a non-linear expression. The expression can be written as $15^4 \cdot x^4$. The exponent of 4 with a base of x is the reason it is not linear.

8.   A number increased by five, divided by two.

Let x be a number, then $\frac{x+5}{2}$ is a linear expression.

9.   Eight times the result of subtracting three from a number.

Let x be a number, then $8(x - 3)$ is a linear expression.

10.   The sum of twice a number and four times a number subtracted from the number squared.

Let x be a number, then $x^2 - (2x + 4x)$ is a non-linear expression. The term x^2 is the reason it is not linear.

11.   One-third of the result of three times a number that is increased by 12.

Let x be a number, then $\frac{1}{3}(3x + 12)$ is a linear expression.

12.   Five times the sum of one-half and a number.

Let x be a number, then $5\left(\frac{1}{2} + x\right)$ is a linear expression.

13.   Three-fourths of a number multiplied by seven.

Let x be a number, then $\frac{3}{4}x \cdot 7$ is a linear expression.

14.   The sum of a number and negative three, multiplied by the number.

Let x be a number, then $(x + (-3))x$ is a non-linear expression because $(x + (-3))x = x^2 - 3x$ after using the distributive property. It is non-linear because the power of x in the term x^2 is greater than 1.

15.   The square of the difference between a number and 10.

Let x be a number, then $(x - 10)^2$ is a non-linear expression because $(x - 10)^2 = x^2 - 20x + 100$. The term x^2 is a positive power of $x > 1$; therefore, this is a not a linear expression.

Lesson 3: Linear Equations in x

Student Outcomes

- Students know that a linear equation is a statement of equality between two expressions.
- Students know that a linear equation in x is actually a question: Can you find all numbers x, if they exist, that satisfy a given equation? Students know that those numbers x that satisfy a given equation are called *solutions*.

Classwork

Concept Development (7 minutes)

- We want to define "linear equation in x." Here are some examples of linear equations in x. Using what you know about the words *linear* (from Lesson 2) and *equation* (from Lesson 1), develop a mathematical definition of "linear equation in x."

> **Scaffolding:**
>
> Consider developing a word bank or word wall to be used throughout the module.

Show students the examples below, and provide them time to work individually or in small groups to develop an appropriate definition. Once students share their definitions, continue with the definition and discussion that follows.

$x + 11 = 15$	$5 + 3 = 8$	$-\frac{1}{2}x = 22$
$15 - 4x = x + \frac{4}{5}$	$3 - (x + 2) = -12x$	$\frac{3}{4}x + 6(x - 1) = 9(2 - x)$

- When two linear expressions are equal, they can be written as a linear equation in x.
- Consider the following equations. Which are true, and how do you know?

  $4 + 1 = 5$

  $6 + 5 = 16$

  $21 - 6 = 15$

  $6 - 2 = 1$

  - *The first and third equations are true because the value on the left side is equal to the number on the right side.*

- Is $4 + 15x = 49$ true? How do you know?

Have a discussion that leads to students developing a list of values for x that make it false, along with one value of x that makes it true. Then, conclude the discussion by making the two points below.

- A linear equation in x is a statement about equality, but it is also an invitation to find all of the numbers x, if they exist, that make the equation true. Sometimes the question is asked in this way: What number(s) x satisfy the equation? The question is often stated more as a directive: Solve. When phrased as a directive, it is still considered a question. Is there a number(s) x that make the statement true? If so, what is the number(s) x?

Lesson 3:	Linear Equations in x
Date:	11/8/13

28

- Equations that contain a variable do not have a definitive truth value; in other words, there are values of the variable that make the equation true and values that make it false. When we say that we have "solved an equation," what we are really saying is that we have found a number (or numbers) x that makes the linear equation true. That number x is called the solution to the linear equation.

Example 1 (4 minutes)

- Here is a linear equation in x: $4 + 15x = 49$. The question is, is there a number x that makes the linear expression $4 + 15x$ equal to the linear expression 49? Suppose you are told this number x has a value of 2, i.e., $x = 2$. We replace any instance of x in the linear equation with the value of 2, as shown:

$$4 + 15 \cdot 2 = 49$$

Next, we evaluate each side of the equation. The left side is

$$4 + 15 \cdot 2 = 4 + 30$$
$$= 34$$

The right side of the equation is 49. Clearly, $34 \neq 49$. Therefore, the number 2 is not a solution to this equation.

> **Scaffolding:**
>
> Remind students that when a number and a symbol are next to one another, such as $15x$, we do not need to use a symbol to represent the multiplication (it is a convention). For clarity, when two numbers are being multiplied, we do use a multiplication symbol. It is necessary to tell the difference between the number, 152 and the product, $15 \cdot 2$.

- Is the number 3 a solution to the equation, i.e., is this equation true when $x = 3$?
  - *Yes, because the left side of the equation equals the right side of the equation:*

    The left side is

    $$4 + 15 \cdot 3 = 4 + 45$$
    $$= 49$$

    The right side is 49. Since $49 = 49$, then we can say that $x = 3$ is a solution to the equation $4 + 15x = 49$.

- 3 is a solution to the equation because it is a value of x that makes the equation true.

Example 2 (4 minutes)

- Here is a linear equation in x: $8x - 19 = -4 - 7x$.
- Is 5 a solution to the equation? That is, is $x = 5$ a solution to the equation?
  - *No, because the left side of the equation does not equal the right side of the equation:*

    The left side is

    $$8 \cdot 5 - 19 = 40 - 19$$
    $$= 21$$

    The right side is

    $$-4 - 7 \cdot 5 = -4 - 35$$
    $$= -39$$

    Since $21 \neq -39$, then $x \neq 5$.

	Lesson 3:	Linear Equations in x	
	Date:	11/8/13	29

- Is 1 a solution to the equation? That is, is this equation true when $x = 1$?

  □ *Yes, the left side and right side of the equation are equal to the same number.*

    The left side is

    $$8 \cdot 1 - 19 = 8 - 19$$
    $$= -11$$

    The right side is

    $$-4 - 7 \cdot 1 = -4 - 7$$
    $$= -11$$

    Since $-11 = -11$, then $x = 1$.

Example 3 (4 minutes)

- Here is a linear equation in x: $3(x + 9) = 4x - 7 + 7x$.

- We can make our work simpler if we use some properties to transform the expression on the right side of the equation into an expression with fewer terms.

Provide students time to transform the equation into fewer terms, then proceed with the points below.

MP.1

- For example, notice that on the right side there are two terms that contain x. First, we will use the Commutative Property to rearrange the terms to better see what we are doing:

  $$4x + 7x - 7$$

  Next, we will use the distributive property to collect the terms that contain x:

  $$4x + 7x - 7 = (4 + 7)x - 7$$
  $$= 11x - 7$$

  Finally, the transformed (but still the same) equation can be written as: $3(x + 9) = 11x - 7$.

- Is $\frac{5}{4}$ a solution to the equation? That is, is this equation true when $x = \frac{5}{4}$?

  □ *No, because the left side of the equation does not equal the right side of the equation:*

    The left side is

    $$3\left(\frac{5}{4} + 9\right) = 3\left(\frac{41}{4}\right)$$
    $$= \frac{123}{4}$$

    The right side is

    $$11 \cdot \frac{5}{4} - 7 = \frac{55}{4} - 7$$
    $$= \frac{27}{4}$$

    Since $\frac{123}{4} \neq \frac{27}{4}$, then $x \neq \frac{5}{4}$.

Lesson 3:	Linear Equations in x
Date:	11/8/13

Example 4 (4 minutes)

- Here is a linear equation in x: $-2x + 11 - 5x = 5 - 6x$.

- We want to check to see if 6 is a solution to the equation, i.e., is $x = 6$ a solution to the equation? Before we do that, what would make our work easier?

  □ *We could use the Commutative and Distributive Properties to transform the left side of the equation into an expression with fewer terms.*

$$-2x + 11 - 5x = -2x - 5x + 11$$
$$= (-2 - 5)x + 11$$
$$= -7x + 11$$

- The transformed equation can be written as: $-7x + 11 = 5 - 6x$. Is 6 a solution to the equation, i.e., is this equation true when $x = 6$?

  □ *Yes, because the left side of the equation is equal to the right side of the equation:*

    The left side is

$$-7x + 11 = -7 \cdot 6 + 11$$
$$= -42 + 11$$
$$= -31$$

    The right side is

$$5 - 6x = 5 - 6 \cdot 6$$
$$= 5 - 36$$
$$= -31$$

    Since $-31 = -31$, then $x = 6$.

Exercises 1–6 (12 minutes)

Students complete Exercises 1–6 independently.

Exercises 1–6

1. **Is the equation true when $x = -3$; in other words, is -3 a solution to the equation: $6x + 5 = 5x + 8 + 2x$? Explain.**

   If we replace x with the number -3, then the left side of the equation is

$$6 \cdot (-3) + 5 = -18 + 5$$
$$= -13$$

   and the right side of the equation is

$$5 \cdot (-3) + 8 + 2 \cdot (-3) = -15 + 8 - 6$$
$$= -7 - 6$$
$$= -13$$

   Since $-13 = -13$, then $x = -3$ is a solution to the equation $6x + 5 = 5x + 8 + 2x$.

   Note: Some students may have transformed the equation.

	Lesson 3:	Linear Equations in x
	Date:	11/8/13

31

2. Does $x = 12$ satisfy the equation: $16 - \frac{1}{2}x = \frac{3}{4}x + 1$? **Explain.**

If we replace x with the number 12, then the left side of the equation is

$$16 - \frac{1}{2}x = 16 - \frac{1}{2} \cdot (12)$$
$$= 16 - 6$$
$$= 10$$

and the right side of the equation is

$$\frac{3}{4}x + 1 = \frac{3}{4} \cdot (12) + 1$$
$$= 9 + 1$$
$$= 10$$

Since $10 = 10$, then $x = 12$ is a solution to the equation $16 - \frac{1}{2}x = \frac{3}{4}x + 1$.

3. Chad solved the equation $24x + 4 + 2x = 3(10x - 1)$ and is claiming that $x = 2$ makes the equation true. **Is Chad correct? Explain.**

If we replace x with the number 2, then the left side of the equation is

$$24x + 4 + 2x = 24 \cdot 2 + 4 + 2 \cdot 2$$
$$= 48 + 4 + 4$$
$$= 56$$

and the right side of the equation is

$$3(10x - 1) = 3(10 \cdot 2 - 1)$$
$$= 3(20 - 1)$$
$$= 3(19)$$
$$= 57$$

Since $56 \neq 57$, then $x = 2$ is not a solution to the equation $24x + 4 + 2x = 3(10x - 1)$, and Chad is not correct.

4. Lisa solved the equation $x + 6 = 8 + 7x$ and claimed that the solution is $x = -\frac{1}{3}$. **Is she correct? Explain.**

If we replace x with the number $-\frac{1}{3}$, then the left side of the equation is

$$x + 6 = -\frac{1}{3} + 6$$
$$= 5\frac{2}{3}$$

and the right side of the equation is

$$8 + 7x = 8 + 7 \cdot \left(-\frac{1}{3}\right)$$
$$= 8 - \frac{7}{3}$$
$$= \frac{24}{3} - \frac{7}{3}$$
$$= \frac{17}{3}$$

Since $5\frac{2}{3} = \frac{17}{3}$, then $x = -\frac{1}{3}$ is a solution to the equation $x + 6 = 8 + 7x$, and Lisa is correct.

5. Angel transformed the following equation from $6x + 4 - x = 2(x + 1)$ to $10 = 2(x + 1)$. He then stated that the solution to the equation is $x = 4$. Is he correct? Explain.

    No, Angel is not correct. He did not transform the equation correctly. The expression on the left side of the equation $6x + 4 - x = 2(x + 1)$ would transform to

    $$6x + 4 - x = 6x - x + 4$$
    $$= (6 - 1)x + 4$$
    $$= 5x + 4$$

    If we replace x with the number 4, then the left side of the equation is

    $$5x + 4 = 5 \cdot 4 + 4$$
    $$= 20 + 4$$
    $$= 24$$

    and the right side of the equation is

    $$2(x + 1) = 2(4 + 1)$$
    $$= 2(5)$$
    $$= 10$$

    Since $24 \neq 10$, then $x = 4$ is not a solution to the equation $6x + 4 - x = 2(x + 1)$, and Angel is not correct.

6. Claire was able to verify that $x = 3$ was a solution to her teacher's linear equation, but the equation got erased from the board. What might the equation have been? Identify as many equations as you can with a solution of $x = 3$.

    Answers will vary. Ask students to share their equations and justifications as to how they knew $x = 3$ would make a true number sentence.

7. Does an equation always have a solution? Could you come up with an equation that does not have a solution?

    Answers will vary Expect students to write equations that are false. Ask students to share their equations and justifications as to how they knew the equation they wrote did not have a solution. The concept of "no solution" is introduced in Lesson 6 and solidified in Lesson 7.

Closing (5 minutes)

Summarize, or ask students to summarize, the main points from the lesson:

- We know that equations are statements about equality. That is, the expression on the left side of the equal sign is equal to the expression on the right side of the equal sign.

- We know that a solution to a linear equation in x will be a number, and that when all instances of x are replaced with the number, the left side will equal the right side.

Lesson Summary

Equations are statements about equality. If the expression on the left side of the equal sign has the same value as the expression on the right side of the equal sign, then you have a true equation.

A solution to a linear equation in x is a number, such that when all instances of x are replaced with the number, the left side will equal the right side. For example, $x = 2$ is a solution to $3x + 4 = x + 8$ because the left side of the equation is

$$3x + 4 = 3(2) + 4$$
$$= 6 + 4$$
$$= 10$$

and the right side of the equation is

$$x + 8 = 2 + 8$$
$$= 10$$

Since $10 = 10$, then $x = 2$ is a solution to the linear equation $3x + 4 = x + 8$.

Exit Ticket (5 minutes)

Name _____   Date_____

Lesson 3: Linear Equations in x

Exit Ticket

1.   Is 8 a solution to $\frac{1}{2}x + 9 = 13$? Explain.

2.   Write three different equations that have $x = 5$ as a solution.

3.   Is -3 a solution to the equation $3x - 5 = 4 + 2x$? Explain.

Exit Ticket Sample Solutions

1.   Is 8 a solution to $\frac{1}{2}x + 9 = 13$? **Explain.**

   If we replace x with the number 8, then the left side is $\frac{1}{2}(8) + 9 = 4 + 9 = 13$ and the right side is 13. Since $13 = 13$, then $x = 8$ is a solution.

2.   Write three different equations that have $x = 5$ as a solution.

   Answers will vary. Accept equations where $x = 5$ makes a true number sentence.

3.   Is -3 a solution to the equation $3x - 5 = 4 + 2x$? **Explain.**

   If we replace x with the number -3, then the left side is $3(-3) - 5 = -9 - 5 = -14$. The right side is $4 + 2(-3) = 4 - 6 = -2$. Since $-14 \neq -2$, then $x = -3$ is not a solution to the equation.

Problem Set Sample Solutions

Students practice determining whether or not a given number is a solution to the linear equation.

1.   Given that $2x + 7 = 27$ and $3x + 1 = 28$, does $2x + 7 = 3x + 1$? **Explain.**

   No, because a linear equation is a statement about equality. We are given that $2x + 7 = 27$, but $3x + 1 = 28$. Since each linear expression is equal to a different number, $2x + 7 \neq 3x + 1$.

2.   Is -5 a solution to the equation: $6x + 5 = 5x + 8 + 2x$? **Explain.**

   If we replace x with the number -5, then the left side of the equation is

$$6 \cdot (-5) + 5 = -30 + 5$$
$$= -25$$

   and the right side of the equation is

$$5 \cdot (-5) + 8 + 2 \cdot (-5) = -25 + 8 - 10$$
$$= -17 - 10$$
$$= -27$$

   Since $-25 \neq -27$, then $x \neq -5$ is not a solution to the equation $6x + 5 = 5x + 8 + 2x$.

   Note: Some students may have transformed the equation.

3.   Does $x = 1.6$ satisfy the equation: $6 - 4x = -\frac{x}{4}$? **Explain.**

   If we replace x with the number 1.6, then the left side of the equation is

$$6 - 4 \cdot 1.6 = 6 - 6.4$$
$$= -0.4$$

   and the right side of the equation is

$$-\frac{1.6}{4} = -0.4$$

   Since $-0.4 = -0.4$, then $x = 1.6$ is a solution to the equation $6 - 4x = -\frac{x}{4}$.

4. Use the linear equation $3(x + 1) = 3x + 3$ to answer parts (a)–(d).

    a.   **Does $x = 5$ satisfy the equation above? Explain.**

        If we replace x with the number 5, then the left side of the equation is

$$3(5 + 1) = 3(6)$$
$$= 18$$

        and the right side of the equation is

$$3x + 3 = 3 \cdot 5 + 3$$
$$= 15 + 3$$
$$= 18$$

        Since $18 = 18$, then $x = 5$ is a solution to the equation $3(x + 1) = 3x + 3$.

    b.   **Is $x = -8$ a solution the equation above? Explain.**

        If we replace x with the number -8, then the left side of the equation is

$$3(-8 + 1) = 3(-7)$$
$$= -21$$

        and the right side of the equation is

$$3x + 3 = 3 \cdot (-8) + 3$$
$$= -24 + 3$$
$$= -21$$

        Since $-21 = -21$, then $x = -8$ is a solution to the equation $3(x + 1) = 3x + 3$.

    c.   **Is $x = \frac{1}{2}$ a solution the equation above? Explain.**

        If we replace x with the number $\frac{1}{2}$, then the left side of the equation is

$$3\left(\frac{1}{2} + 1\right) = 3\left(\frac{1}{2} + \frac{2}{2}\right)$$
$$= 3\left(\frac{3}{2}\right)$$
$$= \frac{9}{2}$$

        and the right side of the equation is

$$3x + 3 = 3 \cdot \left(\frac{1}{2}\right) + 3$$
$$= \frac{3}{2} + 3$$
$$= \frac{3}{2} + \frac{6}{2}$$
$$= \frac{9}{2}$$

        Since $\frac{9}{2} = \frac{9}{2}$, then $x = \frac{1}{2}$ is a solution to the equation $3(x + 1) = 3x + 3$.

    d.   **What interesting fact about the equation $3(x + 1) = 3x + 3$ is illuminated by the answers to parts (a), (b), and (c)? Why do you think this is true?**

        Note to teacher: Ideally students will notice that the equation $3(x + 1) = 3x + 3$ is an identity under the distributive law. The purpose of this problem is to prepare students for the idea that linear equations can have more than one solution, which is a topic of Lesson 7.

Lesson 4: Solving a Linear Equation

Student Outcomes

- Students extend the use of the properties of equality to solve linear equations having rational coefficients.

Classwork

Concept Development (13 minutes)

- To solve an equation means to find all of the numbers x, if they exist, so that the given equation is true.
- In some cases, some simple guess work can lead us to a solution. For example, consider the following equation:

$$4x + 1 = 13$$

  What number x would make this equation true? That is, what value of x would make the left side equal to the right side? (Give students a moment to guess a solution.)

  □ *When $x = 3$, we get a true statement. The left side of the equal sign is equal to 13 and so is the right side of the equal sign.*

  In other cases, guessing the correct answer is not so easy. Consider the following equation:
$$3(4x - 9) + 10 = 15x + 2 + 7x$$

  Can you guess a number for x that would make this equation true? (Give students a minute to guess.)

- Guessing is not always an efficient strategy for solving equations. In the last example, there are several terms in each of the linear expressions comprising the equation. This makes it more difficult to easily guess a solution. For this reason, we want to use what we know about the properties of equality to transform equations into equations with fewer terms.
- The ultimate goal of solving any equation is to get it into the form of x (or whatever symbol is being used in the equation) equal to a constant.

Complete the activity described to remind students of the properties of equality, then proceed with the discussion that follows.

Give students the equation: $4 + 1 = 7 - 2$ and ask them the following questions.

1. Is this equation true?
2. Perform each of the following operations, and state whether or not the equation is still true:
   a. Add three to both sides of the equal sign.
   b. Add three to the left side of the equal sign, and add two to the right side of the equal sign.
   c. Subtract six from both sides of the equal sign.
   d. Subtract three from one side of the equal sign and subtract three from the other side.
   e. Multiply both sides of the equal sign by ten.
   f. Multiply the left side of the equation by ten and the right side by four.
   g. Divide both sides of the equation by two.
   h. Divide the left side of the equation by two and the right side of the equation by five.
3. What do you notice? Describe any patterns you see.

MP.8

- There are four properties of equality that will allow us to transform an equation into the form we want. If A, B, and C are any rational numbers, then

  - If $A = B$, then $A + C = B + C$.
  - If $A = B$, then $A - C = B - C$.
  - If $A = B$, then $A \cdot C = B \cdot C$.
  - If $A = B$, then $\dfrac{A}{C} = \dfrac{B}{C}$, where C is not equal to zero.

  All four of the properties require us to start off with $A = B$. That is, we have to assume that a given equation has an expression on the left side that is equal to the expression on the right side. Working under that assumption, each time we use one of the properties of equality, we are transforming the equation into another equation that is also true, i.e., left side equals right side.

Example 1 (3 minutes)

- Solve the linear equation $2x - 3 = 4x$ for the number x.
- Examine the properties of equality. Choose "something" to add, subtract, multiply, or divide on both sides of the equation.

Validate the use of the properties of equality by having students share their thoughts. Then, discuss the "best" choice for the first step in solving the equation with the points below. Be sure to remind students throughout this and the other examples that our goal is to get x equal to a constant; therefore, the "best" choice is one that gets us to that goal most efficiently.

- First, we must assume that there is a number x that makes the equation true. Working under that assumption, when we use the property, If $A = B$, then $A - C = B - C$, we get an equation that is also true:

$$2x - 3 = 4x$$
$$2x - 2x - 3 = 4x - 2x$$

Now, using the distributive property, we get another set of equations that is also true:

$$(2 - 2)x - 3 = (4 - 2)x$$
$$0x - 3 = 2x$$
$$-3 = 2x$$

Using another property, If $A = B$, then $\dfrac{A}{C} = \dfrac{B}{C}$, we get another true equation:

$$\frac{-3}{2} = \frac{2x}{2}$$

After simplifying the fraction $\dfrac{2}{2}$, we have

$$\frac{-3}{2} = x$$

is also true.

- The last step is to check to see if $x = -\dfrac{3}{2}$ satisfies the equation $2x - 3 = 4x$.

  The left side of the equation is equal to $2 \cdot \left(-\dfrac{3}{2}\right) - 3 = -3 - 3 = -6$.

  The right side of the equation is equal to $4 \cdot \left(-\dfrac{3}{2}\right) = 2 \cdot (-3) = -6$.

  Since the left side equals the right side, we know we have found the correct number x that solves the equation $2x - 3 = 4x$.

Lesson 4:	Solving a Linear Equation
Date:	11/8/13

39

Example 2 (4 minutes)

- Solve the linear equation $\frac{3}{5}x - 21 = 15$. Keep in mind that our goal is to transform the equation so that it is in the form of x equal to a constant. If we assume that the equation is true for some number x, which property should we use to help us reach our goal and how should we use it?

Again, provide students time to decide which property is "best" to use first.

  □   *We should use: If $A = B$, then $A + C = B + C$, where the number C is 21.*

Note to teacher: If students suggest that we subtract 15 from both sides, i.e., make C be -15, then remind them that we want the form of x equal to a constant. Subtracting 15 from both sides of the equal sign puts the x and all of the constants on the same side of the equal sign. There is nothing mathematically incorrect about subtracting 15; it just doesn't get us any closer to reaching our goal.

- If we use $A + C = B + C$, then we have the true statement:

$$\frac{3}{5}x - 21 + 21 = 15 + 21$$

  and

$$\frac{3}{5}x = 36.$$

  Which property should we use to reach our goal, and how should we use it?

  □   *We should use: If $A = B$, then $A \cdot C = B \cdot C$, where C is $\frac{5}{3}$.*

- If we use $A \cdot C = B \cdot C$, then we have the true statement:

$$\frac{3}{5}x \cdot \frac{5}{3} = 36 \cdot \frac{5}{3}$$

  and by the commutative property and the cancellation law we have:

$$x = 12 \cdot 5 = 60.$$

- Does $x = 60$ satisfy the equation $\frac{3}{5}x - 21 = 15$?

  □   *Yes, because the left side of the equation is equal to $\frac{180}{5} - 21 = 36 - 21 = 15$. Since the right side is also 15, then we know that $x = 60$ is a solution to $\frac{3}{5}x - 21 = 15$.*

Example 3 (5 minutes)

- The properties of equality are not the only properties we can use with equations. What other properties do we know that could make solving an equation more efficient?

  □   *We know the distributive property, which allows us to expand and simplify expressions.*

  □   *We know the commutative and associative properties, which allow us to rearrange and group terms within expressions.*

Now we will solve the linear equation $\frac{1}{5}x + 13 + x = 1 - 9x + 22$. Is there anything we can do to the linear expression on the left side to transform it into an expression with fewer terms?

- □ *Yes, we can use the commutative and distributive properties:*

$$\frac{1}{5}x + 13 + x = \frac{1}{5}x + x + 13$$
$$= \frac{6}{5}x + 13$$

- ■ Is there anything we can do to the linear expression on the right side to transform it into an expression with fewer terms?

  - □ *Yes, we can use the commutative property:*

$$1 - 9x + 22 = 1 + 22 - 9x$$
$$= 23 - 9x$$

- ■ Now we have the equation: $\frac{6}{5}x + 13 = 23 - 9x$. What should we do now to solve the equation?

Students should come up with the following four responses as to what should be done first. A case can be made for each of them being the "best" move. In this case, each first move gets us one step closer to our goal of having the solution in the form of x equal to a constant. Select one option and move forward with solving the equation (the notes that follow align to the first choice, subtracting 13 from both sides of the equal sign).

- □ *We should subtract 13 from both sides of the equal sign.*
- □ *We should subtract 23 from both sides of the equal sign.*
- □ *We should add 9x to both sides of the equal sign.*
- □ *We should subtract $\frac{6}{5}x$ from both sides of the equal sign.*

- ■ Let's choose to subtract 13 from both sides of the equal sign. Though all options were generally equal with respect to being the "best" first step, I chose this one because when I subtract 13 on both sides, the value of the constant on the left side is positive. I prefer to work with positive numbers. Then we have

$$\frac{6}{5}x + 13 - 13 = 23 - 13 - 9x$$
$$\frac{6}{5}x = 10 - 9x$$

> **Note to Teacher:**
>
> There are many ways to solve this equation. Any of the actions listed below are acceptable. In fact, a student could say: "add 100 to both sides of the equal sign," and that, too, would be an acceptable action. It may not lead us directly to our answer, but it is still an action that would make a mathematically correct statement. Make clear to students that it doesn't matter which option they choose or in which order; what matters is that they use the properties of equality to make true statements that lead to a solution in the form of x equal to a constant.

- ■ What should we do next? Why?

  - □ *We should add 9x to both sides of the equal sign. We want our solution in the form of x equal to a constant, and this move puts all terms with an x on the same side of the equal sign.*

- ■ Adding $9x$ to both sides of the equal sign, we have:

$$\frac{6}{5}x + 9x = 10 - 9x + 9x$$
$$\frac{51}{5}x = 10$$

> **Note to Teacher:**
>
> We still have options. If students say we should subtract $\frac{6}{5}x$ from both sides of the equal sign, remind them of our goal of obtaining the x equal to a constant.

Lesson 4:	Solving a Linear Equation
Date:	11/8/13

- What do we need to do now?

  ▫ *We should multiply $\frac{5}{51}$ on both sides of the equal sign.*

- Then we have:

$$\frac{51}{5}x \cdot \frac{5}{51} = 10 \cdot \frac{5}{51}$$

By the commutative property and the fact that $\frac{5}{51} \times \frac{51}{5} = 1$, we have

$$x = \frac{50}{51}.$$

- Since all transformed versions of the original equation are true, we can select any of them to check our answer. However, it is best to check the solution in the original equation because we may have made a mistake transforming the equation.

$$\frac{1}{5}x + 13 + x = 1 - 9x + 22$$

$$\frac{1}{5}\left(\frac{50}{51}\right) + 13 + \frac{50}{51} = 1 - 9\left(\frac{50}{51}\right) + 22$$

$$\frac{6}{5}\left(\frac{50}{51}\right) + 13 = 23 - 9\left(\frac{50}{51}\right)$$

$$\frac{300}{255} + 13 = 23 - \frac{450}{51}$$

$$\frac{3615}{255} = \frac{723}{51}$$

$$\frac{723}{51} = \frac{723}{51}$$

Since both sides of our equation equal $\frac{723}{51}$, then we know our answer is correct.

Exercises 1–5 (10 minutes)

Students work on Exercises 1–5 independently.

Exercises 1–5

For each problem, show your work and check that your solution is correct.

1. **Solve the linear equation: $x + x + 2 + x + 4 + x + 6 = -28$. State the property that justifies your first step and why you chose it.**

    The left side of the equation can be transformed from $x + x + 2 + x + 4 + x + 6$ to $4x + 12$ using the commutative and distributive properties. Using these properties decreases the number of terms of the equation. Now we have the equation:

$$4x + 12 = -28$$
$$4x + 12 - 12 = -28 - 12$$
$$4x = -40$$
$$\frac{1}{4} \cdot 4x = -40 \cdot \frac{1}{4}$$
$$x = -10$$

    The left side of the equation is equal to $(-10) + (-10) + 2 + (-10) + 4 + (-10) + 6$ which is -28. Since the left side is equal to the right side, then $x = -10$ is the solution to the equation.

    Note: Students could use the division property in the last step to get the answer.

---

2. Solve the linear equation: $2(3x + 2) = 2x - 1 + x$. State the property that justifies your first step and why you chose it.

Both sides of equation can be rewritten using the distributive property. I have to use it on the left side to expand the expression. I have to use it on the right side to collect like terms.

The left side is:

$$2(3x + 2) = 6x + 4$$

The right side is:

$$2x - 1 + x = 2x + x - 1$$
$$= 3x - 1$$

The equation is:

$$6x + 4 = 3x - 1$$
$$6x + 4 - 4 = 3x - 1 - 4$$
$$6x = 3x - 5$$
$$6x - 3x = 3x - 3x - 5$$
$$3x = -5$$
$$\frac{1}{3} \cdot 3x = \frac{1}{3} \cdot (-5)$$
$$x = -\frac{5}{3}$$

The left side of the equation is equal to $2(-5 + 2) = 2(-3) = -6$. The right side of the equation is equal to $-5 - 1 = -6$. Since both sides are equal to -6, then $x = -\frac{5}{3}$ is a solution to $2(3x + 2) = 2x - 1 + x$.

Note: Students could use the division property in the last step to get the answer.

3. Solve the linear equation: $x - 9 = \frac{3}{5}x$. State the property that justifies your first step and why you chose it.

I chose to use the subtraction property of equality to get all terms with an x on one side of the equal sign.

$$x - 9 = \frac{3}{5}x$$
$$x - x - 9 = \frac{3}{5}x - x$$
$$-9 = -\frac{2}{5}x$$
$$-\frac{5}{2} \cdot (-9) = -\frac{5}{2} \cdot -\frac{2}{5}x$$
$$\frac{45}{2} = x$$

The left side of the equation is $\frac{45}{2} - \frac{18}{2} = \frac{27}{2}$. The right side is $\frac{3}{5} \cdot \frac{45}{2} = \frac{3}{1} \cdot \frac{9}{2} = \frac{27}{2}$. Since both sides are equal to the same number, then $x = \frac{45}{2}$ is a solution to $x - 9 = \frac{3}{5}x$.

4. Solve the linear equation: $29 - 3x = 5x + 5$. State the property that justifies your first step and why you chose it.

I chose to use the addition property of equality to get all terms with an x on one side of the equal sign.

$$29 - 3x = 5x + 5$$
$$29 - 3x + 3x = 5x + 3x + 5$$
$$29 = 8x + 5$$
$$29 - 5 = 8x + 5 - 5$$
$$24 = 8x$$
$$\frac{1}{8} \cdot 24 = \frac{1}{8} \cdot 8x$$
$$3 = x$$

The left side of the equal sign is $29 - 3(3) = 29 - 9 = 20$. The right side is equal to $5(3) + 5 = 15 + 5 = 20$. Since both sides are equal, $x = 3$ is a solution to $29 - 3x = 5x + 5$.

Note: Students could use the division property in the last step to get the answer.

COMMON CORE™

| Lesson 4: | Solving a Linear Equation |
| Date: | 11/8/13 |

43

5. Solve the linear equation: $\frac{1}{3}x - 5 + 171 = x$. State the property that justifies your first step and why you chose it.

I chose to combine the constants −5 and 171. Then, I used the subtraction property of equality to get all terms with an x on one side of the equal sign.

$$\frac{1}{3}x - 5 + 171 = x$$

$$\frac{1}{3}x + 166 = x$$

$$\frac{1}{3}x - \frac{1}{3}x + 166 = x - \frac{1}{3}x$$

$$166 = \frac{2}{3}x$$

$$166 \cdot \frac{3}{2} = \frac{3}{2} \cdot \frac{2}{3}x$$

$$83 \times 3 = x$$

$$249 = x$$

The left side of the equation is $\frac{1}{3} \cdot 249 - 5 + 171 = 83 - 5 + 171 = 78 + 171 = 249$, which is exactly equal to the right side. Therefore, $x = 249$ is a solution to $\frac{1}{3}x - 5 + 171 = x$.

Closing (5 minutes)

Summarize, or ask students to summarize, the main points from the lesson:

- We know that properties of equality, when used to transform equations, make equations with fewer terms that are simpler to solve.

- When solving an equation, we want the answer to be in the form of the symbol x equal to a constant.

Lesson Summary

The properties of equality, shown below, are used to transform equations into simpler forms. If A, B, C are rational numbers, then

- If $A = B$, then $A + C = B + C$ **Addition Property of Equality**
- If $A = B$, then $A - C = B - C$ **Subtraction Property of Equality**
- If $A = B$, then $A \cdot C = B \cdot C$ **Multiplication Property of Equality**
- If $A = B$, then $\frac{A}{C} = \frac{B}{C}$, where C is not equal to zero   **Division Property of Equality**

To solve an equation, transform the equation until you get to the form of x equal to a constant ($x = 5$, for example).

Exit Ticket (5 minutes)

Lesson 4:   Solving a Linear Equation
Date: 11/8/13

Name _____   Date_____

Lesson 4: Solving a Linear Equation

Exit Ticket

1. Guess a number for x that would make the equation true. Check your solution.
$$5x - 2 = 8$$

2. Use the properties of equality to solve the equation: $7x - 4 + x = 12$. State which property justifies your first step and why you chose it. Check your solution.

3. Use the properties of equality to solve the equation: $3x + 2 - x = 11x + 9$. State which property justifies your first step and why you chose it. Check your solution.

Exit Ticket Sample Solutions

1. **Guess a number for x that would make the equation true. Check your solution.**

    $$5x - 2 = 8$$

    When $x = 2$, the left side of the equation is 8, which is the same as the right side. Therefore, $x = 2$ is the solution to the equation.

2. **Use the properties of equality to solve the equation: $7x - 4 + x = 12$. State which property justifies your first step and why you chose it. Check your solution.**

    I used the commutative and distributive properties on the left side of the equal sign to simply the expression to fewer terms.

    $$7x - 4 + x = 12$$
    $$8x - 4 = 12$$
    $$8x - 4 + 4 = 12 + 4$$
    $$8x = 16$$
    $$\frac{8}{8}x = \frac{16}{8}$$
    $$x = 2$$

    The left side of the equation is $7(2) - 4 + 2 = 14 - 4 + 2 = 12$. The right side is also 12. Since the left side equals the right side, $x = 2$ is the solution to the equation.

3. **Use the properties of equality to solve the equation: $3x + 2 - x = 11x + 9$. Check your solution.**

    I used the commutative and distributive properties on the left side of the equal sign to simplify the expression to fewer terms.

    $$3x + 2 - x = 11x + 9$$
    $$2x + 2 = 11x + 9$$
    $$2x - 2x + 2 = 11x - 2x + 9$$
    $$2 = 9x + 9$$
    $$2 - 9 = 9x + 9 - 9$$
    $$-7 = 9x$$
    $$\frac{-7}{9} = \frac{9}{9}x$$
    $$-\frac{7}{9} = x$$

    The left side of the equation is $3\left(\frac{-7}{9}\right) + 2 - \frac{-7}{9} = -\frac{21}{9} + \frac{18}{9} + \frac{7}{9} = \frac{4}{9}$. The right side is $11\left(-\frac{7}{9}\right) + 9 = \frac{-77}{9} + \frac{81}{9} = \frac{4}{9}$.

    Since the left side equals the right side, $x = -\frac{7}{9}$ is the solution to the equation.

Problem Set Sample Solutions

Students solve equations using properties of equality.

For each problem, show your work and check that your solution is correct.

1. Solve the linear equation: $x + 4 + 3x = 72$. State the property that justifies your first step and why you chose it.

    I used the commutative and distributive properties on the left side of the equal sign to simplify the expression to fewer terms.

    $$x + 4 + 3x = 72$$
    $$4x + 4 = 72$$
    $$4x + 4 - 4 = 72 - 4$$
    $$4x = 68$$
    $$\frac{4}{4}x = \frac{68}{4}$$
    $$x = 17$$

    The left side is equal to $17 + 4 + 3(17) = 21 + 51 = 72$, which is what the right side is. Therefore, $x = 17$ is a solution to the equation $x + 4 + 3x = 72$.

2. Solve the linear equation: $x + 3 + x - 8 + x = 55$. State the property that justifies your first step and why you chose it.

    I used the commutative and distributive properties on the left side of the equal sign to simplify the expression to fewer terms.

    $$x + 3 + x - 8 + x = 55$$
    $$3x - 5 = 55$$
    $$3x - 5 + 5 = 55 + 5$$
    $$3x = 60$$
    $$\frac{3}{3}x = \frac{60}{3}$$
    $$x = 20$$

    The left side is equal to $20 + 3 + 20 - 8 + 20 = 43 - 8 + 20 = 35 + 20 = 55$, which is equal to the right side. Therefore, $x = 20$ is a solution to $x + 3 + x - 8 + x = 55$.

3. Solve the linear equation: $\frac{1}{2}x + 10 = -\frac{1}{4}x + 54$. State the property that justifies your first step and why you chose it.

    I chose to use the subtraction property of equality to get all of the constants on one side of the equal sign.

    $$\frac{1}{2}x + 10 = \frac{1}{4}x + 54$$
    $$\frac{1}{2}x + 10 - 10 = \frac{1}{4}x + 54 - 10$$
    $$\frac{1}{2}x = -\frac{1}{4}x + 44$$
    $$\frac{1}{2}x - \frac{1}{4}x = \frac{1}{4}x - \frac{1}{4}x + 44$$
    $$\frac{1}{4}x = 44$$
    $$4 \cdot \frac{1}{4}x = 4 \cdot 44$$
    $$x = 176$$

    The left side of the equation is $\frac{1}{2}(176) + 10 = 88 + 10 = 98$. The right side of the equation is $\frac{1}{4}(176) + 54 = 44 + 54 = 98$. Since both sides equal 98, $x = 176$ is a solution to the equation $\frac{1}{2}x + 10 = \frac{1}{4}x + 54$.

Lesson 4:	Solving a Linear Equation
Date:	11/8/13

4. Solve the linear equation: $\frac{1}{4}x + 18 = x$. State the property that justifies your first step and why you chose it.

    I chose to use the subtraction property of equality to get all terms with an x on one side of the equal sign.

    $$\frac{1}{4}x + 18 = x$$
    $$\frac{1}{4}x - \frac{1}{4}x + 18 = x - \frac{1}{4}x$$
    $$18 = \frac{3}{4}x$$
    $$\frac{4}{3} \cdot 18 = \frac{4}{3} \cdot \frac{3}{4}x$$
    $$24 = x$$

    The left side of the equation is $\frac{1}{4}(24) + 18 = 6 + 18 = 24$, which is what the right side is equal to. Therefore, $x = 24$ is a solution to $\frac{1}{4}x + 18 = x$.

5. Solve the linear equation: $17 - x = \frac{1}{3} \cdot 15 + 6$. State the property that justifies your first step and why you chose it.

    The right side of the equation can be simplified to 11. Then the equation is

    $$17 - x = 11$$

    and $x = 6$. Both sides of the equation equal 11; therefore, $x = 6$ is a solution to the equation $17 - x = \frac{1}{3} \cdot 15 + 6$. I was able to solve the equation mentally without using the properties of equality.

6. Solve the linear equation: $\frac{x+x+2}{4} = 189.5$. State the property that justifies your first step and why you chose it.

    $$\frac{x+x+2}{4} = 189.5$$
    $$x + x + 2 = 4(189.5)$$
    $$2x + 2 = 758$$
    $$2x + 2 - 2 = 758 - 2$$
    $$2x = 756$$
    $$\frac{2}{2}x = \frac{756}{2}$$
    $$x = 378$$

    The left side of the equation is $\frac{378+378+2}{4} = \frac{758}{4} = 189.5$, which is equal to the right side of the equation. Therefore, $x = 378$ is a solution to $\frac{x+x+2}{4} = 189.5$.

7. Alysha solved the linear equation: $2x - 3 - 9x = 14 + x - 1$. Her work is shown below. When she checked her answer, the left side of the equation did not equal the right side. Find and explain Alysha's error, and then solve the equation correctly.

$$2x - 3 - 9x = 14 + x - 1.$$
$$-6x - 3 = 13 + 2x$$
$$-6x - 3 + 3 = 13 + 3 + 2x$$
$$-6x = 16 + 2x$$
$$-6x + 2x = 16$$
$$-4x = 16$$
$$\frac{-4}{-4}x = \frac{16}{-4}$$
$$x = -4$$

Alysha made a mistake on the 5th line. She added $2x$ to the left side of the equal sign and subtracted $2x$ on the right side of the equal sign. To use the property correctly, she should have subtracted $2x$ on both sides of the equal sign, making the equation at that point:

$$-6x - 2x = 16 + 2x - 2x$$
$$-8x = 16$$
$$\frac{-8}{-8}x = \frac{16}{-8}$$
$$x = -2$$

Lesson 5: Writing and Solving Linear Equations

Student Outcomes

- Students apply knowledge of geometry to writing and solving linear equations.

Lesson Notes

All of the problems in this lesson relate to what students have learned about geometry in recent modules and previous years. The purpose is two-fold, first, we want to reinforce what students have learned about geometry, and second, we want to demonstrate a need for writing and solving an equation in a context that is familiar. Throughout the lesson students solve mathematical problems that relate directly to what students have learned about angle relationships, congruence, and the triangle sum theorem. Encourage students to draw a diagram to represent the situation presented in the word problems.

Classwork

Example 1 (5 minutes)

- Solve the following:

> **Example 1**
>
> One angle is five less than three times the size of another angle. Together they have a sum of $143°$. What are the sizes of each angle?

MP.1

Provide students with time to make sense of the problem and persevere in solving it. They could begin their work by guessing and checking, drawing a diagram, or other methods as appropriate. Then move to the algebraic method shown below.

- What do we need to do first to solve this problem?
  - *First we need to define our variable (symbol). Let x be the size of the first angle.*
- If x is the size of the first angle, how do you represent the size of the second angle?
  - *The second angle is $3x - 5$.*
- What is the equation that represents this situation?
  - *The equation is: $x + 3x - 5 = 143$.*
- The equation that represents this situation is: $x + 3x - 5 = 143$. Solve for x, then determine the size of each angle.

> *Scaffolding:*
>
> Model for students how to use diagrams to help make sense of the problems throughout this lesson. Encourage students to use diagrams to help them understand the situation.

As students share their solutions for this and subsequent problems, ask them a variety of questions to reinforce the learning of the last few lessons. For example, you can ask students whether or not this is a linear equation and how they know, to justify their steps and explain why they chose their particular first step, what the solution means, or how they know their answer is correct.

Student work:

$$x + 3x - 5 = 143$$
$$(1 + 3)x - 5 = 143$$
$$4x - 5 = 143$$
$$4x - 5 + 5 = 143 + 5$$
$$4x = 148$$
$$x = 37$$

The size of the first angle is $37°$. *The second angle is* $3(37) - 5 = 111 - 5 = 106°$.

- Compare the method you tried at the beginning of the problem with the algebraic method. What advantage does writing and solving an equation have?

  - *Writing and solving an equation is a more direct method than the one I tried before. It allows me to find the answer more quickly.*

- Could we have defined x to be the size of the second angle? If so, what, if anything, would change?

  - *If we let x be the size of the second angle, then the equation would change, but the answers for the sizes of the angles should remain the same.*

- If x is the size of the second angle, how would we write the size of the first angle?

  - *The first angle would be $\frac{x+5}{3}$.*

- The equation that represents the situation is $x + \frac{x+5}{3} = 143$. How should we solve this equation?

  - *We could add the fractions together, then solve for x.*

  - *We could multiply every term by 3 to change the fraction to a whole number.*

- Using either method, solve the equation. Verify that the sizes of the angles are the same as before.

  -

$$x + \frac{x + 5}{3} = 143$$
$$\frac{3x}{3} + \frac{x + 5}{3} = 143$$
$$\frac{3x + x + 5}{3} = 143$$
$$3x + x + 5 = 143(3)$$
$$(3 + 1)x + 5 = 429$$
$$4x + 5 = 429$$
$$4x + 5 - 5 = 429 - 5$$
$$4x = 424$$
$$x = 106$$

> **Scaffolding:**
> You may need to remind students how to add fractions by rewriting term(s) as equivalent fractions then adding the numerators. Provide support as needed.

COMMON CORE™

Lesson 5:	Writing and Solving Linear Equations
Date:	11/8/13

     ◻   *The size of the second angle is* 106°. *The measure of the first angle is* $\frac{x+5}{3} = \frac{106+5}{3} = \frac{111}{3} = 37°$.

          OR

$$x + \frac{x+5}{3} = 143$$

$$3\left(x + \frac{x+5}{3} = 143\right)$$

$$3x + x + 5 = 429$$

$$4x + 5 = 429$$

$$4x + 5 - 5 = 429 - 5$$

$$4x = 424$$

$$x = 106$$

The size of the second angle is 106°. *The measure of the first angle is* $\frac{x+5}{3} = \frac{106+5}{3} = \frac{111}{3} = 37°$.

- ▪ Whether we let x represent the first angle or the second angle does not change our answers. Whether we solve the equation using the first or second method does not change our answers. What matters is that we accurately write the information in the problem and correctly use the properties of equality. You may solve a problem differently than your classmates or teachers. Again, what matters most is that what you do is accurate and correct.

Example 2 (12 minutes)

- ▪ Solve the following:

> **Example 2**
>
> **Given a right triangle, find the size of the angles if one angle is ten more than four times the other angle and the third angle is the right angle.**

Give students time to work. As they work, walk around and identify students who are writing and solving the problem in different ways. The instructional goal of this example is to make clear that there are different ways to solve a linear equation as opposed to one "right way". Select students to share their work with the class. If students don't come up with different ways of solving the equation, talk them through the following student work samples.

Again, as students share their solutions, ask them a variety of questions to reinforce the learning of the last few lessons. For example, you can ask students whether or not this is a linear equation and how they know, or to justify their steps and explain why they chose their particular first step, what the solution means, or how they know their answer is correct.

Solution One

Let x be the size of the first angle. Then the second angle is $4x + 10$. The sum of the measures for the angles for this right triangle is as follows: $x + 4x + 10 + 90 = 180$.

$$x + 4x + 10 + 90 = 180$$
$$(1 + 4)x + 100 = 180$$
$$5x + 100 = 180$$
$$5x + 100 - 100 = 180 - 100$$
$$5x = 80$$
$$x = 16$$

The measure of the first angle is $16°$, the measure of the second angle is $4(16) + 10 = 64 + 10 = 74°$, and the third angle is $90°$.

Solution Two

Let x be the size of the first angle. Then the second angle is $4x + 10$. Since we have a right triangle we already know that one angle is $90°$ which means that the sum of the other two angles is 90: $x + 4x + 10 = 90$.

$$x + 4x + 10 = 90$$
$$(1 + 4)x + 10 = 90$$
$$5x + 10 = 90$$
$$5x + 10 - 10 = 90 - 10$$
$$5x = 80$$
$$x = 16$$

The measure of the first angle is $16°$, the measure of the second angle is $4(16) + 10 = 64 + 10 = 74°$, and the third angle is $90°$.

Solution Three

Let x be the size of the second angle. Then the first angle is $\frac{x-10}{4}$. Since we have a right triangle we already know that one angle is $90°$ which means that the sum of the other two angles is 90: $x + \frac{x-10}{4} = 90$.

$$x + \frac{x-10}{4} = 90$$
$$4\left(x + \frac{x-10}{4} = 90\right)$$
$$4x + x - 10 = 360$$
$$(4 + 1)x - 10 = 360$$
$$5x - 10 = 360$$
$$5x - 10 + 10 = 360 + 10$$
$$5x = 370$$
$$x = 74$$

The measure of the second angle is $74°$, the measure of the first angle is $\frac{74-10}{4} = \frac{64}{4} = 16°$, and the third angle is $90°$.

<u>Solution Four</u>

Let x be the size of the second angle. Then the first angle is $\frac{x-10}{4}$. The sum of the three angles is as follows: $x + \frac{x-10}{4} +$
$90 = 180$.

$$x + \frac{x-10}{4} + 90 = 180$$
$$x + \frac{x-10}{4} + 90 - 90 = 180 - 90$$
$$x + \frac{x-10}{4} = 90$$
$$\frac{4x}{4} + \frac{x-10}{4} = 90$$
$$\frac{4x+x-10}{4} = 90$$
$$4x + x - 10 = 360$$
$$5x - 10 + 10 = 360 + 10$$
$$5x = 370$$
$$x = 74$$

The second angle is 74°, the first angle is $\frac{74-10}{4} = \frac{64}{4} = 16°$, and the third angle is 90°.

Make sure students see at least four different methods of solving the problem. Conclude this example with the statements below.

- Each method was slightly different either in terms of how the variable was defined or how the properties of equality were used to solve the equation. The way you find the answer may be different than your classmates or your teacher.

- As long as you write accurately and do what is mathematically correct, you will find the correct answer.

Example 3 (4 minutes)

- A pair of alternate interior angles are described as follows. One angle is fourteen more than half a number. The other angle is six less than half a number. Are the angles congruent?

- We will begin by assuming that the angles are congruent. If the angles are congruent, what does that mean about their measures?

  □ *It means that they are equal in measure.*

- Write an expression that describes each angle.

  □ *One angle is $\frac{x}{2} + 14$ and the other angle is $\frac{x}{2} - 6$.*

- If the angles are congruent, we can write the equation is $\frac{x}{2} + 14 = \frac{x}{2} - 6$. We know that our properties of equality allow us to transform equations while making sure that they remain true.

$$\frac{x}{2} + 14 = \frac{x}{2} - 6$$
$$\frac{x}{2} - \frac{x}{2} + 14 = \frac{x}{2} - \frac{x}{2} - 6,$$
$$14 \neq -6.$$

Therefore, our assumption was not correct and the angles are not congruent.

Lesson 5:   Writing and Solving Linear Equations
Date: 11/8/13

54

Exercises 1–6 (16 minutes)

Students complete Exercises 1–6 independently or in pairs.

Exercises 1–6

For each of the following problems, write an equation and solve.

1. A pair of congruent angles are described as follows: the measure of one angle is three more than twice a number and the other angle's measure is 54.5 less than three times the number. Determine the size of the angles.

   Let x be the number. Then the measure of one angle is $3 + 2x$ and the measure of the other angle is $3x - 54.5$. Because the angles are congruent, their measures are equal. Therefore,

$$3 + 2x = 3x - 54.5$$
$$3 + 2x - 2x = 3x - 2x - 54.5$$
$$3 = x - 54.5$$
$$3 + 54.5 = x - 54.5 + 54.5$$
$$57.5 = x$$

   Then each angle is $3 + 2(57.5) = 3 + 115 = 118°$.

2. The measure of one angle is described as twelve more than four times a number. Its supplement is twice as large. Find the measure of each angle.

   Let x be the number. Then the measure of one angle is $4x + 12$. The other angle is $2(4x + 12) = 8x + 24$. Since the angles are supplementary, their sum must be 180:

$$4x + 12 + 8x + 24 = 180$$
$$12x + 36 = 180$$
$$12x + 36 - 36 = 180 - 36$$
$$12x = 144$$
$$x = 12$$

   One angle is $4(12) + 12 = 48 + 12 = 60°$ and the other angle is $180 - 60 = 120°$.

3. A triangle has angles described as follows: the first angle is four more than seven times a number, another angle is four less than the first and the third angle is twice as large as the first. What are the sizes of each of the angles?

   Let x be the number. The measure of the first angle is $7x + 4$. The measure of the second angle is $7x + 4 - 4 = 7x$. The measure of the third angle is $2(7x + 4) = 14x + 8$. The sum of the angles of a triangle must be $180°$.

$$7x + 4 + 7x + 14x + 8 = 180$$
$$28x + 12 = 180$$
$$28x + 12 - 12 = 180 - 12$$
$$28x = 168$$
$$x = 6$$

   The measure of the first angle is $7(6) + 4 = 42 + 4 = 46°$. The measure of the second angle is $7(6) = 42°$. The measure of the third angle is $2(46) = 92°$.

4. One angle measures nine more than six times a number. A sequence of rigid motions maps the angle onto another angle that is described as being thirty less than nine times the number. What is the measure of the angles?

   Let x be the number. Then the measure of one angle is $6x + 9$. The measure of the other angle is $9x - 30$. Since rigid motions preserve the measures of angles, then the measure of these angles is equal.

$$6x + 9 = 9x - 30$$
$$6x + 9 - 9 = 9x - 30 - 9$$
$$6x = 9x - 39$$
$$6x - 9x = 9x - 9x - 39$$
$$-3x = -39$$
$$x = 13$$

   The angles measure $6(13) + 9 = 78 + 9 = 87°$.

---

5. A right triangle is described as having an angle of size "six less than negative two times a number," another angle that is "three less than negative one-fourth the number", and a right angle. What are the measures of the angles?

Let x be a number. Then one angle is $-2x - 6$. The other angle is $-\frac{x}{4} - 3$. The sum of the two angles must be $90°$.

$$-2x - 6 + \left(-\frac{x}{4}\right) - 3 = 90$$
$$\left(-\frac{8x}{4}\right) + \left(-\frac{x}{4}\right) - 9 = 90$$
$$\left(-\frac{9x}{4}\right) - 9 + 9 = 90 + 9$$
$$-\frac{9x}{4} = 99$$
$$-9x = 396$$
$$x = -44$$

One of the angles is $-2(-44) - 6 = 88 - 6 = 82°$. The other angle is $90 - 82 = 8°$.

6. One angle is one less than six times the size of another. The two angles are complementary angles. Find the size of each angle.

Let x be the measure of the first angle. Then the measure of the second angle is $6x - 1$. The sum of the measures will be 90 because the angles are complementary.

$$x + 6x - 1 = 90$$
$$7x - 1 = 90$$
$$7x - 1 + 1 = 90 + 1$$
$$7x = 91$$
$$x = 13$$

One angle is $13°$ and the other angle is $6(13) - 1 = 78 - 1 = 77°$.

Closing (4 minutes)

Summarize, or ask students to summarize, the main points from the lesson:

- We know that an algebraic method for solving equations is more efficient than guessing and checking.
- We know how to write and solve equations that relate to angles, triangles, and geometry in general.
- We know that drawing a diagram can sometimes make it easier to understand a problem and that there is more than one way to solve an equation.

Exit Ticket (4 minutes)

Name _____   Date _____

Lesson 5: Writing and Solving Linear Equations

Exit Ticket

For each of the following problems, write an equation and solve.

1. Given a right triangle, find the measures of all the angles if one angle is a right angle and the measure of the second angle is six less than seven times the measure of the third angle.

2. In a triangle, the measure of the first angle is six times a number. The measure of the second angle is nine less than the first angle. The measure of the third angle is three times the number more than the measure of the first angle. Determine the measures of each of the angles.

Exit Ticket Sample Solutions

1. Given a right triangle, find the measures of all of the angles if one angle is a right angle and the measure of a second angle is six less than seven times the measure of the third angle.

    Let x represent the measure of the third angle. Then $7x - 6$ can represent the measure of the second angle. The sum of the two angles in the right triangles will be $90°$.

    $$7x - 6 + x = 90$$
    $$8x - 6 = 90$$
    $$8x - 6 + 6 = 90 + 6$$
    $$8x = 96$$
    $$\frac{8}{8}x = \frac{96}{8}$$
    $$x = 12$$

    The measure of the third angle is $12°$ and the measure of the second angle is $7(12) - 6 = 84 - 6 = 78°,$. The measure of the third angle is $90°$.

2. In a triangle, the measure of the first angle is six times a number. The measure of the second angle is nine less than the first angle. The measure of the third angle is three times the number more than the measure of the first angle. Determine the measures of each of the angles.

    Let x be the number. Then the measure of the first angles is $6x$, the measure of the second angle is $6x - 9$, and the measure of the third angle is $3x + 6x$. The sum of the measures of the angles in a triangle is $180°$.

    $$6x + 6x - 9 + 3x + 6x = 180$$
    $$21x - 9 = 180$$
    $$21x - 9 + 9 = 180 + 9$$
    $$21x = 189$$
    $$\frac{21}{21}x = \frac{189}{21}$$
    $$x = 9$$

    The measure of the first angle is $6(9) = 54°$. The measure of the second angle is $54 - 9 = 45°$. The measure of the third angle is $54 + 3(9) = 54 + 27 = 81°$.

Note to teacher: There are several ways to solve problems like these. For example, a student may let x be the size of the first angle, and write the size of the other angles accordingly. Either way, make sure that students are defining their symbols and correctly using the properties of equality to solve.

Problem Set Sample Solutions

Students practice writing and solving linear equations.

For each of the following problems, write an equation and solve.

1. The measure of one angle is thirteen less than five times the measure of another angle. The sum of the measures of the two angles is $140°$. Determine the measures of each of the angles.

    Let x be the size of the one angle. Then the measure of the other angle is $5x - 13$.

    $$x + 5x - 13 = 140$$
    $$6x - 13 = 140$$
    $$6x - 13 + 13 = 140 + 13$$
    $$6x = 153$$
    $$x = 25.5$$

    The measure of one angle is $25.5°$ and the measure of the other angle is $140 - 25.5 = 114.5°$.

Lesson 5:   Writing and Solving Linear Equations
Date: 11/8/13

2. An angle measures seventeen more than three times a number. Its supplement is three more than seven times the number. What is the measure of each angle?

Let x be the number. Then one angle is $3x + 17$. The other angle is $7x + 3$. Since the angles are supplementary, the sum of their measures will be 180.

$$3x + 17 + 7x + 3 = 180$$
$$10x + 20 = 180$$
$$10x + 20 - 20 = 180 - 20$$
$$10x = 160$$
$$x = 16$$

One angle is $3(16) + 17 = 65°$. The other angle is $180 - 65 = 115°$.

3. The angles of a triangle are described as follows: $\angle A$ is the largest angle, its measure is twice the measure of $\angle B$. The measure of $\angle C$ is 2 less than half the measure of $\angle B$. Find the measures of the three angles.

Let x be the measure of $\angle B$. Then the measure of $\angle A = 2x$ and $\angle C = \frac{x}{2} - 2$. The sum of the measures of the angles must be 180.

$$x + 2x + \frac{x}{2} - 2 = 180$$
$$3x + \frac{x}{2} - 2 + 2 = 180 + 2$$
$$3x + \frac{x}{2} = 182$$
$$\frac{6x}{2} + \frac{x}{2} = 182$$
$$\frac{7x}{2} = 182$$
$$7x = 364$$
$$x = 52$$

The measures of the angles are as follows: $\angle A = 104°, \angle B = 52°, and \angle C = \frac{52}{2} - 2 = 26 - 2 = 24°$.

4. A pair of corresponding angles are described as follows: the measure of one angle is five less than seven times a number and the measure of the other angle is eight more than seven times the number. Are the angles congruent? Why or why not?

Let x be the number. Then measure of one angle is $7x - 5$ and the measure of the other angle is $7x + 8$. Assume they are congruent, which means their measures are equal.

$$7x - 5 = 7x + 8$$
$$7x - 7x - 5 = 7x - 7x + 8$$
$$-5 \neq 8$$

Since $-5 \neq 8$, the angles are not congruent.

5. The measure of one angle is eleven more than four times a number. Another angle is twice the first angle's measure. The sum of the measures of the angles is $195°$. What is the measure of each angle?

Let x be the number. The measure of one angle can be represented with $4x + 11$ and the other angle's measure can be represented as $2(4x + 11) = 8x + 22$.

$$4x + 11 + 8x + 22 = 195$$
$$12x + 33 = 195$$
$$12x + 33 - 33 = 195 - 33$$
$$12x = 162$$
$$x = 13.5$$

The measure of one angle is $4(13.5) + 11 = 54 + 11 = 65°$ and the measure of the other angle is $130°$.

6. Three angles are described as follows: $\angle B$ is half the size of $\angle A$. The measure of $\angle C$ is equal to one less than 2 times the measure of $\angle B$. The sum of $\angle A$ and $\angle B$ is 114. Can the three angles form a triangle? Why or why not?

    Let x represent the measure of $\angle A$. Then the measure of $\angle B = \frac{x}{2}$ and the measure of $\angle C = 2\left(\frac{x}{2}\right) - 1 = x - 1$.

    The sum of $\angle A + \angle B = 114$.

    $$x + \frac{x}{2} = 114$$
    $$\frac{3x}{2} = 114$$
    $$3x = 228$$
    $$x = 76$$

    The measure of $\angle A = 76°$, $\angle B = \frac{76}{2} = 38°$, and $\angle C = 75°$. The sum of the three angles is $76 + 38 + 75 = 189$. Since the sum of the measures of the interior angles of a triangle must sum to $180°$, these angles do not form a triangle. Their sum is too large.

Lesson 6: Solutions of a Linear Equation

Student Outcomes

- Students transform equations into simpler forms using the distributive property.
- Students learn that not every linear equation has a solution.

Lesson Notes

The distributive property can be used to both expand and simplify expressions. Students have already used the distributive Property to "collect like terms." For example, $2x + 6x = (2 + 6)x = 8x$. Students have also used the distributive property to expand expressions. For example, $2(x + 5) = 2x + 10$. In this lesson students continue to use the distributive property to solve more complicated equations. Also highlighted in this lesson is a common error that students make when using the distributive property, which is multiplying a factor to terms that are not part of the group. For example, in the expression $3(x + 1) - 5$, students should know that they do not distribute the factor 3 to the term -5 because it is not in the group $(x + 1)$.

Classwork

Example 1 (4 minutes)

- What value of x would make the linear equation $4x + 3(4x + 7) = 4(7x + 3) - 3$ true? What is the "best" first step and why?

Have a discussion with students about what the "best" first step is and why. Make clear that the distributive property will allow us to better see and work with the terms of the linear equation. Proceed with the following discussion.

- In order to find out what that solution might be, we must use the distributive property. The left side of the equation has the following expression:

$$4x + 3(4x + 7)$$

Where and how will the distributive property be used?

  □ *We will need to use the distributive property to expand $3(4x + 7)$ and then again to collect like terms.*

- Our work for now is just on the left side of the equation, the right side will remain unchanged for the moment.

$$4x + 3(4x + 7) = 4(7x + 3) - 3$$
$$4x + 12x + 21 = 4(7x + 3) - 3$$
$$(4 + 12)x + 21 = 4(7x + 3) - 3$$
$$16x + 21 = 4(7x + 3) - 3$$

- Now we need to rewrite the right side. Again we will use the distributive property. The left side of the equation will remain unchanged.

$$16x + 21 = 4(7x + 3) - 3$$
$$16x + 21 = 28x + 12 - 3$$

- Notice that we did not apply the distributive property to the term -3. Since it was not part of the group $(7x + 3)$, it is not multiplied by 4.

$$16x + 21 = 28x + 9$$

- Now we have the transformed the given equation into the following form: $16x + 21 = 28x + 9$. Solve the equation.

  □   *Student work:*

$$16x + 21 = 28x + 9$$
$$16x - 16x + 21 = 28x - 16x + 9$$
$$21 = 12x + 9$$
$$21 - 9 = 12x + 9 - 9$$
$$12 = 12x$$
$$x = 1$$

- Is $x = 1$ really a solution to the equation $4x + 3(4x + 7) = 4(7x + 3) - 3$? How do you know?

  □   *Yes, $x = 1$ is a solution because $4 + 3(11) = 37$ and $4(10) - 3 = 37$. Since both expressions are equal to 37, then $x = 1$ is a solution to the equation.*

Example 2 (4 minutes)

- What value of x would make the following linear equation true: $20 - (3x - 9) - 2 = -(-11x + 1)$? Since we have a group of terms that is preceded by a "$-$" sign, we will simplify this first. The "$-$" sign means we need to take the opposite of each of the terms within the group, i.e., parentheses.

- We begin with the left side of the equation:

  $20 - (3x - 9) - 2 = -(-11x + 1)$

  We need only to take the opposite of the terms within the grouping symbols. Is the term -2 within the grouping symbol?

  □   *No.*

- For that reason, we need only find the opposite of $3x - 9$. What is the opposite of $3x - 9$?

  □   *The opposite of $3x - 9$ is $-3x + 9$.*

- The left side of the equation is rewritten as

$$20 - (3x - 9) - 2 = -(-11x + 1)$$
$$20 - 3x + 9 - 2 = -(-11x + 1)$$
$$20 + 9 - 2 - 3x = -(-11x + 1)$$
$$27 - 3x = -(-11x + 1)$$

- Now we rewrite the right side of the equation: $-(-11x + 1)$.

$$27 - 3x = -(-11x + 1)$$
$$27 - 3x = 11x - 1$$

> **Scaffolding:**
>
> The equation in this example can be modified to $20 - (3x - 9 + 1) = 10$ to meet the needs of diverse learners. Also consider having students fold a piece of paper in half, solving on the left side and justifying their steps on the right side.

- The transformed equation is $27 - 3x = 11x - 1$.

$$27 - 3x = 11x - 1$$
$$27 - 3x + 3x = 11x + 3x - 1$$
$$27 = 14x - 1$$
$$27 + 1 = 14x - 1 + 1$$
$$28 = 14x$$
$$2 = x$$

- Check: The left side is: $27 - 3(2) = 27 - 6 = 21$. The right side is: $11(2) - 1 = 22 - 1 = 21$. Since $21 = 21$, $x = 2$ is the solution.

Example 3 (4 minutes)

- What value of x would make the following linear equation true: $\frac{1}{2}(4x + 6) - 2 = -(5x + 9)$? Begin by transforming both sides of the equation into a simpler form.

  - *Student work:*

$$\frac{1}{2}(4x + 6) - 2 = -(5x + 9)$$
$$2x + 3 - 2 = -5x - 9$$

> *Scaffolding:*
> The equation in this example can be modified to $2x + 1 = -(5x + 9)$ to meet the needs of diverse learners.

Make sure that students do not distribute the factor $\frac{1}{2}$ to the term -2, and that they have, in general, transformed the equation correctly.

- Now that we have the simpler equation, $2x + 3 - 2 = -5x - 9$, complete the solution.

  - *Student work:*

$$2x + 3 - 2 = -5x - 9$$
$$2x + 1 = -5x - 9$$
$$2x + 1 - 1 = -5x - 9 - 1$$
$$2x + 0 = -5x - 10$$
$$2x = -5x - 10$$
$$2x + 5x = -5x + 5x - 10$$
$$(2 + 5)x = (-5 + 5)x - 10$$
$$7x = 0x - 10$$
$$7x = -10$$
$$\frac{7}{7}x = -\frac{10}{7}$$
$$x = -\frac{10}{7}$$

- Check: The left side is: $2\left(-\frac{10}{7}\right) + 1 = -\frac{20}{7} + \frac{7}{7} = -\frac{13}{7}$. The right side is: $-5\left(-\frac{10}{7}\right) - 9 = \frac{50}{7} - \frac{63}{7} = -\frac{13}{7}$. Since $-\frac{13}{7} = -\frac{13}{7}$, $x = -\frac{10}{7}$ is the solution.

Example 4 (11 minutes)

- ▪ Consider the following equation: $2(x + 1) = 2x - 3$. What value of x makes the equation true?

  - ▫ *Student work:*

$$2(x + 1) = 2x - 3$$
$$2x + 2 = 2x - 3$$
$$2x - 2x + 2 = 2x - 2x - 3$$
$$2 = -3$$

- ▪ How should we interpret $2 = -3$?

Lead a discussion with the conclusion that since $2 \neq -3$, then the equation has no solution. Allow students time to try to find a value of x that would make it true by guessing and checking. After they realize that there is no such number x, make it clear to students that some equations have no solution. Ask the following question.

MP.3

- ▪ Why do you think this happened?

  - ▫ *We know that an equation is a statement of equality. The linear expressions were such that they could not be equal to each other, no matter what value was substituted for x.*

- ▪ What value of x would make the following linear equation true: $9(4 - 2x) - 3 = 4 - 6(3x - 5)$? Transform the equation by simplifying both sides.

  - ▫ *Student work:*

$$9(4 - 2x) - 3 = 4 - 6(3x - 5)$$
$$36 - 18x - 3 = 4 - 18x + 30$$

> *Scaffolding:*
>
> The equation in this example can be modified to $9(4 - 2x) - 3 = -18x$ to meet the needs of diverse learners.

Be sure to check that students did not subtract $4 - 6$ on the right side, then distribute -2. This is a common error. Remind students that we must multiply first, then add or subtract, just like we would to simply expressions using the correct order of operations.

- ▪ The transformed equation is $36 - 18x - 3 = 4 - 18x + 30$. Now complete the solution.

  - ▫ *Student work:*

$$36 - 18x - 3 = 4 - 18x + 30$$
$$33 - 18x = 34 - 18x$$
$$33 - 18x + 18x = 34 - 18x + 18x$$
$$33 = 34$$

    Like the last problem, there is no value of x that can be substituted into the equation to make it true. Therefore this equation has no solution.

- ▪ Write at least one equation that has no solution. It does not need to be complicated, but the result should be similar to the last two problems. The result from the first equation was $2 \neq -3$ and the second was $33 \neq 34$.

Have students share their equations and verify that they have no solution.

Optional Example 5 (4 minutes)

- So far we have used the distributive property to simplify expressions when solving equations. In some cases, we can use the distributive property to make our work even simpler. Consider the following equation:

$$3x + 15 = -6$$

Notice that each term has a common factor of 3. We will use the distributive property and what we know about the properties of equality to solve this equation quickly.

$$3x + 15 = -6$$
$$3(x + 5) = 3 \cdot (-2)$$

Notice that the expressions on both sides of equal sign have a factor of 3. We can use the multiplication property of equality, *if* $A = B$, *then* $A \cdot C = B \cdot C$ *as follows*:

$$3(x + 5) = 3 \cdot (-2)$$
$$x + 5 = -2$$
$$x + 5 - 5 = -2 - 5$$
$$x = -7$$

- This isn't something that we can expect to do every time we solve an equation, but it is good to keep an eye out for it.

Exercises 1–6 (12 minutes)

Students complete Exercises 1–6 independently.

Exercises

Find the value of x that makes the equation true.

1. $17 - 5(2x - 9) = -(-6x + 10) + 4$

    Sample student work:

    $$17 - 5(2x - 9) = -(-6x + 10) + 4$$
    $$17 - 10x + 45 = 6x - 10 + 4$$
    $$62 - 10x = 6x - 6$$
    $$62 - 10x + 10x = 6x + 10x - 6$$
    $$62 = 16x - 6$$
    $$62 + 6 = 16x - 6 + 6$$
    $$68 = 16x$$
    $$\frac{68}{16} = \frac{16}{16}x$$
    $$\frac{68}{16} = x$$
    $$\frac{17}{4} = x$$

---

2. $-(x - 7) + \dfrac{5}{3} = 2(x + 9)$

Sample student work:

$$-(x - 7) + \dfrac{5}{3} = 2(x + 9)$$

$$-x + 7 + \dfrac{5}{3} = 2x + 18$$

$$-x + \dfrac{26}{3} = 2x + 18$$

$$-x + x + \dfrac{26}{3} = 2x + x + 18$$

$$\dfrac{26}{3} = 3x + 18$$

$$\dfrac{26}{3} - 18 = 3x + 18 - 18$$

$$-\dfrac{28}{3} = 3x$$

$$\dfrac{1}{3} \cdot \dfrac{-28}{3} = \dfrac{1}{3} \cdot 3x$$

$$-\dfrac{28}{9} = x$$

3. $\dfrac{4}{9} + 4(x - 1) = \dfrac{28}{9} - (x - 7x) + 1$

Sample student work:

$$\dfrac{4}{9} + 4(x - 1) = \dfrac{28}{9} - (x - 7x) + 1$$

$$\dfrac{4}{9} - \dfrac{4}{9} + 4(x - 1) = \dfrac{28}{9} - \dfrac{4}{9} - (x - 7x) + 1$$

$$4x - 4 = \dfrac{24}{9} - x + 7x + 1$$

$$4x - 4 = \dfrac{33}{9} + 6x$$

$$4x - 4 + 4 = \dfrac{33}{9} + \dfrac{36}{9} + 6x$$

$$4x = \dfrac{69}{9} + 6x$$

$$4x - 6x = \dfrac{69}{9}$$

$$-2x = \dfrac{23}{3}$$

$$\dfrac{1}{-2} \cdot -2x = \dfrac{1}{-2} \cdot \dfrac{23}{3}$$

$$x = -\dfrac{23}{6}$$

4. $5(3x + 4) - 2x = 7x - 3(-2x + 11)$

$$5(3x + 4) - 2x = 7x - 3(-2x + 11)$$

$$15x + 20 - 2x = 7x + 6x - 33$$

$$13x + 20 = 13x - 33$$

$$13x - 13x + 20 = 13x - 13x - 33$$

$$20 \neq -33$$

This equation has no solution.

5. $7x - (3x + 5) - 8 = \frac{1}{2}(8x + 20) - 7x + 5$

     Sample student work:

$$7x - (3x + 5) - 8 = \frac{1}{2}(8x + 20) - 7x + 5$$
$$7x - 3x - 5 - 8 = 4x + 10 - 7x + 5$$
$$4x - 13 = -3x + 15$$
$$4x - 13 + 13 = -3x + 15 + 13$$
$$4x = -3x + 28$$
$$4x + 3x = -3x + 3x + 28$$
$$7x = 28$$
$$x = 4$$

6.   Write at least three equations that have no solution.

     Answers will vary. Verify that the equations written have no solution.

Closing (5 minutes)

Summarize, or ask students to summarize, the following main points from the lesson:

- We know how to transform equations into simpler forms using the distributive property.
- We now know that there are some equations that do not have solutions.

Lesson Summary

The distributive property is used to expand expressions. For example, the expression $2(3x - 10)$ is rewritten as $6x - 20$ after the distributive property is applied.

The distributive property is used to simply expressions. For example, the expression $7x + 11x$ is rewritten as $(7 + 11)x$ and $18x$ after the distributive property is applied.

The distributive property is applied only to terms within a group:

$$4(3x + 5) - 2 = 12x + 20 - 2$$

Notice that the term -2 is not part of the group and therefore not multiplied by 4.

When an equation is transformed into an untrue sentence, like $5 \neq 11$, we say the equation has <u>no solution</u>.

Exit Ticket (5 minutes)

Name _____   Date _____

Lesson 6: Solutions of a Linear Equation

Exit Ticket

Transform the equation if necessary, then solve to find the value of x that makes the equation true.

1. $5x - (x + 3) = \frac{1}{3}(9x + 18) - 5$

2. $5(3x + 9) - 2x = 15x - 2(x - 5)$

Exit Ticket Sample Solutions

> Transform the equation if necessary, then solve to find the value of x that makes the equation true.
>
> 1. $5x - (x + 3) = \frac{1}{3}(9x + 18) - 5$
>
> $$5x - (x + 3) = \frac{1}{3}(9x + 18) - 5$$
> $$5x - x - 3 = 3x + 6 - 5$$
> $$4x - 3 = 3x + 1$$
> $$4x - 3x - 3 = 3x - 3x + 1$$
> $$x - 3 = 1$$
> $$x = 4$$
>
> 2. $5(3x + 9) - 2x = 15x - 2(x - 5)$
>
> $$5(3x + 9) - 2x = 15x - 2(x - 5)$$
> $$15x + 45 - 2x = 15x - 2x + 10$$
> $$13x + 45 = 13x + 10$$
> $$45 \neq 10$$
>
> *Since* $45 \neq 10$*, then the equation has no solution.*

Problem Set Sample Solutions

Students practice using the distributive property to transform equations and solve.

> Transform the equation if necessary, then solve it to find the value of x that makes the equation true.
>
> 1. $x - (9x - 10) + 11 = 12x + 3\left(-2x + \frac{1}{3}\right)$
>
>   *Sample student work:*
>
> $$x - (9x - 10) + 11 = 12x + 3\left(-2x + \frac{1}{3}\right)$$
> $$x - 9x + 10 + 11 = 12x - 6x + 1$$
> $$-8x + 21 = 6x + 1$$
> $$-8x + 8x + 21 = 6x + 8x + 1$$
> $$21 = 14x + 1$$
> $$21 - 1 = 14x + 1 - 1$$
> $$20 = 14x$$
> $$\frac{20}{14} = \frac{14}{14}x$$
> $$\frac{10}{7} = x$$
>
> 2. $7x + 8\left(x + \frac{1}{4}\right) = 3(6x - 9) - 8$
>
>   *Sample student work:*
>
> $$7x + 8\left(x + \frac{1}{4}\right) = 3(6x - 9) - 8$$
> $$7x + 8x + 2 = 18x - 27 - 8$$
> $$15x + 2 = 18x - 35$$
> $$15x - 15x + 2 = 18x - 15x - 35$$
> $$2 = 3x - 35$$
> $$2 + 35 = 3x - 35 + 35$$
> $$37 = 3x$$
> $$\frac{37}{3} = \frac{3}{3}x$$
> $$\frac{37}{3} = x$$

Lesson 6:	Solutions of a Linear Equation
Date:	11/8/13

69

3. $-4x - 2(8x + 1) = -(-2x - 10)$

Sample student work:

$$-4x - 2(8x + 1) = -(-2x - 10)$$
$$-4x - 16x - 2 = 2x + 10$$
$$-20x - 2 = 2x + 10$$
$$-20x + 20x - 2 = 2x + 20x + 10$$
$$-2 = 22x + 10$$
$$-2 - 10 = 22x + 10 - 10$$
$$-12 = 22x$$
$$-\frac{12}{22} = \frac{22}{22}x$$
$$-\frac{6}{11} = x$$

4. $11(x + 10) = 132$

Sample student work:

$$11(x + 10) = 132$$
$$x + 10 = 12$$
$$x = 2$$

5. $37x + \frac{1}{2} - \left(x + \frac{1}{4}\right) = 9(4x - 7) + 5$

Sample student work:

$$37x + \frac{1}{2} - \left(x + \frac{1}{4}\right) = 9(4x - 7) + 5$$
$$37x + \frac{1}{2} - x - \frac{1}{4} = 36x - 63 + 5$$
$$36x + \frac{1}{4} = 36x - 58$$
$$36x - 36x + \frac{1}{4} = 36x - 36x - 58$$
$$\frac{1}{4} \neq -58$$

This equation has no solution.

6. $3(2x - 14) + x = 15 - (-9x - 5)$

Sample student work:

$$3(2x - 14) + x = 15 - (-9x - 5)$$
$$6x - 42 + x = 15 + 9x + 5$$
$$7x - 42 = 20 + 9x$$
$$7x - 7x - 42 = 20 + 9x - 7x$$
$$-42 = 20 + 2x$$
$$-42 - 20 = 20 - 20 + 2x$$
$$-62 = 2x$$
$$-31 = x$$

7. $8(2x + 9) = 56$

Sample student work:

$$8(2x + 9) = 56$$
$$2x + 9 = 7$$
$$2x + 9 - 9 = 7 - 9$$
$$2x = -2$$
$$x = -1$$

Lesson 6: Solutions of a Linear Equation
Date: 11/8/13

70

Lesson 7: Classification of Solutions

Student Outcomes

- Students know the conditions for which a linear equation will have a unique solution, no solution, or infinitely many solutions.

Lesson Notes

Part of the discussion on the second page in this lesson is optional. The key parts of the discussion are those that point out the characteristics of the constants and coefficients of an equation that allow students to see the structure in equations that lead to a unique solution, no solution, or infinitely many solutions. You can choose to go through the discussion with your students or choose to use the activity at the top of the fourth page of this lesson. The activity requires students to examine groups of equations and make conclusions about the nature of their solutions based on what they observe, leading to the same result as discussion.

Classwork

Exercises 1–3 (6 minutes)

Students complete Exercises 1–3 independently in preparation for the discussion that follows.

Exercises 1–3

Solve each of the following equations for x.

1. $7x - 3 = 5x + 5$

    Sample student work:

    $$7x - 3 = 5x + 5$$
    $$7x - 3 + 3 = 5x + 5 + 3$$
    $$7x = 5x + 8$$
    $$7x - 5x = 5x - 5x + 8$$
    $$2x = 8$$
    $$x = 4$$

2. $7x - 3 = 7x + 5$

    Sample student work:

    $$7x - 3 = 7x + 5$$
    $$7x - 7x - 3 = 7x - 7x + 5$$
    $$-3 \neq 5$$

    This equation has no solution.

---

3. $7x - 3 = -3 + 7x$

Sample student work:

$$7x - 3 = -3 + 7x$$
$$7x - 3 + 3 = -3 + 3 + 7x$$
$$7x = 7x$$

OR

$$7x - 3 = -3 + 7x$$
$$7x - 7x - 3 = -3 + 7x - 7x$$
$$-3 = -3$$

Discussion (15 minutes)

Display the three equations so that students can easily see and compare them throughout the discussion.

$7x - 3 = 5x + 5$	$7x - 3 = 7x + 5$	$7x - 3 = -3 + 7x$

- Was there anything new or unexpected about Exercise 1?
    - *No. We solved the equation for x and x = 4.*

You may choose to continue with the discussion of Exercise 1 or complete the activity described at the end of the discussion on page 74. Be sure to revisit Exercises 2 and 3 and classify the solution to those equations.

- What can you say about the coefficients of terms with x in the equation?
    - *They are different.*
- Do you think any number other than 4 would make the equation true?
    - *I don't think so, but I'd have to try different numbers in order to find out.*
- Instead of having to check every single number to see if it makes the equation true, we can look at a general form of an equation to show there can be only one solution.
- Given a linear equation that has been simplified on both sides, $ax + b = cx + d$, where $a, b, c,$ and d are constants and $a \neq c$, we can use use our normal properties of equality to solve for x:

$$ax + b = cx + d$$
$$ax + b - b = cx + d - b$$
$$ax = cx + d - b$$
$$ax - cx = cx - cx + d - b$$
$$(a - c)x = d - b$$
$$\frac{a - c}{a - c}x = \frac{d - b}{a - c}$$
$$x = \frac{d - b}{a - c}$$

- The only value of x that will make the equation true is the division of the difference of the constants by the difference of the coefficients of x. In other words, if the coefficients of x are different on each side of the equal sign, then the equation will have one solution.

- As an aside, if the coefficients of x are different and the value of the constants are the same, the only solution is $x = 0$. Consider the following equation:

$$2x + 12 = x + 12$$
$$2x + 12 - 12 = x + 12 - 12$$
$$2x = x$$
$$2x - x = x - x$$
$$x = 0$$

- The only value of x that will make $2x + 12 = x + 12$ true, is $x = 0$.

- Was there anything new or unexpected about Exercise 2?

   □ *No. We tried to solve the equation and got an untrue statement, $-3 \neq 5$; therefore, the equation had no solutions.*

- What can you say about the coefficients of the terms with x in the second equation?

   □ *The coefficients were the same.*

- What can you say about the constants in the second equation?

   □ *The constants were different.*

- It is time to begin formalizing what we have observed as we have solved equations. To begin with, we have learned that some linear equations have no solutions. That is, when we solve an equation using our properties of equality and end up with a statement like $a = b$, where a, b are different numbers, we say that the equation has no solution.

- To produce and/or recognize an equation with no solutions, consider the equation with both sides simplified. The coefficients of the variable x will be the same on both sides of the equal sign and the value of the constants on each side will be different. This type of equation has no solution because there is no value of x in an equation such as $x + a = x + b$ that will make the equation true.

Give students a moment to compare the equation $x + a = x + b$ with Exercise 2.

- Was there anything new or unexpected about Exercise 3?

   □ *Yes. When solving the equation we got $-3 = -3$, which did not give us a value for x.*

   □ *Yes. When solving the equation we got to $7x = 7x$ and we weren't sure what to do next or what it meant.*

Provide students with time to discuss in small groups how they should interpret the meaning of such statements. Students have yet to work with equations that yield such results and they need the time to make sense of the statements. If necessary, ask the questions in the next two bullet points to guide their thinking. Give them time to try different values of x in the both equations to verify that it is always true. Next, have students share their thoughts and interpretations and resume the discussion below.

- Is $-3 = -3$ a true statement? Is it always true?

   □ *Yes.*

- If $7x = 7x$, will we always have an equality, no matter which number we choose for x?

   □ *Yes. This is an identity because the same expression is on both sides of the equal sign.*

- What can you say about the coefficients of the terms with x in the equation in Exercise 3?

   □ *The coefficients are the same.*

| **Lesson 7:** | Classification of Solutions |
| **Date:** | 11/8/13 |

73

- What can you say about the constants in the equation?

  □ *The constants are the same.*

- We now know that there are equations that produce statements that are always true. That is, -3 will always equal -3, 0 is always equal to 0, and $7x$ will always equal $7x$ no matter what number x happens to be (because 7 times a number is just a number). When we solve an equation using our properties of equality and end up with a statement like $a = a$ where a is a number, then we say that the equation has infinitely many solutions.

- To produce and/or recognize an equation with infinitely many solutions, the coefficients of the variable x and the value of the constants will be the same in the simplified expressions on both sides of the equal sign. This type of equation has infinitely many solutions because *any value* of x in an equation like $x + a = x + a$ will make the equation true.

Give students a moment to compare the equation $x + a = x + a$ with Exercise 3.

Activity: Display the table below. Provide students time to work independently to solve the equations, then in small groups to generalize what they notice about each of the equations, that is, they should answer the question: What can we see in an equation that will tell us about the solution to the equation?

MP.8

$3x + 4 = 8x - 9$	$6x + 5 = 8 + 6x$	$10x - 4 = -4 + 10x$
$-4x - 5 = 6 - 11x$	$12 - 15x = -2 - 15x$	$-2x + 5 = -2x + 5$
$9 + \dfrac{1}{2}x = 5x - 1$	$\dfrac{5}{4}x - 1 = 1 + \dfrac{5}{4}x$	$7 + 9x = 9x + 7$

The goal of the activity is for students to make the following three observations. (1) In equations where both sides are simplified, when the coefficients of x and the constants in the equation are unique, i.e., $ax + b = cx + d$, there will be a unique solution, i.e., $x = \dfrac{d-b}{a-c}$, as in the first column. (2) Similarly, we want students to observe that when an equation is of the form $x + b = x + c$, that there will be no solution, as in the second column. (3) Lastly, when an equation is of the form $x + a = x + a$, then there are infinitely many solutions, as in the third column.

Exercises 4–10 (14 minutes)

Students complete Exercises 4–10 independently or in pairs.

Exercises 4–10

Give a brief explanation as to what kind of solution(s) you expect the following linear equations to have. Transform the equation into a simpler form if necessary.

4. $11x - 2x + 15 = 8 + 7 + 9x$

  If I use the distributive property on the left side I notice that the coefficients of the x are the same, specifically 9, and when I simplify the constants on the right side, I notice that they are the same. Therefore, this equation has infinitely many solutions.

---

5. $3(x - 14) + 1 = -4x + 5$

   If I use the distributive property on the left side I notice that the coefficients of the x are the different. Therefore, the equation has one solution.

6. $-3x + 32 - 7x = -2(5x + 10)$

   If I use the distributive property on the each side of the equation I notice that the coefficients of x are the same, but the constants are different. Therefore, this equation has no solutions.

7. $\frac{1}{2}(8x + 26) = 13 + 4x$

   If I use the distributive property on the left side I notice that the coefficients of the x are the same, specifically 4, and the constants are also the same, 13. Therefore, this equation has infinitely many solutions.

8. Write two equations that have no solutions.

   Answers will vary. Verify that students have written equations where the coefficients of x on each side of the equal sign are the same and the constants on each side are unique.

9. Write two equations that have one unique solution each.

   Answers will vary. Accept equations where the coefficients of x on each side of the equal sign are unique.

10. Write two equations that have infinitely many solutions.

    Answers will vary. Accept equations where the coefficients of x and constants on each side of the equal sign are the same.

Closing (5 minutes)

Summarize, or ask students to summarize, the main points from the lesson:

- We know that equations will either have a unique solution, no solution, or infinitely many solutions.
- We know that equations with no solution will, after being simplified on both sides, have coefficients of x that are the same on both sides of the equal sign and constants that are different.
- We know that equations with infinitely many solutions will, after being simplified on both sides, have coefficients of x and constants that are the same on both sides of the equal sign.

Lesson Summary

There are three classifications of solutions to linear equations: one solution (unique solution), no solution, or infinitely many solutions.

Equations with no solution will, after being simplified, have coefficients of x that are the same on both sides of the equal sign and constants that are different. For example, $x + b = x + c$, where b, c are constants that are not equal. A numeric example is $8x + 5 = 8x - 3$.

Equations with infinitely many solutions will, after being simplified, have coefficients of x and constants that are the same on both sides of the equal sign. For example, $x + a = x + a$, where a is a constant. A numeric example is $6x + 1 = 1 + 6x$.

Exit Ticket (5 minutes)

Lesson 7:	Classification of Solutions
Date:	11/8/13

Name _____   Date _____

Lesson 7: Classification of Solutions

Exit Ticket

Give a brief explanation as to what kind of solution(s) you expect the following linear equations to have. Transform the equation into a simpler form if necessary.

1. $3(6x + 8) = 24 + 18x$

2. $12(x + 8) = 11x - 5$

3. $5x - 8 = 11 - 7x + 12x$

Exit Ticket Sample Solutions

> Give a brief explanation as to what kind of solution(s) you expect the following linear equations to have. Transform the equation into a simpler form if necessary.
>
> 1. $3(6x + 8) = 24 + 18x$
>
>   *If I use the distributive property on the left side I notice that the coefficients of the x are the same and the constants are the same. Therefore, this equation has infinitely many solutions.*
>
> 2. $12(x + 8) = 11x - 5$
>
>   *If I use the distributive property on the left side I notice that the coefficients of the x are different and the constants are different. Therefore, this equation has a unique solution.*
>
> 3. $5x - 8 = 11 - 7x + 12x$
>
>   *If I collect the like terms on the right side I notice that the coefficients of x are the same, but the constants are different. Therefore, this equation has no solution.*

Problem Set Sample Solutions

Students apply their knowledge of solutions to linear equations by writing equations with unique solutions, no solutions, and infinitely many solutions.

> 1. Give a brief explanation as to what kind of solution(s) you expect the linear equation to have:
> $18x + \frac{1}{2} = 6(3x + 25)$. Transform the equation into a simpler form if necessary.
>
>   *If I use the distributive property on the right side of the equation I notice that the coefficients of x are the same, but the constants are different. Therefore, this equation has no solutions.*
>
> 2. Give a brief explanation as to what kind of solution(s) you expect the linear equation to have:
> $8 - 9x = 15x + 7 + 3x$. Transform the equation into a simpler form if necessary.
>
>   *If I collect the like terms on the right side of the equation then I notice that the coefficients of x are different and so are the constants. Therefore, this equation will have a unique solution.*
>
> 3. Give a brief explanation as to what kind of solution(s) you expect the linear equation to have:
> $5(x + 9) = 5x + 45$. Transform the equation into a simpler form if necessary.
>
>   *This is an identity under the distributive property. Therefore, this equation will have infinitely many solutions.*
>
> 4. Give three examples of equations where the solution will be unique, that is, only one solution is possible.
>
>   *Accept equations where the coefficients of x on each side of the equal sign are unique.*
>
> 5. Solve one of the equations you wrote in problem 4 and explain why it is the only solution.
>
>   *Verify that students solved one of the equations. They should have an explanation that includes the statement that there is only one possible number that could make the equation true. They may have referenced one of the simpler forms of their transformed equation to make their case.*

	Lesson 7:	Classification of Solutions
	Date:	11/8/13

6. Give three examples of equations where there will be no solution.

    Accept equations where the coefficients of x on each side of the equal sign are the same and the constants on each side are unique.

7. Attempt to solve one of the equations you wrote in problem 6 and explain why it has no solution.

    Verify that students have solved one of the equations. They should have an explanation that includes the statement about getting a false equation, e.g., $6 \neq 10$.

8. Give three examples of equations where there will be infinitely many solutions.

    Accept equations where the coefficients of x and constants on each side of the equal sign are the same.

9. Attempt to solve one of the equations you wrote in problem 8 and explain why it has infinitely many solutions.

    Verify that students have solved one of the equations. They should have an explanation that includes the statement about the linear expressions being exactly the same, an identity; therefore, any rational number x would make the equation true.

Lesson 7:   Classification of Solutions
Date: 11/8/13

78

Lesson 8: Linear Equations in Disguise

Student Outcomes

- Students rewrite and solve equations that are not obviously linear equations using properties of equality.

Lesson Notes

In this lesson, students learn that some equations that may not look like linear equations are, in fact, linear. This lesson on solving rational equations is included because of the types of equations students will see in later topics of this module related to slope. Students will recognize these equations as proportions. It is not necessary to refer to these types of equations as equations that contain rational expressions. They can be referred to simply as proportions since students are familiar with this terminology. Expressions of this type will be treated carefully in algebra as they involve a discussion about why the denominator of such expressions cannot be equal to zero. That discussion is not included in this lesson.

Classwork

Concept Development (3 minutes)

- Some linear equations may not look like linear equations upon first glance. A simple example that you should recognize is

$$\frac{x}{5} = \frac{6}{12}$$

- What do we call this kind of problem and how do we solve it?

  □ *This is a proportion. We can solve this by multiplying both sides of the equation by 5. We can also solve it by multiplying each numerator with the other fraction's denominator.*

Students may not think of multiplying each numerator with the other fraction's denominator because multiplying both sides by 5 requires fewer steps and uses the multiplication property of equality that has been used to solve other equations. If necessary, state the theorem and give a brief explanation.

Theorem. Given rational numbers A, B, C, and D, so that $B \neq 0$ and $D \neq 0$, the property states

$$\text{If } \frac{A}{B} = \frac{C}{D}, \text{ then } AD = BC.$$

- To find the value of x, we can multiply each numerator by the other fraction's denominator.

$$\frac{x}{5} = \frac{6}{12}$$
$$12x = 6(5)$$

- It should be more obvious now that we have a linear equation. We can now solve it as usual using the properties of equality.

$$12x = 30$$
$$x = \frac{30}{12}$$
$$x = \frac{5}{2}$$

- In this lesson, our work will be similar, but the numerator and/or the denominator of the fractions may contain more than one term. However, the way we solve these kinds of problems remain the same.

Example 1 (5 minutes)

- Given a linear equation in disguise, we will *try* to solve it. To do so, we must first assume that the following equation is true for some number x.

$$\frac{x-1}{2} = \frac{x + \frac{1}{3}}{4}$$

- We want to make this equation look like the linear equations we are used to. For that reason, we will multiply both sides of the equation by 2 and 4, as we normally do with proportions:

$$2\left(x + \frac{1}{3}\right) = 4(x-1)$$

- Is this a linear equation? How do you know?
  - *Yes, this is a linear equation because the expressions on the left and right of the equal sign are linear expressions.*

- Notice that the expressions that contained more than one term were put in parentheses. We do that so we don't make a mistake and forget to use the distributive property.

- Now that we have a linear equation. We will use the distributive property and solve as usual.

$$2\left(x + \frac{1}{3}\right) = 4(x-1)$$
$$2x + \frac{2}{3} = 4x - 4$$
$$2x - 2x + \frac{2}{3} = 4x - 2x - 4$$
$$\frac{2}{3} = 2x - 4$$
$$\frac{2}{3} + 4 = 2x - 4 + 4$$
$$\frac{14}{3} = 2x$$
$$\frac{1}{2} \cdot \frac{14}{3} = \frac{1}{2} \cdot 2x$$
$$\frac{7}{3} = x$$

- How can we verify that $\frac{7}{3}$ is the solution to the equation?

  - We can replace x with $\frac{7}{3}$ in the original equation:

$$\frac{x-1}{2} = \frac{x+\frac{1}{3}}{4}$$

$$\frac{\frac{7}{3}-1}{2} = \frac{\frac{7}{3}+\frac{1}{3}}{4}$$

$$\frac{\frac{4}{3}}{2} = \frac{\frac{8}{3}}{4}$$

$$4\left(\frac{4}{3}\right) = 2\left(\frac{8}{3}\right)$$

$$\frac{16}{3} = \frac{16}{3}$$

- Since $\frac{7}{3}$ made the equation true, then we know it is the solution to the equation.

Example 2 (4 minutes)

- Can we solve the following equation? Explain.

$$\frac{\frac{1}{5}-x}{7} = \frac{2x+9}{3}$$

  - We need to multiply each numerator with the other fraction's denominator.

- So,

$$\frac{\frac{1}{5}-x}{7} = \frac{2x+9}{3}$$

$$7(2x+9) = 3\left(\frac{1}{5}-x\right)$$

- What would be the next step?

  - Use the distributive property.

- Now we have

$$7(2x+9) = 3\left(\frac{1}{5}-x\right)$$

$$14x+63 = \frac{3}{5}-3x$$

- Is this a linear equation? How do you know?

  - Yes, this is a linear equation because the left and right side are linear expressions.

Example 3 (5 minutes)

- ▪ Can we solve the following equation? If so, go ahead and solve it. If not, explain why not.

> **Example 3**
>
> **Can this equation be solved?**
>
> $$\frac{6+x}{7x+\frac{2}{3}} = \frac{3}{8}$$

Give students a few minutes to work. Provide support to students as needed.

- □ *Yes, we can solve the equation because we can multiply each numerator with the other fraction's denominator and then use the distributive property to begin solving it:*

> $$\frac{6+x}{7x+\frac{2}{3}} = \frac{3}{8}$$
> $$(6+x)8 = \left(7x + \frac{2}{3}\right)3$$
> $$48 + 8x = 21x + 2$$
> $$48 + 8x - 8x = 21x - 8x + 2$$
> $$48 = 13x + 2$$
> $$48 - 2 = 13x + 2 - 2$$
> $$46 = 13x$$
> $$\frac{46}{13} = x$$

Example 4 (5 minutes)

- ▪ Can we solve the following equation? If so, go ahead and solve it. If not, explain why not.

> **Example 4**
>
> **Can this equation be solved?**
>
> $$\frac{7}{3x+9} = \frac{1}{8}$$

Give students a few minutes to work. Provide support to students as needed.

- □ *Yes, we can solve the equation because we can multiply each numerator with the other fractions denominator and then use the distributive property to begin solving it.*

> $$\frac{7}{3x+9} = \frac{1}{8}$$
> $$7(8) = (3x+9)1$$
> $$56 = 3x + 9$$
> $$56 - 9 = 3x + 9 - 9$$
> $$47 = 3x$$
> $$\frac{47}{3} = x$$

Example 5 (5 minutes)

Example 5

In the diagram below, $\triangle ABC \sim \triangle A'B'C'$. Using what we know about similar triangles, we can determine the value of x.

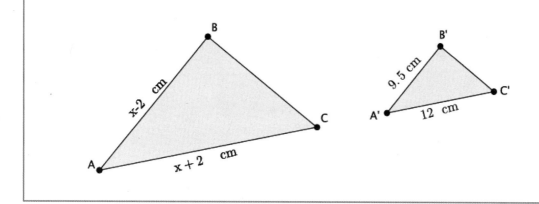

- Begin by writing the ratios that represent the corresponding sides.

$$\frac{x-2}{9.5} = \frac{x+2}{12}$$

It is possible to write several different proportions in this case. If time, discuss this fact with students.

- Now that we have the ratios, solve for x and find the lengths of AB and AC.

$$\frac{x-2}{9.5} = \frac{x+2}{12}$$
$$(x-2)12 = 9.5(x+2)$$
$$12x - 24 = 9.5x + 19$$
$$12x - 24 + 24 = 9.5x + 19 + 24$$
$$12x = 9.5x + 43$$
$$12x - 9.5x = 9.5x - 9.5x + 43$$
$$2.5x = 43$$
$$x = \frac{43}{2.5}$$
$$x = 17.2$$

The length of $|AB| = 15.2$ cm and the length of $|AC| = 19.2$ cm.

Exercises 1–4 (8 minutes)

Students complete Exercises 1–4 independently.

Exercises 1–4

Solve the following equations of rational expressions, if possible.

1. $\dfrac{2x+1}{9} = \dfrac{1-x}{6}$

    Sample student work:

    $$\frac{2x+1}{9} = \frac{1-x}{6}$$
    $$9(1-x) = (2x+1)6$$
    $$9 - 9x = 12x + 6$$
    $$9 - 9x + 9x = 12x + 9x + 6$$
    $$9 = 21x + 6$$
    $$9 - 6 = 21x + 6 - 6$$
    $$3 = 21x$$
    $$\frac{3}{21} = \frac{21}{21}x$$
    $$\frac{1}{7} = x$$

2. $\dfrac{5+2x}{3x-1} = \dfrac{6}{7}$

    Sample student work:

    $$\frac{5+2x}{3x-1} = \frac{6}{7}$$
    $$(5+2x)7 = (3x-1)6$$
    $$35 + 14x = 18x - 6$$
    $$35 - 35 + 14x = 18x - 6 - 35$$
    $$14x = 18x - 41$$
    $$14x - 18x = 18x - 18x - 41$$
    $$-4x = -41$$
    $$\frac{-4}{-4}x = \frac{-41}{-4}$$
    $$x = \frac{41}{4}$$

3. $\dfrac{x+9}{12} = \dfrac{-2x-\frac{1}{2}}{3}$

    Sample student work:

    $$\frac{x+9}{12} = \frac{-2x-\frac{1}{2}}{3}$$
    $$12\left(-2x-\frac{1}{2}\right) = (x+9)3$$
    $$-24x - 6 = 3x + 27$$
    $$-24x + 24x - 6 = 3x + 24x + 27$$
    $$-6 = 27x + 27$$
    $$-6 - 27 = 27x + 27 - 27$$
    $$-33 = 27x$$
    $$\frac{-33}{27} = \frac{23}{27}x$$
    $$-\frac{11}{9} = x$$

---

4. $\dfrac{8}{3-4x} = \dfrac{5}{2x+\frac{1}{4}}$

Sample student work:

$$\frac{8}{3-4x} = \frac{5}{2x+\frac{1}{4}}$$

$$8\left(2x+\frac{1}{4}\right) = (3-4x)5$$

$$16x + 2 = 15 - 20x$$

$$16x + 2 - 2 = 15 - 2 - 20x$$

$$16x = 13 - 20x$$

$$16x + 20x = 13 - 20x + 20x$$

$$36x = 13$$

$$\frac{36}{36}x = \frac{13}{36}$$

$$x = \frac{13}{36}$$

Closing (5 minutes)

Summarize, or ask students to summarize, the main points from the lesson:

- We know that proportions that have more than one term in the numerator and/or denominator can be solved the same way we normally solve a proportion.

- When multiplying a fraction with more than one term in the numerator and/or denominator by a number, we should put the expressions with more than one term in parentheses, so we are less likely to forget to use the distributive property.

Lesson Summary

Proportions are linear equations in disguise and are solved the same way we normally solve proportions.

When multiplying a fraction with more than one term in the numerator and/or denominator by a number, put the expressions with more than one term in parentheses so you remember to use the distributive property when transforming the equation. For example:

$$\frac{x+4}{2x-5} = \frac{3}{5}$$

$$5(x+4) = 3(2x-5)$$

The equation $5(x+4) = 3(2x-5)$ is now clearly a linear equation and can be solved using the properties of equality.

Exit Ticket (5 minutes)

	Lesson 8:	Linear Equations in Disguise
	Date:	11/8/13

85

Name _____   Date _____

Lesson 8: Linear Equations in Disguise

Exit Ticket

Solve the following equations for x.

1. $\dfrac{5x-8}{3} = \dfrac{11x-9}{5}$

2. $\dfrac{x+11}{7} = \dfrac{2x+1}{-8}$

3. $\dfrac{-x-2}{-4} = \dfrac{3x+6}{2}$

Exit Ticket Sample Solutions

1. $\dfrac{5x-8}{3} = \dfrac{11x-9}{5}$

$$\frac{5x-8}{3} = \frac{11x-9}{5}$$

$$5(5x-8) = 3(11x-9)$$

$$25x - 40 = 33x - 27$$

$$25x - 25x - 40 = 33x - 25x - 27$$

$$-40 = 8x - 27$$

$$-40 + 27 = 8x - 27 + 27$$

$$-13 = 8x$$

$$-\frac{13}{8} = x$$

2. $\dfrac{x+11}{7} = \dfrac{2x+1}{-8}$

$$\frac{x+11}{7} = \frac{2x+1}{-8}$$

$$7(2x+1) = -8(x+11)$$
$$14x + 7 = -8x - 88$$
$$14x + 7 - 7 = -8x - 88 - 7$$
$$14x = -8x - 95$$
$$14x + 8x = -8x + 8x - 95$$
$$22x = -95$$
$$x = -\frac{95}{22}$$

3. $\dfrac{-x-2}{-4} = \dfrac{3x+6}{2}$

$$\frac{-x-2}{-4} = \frac{3x+6}{2}$$
$$-4(3x+6) = 2(-x-2)$$

$$-12x - 24 = -2x - 4$$
$$-12x - 24 + 24 = -2x - 4 + 24$$
$$-12x = -2x + 20$$
$$-12x + 2x = -2x + 2x + 20$$
$$-10x = 20$$
$$x = -2$$

COMMON CORE™   Lesson 8:   Linear Equations in Disguise
                    Date: 11/8/13

Problem Set Sample Solutions

Students practice solving equations with rational expressions, if a solution possible.

Solve the following equations of rational expressions, if possible. If it cannot be solved, explain why.

1. $\dfrac{5}{6x-2} = \dfrac{-1}{x+1}$

   Sample student work:

   $$\frac{5}{6x-2} = \frac{-1}{x+1}$$
   $$5(x+1) = -1(6x-2)$$
   $$5x+5 = -6x+2$$
   $$5x+5-5 = -6x+2-5$$
   $$5x = -6x-3$$
   $$5x+6x = -6x+6x-3$$
   $$11x = -3$$
   $$x = -\frac{3}{11}$$

2. $\dfrac{4-x}{8} = \dfrac{7x-1}{3}$

   Sample student work:

   $$\frac{4-x}{8} = \frac{7x-1}{3}$$
   $$8(7x-1) = (4-x)3$$
   $$56x-8 = 12-3x$$
   $$56x-8+8 = 12+8-3x$$
   $$56x = 20-3x$$
   $$56x+3x = 20-3x+3x$$
   $$59x = 20$$
   $$\frac{59}{59}x = \frac{20}{59}$$
   $$x = \frac{20}{59}$$

3. $\dfrac{3x}{x+2} = \dfrac{5}{9}$

   Sample student work:

   $$\frac{3x}{x+2} = \frac{5}{9}$$
   $$9(3x) = (x+2)5$$
   $$27x = 5x+10$$
   $$27x-5x = 5x-5x+10$$
   $$22x = 10$$
   $$\frac{22}{22}x = \frac{10}{22}$$
   $$x = \frac{5}{11}$$

COMMON CORE

Lesson 8:   Linear Equations in Disguise
Date: 11/8/13

Lesson 8

4. $\dfrac{\frac{1}{2}x+6}{3}=\dfrac{x-3}{2}$

Sample student work:

$$\dfrac{\frac{1}{2}x+6}{3}=\dfrac{x-3}{2}$$
$$3(x-3)=2\left(\dfrac{1}{2}x+6\right)$$
$$3x-9=x+12$$
$$3x-9+9=x+12+9$$
$$3x=x+21$$
$$3x-x=x-x+21$$
$$2x=21$$
$$x=\dfrac{21}{2}$$

5. $\dfrac{7-2x}{6}=\dfrac{x-5}{1}$

Sample student work:

$$\dfrac{7-2x}{6}=\dfrac{x-5}{1}$$
$$6(x-5)=(7-2x)1$$
$$6x-30=7-2x$$
$$6x-30+30=7+30-2x$$
$$6x=37-2x$$
$$6x+2x=37-2x+2x$$
$$8x=37$$
$$\dfrac{8}{8}x=\dfrac{37}{8}$$
$$x=\dfrac{37}{8}$$

6. $\dfrac{2x+5}{2}=\dfrac{3x-2}{6}$

Sample student work:

$$\dfrac{2x+5}{2}=\dfrac{3x-2}{6}$$
$$2(3x-2)=6(2x+5)$$
$$6x-4=12x+30$$
$$6x-4+4=12x+30+4$$
$$6x=12x+34$$
$$6x-12x=12x-12x+34$$
$$-6x=34$$
$$x=-\dfrac{34}{6}$$
$$x=-\dfrac{17}{3}$$

7. $\dfrac{6x+1}{3} = \dfrac{9-x}{7}$

Sample student work:

$$\frac{6x+1}{3} = \frac{9-x}{7}$$
$$(6x+1)7 = 3(9-x)$$
$$42x+7 = 27-3x$$
$$42x+7-7 = 27-7-3x$$
$$42x = 20-3x$$
$$42x+3x = 20-3x+3x$$
$$45x = 20$$
$$\frac{45}{45}x = \frac{20}{45}$$
$$x = \frac{4}{9}$$

8. $\dfrac{\frac{1}{3}x-8}{12} = \dfrac{-2-x}{15}$

Sample student work:

$$\frac{\frac{1}{3}x-8}{12} = \frac{-2-x}{15}$$
$$12(-2-x) = \left(\frac{1}{3}x-8\right)15$$
$$-24-12x = 5x-120$$
$$-24-12x+12x = 5x+12x-120$$
$$-24 = 17x-120$$
$$-24+120 = 17x-120+120$$
$$96 = 17x$$
$$\frac{96}{17} = \frac{17}{17}x$$
$$\frac{96}{17} = x$$

9. $\dfrac{3-x}{1-x} = \dfrac{3}{2}$

Sample student work:

$$\frac{3-x}{1-x} = \frac{3}{2}$$
$$(3-x)2 = (1-x)3$$
$$6-2x = 3-3x$$
$$6-2x+2x = 3-3x+2x$$
$$6 = 3-x$$
$$6-3 = 3-3-x$$
$$3 = -x$$
$$-3 = x$$

10. In the diagram below, $\triangle ABC \sim \triangle A'B'C'$. Determine the lengths of AC and BC.

 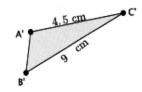

Sample student work:

$$\frac{x+4}{4.5} = \frac{3x-2}{9}$$
$$9(x+4) = 4.5(3x-2)$$
$$9x+36 = 13.5x-9$$
$$9x+36+9 = 13.5x-9+9$$
$$9x+45 = 13.5x$$
$$9x-9x+45 = 13.5x-9x$$
$$45 = 4.5x$$
$$10 = x$$

The length of $|AC| = 14\ cm$ and the length of $|BC| = 28\ cm$.

Lesson 9: An Application of Linear Equations

Student Outcomes

- Students know how to rewrite an exponential expression that represents a series as a linear equation.

Lesson Notes

The purpose of this lesson is to expose students to applications of linear equations. The discussion below revisits the Facebook problem from Module 1, but this time in the context of a linear equation. This is an opportunity to highlight MP 1: Make sense of problems and persevere in solving them, as the discussion requires students to work with equations in ways they have not before. If you feel that the discussion is too challenging for your students you can choose to use the series of more accessible applications of linear equations beginning on page 94 of this lesson.

Classwork

Discussion (30 minutes)

- In Module 1, you saw the following problem:

  You sent a photo of you and your family on vacation to seven Facebook friends. If each of them sends it to five of their friends, and each of those friends sends it to five of their friends, and those friends send it to five more, how many people (not counting yourself) will see your photo? Assume that no friend received the photo twice.

  In Module 1 you were asked to express your answer in exponential notation. The solution is the given here:

  (1) The number of friends you sent a photo to $= 7$.

  (2) The number of friends 7 people sent the photo to $- 7 \cdot 5$

  (3) The number of friends $7 \cdot 5$ people sent the photo to $= (7 \cdot 5) \cdot 5$

  (4) The number of friends $(7 \cdot 5) \cdot 5$ people sent the photo to $= \big((7 \cdot 5) \cdot 5\big) \cdot 5$

  Therefore, the total number of people who received the photo is:

  $$7 + 7 \cdot 5 + 7 \cdot 5^2 + 7 \cdot 5^3$$

- Let's refer to "you sending the photo" as the first step. Then "your friends sending the photo to their friends" is the second step, and so on. In the original problem, there were four steps. Assuming the trend continues, how would you find the sum after ten steps?

  ▫ *We would continue the pattern until we got to the 10th step.*

- What if I asked you how many friends received the photo after 100 steps?

  ▫ *It would take a long time to continue the pattern to the 100th step.*

- We want to be able to answer the question for any number of steps. For that reason, we will work towards expressing our answer as a linear equation.

- For convenience, let's introduce some symbols. Since we are talking about steps, we will refer to the sum after step one as S_1. Then the sum after step two is S_2, the sum after step three is S_3, and so on. Thus,

$$S_1 = 7 \tag{1}$$
$$S_2 = 7 + 7 \cdot 5 \tag{2}$$
$$S_3 = 7 + 7 \cdot 5 + 7 \cdot 5^2 \tag{3}$$
$$S_4 = 7 + 7 \cdot 5 + 7 \cdot 5^2 + 7 \cdot 5^3 \tag{4}$$

- What patterns do you notice within each of the equations (1)–(4)?

  - *They contain some of the same terms. For example, equation (2) is the same as (1), except equation (2) has the term $7 \cdot 5$. Similarly, equation (3) is the same as (2), except equation (3) has the term $7 \cdot 5^2$.*

- What you noticed is true. However, we want to generalize in a way that doesn't require us to know one step before getting to the next step. Let's see what other hidden patterns there are.

- Let's begin with equation (2):

$$S_2 = 7 + 7 \cdot 5$$
$$S_2 - 7 = 7 \cdot 5$$
$$S_2 - 7 + 7 \cdot 5^2 = 7 \cdot 5 + 7 \cdot 5^2$$
$$S_2 - 7 + 7 \cdot 5^2 = 5(7 + 7 \cdot 5)$$

> **Scaffolding:**
>
> Talk students through the manipulation of the equation. For example, "We begin by subtracting 7 from both sides. Next, we will add the number 7 times 5^2 to both sides of the equation. Then, using the distributive property…"

Notice that the grouping on the right side of the equation is exactly S_2, so we have the following:

$$S_2 - 7 + 7 \cdot 5^2 = 5S_2$$

This linear equation is a linear equation in S_2. It is an equation we know how to solve (pretend S_2 is an x if that helps).

- Let's do something similar with equation (3):

$$S_3 = 7 + 7 \cdot 5 + 7 \cdot 5^2$$
$$S_3 - 7 = 7 \cdot 5 + 7 \cdot 5^2$$
$$S_3 - 7 + 7 \cdot 5^3 = 7 \cdot 5 + 7 \cdot 5^2 + 7 \cdot 5^3$$
$$S_3 - 7 + 7 \cdot 5^3 = 5(7 + 7 \cdot 5 + 7 \cdot 5^2)$$

Again, the grouping on the right side of the equation is exactly the equation we began with, S_3, so we have the following:

$$S_3 - 7 + 7 \cdot 5^3 = 5S_3$$

This is a linear equation in S_3.

- Let's work together to do something similar with equation (4):

$$S_4 = 7 + 7 \cdot 5 + 7 \cdot 5^2 + 7 \cdot 5^3$$

- What did we do first in each of the equations (2) and (3)?

  - *Subtract 7 from both sides of the equation.*

- Now we have the following:

$$S_4 - 7 = 7 \cdot 5 + 7 \cdot 5^2 + 7 \cdot 5^3$$

- What did we do next?
  - *We added $7 \cdot 5$ raised to a power to both sides of the equation. When it was the second step, the power of 5 was 2. When it was the third step, the power of 5 was 3. Now that it's the fourth step, the power of 5 should be 4.*

- Now we have
$$S_4 - 7 + 7 \cdot 5^4 = 7 \cdot 5 + 7 \cdot 5^2 + 7 \cdot 5^3 + 7 \cdot 5^4$$

- What did we do after that?
  - *We used the distributive property to rewrite the right side of the equation.*

- Now we have
$$S_4 - 7 + 7 \cdot 5^4 = 5(7 \cdot 5 + 7 \cdot 5^2 + 7 \cdot 5^3)$$

- What do we do now?
  - *We substitute the grouping on the right side of the equation with S_4.*

- Finally, we have a linear equation in S_4:
$$S_4 - 7 + 7 \cdot 5^4 = 5S_4$$

- Let's look at the linear equations altogether:
$$S_2 - 7 + 7 \cdot 5^2 = 5S_2$$
$$S_3 - 7 + 7 \cdot 5^3 = 5S_3$$
$$S_4 - 7 + 7 \cdot 5^4 = 5S_4$$

What do you think the equation would be for S_{10}?
  - *According to the pattern, it would be $S_{10} - 7 + 7 \cdot 5^{10} = 5S_{10}$.*

- Now let's solve the equation. (Note again that we do not simplify $(1 - 5)$ for the reason explained above.):

$$S_{10} - 7 + 7 \cdot 5^{10} = 5S_{10}$$
$$S_{10} - 5S_{10} - 7 + 7 \cdot 5^{10} = 5S_{10} - 5S_{10}$$
$$S_{10}(1 - 5) - 7 + 7 \cdot 5^{10} = 0$$
$$S_{10}(1 - 5) - 7 + 7 + 7 \cdot 5^{10} - 7 \cdot 5^{10} = 7 - 7 \cdot 5^{10}$$
$$S_{10}(1 - 5) = 7(1 - 5^{10})$$
$$S_{10} = \frac{7(1 - 5^{10})}{(1 - 5)}$$
$$S_{10} = 17{,}089{,}842$$

> **Note to teacher:**
> This equation is solved differently than the equations we have been solving because we want to show students the normal form of an equation for the summation of a geometric series. In general, if $a \neq 1$, then
> $$1 + a + a^2 + \cdots + a^{n-1} + a^n = \frac{1 - a^{n+1}}{1 - a}$$

After ten steps, 17,089,842 will see the photo!

Exercises 1–2 (5 minutes)

Students complete Exercises 1–2 independently.

> **Exercises 1–2**
>
> 1. Write the equation for the fifteenth step.
> $$S_{15} - 7 + 7 \cdot 5^{15} = 5S_{15}$$

2.   How many people would see the photo after fifteen steps? Use a calculator if needed.

$$S_{15} - 7 + 7 \cdot 5^{15} = 5S_{15}$$

$$S_{15} - 5S_{15} - 7 + + 7 \cdot 5^{15} = 5S_{15} - 5S_{15}$$

$$S_{15}(1 - 5) - 7 + 7 \cdot 5^{15} = 0$$

$$S_{15}(1 - 5) - 7 + 7 + 7 \cdot 5^{15} - 7 \cdot 5^{15} = 7 - 7 \cdot 5^{15}$$

$$S_{15}(1 - 5) = 7(1 - 5^{15})$$

$$S_{15} = \frac{7(1 - 5^{15})}{(1 - 5)}$$

$$S_{15} = 53,405,761,717$$

Exercises 3–11 as Alternative to Discussion (30 minutes)

Students should be able to complete the following problems independently as they are an application of skills learned to this point, namely transcription and solving linear equations in one-variable. You can choose to have students work on the problems one at a time and share their work with the whole class, or assign the entire set and allow students to work at their own pace. Provide correct solutions at the end of the lesson.

Exercises 3–11

3.   Marvin paid an entrance fee of $5 plus an additional $1.25 per game at a local arcade. Altogether he spent $26.25. Write and solve an equation to determine how many games Marvin played.

   Let x represent the number of games he played.

$$5 + 1.25x = 26.25$$

$$1.25x = 21.25$$

$$x = \frac{21.25}{1.25}$$

$$x = 17$$

   Marvin played 17 games.

4.   The sum of four consecutive numbers is -26. What are the numbers?

   Let x be a number

$$x + x + 1 + x + 2 + x + 3 = -26$$
$$4x + 6 = -26$$
$$4x = -32$$
$$x = -8$$

   The numbers are $-8, -7, -6,$ and -5.

---

5. A book has x pages. How many pages are in the book if Maria read 45 pages of a book Monday, $\frac{1}{2}$ the book Tuesday, and the remaining 72 pages Wednesday?

Let x be the number of pages in the book.

$$x = 45 + \frac{1}{2}x + 72$$
$$x = 117 + \frac{1}{2}x$$
$$\frac{1}{2}x = 117$$
$$x = 234$$

The book has 234 pages.

6. A number increased by 5 and divided by 2 is equal to 75.

Let x be the number.

$$\frac{x + 5}{2} = 75$$
$$x + 5 = 150$$
$$x = 145$$

The number is 145.

7. The sum of thirteen and twice a number is seven less than six times a number. What is the number?

Let x be the number.

$$13 + 2x = 6x - 7$$
$$20 + 2x = 6x$$
$$20 = 4x$$
$$5 = x$$

The number is 5.

8. The width of a rectangle is 7 less than twice the length. If the perimeter of the rectangle is 43.6 inches, what is the area of the rectangle?

Let x represent the length of the rectangle.

$$2x + 2(2x - 7) = 43.6$$
$$2x + 4x - 14 = 43.6$$
$$6x - 14 = 43.6$$
$$6x = 57.6$$
$$x = \frac{57.6}{6}$$
$$x = 9.6$$

The length of the rectangle is 9.6 inches and the width is 12.2 inches, so the area is 117.12 in².

9. Two hundred and fifty tickets are available for sale for a school dance. On Monday 35 tickets were sold. An equal number of tickets were sold each day for the next 5 days. How many tickets were sold on one of those 5 days?

Let x be the number of tickets sold on one of those 5 days.

$$250 = 35 + 5x$$
$$215 = 5x$$
$$43 = x$$

43 tickets were sold on each of the 5 days.

10. Shonna skateboarded for some number of minutes on Monday. On Tuesday, she skateboarded for twice as many minutes as she did on Monday, and on Wednesday, she skateboarded for half the sum of minutes from Monday and Tuesday. Altogether she skateboarded for a total of 3 hours. How many minutes did she skateboard each day?

Let x be the number of minutes she skateboarded on Monday.

$$x + 2x + \frac{2x + x}{2} = 180$$
$$\frac{2x}{2} + \frac{4x}{2} + \frac{2x + x}{2} = 180$$
$$\frac{9x}{2} = 180$$
$$9x = 360$$
$$x = 40$$

Shonna skateboarded 40 minutes on Monday, 80 minutes on Tuesday, and 60 minutes on Wednesday.

11. In the diagram below, $\triangle ABC \sim \triangle A'B'C'$. Determine the length of AC and BC.

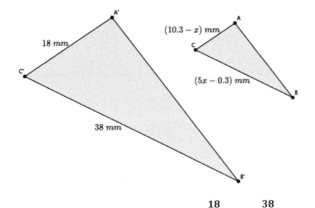

$$\frac{18}{10.3 - x} = \frac{38}{5x - 0.3}$$
$$18(5x - 0.3) = 38(10.3 - x)$$
$$90x - 5.4 = 391.4 - 38x$$
$$128x - 5.4 = 391.4$$
$$128x = 396.8$$
$$x = \frac{396.8}{128}$$
$$x = 3.1$$

The length of AC is 7.2 mm and the length of BC is 15.2 mm.

Closing (5 minutes)

Summarize, or ask students to summarize, the main points from the lesson:

- We can rewrite equations to develop a pattern and make predictions.
- We know that for problems like these we can generalize equations so that we do not have to do each step to get our answer.
- We learned how equations can be used to solve problems.

Exit Ticket (5 minutes)

Name _____   Date _____

Lesson 9: An Application of Linear Equations

Exit Ticket

1. Rewrite the equation that would represent the fifth step of the Facebook problem:

$$S_5 = 7 + 7 \cdot 5 + 7 \cdot 5^2 + 7 \cdot 5^3 + 7 \cdot 5^4$$

2. The sum of four consecutive integers is 74. Write an equation and solve to find the numbers?

Exit Ticket Sample Solutions

1. Rewrite the equation that would represent the fifth step of the Facebook problem:

$$S_5 = 7 + 7 \cdot 5 + 7 \cdot 5^2 + 7 \cdot 5^3 + 7 \cdot 5^4$$

$$S_5 = 7 + 7 \cdot 5 + 7 \cdot 5^2 + 7 \cdot 5^3 + 7 \cdot 5^4$$

$$S_5 - 7 = 7 \cdot 5 + 7 \cdot 5^2 + 7 \cdot 5^3 + 7 \cdot 5^4$$

$$S_5 - 7 + 7 \cdot 5^5 = 7 \cdot 5 + 7 \cdot 5^2 + 7 \cdot 5^3 + 7 \cdot 5^4 + 7 \cdot 5^5$$

$$S_5 - 7 + 7 \cdot 5^5 = 5(7 + 7 \cdot 5 + 7 \cdot 5^2 + 7 \cdot 5^3 + 7 \cdot 5^4)$$

$$S_5 - 7 + 7 \cdot 5^5 = 5(S_5)$$

$$S_5 - 5S_5 - 7 + 7 \cdot 5^5 = 0$$

$$S_5 - 5S_5 = 7 - (7 \cdot 5^5)$$

$$(1 - 5)S_5 = 7 - (7 \cdot 5^5)$$

$$(1 - 5)S_5 = 7(1 - 5^5)$$

$$S_5 = \frac{7(1 - 5^5)}{1 - 5}$$

2. The sum of four consecutive integers is 74. Write an equation and solve to find the numbers?

Let x be the first number

$$x + x + 1 + x + 2 + x + 3 = 74$$
$$4x + 6 = 74$$
$$4x = 68$$
$$x = 17$$

The numbers are 17, 18, 19, and 20.

Problem Set Sample Solutions

Assign the problems that relate to the elements of the lesson you chose to use with students.

1. You forward an e-card you found online to three of your friends. They liked it so much that they forwarded it on to four of their friends, who then forwarded it on to four of their friends, and so on. The number of people who saw the e-card is shown below. Let S_1 represent the number of people who saw the e-card after one step, let S_2 represent the number of people who saw the e-card after two steps, and so on.

$$S_1 = 3$$
$$S_2 = 3 + 3 \cdot 4$$
$$S_3 = 3 + 3 \cdot 4 + 3 \cdot 4^2$$
$$S_4 = 3 + 3 \cdot 4 + 3 \cdot 4^2 + 3 \cdot 4^3$$

a. Find the pattern in the equations.

$$S_2 = 3 + 3 \cdot 4$$
$$S_2 - 3 = 3 \cdot 4$$
$$S_2 - 3 + 3 \cdot 4^2 = 3 \cdot 4 + 3 \cdot 4^2$$
$$S_2 - 3 + 3 \cdot 4^2 = 4(3 + 3 \cdot 4)$$
$$S_2 - 3 + 3 \cdot 4^2 = 4S_2$$

$$S_3 = 3 + 3 \cdot 4 + 3 \cdot 4^2$$
$$S_3 - 3 = 3 \cdot 4 + 3 \cdot 4^2$$
$$S_3 - 3 + 3 \cdot 4^3 = 3 \cdot 4 + 3 \cdot 4^2 + 3 \cdot 4^3$$
$$S_3 - 3 + 3 \cdot 4^3 = 4(3 + 3 \cdot 4 + 3 \cdot 4^2)$$
$$S_3 - 3 + 3 \cdot 4^3 = 4S_3$$

$$S_4 = 3 + 3 \cdot 4 + 3 \cdot 4^2 + 3 \cdot 4^3$$
$$S_4 - 3 = 3 \cdot 4 + 3 \cdot 4^2 + 3 \cdot 4^3$$
$$S_4 - 3 + 3 \cdot 4^4 = 3 \cdot 4 + 3 \cdot 4^2 + 3 \cdot 4^3 + 3 \cdot 4^4$$
$$S_4 - 3 + 3 \cdot 4^4 = 4(3 + 3 \cdot 4 + 3 \cdot 4^2 + 3 \cdot 4^3)$$
$$S_4 - 3 + 3 \cdot 4^4 = 4S_4$$

b.   Assuming the trend continues, how many people will have seen the e-card after 10 steps?

$$S_{10} - 3 + 3 \cdot 4^{10} = 4S_{10}$$
$$S_{10} - 4S_{10} - 3 + 3 \cdot 4^{10} = 0$$
$$S_{10}(1 - 4) = 3 - 3 \cdot 4^{10}$$
$$S_{10}(1 - 4) = 3(1 - 4^{10})$$
$$S_{10} = \frac{3(1 - 4^{10})}{(1 - 4)}$$
$$S_{10} = 1048575$$

After ten steps, $1,048,575$ people will have seen the e-card.

c.   How many people will have seen the e-card after n steps?

$$S_n = \frac{3(1 - 4^n)}{(1 - 4)}$$

For each of the following questions, write an equation and solve to find each answer.

2.   Lisa has a certain amount of money. She spent 39 dollars and has $\frac{3}{4}$ of the original amount left. How much money did she have originally?

Let x be the amount of money Lisa had originally.

$$x - 39 = \frac{3}{4}x$$
$$-39 = -\frac{1}{4}x$$
$$156 = x$$

Lisa had $\$156$ originally.

3. The length of a rectangle is 4 more than 3 times the width. If the perimeter of the rectangle is 18.4 cm, what is the area of the rectangle?

    Let x represent the width of the rectangle.

    $$2(4 + 3x) + 2x = 18.4$$
    $$8 + 6x + 2x = 18.4$$
    $$8 + 8x = 18.4$$
    $$8x = 10.4$$
    $$x = \frac{10.4}{8}$$
    $$x = 1.3$$

    The width of the rectangle is 1.3 cm and the length is 7.9 cm, so the area is 10.27 cm².

4. Eight times the result of subtracting 3 from a number is equal to the number increased by 25.

    Let x be the number.

    $$8(x - 3) = x + 25$$
    $$8x - 24 = x + 25$$
    $$7x - 24 = 25$$
    $$7x = 49$$
    $$x = 7$$

    The number is 7.

5. Three consecutive odd integers have a sum of 3. What are the numbers?

    Let x be the first number.

    $$x + x + 2 + x + 4 = 3$$
    $$3x + 6 = 3$$
    $$3x = -3$$
    $$x = -1$$

    The numbers are $-1, 1$, and 3.

6. Each month Liz pays \$35 to her phone company just to use the phone. Each text she sends costs her an additional \$0.05. In March her phone bill was \$72.60. In April her phone bill was \$65.85. How many texts did she send each month?

    Let x be the number of texts she sent in March.

    $$35 + 0.05x = 72.60$$
    $$0.05x = 37.6$$
    $$x = \frac{37.6}{0.05}$$
    $$x = 752$$

    She sent 752 texts in March.

    Let y be the number of texts she sent in April.

    $$35 + 0.05y = 65.85$$
    $$0.05y = 30.85$$
    $$y = \frac{30.85}{0.05}$$
    $$y = 617$$

    She sent 617 texts in April.

Lesson 9:	An Application of Linear Equations
Date:	11/8/13

102

7. Claudia is reading a book that has 360 pages. She has already read some of the book last week. She plans to read 46 pages today. When she does, she will be $\frac{4}{5}$ of the way through the book. How many pages did she read last week?

    Let x be the number of pages she read last week.

    $$x + 46 = \frac{4}{5}(360)$$
    $$x + 46 = 288$$
    $$x = 242$$

    Claudia read 242 pages last week.

8. In the diagram below, $\triangle ABC \sim \triangle A'B'C'$. Determine the measure of $\angle A$.

    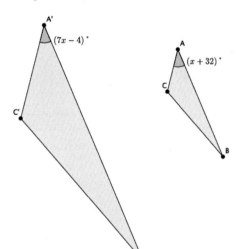

    $$7x - 4 = x + 32$$
    $$6x - 4 = 32$$
    $$6x = 36$$
    $$x = 6$$

    The measure of $\angle A$ is $38°$.

9. In the diagram below, $\triangle ABC \sim \triangle A'B'C'$. Determine the measure of $\angle A$.

    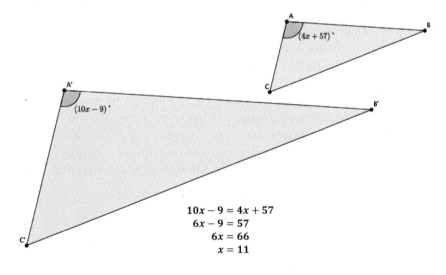

    $$10x - 9 = 4x + 57$$
    $$6x - 9 = 57$$
    $$6x = 66$$
    $$x = 11$$

    The measure of $\angle A$ is $101°$.

Topic B:

Linear Equations in Two Variables and Their Graphs

8.EE.B.5

Focus Standard:	8.EE.B.5	Graph proportional relationships, interpreting the unit rate as the slope of the graph. Compare two different proportional relationships represented in different ways.
Instructional Days:	5	
Lesson 10:	A Critical Look at Proportional Relationships (S)[1]	
Lesson 11:	Constant Rate (P)	
Lesson 12:	Linear Equations in Two Variables (E)	
Lesson 13:	The Graph of a Linear Equation in Two Variables (S)	
Lesson 14:	The Graph of a Linear Equation—Horizontal and Vertical Lines (S)	

Topic B begins with students working with proportional relationships related to average speed and constant speed. In Lesson 10, students use information that is organized in the form of a table to write linear equations. In Lesson 11, students learn how to apply the concept of constant rate to a variety of contexts requiring two variables (**8.EE.B.5**). Lesson 12 introduces students to the standard form of an equation in two variables. At this point, students use a table to help them find and organize solutions to a linear equation in two variables. Students then use the information from the table to begin graphing solutions on a coordinate plane. Lesson 13 is when students begin to question whether or not the graph of a linear equation is a line as opposed to something that is curved. Lesson 14 presents students with equations in standard form, $ax + by = c$, where $a = 0$ or $b = 0$, which produces lines that are either vertical or horizontal.

---

[1] Lesson Structure Key: **P**-Problem Set Lesson, **M**-Modeling Cycle Lesson, **E**-Exploration Lesson, **S**-Socratic Lesson

Lesson 10: A Critical Look at Proportional Relationships

Student Outcomes

- Students work with proportional relationships in terms of average speed and constant speed in order to write a linear equation in two variables.
- Students use linear equations in two variables to answer questions about distance and time.

Classwork

Discussion (25 minutes)

Example 1

- Consider the word problem below. We can do several things to answer this problem, but let's begin to organize our work using a table for time and distance:

> *Scaffolding:*
> It may be necessary to remind students of the relationship between distance traveled, rate, and time spent traveling at that rate.

Example 1

Paul walks 2 miles in 25 minutes. How many miles can Paul walk in 137. 5 minutes?

Time (in minutes)	Distance (in miles)
25	2
50	4
75	6
100	8
125	10

As students answer the questions below, fill in the table.

- How many miles would Paul be able to walk in 50 minutes? Explain.
    - *Paul could walk 4 miles in 50 minutes because 50 minutes is twice the time we were given, so we can calculate twice the distance, which is 4.*
- How many miles would Paul be able to walk in 75 minutes? Explain.
    - *Paul could walk 6 miles in 75 minutes because 75 minutes is three times the number of minutes we were given, so we can calculate three times the distance, which is 6.*
- How many miles would Paul be able to walk in 100 minutes?
    - *He could walk 8 miles.*
- How many miles would he walk in 125 minutes?
    - *He could walk 10 miles.*
- How could we determine the number of miles Paul could walk in 137.5 minutes?

Provide students time to think about the answer to this question. They will likely say that they can write a proportion to figure it out. Allow them to share and demonstrate their solutions. Then proceed with the discussion below, if necessary.

- Since the relationship between the distance Paul walks and the time it takes him to walk that distance is proportional, we let y represent the distance Paul walks in 137.5 minutes and write:

$$\frac{25}{2} = \frac{137.5}{y}$$
$$25y = 137.5(2)$$
$$25y = 275$$
$$y = 11$$

Therefore, Paul can walk 11 miles in 137.5 minutes.

- How many miles y can Paul walk in x minutes?

Provide students time to think about the answer to this question. Allow them to share their ideas and then proceed with the discussion below, if necessary.

- We know for a fact that Paul can walk 2 miles in 25 minutes, so we can write the ratio $\frac{25}{2}$ as we did with the proportion. We can write another ratio for the number of miles y Paul walks in x minutes. It is $\frac{x}{y}$. For the same reason we could write the proportion before, we can write one now with these two ratios:

$$\frac{25}{2} = \frac{x}{y}$$

Does this remind you of something we've done recently? Explain.

  □ *This is a linear equation in disguise. All we need to do is multiply each numerator by the other fractions denominator, then we will have a linear equation.*

$$25y = 2x$$

- Recall our original question: How many miles y can Paul walk in x minutes? We need to solve this equation for y.

$$25y = 2x$$
$$y = \frac{2}{25}x$$
$$y = 0.08x$$

Paul can walk y miles in $0.08x$ minutes. This equation will allow us to answer all kinds of questions about Paul with respect to any given number of minutes or miles.

- Let's go back to the table and look for $y = 0.08x$ or its equivalent $y = \frac{2}{25}x$ there. What do you notice?

Time (in minutes)	Distance (in miles)
25	2
50	4
75	6
100	8
125	10

- *The fraction $\frac{2}{25}$ came from the first row in the table. It's the distance traveled divided by the time it took to travel that distance. It is also in between each row of the table. For example, the difference between 4 miles and 2 miles is 2, and the difference between the associated times 50 and 25 is 25. The pattern repeats throughout the table.*

Show on the table the +2 between each distance interval and the +25 between each time interval. Remind students that they have done work like this before, specifically finding a unit rate for a proportional relationship. Make clear that the unit rate found in the table was exactly the same as the unit rate found using the proportion and that the unit rate is the rate at which Paul walks.

- Let's look at another problem where only a table is provided:

Time (in hours)	Distance (in miles)
3	123
6	246
9	369
12	492
	y

We want to know how many miles y can be traveled in any number of hours x. Using our previous work, what should we do?

- *We can write and solve a proportion that contains both x and y or use the table to help us determine the unit rate.*

- How many miles y can be traveled in any number of hours x?

- *Student work:*

$$\frac{123}{3} = \frac{y}{x}$$
$$123x = 3y$$
$$\frac{123}{3}x = y$$
$$41x = y$$

- What does the equation $y = 41x$ mean?

- *It means that the distance traveled y is equal to the rate of 41 multiplied by the number of hours x traveled at that rate.*

Lesson 10:	A Critical Look at Proportional Relationships
Date:	11/8/13

107

Example 2

The point of this problem is to make clear to students that we must assume constant rate in order to write linear equations in two variables and to use those equations to answer questions about distance, time, and rate.

- Consider the following word problem: Alexxa walked from the Grand Central Station on 42nd street to the Penn Station on 7th avenue. The total distance traveled was 1.1 miles. It took Alexxa 25 minutes to make the walk. How many miles did she walk in the first 10 minutes?

Give students a minute to think and/or work on the problem. Expect them to write a proportion and solve the problem. The next part of the discussion will get them to think about what is meant by "constant" speed or rather lack of it.

  □ *She walked 0.44 miles. (Assuming students used a proportion to solve.)*

- Are you sure about your answer? How often do you walk at a constant speed? Notice the problem did not even mention that she was walking at the same rate throughout the entire 1.1 miles. What if you have more information about her walk: Alexxa walked from Grand Central Station (GCS) along 42nd street to an ATM machine 0.3 miles away in 8 minutes. It took her 2 minutes to get some money out of the machine. Do you think your answer is still correct?

  □ *Probably not since now that we know she had to stop at the ATM.*

- Let's continue with Alexxa's walk: She reached the 7th avenue junction 13 minutes after she left GCS, a distance of 0.6 miles. There she met her friend Karen with whom she talked for 2 minutes. After leaving her friend she finally got to Penn Station 25 minutes after her walk began.

- Isn't this a more realistic situation than believing that she walked the exact same speed throughout the entire trip? What other events typically occur during walks in the city?

  □ *Stop lights at crosswalks, traffic, maybe a trip/fall, running an errand, etc.*

- This is precisely the reason we need to take a critical look at what we call "proportional relationships" and constant speed, in general.

- The following table shows an accurate picture of Alexxa's walk:

Time(in minutes)	Distance Traveled (in miles)
0	0
8	0.3
10	0.3
13	0.6
15	0.6
25	1.1

With this information, we can answer the question. Alexxa walked *exactly* 0.3 miles in 10 minutes.

- Now that we have an idea of what could go wrong when we assume a person walks at a constant rate or that a proportion can give us the correct answer all of the time, let's define what is called *average speed*.

  Suppose a person walks a distance of d (miles) in a given time interval t (minutes). Then the **average speed** in the given time interval is $\dfrac{d}{t}$ in miles per minute.

- With this definition we can calculate Alexxa's average speed: The distance that Alexxa traveled divided by the time interval she walked is $\dfrac{1.1}{25}$ miles per minute.

- If we assume that someone can actually walk at the same average speed over *any* time interval, then we say that the person is walking at a *constant speed*.

  Suppose the average speed of a person is the *same* constant C for *any* given time interval. Then we say that the person is walking at a **constant speed C.**

- If the original problem included information specifying constant speed, then we could write the following:

  Alexxa's average speed for 25 minutes is $\dfrac{1.1}{25}$.

  Let y represent the distance Alexxa walked in 10 minutes. Then her average speed for 10 minutes is $\dfrac{y}{10}$.

  Since Alexxa is walking at a constant speed of C miles per minute, then we know that

  $$\dfrac{1.1}{25} = C \qquad \text{and} \qquad \dfrac{y}{10} = C$$

  Since both fractions are equal to C, then we can write

  $$\dfrac{1.1}{25} = \dfrac{y}{10}.$$

  With the assumption of constant speed, we now have a "proportional relationship," which would make the answer you came up with in the beginning correct.

- We can go one step further and write a statement in general. If Alexxa walks y miles in x minutes, then

  $$\dfrac{y}{x} = C \qquad \text{and} \qquad \dfrac{1.1}{25} = \dfrac{y}{x}$$

  To find how many miles y, Alexxa walks in x miles, we solve the equation for y:

  $$\dfrac{1.1}{25} = \dfrac{y}{x}$$

  $$25y = 1.1x$$

  $$\dfrac{25}{25}y = \dfrac{1.1}{25}x$$

  $$y = \dfrac{1.1}{25}x$$

  where the last equation is an example of a linear equation in two variables x and y. With this general equation, we can find the distance y Alexxa walks in any given time x. Since we have more information about Alexxa's walk, that is where and when she stopped, we know that the equation cannot accurately predict the distance she walks after a certain number of minutes. To do so requires us to assume that she walks at a constant rate. This is an assumption we generally take for granted when solving problems about rate.

Exercises 1–2 (5 minutes)

Students complete Exercises 1–2 independently or in pairs.

Exercises 1–2

1. Wesley walks at a constant speed from his house to school 1.5 miles away. It took him 25 minutes to get to school.

   a. What fraction represents his constant speed, C?

   $$\frac{1.5}{25} = C$$

   b. You want to know how many miles he has walked after 15 minutes. Let y represent the distance he traveled after 15 minutes of walking at the given constant speed. Write a fraction that represents the constant speed, C in terms of y.

   $$\frac{y}{15} = C$$

   c. Write the fractions from parts (a) and (b) as a proportion and solve to find out many miles Wesley walked after 15 minutes.

   $$\frac{1.5}{25} = \frac{y}{15}$$
   $$25y = 22.5$$
   $$\frac{25}{25}y = \frac{22.5}{25}$$
   $$y = 0.9$$

   Wesley walks 0.9 miles in 15 minutes.

   d. Let y be the distance in miles that Wesley traveled after x minutes. Write a linear equation in two variables that represents how many miles Wesley walked after x minutes.

   $$\frac{1.5}{25} = \frac{y}{x}$$
   $$25y - 1.5x$$
   $$\frac{25}{25}y = \frac{1.5}{25}x$$
   $$y = \frac{1.5}{25}x$$

2. Stefanie drove at a constant speed from her apartment to her friend's house 20 miles away. It took her 45 minutes to reach her destination.

   a. What fraction represents her constant speed, C?

   $$\frac{20}{45} = C$$

   b. What fraction represents constant speed, C, if it takes her x number of minutes to get half-way to her friend's house?

   $$\frac{10}{x} = C$$

---

c.   Write a proportion using the fractions from parts (a) and (b) to determine how many minutes it takes her to get to the half-way point.

$$\frac{20}{45} = \frac{10}{x}$$
$$20x = 450$$
$$\frac{20}{20}x = \frac{450}{20}$$
$$x = 22.5$$

Stefanie gets half-way to her friend's house, 10 miles away, after 22.5 minutes.

d.   Write a two variable equation to represent how many miles Stefanie can drive over any time interval.

Let y represent the distance traveled over any time interval x. Then,

$$\frac{20}{45} = \frac{y}{x}$$
$$20x = 45y$$
$$\frac{20}{45}x = \frac{45}{45}y$$
$$\frac{4}{9}x = y$$

Discussion (4 minutes)

- Consider the problem: Dave lives 15 miles from town A. He is driving at a constant speed of 50 miles per hour from his home away from (in the opposite direction of) the city. How far away is Dave from the town after x hours of driving?

- Since we know he is driving at a constant speed of 50 miles per hour, then we need to determine the distance he travels over a time interval.

- If we say that Dave is y miles from town A after driving x hours, how can we express the actual number of miles that Dave traveled?

  □   *Dave is 15 miles from town A to begin with, so the total number of miles Dave traveled is $y - 15$.*

- If Dave's average speed in x hours is $\dfrac{y-15}{x}$, which is equal to a constant, i.e., his constant speed, then we have the equation

$$\frac{y - 15}{x} = 50$$

- We want to know how many miles Dave is from town A, y, after driving for x hours. Solve this equation for y.

  □   *Student work:*

$$\frac{y - 15}{x} = 50$$
$$y - 15 = 50x$$
$$y - 15 + 15 = 50x + 15$$
$$y = 50x + 15$$

Lesson 10:   A Critical Look at Proportional Relationships
Date: 11/8/13

111

- With this equation, $y = 50x + 15$, we can find the distance Dave is from town A for any given time x. How far away is Dave from town A after one hour?

  □ *Student work:*

    If $x = 1$, then

    $y = 50(1) + 15$
    $y = 65$

    Dave is 65 miles from town A after one hour.

Exercise 3 (4 minutes)

Students complete Exercise 3 independently or in pairs.

Exercise 3

3. **The equation that represents how many miles, y, Dave travels after x hours is $y = 50x + 15$. Use the equation to complete the table below.**

x (hours)	Linear equation in y: $y = 50x + 15$	y (miles)
1	$y = 50(1) + 15$	65
2	$y = 50(2) + 15$	115
3	$y = 50(3) + 15$	165
3.5	$y = 50(3.5) + 15$	190
4.1	$y = 50(4.1) + 15$	220

Closing (3 minutes)

Summarize, or ask students to summarize, the main points from the lesson:

- Average speed is found by taking the total distance traveled in a given time interval, divided by the time interval.

- If we assume the same average speed over any time interval, then we have constant speed, which can then be used to express a linear equation in two variables relating distance and time.

- We know how to use linear equations to answer questions about distance and time.

- We cannot assume that a problem can be solved using a proportion unless we know that the situation involves constant speed (or rate).

Lesson Summary

Average speed is found by taking the total distance traveled in a given time interval, divided by the time interval.

If y is the total distance traveled in a given time interval x, then $\frac{y}{x}$ is the average speed.

If we assume the same average speed over any time interval, then we have constant speed, which can then be used to express a linear equation in two variables relating distance and time.

If $\frac{y}{x} = C$, where C is a constant, then you have constant speed.

Exit Ticket (4 minutes)

Name _____   Date _____

Lesson 10: A Critical Look at Proportional Relationships

1. Alex skateboards at a constant speed from his house to school 3.8 miles away. It takes him 18 minutes.

    a.   What fraction represents his constant speed, C?

    b.   After school, Alex skateboards at the same constant speed to his friend's house. It takes him 10 minutes. Write the fraction that represents constant speed, C, if he travels a distance of y.

    c.   Write the fractions from part (a) and (b) as a proportion, and solve to find out how many miles Alex's friend's house is from school. Round your answer to the tenths place.

Exit Ticket Sample Solutions

1. Alex skateboards at a constant speed from his house to school 3.8 miles away. It takes him 18 minutes.

    a. What fraction represents his constant speed, C?

    $$\frac{3.8}{18} = C$$

    b. After school, Alex skateboards at the same constant speed to his friend's house. It takes him 10 minutes. Write the fraction that represents constant speed, C, if he travels a distance of y.

    $$\frac{y}{10} = C$$

    c. Write the fractions from part (a) and (b) as a proportion and solve to find out how many miles Alex's friend's house is from school. Round your answer to the tenths place.

    $$\frac{3.8}{18} = \frac{y}{10}$$
    $$3.8(10) = 18y$$
    $$38 = 18y$$
    $$\frac{38}{18} = y$$
    $$2.1 \approx y$$

    Alex's friend lives about 2.1 miles from school.

Problem Set Sample Solutions

Students practice writing and solving proportions to solve constant speed problems. Students write two variable equations to represent situations generally.

1. Eman walks from the store to her friend's house, 2 miles away. It takes her 35 minutes.

    a. What fraction represents her constant speed, C?

    $$\frac{2}{35} = C$$

    b. Write the fraction that represents her constant speed, C, if she walks y miles in 10 minutes.

    $$\frac{y}{10} = C$$

    c. Write a proportion using the fractions from parts (a) and (b) to determine how many miles she walks after 10 minutes. Round your answer to the hundredths place.

    $$\frac{2}{35} = \frac{y}{10}$$
    $$35y = 20$$
    $$\frac{35}{35}y = \frac{20}{35}$$
    $$y = 0.57142\ldots$$

    Eman walks about 0.57 miles after 10 minutes.

Lesson 10:   A Critical Look at Proportional Relationships
Date: 11/8/13

114

d. Write a two-variable equation to represent how many miles Eman can walk over any time interval.

Let y represent the distance Eman walks in x minutes.

$$\frac{2}{35} = \frac{y}{x}$$
$$35y = 2x$$
$$\frac{35}{35}y = \frac{2}{35}x$$
$$y = \frac{2}{35}x$$

2. Erika drives from school to soccer practice 1.3 miles away. It takes her 7 minutes.

   a. What fraction represents her constant speed, C?

   $$\frac{1.3}{7} = C$$

   b. What fraction represents her constant speed, C, if it takes her x minutes to drive exactly 1 mile?

   $$\frac{1}{x} = C$$

   c. Write a proportion using the fractions from parts (a) and (b) to determine how much time it takes her to drive exactly 1 mile. Round your answer to the tenths place.

   $$\frac{1.3}{7} = \frac{1}{x}$$
   $$1.3x = 7$$
   $$\frac{1.3}{1.3}x = \frac{7}{1.3}$$
   $$x = 5.38461\ldots$$

   It takes Erika about 5.4 minutes to drive exactly 1 mile.

   d. Write a two-variable equation to represent how many miles Erika can drive over any time interval.

   Let y be the number of miles Erika travels in x minutes.

   $$\frac{1.3}{7} = \frac{y}{x}$$
   $$7y = 1.3x$$
   $$\frac{7}{7}y = \frac{1.3}{7}x$$
   $$y = \frac{1.3}{7}x$$

3. Darla drives at a constant speed of 45 miles per hour.

   a. If she drives for y miles and it takes her x hours, write the two-variable equation to represent the number of miles Darla can drive in x hours.

   $$\frac{y}{x} = 45$$
   $$y = 45x$$

b.   Darla plans to drive to the market 14 miles from her house, then to the post office 3 miles from the market, and then return home, which is 15 miles from the post office. Assuming she drives at a constant speed the entire time, how long will it take her to get back home after running her errands? Round your answer to the hundredths place.

Altogether, Darla plans to drive $14 + 3 + 15 = 32$ miles.

$$32 = 45x$$
$$\frac{32}{45} = \frac{45}{45}x$$
$$0.71111\ldots = x$$

It will take Darla about 0.71 hours to get home after running her errands.

4.   Aaron walks from his sister's house to his cousin's house, a distance of 4 miles, in 80 minutes. How far does he walk in 30 minutes?

I cannot say for sure how far Aaron walks in 30 minutes because I don't know if he is walking at a constant speed. Maybe he stopped at his friend's house for 20 minutes or something.

5.   Carlos walks 4 miles every night for exercise. It takes him exactly 63 minutes to finish his walk.

a.   Assuming he walks at a constant rate, write an equation that represents how many miles, y, Carlos can walk in x minutes.

Since $\frac{4}{63} = C$ and $\frac{y}{x} = C$, then

$$\frac{4}{63} = \frac{y}{x}$$
$$63y = 4x$$
$$\frac{63}{63}y = \frac{4}{63}x$$
$$y = \frac{4}{63}x$$

b.   Use your equation from part (a) to complete the table below. Use a calculator and round all values to the hundredths place.

x (minutes)	Linear equation in y: $y = \dfrac{4}{63}x$	y (miles)
15	$y = \dfrac{4}{63}(15)$	0.95
30	$y = \dfrac{4}{63}(30)$	1.90
40	$y = \dfrac{4}{63}(40)$	2.54
60	$y = \dfrac{4}{63}(60)$	3.81
75	$y = \dfrac{4}{63}(75)$	4.76

Lesson 11: Constant Rate

Student Outcomes

- Students know the definition of constant rate in varied contexts as expressed using two variables where one is representing a time interval.
- Students graph points on a coordinate plane related to constant rate problems.

Classwork

Example 1 (6 minutes)

Give students the first question below and allow them time to work. Ask them to share their solutions with the class and then proceed with the discussion, table, and graph to finish Example 1.

Example 1

Pauline mows a lawn at a constant rate. Suppose she mows a 35 square foot lawn in 2.5 minutes. What area, in square feet, can she mow in 10 minutes? t minutes?

- What is Pauline's average rate in 2.5 minutes?
  - *Pauline's average rate in 2.5 minutes is $\dfrac{35}{2.5}$ square feet per minute.*
- What is Pauline's average rate in 10 minutes?
  - *Let A represent area mowed. Pauline's average rate in 10 minutes is $\dfrac{A}{10}$ square feet per mintute.*
- Since Pauline mows at a constant rate, C, then $\dfrac{35}{2.5} = C$ and $\dfrac{A}{10} = C$. Therefore,

---

$$\frac{35}{2.5} = \frac{A}{10}$$
$$350 = 2.5A$$
$$\frac{350}{2.5} = \frac{2.5}{2.5}A$$
$$140 = A$$

Pauline mows 140 square feet of lawn in 10 minutes.

- If we let y represent the number of square feet Pauline can mow in t minutes, then Pauline's average rate in minutes is $\dfrac{y}{t}$ square feet per minute.
- Write the two variable equation that represents the area of lawn, y, Pauline can mow in t minutes.

Sample student work:

$$\frac{35}{2.5} = \frac{y}{t}$$
$$2.5y = 35t$$
$$\frac{2.5}{2.5}y = \frac{35}{2.5}t$$
$$y = \frac{35}{2.5}t$$

- What is the meaning of $\frac{35}{2.5}$ in the equation $y = \frac{35}{2.5}$?

  □ *The number $\frac{35}{2.5}$ represents the rate at which Pauline can mow a lawn.*

- We can organize the information in a table:

t (time in minutes)	Linear equation: $y = \frac{35}{2.5}t$	y (area in square feet)
0	$y = \frac{35}{2.5}(0)$	0
1	$y = \frac{35}{2.5}(1)$	$\frac{35}{2.5} = 14$
2	$y = \frac{35}{2.5}(2)$	$\frac{70}{2.5} = 28$
3	$y = \frac{35}{2.5}(3)$	$\frac{105}{2.5} = 42$
4	$y = \frac{35}{2.5}(4)$	$\frac{140}{2.5} = 56$

- On a coordinate plane, we will let the x-axis represent time t, in minutes, and the y-axis represent the area of mowed lawn in square feet. Then we have the following graph:

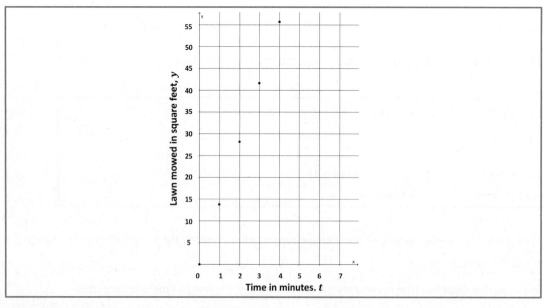

- Because Pauline mows at a constant rate, we would expect the square feet of mowed lawn to continue to rise as the time in minutes increases.

Concept Development (6 minutes)

- In the last lesson, we learned about average speed and constant speed. Constant speed problems are just a special case of a larger variety of problems known as constant rate problems. Some of these problems such as water pouring out of a faucet into a tub, painting a house, and mowing a lawn were topics in Grade 7.

- First, we define the average rate:

  Suppose V gallons of water flow from a faucet in a given time interval t (minutes). Then the *average rate* of water flow in the given time interval is $\frac{V}{t}$ in gallons per minute.

- Then, we define the constant rate:

  Suppose the average rate of water flow is the same constant C for *any* given time interval. Then we say that the water is flowing at a *constant rate, C*.

- Similarly, suppose A square feet of lawn are mowed in a given time interval t (minutes). Then the *average rate* of lawn mowing in the given time interval is $\frac{A}{t}$ square feet per minute. If we assume that the average rate of lawn mowing is the same constant C for *any* given time interval, then we say that the lawn is mowed at a constant rate, C.

- Describe the average rate of painting a house.

  - *Suppose A square feet of house are painted in a given time interval t (minutes). Then the average rate of house painting in the given time interval is $\frac{A}{t}$ square feet per minute.*

- Describe the constant rate of painting a house.

  - *If we assume that the average rate of house painting is the same constant C over any given time interval, then we say that the wall is painted at a constant rate, C.*

- What is the difference between average rate and constant rate?

  - *Average rate is the rate in which something can be done over a specific time interval. Constant rate assumes that the average rate is the same over any time interval.*

- As you can see, the way we define average rate and constant rate for a given situation is very similar. In each case, a transcription of the given information leads to an expression in two variables.

Example 2 (8 minutes)

> **Example 2**
>
> Water flows at a constant rate out of a faucet. Suppose the volume of water that comes out in three minutes is 10.5 gallons. How many gallons of water comes out of the faucet in t minutes?

- Write the linear equation that represents the volume of water, V, that comes out in t minutes.

	Lesson 11:	Constant Rate
	Date:	11/8/13

> **Let C represent the constant rate of water flow.**
>
> $\frac{10.5}{3} = C$ and $\frac{V}{t} = C$, then $\frac{10.5}{3} = \frac{V}{t}$.
>
> $$\frac{10.5}{3} = \frac{V}{t}$$
> $$3V = 10.5t$$
> $$\frac{3}{3}V = \frac{10.5}{3}t$$
> $$V = \frac{10.5}{3}t$$

MP.7

- What is the meaning of the number $\frac{10.5}{3}$ in the equation $V = \frac{10.5}{3}$?

  □ *The number $\frac{10.5}{3}$ represents the rate at which water flows from a faucet.*

- Using the linear equation $V = \frac{10.5}{3}t$, complete the table:

t (time in minutes)	Linear equation: $V = \frac{10.5}{3}t$	V (in gallons)
0	$V = \frac{10.5}{3}(0)$	0
1	$V = \frac{10.5}{3}(1)$	$\frac{10.5}{3} = 3.5$
2	$V = \frac{10.5}{3}(2)$	$\frac{21}{3} = 7$
3	$V = \frac{10.5}{3}(3)$	$\frac{31.5}{3} = 10.5$
4	$V = \frac{10.5}{3}(4)$	$\frac{42}{3} = 14$

- On a coordinate plane, we will let the x-axis represent time t in minutes and the y-axis represent the volume of water. Graph the data from the table.

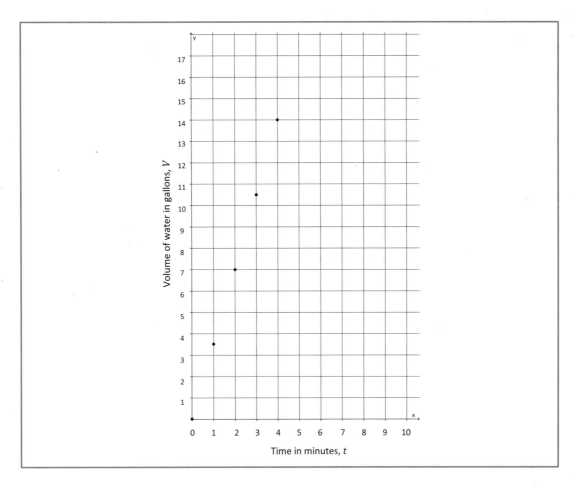

- Using the graph, about how many gallons of water do you think would flow after $1\frac{1}{2}$ minutes? Explain.

  - *After $1\frac{1}{2}$ minutes, between $3\frac{1}{2}$ and 7 gallons of water will flow. Since the water is flowing at a constant rate, we can expect the volume of water to rise between 1 and 2 minutes. The number of gallons that flows after $1\frac{1}{2}$ minutes then would have to be between the number of gallons that flows out after 1 minute and 2 minutes.*

- Using the graph, about how long would it take for 15 gallons of water to flow out of the faucet? Explain.

  - *It would take between 4 and 5 minutes for 15 gallons of water to flow out of the faucet. It takes 4 minutes for 14 gallons to flow; therefore, it must take more than 4 minutes for 15 gallons to come out. It must take less than 5 minutes because $3\frac{1}{2}$ gallons flow out every minute.*

- Graphing proportional relationships like these last two constant rate problems provide us more information than simply solving an equation and calculating one value. The graph provides information that is not so obvious in an equation.

Exercises 1–3 (15 minutes)

Students complete Exercises 1–3 independently.

Exercises 1–3

1. Jesus types at a constant rate. He can type a full page of text in $3\frac{1}{2}$ minutes. We want to know how many pages, p, Jesus can type after t minutes.

    a. Write the linear equation in two variables that represents the number of pages Jesus types in any given time interval.

    Let C represent the constant rate that Jesus types. Then,

    $\frac{1}{3.5} = C$ *and* $\frac{p}{t} = C$, *therefore* $\frac{1}{3.5} = \frac{p}{t}$.

    $$\frac{1}{3.5} = \frac{p}{t}$$
    $$3.5p = t$$
    $$\frac{3.5}{3.5}p = \frac{1}{3.5}t$$
    $$p = \frac{1}{3.5}t$$

    b. Complete the table below. Use a calculator and round answers to the tenths place.

t (time in minutes)	Linear equation: $p = \frac{1}{3.5}t$	p (pages typed)
0	$p = \frac{1}{3.5}(0)$	0
5	$p = \frac{1}{3.5}(5)$	$\frac{5}{3.5} \cong 1.4$
10	$p = \frac{1}{3.5}(10)$	$\frac{10}{3.5} \cong 2.9$
15	$p = \frac{1}{3.5}(15)$	$\frac{15}{3.5} \cong 4.3$
20	$p = \frac{1}{3.5}(20)$	$\frac{20}{3.5} \cong 5.7$

    c. Graph the data on a coordinate plane.

    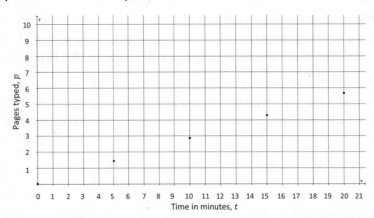

---

    d.   About how long would it take Jesus to type a 5-page paper? Explain.

It would take him between 15 and 20 minutes. After 15 minutes he will have typed 4.3 pages. In 20 minutes he can type 5.7 pages. Since 5 pages is between 4.3 and 5.7, then it will take him between 15 and 20 minutes.

2.   Emily paints at a constant rate. She can paint 32 square feet in five minutes. What area, A, can she paint in t minutes?

    a.   Write the linear equation in two variables that represents the number of square feet Emily can paint in any given time interval.

Let C be the constant rate that Emily paints. Then,

$$\frac{32}{5} = C \text{ and } \frac{A}{t} = C, \text{ therefore } \frac{32}{5} = \frac{A}{t}.$$

$$\frac{32}{5} = \frac{A}{t}$$
$$5A = 32t$$
$$\frac{5}{5}A = \frac{32}{5}t$$
$$A = \frac{32}{5}t$$

    b.   Complete the table below. Use a calculator and round answers to the tenths place.

t (time in minutes)	Linear equation: $A = \frac{32}{5}t$	A (area painted in square feet)
0	$A = \frac{32}{5}(0)$	0
1	$A = \frac{32}{5}(1)$	$\frac{32}{5} = 6.4$
2	$A = \frac{32}{5}(2)$	$\frac{64}{5} = 12.8$
3	$A = \frac{32}{5}(3)$	$\frac{96}{5} = 19.2$
4	$A = \frac{32}{5}(4)$	$\frac{128}{5} = 25.6$

    c.   Graph the data on a coordinate plane.

   d.   **About how many square feet can Emily paint in $\frac{1}{2}$ minutes? Explain.**

Emily can paint between 12.8 and 19.2 square feet in $2\frac{1}{2}$ minutes. After 2 minutes she paints 12.8 square feet and at 3 minutes she will have painted 19.2 square feet.

3.   Joseph walks at a constant speed. He walked to the store, one-half mile away, in 6 minutes. How many miles, m, can he walk in t minutes?

   a.   Write the linear equation in two variables that represents the number of miles Joseph can walk in any given time interval, t.

Let C be the constant rate that Joseph walks. Then,

$$\frac{0.5}{6} = C \text{ and } \frac{m}{t} = C, \text{ therefore } \frac{0.5}{6} = \frac{m}{t}.$$

$$\frac{0.5}{6} = \frac{m}{t}$$
$$6m = 0.5t$$
$$\frac{6}{6}m = \frac{0.5}{6}t$$
$$m = \frac{0.5}{6}t$$

   b.   Complete the table below. Use a calculator and round answers to the tenths place.

t (time in minutes)	Linear equation: $m = \dfrac{0.5}{6}t$	m (distance in miles)
0	$m = \dfrac{0.5}{6}(0)$	0
30	$m = \dfrac{0.5}{6}(30)$	$\dfrac{15}{6} = .5$
60	$m = \dfrac{0.5}{6}(60)$	$\dfrac{30}{6} = 5$
90	$m = \dfrac{0.5}{6}(90)$	$\dfrac{45}{6} = 7.5$
120	$m = \dfrac{0.5}{6}(120)$	$\dfrac{60}{6} = 10$

   c.   Graph the data on a coordinate plane.

> d.   Joseph's friend lives 4 miles away from him. About how long would it take Joseph to walk to his friend's
> house? Explain.
>
> *It will take Joseph a little less than an hour to walk to his friend's house. Since it takes* 30 *minutes for him to
> walk* 2.5 *miles, and* 60 *minutes to walk 5 miles, and 4 is closer to 5 than* .5*, it will take Joseph less than an
> hour to walk the 4 miles.*

Closing (5 minutes)

Summarize, or ask students to summarize, the main points from the lesson:

- Constant rate problems appear in a variety of contexts like painting a house, typing, walking, water flow, etc.
- We can express the constant rate as a two variable equation representing proportional change.
- We can graph the constant rate situation by completing a table to compute data points.

Lesson Summary

When constant rate is stated for a given problem, then you can express the situation as a two variable equation.
The equation can be used to complete a table of values that can then be graphed on a coordinate plane.

Exit Ticket (5 minutes)

Name _____   Date _____

Lesson 11: Constant Rate

Exit Ticket

1. Vicky reads at a constant rate. She can read 5 pages in 9 minutes. We want to know how many pages, p, Vicky can read after t minutes.

    a. Write a linear equation in two variables that represents the number of pages Vicky reads in any given time interval.

    b. Complete the table below. Use a calculator and round answers to the tenths place.

(time in minutes)	Linear equation:	p (pages read)
0		
20		
40		
60		

    c. About how long would it take Vicky to read 25 pages? Explain.

Exit Ticket Sample Solutions

1. Vicky reads at a constant rate. She can read 5 pages in 9 minutes. We want to know how many pages, p, Vicky can read after t minutes.

   a. Write a linear equation in two variables that represents the number of pages Vicky reads in any given time interval.

   Let C represent the constant rate that Vicky reads. Then,

   $\frac{5}{9} = C$ and $\frac{p}{t} = C$, therefore $\frac{5}{9} = \frac{p}{t}$.

   $$\frac{5}{9} = \frac{p}{t}$$
   $$9p = 5t$$
   $$\frac{9}{9}p = \frac{5}{9}t$$
   $$p = \frac{5}{9}t$$

   b. Complete the table below. Use a calculator and round answers to the tenths place.

t (time in minutes)	Linear equation: $p = \frac{5}{9}t$	p (pages read)
0	$p = \frac{5}{9}(0)$	0
20	$p = \frac{5}{9}(20)$	$\frac{100}{9} \cong 11.1$
40	$p = \frac{5}{9}(40)$	$\frac{200}{9} \cong\ \ .2$
60	$p = \frac{5}{9}(60)$	$\frac{300}{9} \cong 33.3$

   c. About how long would it take Vicky to read 25 pages? Explain.

   It would take her a little over 40 minutes. After 40 minutes she can read about 22.2 pages, and after 1 hour she can read about 33.3 pages. Since 25 pages is between 22.2 and 33.3, then it will take her between 40 and 60 minutes to read 25 pages.

Problem Set Sample Solutions

Students practice writing two variable equations that represent a constant rate.

1. A train travels at a constant rate of 45 miles per hour.

   a. What is the distance, d, in miles, that the train travels in t hours?

   Let C be the constant rate the train travels. Then, $\frac{45}{1} = C$ and $\frac{d}{t} = C$; therefore, $\frac{45}{1} = \frac{d}{t}$.

   $$\frac{45}{1} = \frac{d}{t}$$
   $$d = 45t$$

	Lesson 11:	Constant Rate
	Date:	11/8/13

127

b.   How many miles will it have traveled in 2.5 hours?

$$d = 45(2.5)$$
$$= 112.5$$

The train will travel 112.5 miles in 2.5 hours.

2.   Water is leaking from a faucet at a constant rate of $\frac{1}{3}$ gallons per minute.

a.   What is the amount of water, w, that is leaked from the faucet after t minutes?

Let C be the constant rate the water leaks from the faucet. Then,

$$\frac{\frac{1}{3}}{1} = C \text{ and } \frac{w}{t} = C; \text{ therefore, } \frac{\frac{1}{3}}{1} = \frac{w}{t}.$$

$$\frac{\frac{1}{3}}{1} = \frac{w}{t}$$
$$w = \frac{1}{3}t$$

b.   How much water is leaked after an hour?

$$w = \frac{1}{3}t$$
$$= \frac{1}{3}(60)$$
$$= 20$$

The faucet will leak 20 gallons in one hour.

3.   A car can be assembled on an assembly line in 6 hours. Assume that the cars are assembled at a constant rate.

a.   How many cars, y, can be assembled in t hours?

Let C be the constant rate the cars are assembled. Then,

$$\frac{1}{6} = C \text{ and } \frac{y}{t} = C, \text{ therefore } \frac{1}{6} = \frac{y}{t}.$$

$$\frac{1}{6} = \frac{y}{t}$$
$$6y = t$$
$$\frac{6}{6}y = \frac{1}{6}t$$
$$y = \frac{1}{6}t$$

b.   How many cars can be assembled in a week?

A week is $24 \times 7 = 268$ hours. So $y = \frac{1}{6}(168) = 28$. Twenty-eight cars can be assembled in a week.

4.   A copy machine makes copies at a constant rate. The machine can make 80 copies in $2\frac{1}{2}$ minutes.

   a.   Write an equation to represent the number of copies, n, that can be made over any time interval, t.

   Let C be the constant rate that copies can be made. Then

   $\frac{80}{2\frac{1}{2}} = C$ *and* $\frac{n}{t} = C$*, therefore* $\frac{80}{2\frac{1}{2}} = \frac{n}{t}$.

   $$\frac{80}{2\frac{1}{2}} = \frac{n}{t}$$

   $$2\frac{1}{2}n = 80t$$

   $$\frac{5}{2}n = 80t$$

   $$\frac{2}{5} \cdot \frac{5}{2}n = \frac{2}{5} \cdot 80t$$

   $$n = 32t$$

   b.   Complete the table below.

t (time in minutes)	Linear equation: $n = 32t$	n (number of copies)
0	$n = 32(0)$	0
0.25	$n = 32(0.25)$	8
0.5	$n = 32(0.5)$	16
0.75	$n = 32(0.75)$	24
1	$n = 32(1)$	32

   c.   Graph the data on a coordinate plane.

d.   The copy machine runs for 20 seconds, then jams. About how many copies were made before the jam occurred? Explain.

Since 20 *seconds is* 0.3 *of a minute, then the number of copies made will be between* 8 *and* 16 *because* 0.3 *is between* 0.25 *and* 0.5.

5.   Connor runs at a constant rate. It takes him 34 minutes to run four miles.

a.   Write the linear equation in two variables that represents the number of miles Connor can run in any given time interval, t.

Let C be the constant rate that Connor runs and m represent the number of miles. Then
$$\frac{4}{34} = C \text{ and } \frac{m}{t} = C, \text{ therefore } \frac{4}{34} = \frac{m}{t}.$$

$$\frac{4}{34} = \frac{m}{t}$$
$$34m = 4t$$
$$\frac{34}{34}m = \frac{4}{34}t$$
$$m = \frac{4}{34}t$$
$$m = \frac{2}{17}t$$

b.   Complete the table below. Use a calculator and round answers to the tenths place.

t (time in minutes)	Linear equation: $m = \frac{2}{17}t$	m (distance in miles)
0	$m = \frac{2}{17}(0)$	0
15	$m = \frac{2}{17}(15)$	$\frac{30}{17} \cong 1.8$
30	$m = \frac{2}{17}(30)$	$\frac{60}{17} \cong 3.5$
45	$m = \frac{2}{17}(45)$	$\frac{90}{17} \cong 5.3$
60	$m = \frac{2}{17}(60)$	$\frac{120}{17} \cong 7.1$

c.   Graph the data on a coordinate plane.

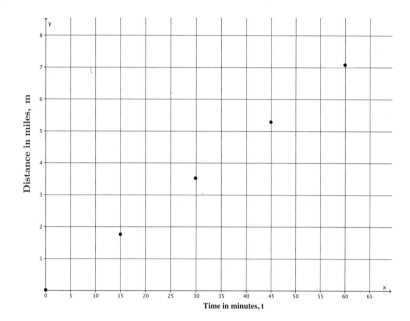

d.   Connor ran for 40 minutes before tripping and spraining his ankle. About how many miles did he run before he had to stop? Explain.

Since Connor ran for 40 minutes, that means that he ran more than 3.5 miles, but less than 5.3 miles. Since 40 is between 30 and 45, then we can use those reference points to make an estimate of how many miles he ran in 40 minutes, probably about 5 miles.

Lesson 12: Linear Equations in Two Variables

Student Outcomes

- Students use a table to find solutions to a given linear equation and plot the solutions on a coordinate plane.

Lesson Notes

In this lesson students will find solutions to a linear equation in two variables using a table, then plot the solutions as points on the coordinate plane. Students will need graph paper in order to complete the Exercises and the Problem Set.

Classwork

Opening Exercise (5 minutes)

Students complete the Opening Exercise independently in preparation for the discussion about standard form and solutions that follows.

Opening Exercise

Emily tells you that she scored 32 points in a basketball game with only two- and three-point baskets (no free throws). How many of each type of basket did she score? Use the table below to organize your work.

Number of Two-Pointers	Number of Three-Pointers
16	0
13	2
10	4
7	6
4	8
1	10

Let x be the number of two-pointers and y be the number of three-pointers that Emily scored. Write an equation to represent the situation.

$$2x + 3y = 32$$

Discussion (10 minutes)

- An equation in the form of $ax + by = c$ is called a *linear equation in two variables*, where a, b, and c are constants, and at least one of a and b are not zero. In this lesson, neither a or b will be equal to zero. In the opening exercise, what equation did you write to represent Emily's score at the basketball game?
  - $2x + 3y = 32$
- The equation $2x + 3y = 32$ is an example of a linear equation in two variables.

- An equation of this form, $ax + by = c$, is also referred to as an equation in *standard form*. Is the equation you wrote in the opening exercise in standard form?

  - *Yes, it is in the same form as $ax + by = c$.*

- In the equation $ax + by = c$, the symbols a, b, and c are constants. What then are x and y?

  - *The symbols x and y are numbers. Since they are not constants, it means they are unknown numbers, typically called variables, in the equation $ax + by = c$.*

- For example, $-50x + y = 15$ is a linear equation in x and y. As you can easily see, not just *any* pair of numbers x and y will make the equation true. Consider $x = 1$ and $y = 2$. Does it make the equation true?

  - *No, because $-50(1) + 2 = -50 + 2 = -48 \neq 15$.*

- What pairs of numbers did you find that worked for Emily's basketball score? Did just any pair of numbers work? Explain.

  - *Students should identify the pairs of numbers in the table of the opening exercise. No, not just any pair of numbers worked. For example, I couldn't say that Emily scored 15 two-pointers and 1 three-pointer because that would mean she scored 33 points in the game, and I know she only scored 32 points.*

- A *solution* to the linear equation in two variables is an ordered pair of numbers (x, y) so that x and y makes the equation a true statement. The pairs of numbers that you wrote in the table for Emily are solutions to the equation $2x + 3y = 32$ because they are pairs of numbers that make the equation true. The question becomes, how do we find an unlimited number of solutions to a given linear equation?

  - *Guess numbers until you find a pair that makes the equation true.*

- A strategy that will help us find solutions to a linear equation in two variables is as follows: We fix a number for x. That means we pick any number we want and call it x. Since we know how to solve a linear equation in one variable, then we solve for y. The number we picked for x and the number we get when we solve for y is the ordered pair (x, y), which is a solution to the two variable linear equation.

- For example, let $x = 5$. Then in the equation $-50x + y = 15$ we have

$$-50(5) + y = 15$$
$$-250 + y = 15$$
$$-250 + 250 + y = 15 + 250$$
$$y = 265$$

Therefore, $(5, 265)$ is a solution to the equation $-50x + y = 15$.

- Similarly, we can fix a number for y and solve for x. Let $y = 10$, then

$$-50x + 10 = 15$$
$$-50x + 10 - 10 = 15 - 10$$
$$-50x = 5$$
$$\frac{-50}{-50}x = \frac{5}{-50}$$
$$x = -\frac{1}{10}$$

Therefore, $(-\frac{1}{10}, 10)$ is a solution to the equation $-50x + y = 15$.

Ask students to provide you with a number for x or y and demonstrate how to find a solution. You can do this more than once in order to prove to students that you can find a solution no matter which number you choose to fix for x or y. Once they are convinced, allow them to work on the exploratory exercises.

Lesson 12:	Linear Equations in Two Variables
Date:	11/8/13

133

Exploratory Challenge/Exercises 1–5 (20 minutes)

Students can work independently or in pairs to complete the exercises. Every few minutes, have students share their tables and graphs with the class. Make suggestions to students as they work as to which values for x or y they could choose. For example, in Exercises 1 and 2, small numbers would ease the mental math work. Exercise 3 may be made easier if they choose a number for y and solve for x. Exercise 4 can be made easier if students choose values for x that are multiples of 5. As you make suggestions, ask students why your suggestions would make the work easier.

Exploratory Challenge/Exercises 1–5

1. Find five solutions for the linear equation $x + y = 3$, and plot the solutions as points on a coordinate plane.

   Sample student work:

x	Linear equation: $x + y = 3$	y
1	$1 + y = 3$	2
2	$2 + y = 3$	1
3	$3 + y = 3$	0
4	$4 + y = 3$	−1
5	$5 + y = 3$	−2

   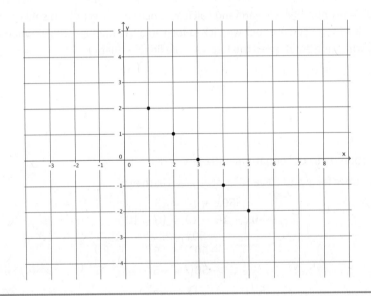

---

2. Find five solutions for the linear equation $2x - y = 10$, and plot the solutions as points on a coordinate plane.

Sample student work:

x	Linear equation: $2x - y = 10$	y
1	$2(1) - y = 10$ $2 - y = 10$ $2 - 2 - y = 10 - 2$ $-y = 8$ $y = -8$	-8
2	$2(2) - y = 10$ $4 - y = 10$ $4 - 4 - y = 10 - 4$ $-y = 6$ $y = -6$	-6
3	$2(3) - y = 10$ $6 - y = 10$ $6 - 6 - y = 10 - 6$ $-y = 4$ $y = -4$	-4
4	$2(4) - y = 10$ $8 - y = 10$ $8 - 8 - y = 10 - 8$ $-y = 2$ $y = -2$	-2
5	$2(5) - y = 10$ $10 - y = 10$ $y = 0$	0

3.   Find five solutions for the linear equation $x + 5y = 21$, and plot the solutions as points on a coordinate plane.

Sample student work:

x	Linear equation: $x + 5y = 21$	y
16	$x + 5(1) = 21$ $x + 5 = 21$ $x = 16$	1
11	$x + 5(2) = 21$ $x + 10 = 21$ $x = 11$	2
6	$x + 5(3) = 21$ $x + 15 = 21$ $x = 6$	3
1	$x + 5(4) = 21$ $x + 20 = 21$ $x = 1$	4
-4	$x + 5(5) = 21$ $x + 25 = 21$ $x = -4$	5

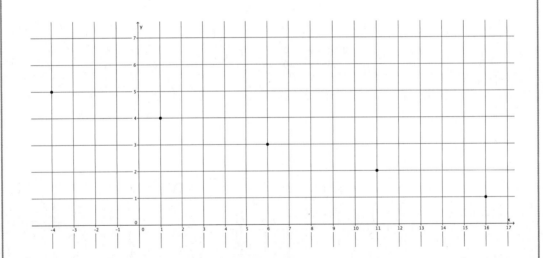

4.   Consider the linear equation $\frac{2}{5}x + y = 11$.

    a.   Will you choose to fix values for x or y? Explain.

       If I fix values for x, it will make the computations easier. Solving for y can be done in one step.

    b.   Are there specific numbers that would make your computational work easier? Explain.

       Values for x that are multiples of 5 will make the computations easier. When I multiply $\frac{2}{5}$ by a multiple of 5, I will get an integer.

COMMON CORE™

Lesson 12:	Linear Equations in Two Variables
Date:	11/8/13

136

c. Find five solutions to the linear equation $\frac{2}{5}x + y = 11$, and plot the solutions as points on a coordinate plane.

Sample student work:

x	Linear equation: $\frac{2}{5}x + y = 11$	y
5	$\frac{2}{5}(5) + y = 11$ $2 + y = 11$ $y = 9$	9
10	$\frac{2}{5}(10) + y = 11$ $4 + y = 11$ $y = 7$	7
15	$\frac{2}{5}(15) + y = 11$ $6 + y = 11$ $y = 5$	5
20	$\frac{2}{5}(20) + y = 11$ $8 + y = 11$ $y = 3$	3
25	$\frac{2}{5}(25) + y = 11$ $10 + y = 11$ $y = 1$	1

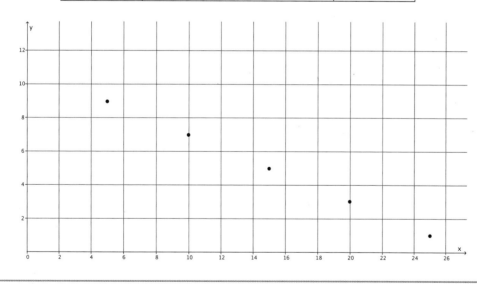

5. At the store you see that you can buy a bag of candy for $2 and a drink for $1. Assume you have a total of $35 to spend. You are feeling generous and want to buy some snacks for you and your friends.

   a. Write an equation in standard form to represent the number of bags of candy, x, and the number of drinks, y, you can buy with $35.

$$2x + y = 35$$

   b. Find five solutions to the linear equation, and plot the solutions as points on a coordinate plane.

   Sample student work:

x	Linear equation: $2x + y = 35$	y
4	$2(4) + y = 35$ $8 + y = 35$ $y = 27$	27
5	$2(5) + y = 35$ $10 + y = 35$ $y = 25$	25
8	$2(8) + y = 35$ $16 + y = 35$ $y = 19$	19
10	$2(10) + y = 35$ $20 + y = 35$ $y = 15$	15
15	$2(15) + y = 35$ $30 + y = 35$ $y = 5$	5

Closing (5 minutes)

Summarize, or ask students to summarize, the main points from the lesson:

- A two variable equation in the form of $ax + by = c$ is known as a linear equation in standard form.

- A solution to a linear equation in two variables is an ordered pair (x, y) that makes the given equation true.

- We can find solutions by fixing a number for x or y, then solving for the other variable. Our work can be made easier by thinking about the computations we will need to make before fixing a number for x or y. For example, if x has a coefficient of $\frac{1}{3}$ we should select values for x that are multiples of 3.

Lesson Summary

A two-variable linear equation in the form $ax + by = c$ is said to be in *standard form*.

A solution to a linear equation in two variables is the ordered pair (x, y) that makes the given equation true. Solutions can be found by fixing a number for x and solving for y or fixing a number for y and solving for x.

Exit Ticket (5 minutes)

    Lesson 12:   Linear Equations in Two Variables
                  Date: 11/8/13   139

Name _____   Date _____

Lesson 12: Linear Equations in Two Variables

Exit Ticket

1.   Is the point $(1, 3)$ a solution to the linear equation $5x - 9y = 32$? Explain.

2.   Find three solutions for the linear equation $4x - 3y = 1$, and plot the solutions as points on a coordinate plane.

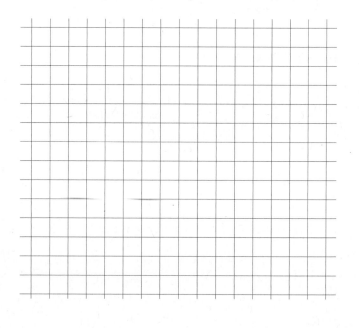

x	Linear equation: $4x - 3y = 1$	y

Exit Ticket Sample Solutions

1. Is the point $(1, 3)$ a solution to the linear equation $5x - 9y = 32$? Explain.

   No, $(1, 3)$ is not a solution to $5x - 9y = 32$ because $5(1) - 9(3) = 5 - 27 = -22$ and $-22 \neq 32$.

2. Find three solutions for the linear equation $4x - 3y = 1$, and plot the solutions as points on a coordinate plane.

   Sample student work.

x	Linear equation: $4x - 3y = 1$	y
1	$4(1) - 3y = 1$ $4 - 3y = 1$ $-3y = -3$ $y = 1$	1
4	$4x - 3(5) = 1$ $4x - 15 = 1$ $4x = 16$ $x = 4$	5
7	$4(7) - 3y = 1$ $28 - 3y = 1$ $-3y = -27$ $y = 9$	9

Problem Set Sample Solutions

Students practice finding and graphing solutions for linear equations that are in standard form.

1. Consider the linear equation $x - \dfrac{3}{2}y = -2$.

   a. Will you choose to fix values for x or y? Explain.

   If I fix values for y, it will make the computations easier. Solving for x can be done in one step.

   b. Are there specific numbers that would make your computational work easier? Explain.

   Values for y that are multiples of 2 will make the computations easier. When I multiply $\dfrac{3}{2}$ by a multiple of 2, I will get a whole number.

Lesson 12:   Linear Equations in Two Variables
Date: 11/8/13

c. Find five solutions to the linear equation $x - \frac{3}{2}y = -2$, and plot the solutions as points on a coordinate plane.

Sample student work:

x	Linear equation: $x - \frac{3}{2}y = -2$	y
1	$x - \frac{3}{2}(2) = -2$ $x - 3 = -2$ $x - 3 + 3 = -2 + 3$ $x = 1$	2
4	$x - \frac{3}{2}(4) = -2$ $x - 6 = -2$ $x - 6 + 6 = -2 + 6$ $x = 4$	4
7	$x - \frac{3}{2}(6) = -2$ $x - 9 = -2$ $x - 9 + 9 = -2 + 9$ $x = 7$	6
10	$x - \frac{3}{2}(8) = -2$ $x - 12 = -2$ $x - 12 + 12 = -2 + 12$ $x = 10$	8
13	$x - \frac{3}{2}(10) = -2$ $x - 15 = -2$ $x - 15 + 15 = -2 + 15$ $x = 13$	10

2.   Find five solutions for the linear equation $\frac{1}{3}x + y = 12$, and plot the solutions as points on a coordinate plane.

Sample student work:

x	Linear equation: $\frac{1}{3}x + y = 12$	y
3	$\frac{1}{3}(3) + y = 12$ $1 + y = 12$ $y = 11$	11
6	$\frac{1}{3}(6) + y = 12$ $2 + y = 12$ $y = 10$	10
9	$\frac{1}{3}(9) + y = 12$ $3 + y = 12$ $y = 9$	9
12	$\frac{1}{3}(12) + y = 12$ $4 + y = 12$ $y = 8$	8
15	$\frac{1}{3}(15) + y = 12$ $5 + y = 12$ $y = 7$	7

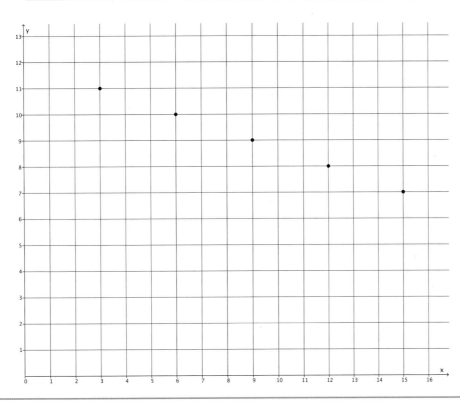

3. Find five solutions for the linear equation $-x + \frac{3}{4}y = -6$, and plot the solutions as points on a coordinate plane.

Sample student work:

x	Linear equation: $-x + \frac{3}{4}y = -6$	y
9	$-x + \frac{3}{4}(4) = -6$ $-x + 3 = -6$ $-x + x + 3 = -6 + x$ $3 = -6 - x$ $3 + 6 = -6 + 6 + x$ $9 - x$	4
12	$-x + \frac{3}{4}(8) = -6$ $-x + 6 = -6$ $-x + x + 6 = -6 + x$ $6 = -6 + x$ $6 + 6 = -6 + 6 + x$ $12 = x$	8
15	$-x + \frac{3}{4}(12) = -6$ $-x + 9 = -6$ $-x + x + 9 = -6 + x$ $9 = -6 + x$ $9 + 6 = -6 + 6 + x$ $15 = x$	12
18	$-x + \frac{3}{4}(16) = -6$ $-x + 12 = -6$ $-x + x + 12 = -6 + x$ $12 = -6 + x$ $12 + 6 = -6 + 6 + x$ $18 = x$	16
21	$-x + \frac{3}{4}(20) = -6$ $-x + 15 = -6$ $-x + x + 15 = -6 + x$ $15 = -6 + x$ $15 + 6 = -6 + 6 + x$ $21 = x$	20

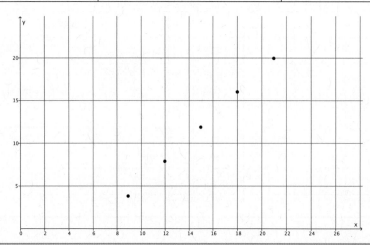

4. Find five solutions for the linear equation $2x + y = 5$, and plot the solutions as points on a coordinate plane.

Sample student work:

x	Linear equation: $2x + y = 5$	y
1	$2(1) + y = 5$ $2 + y = 5$ $y = 3$	3
2	$2(2) + y = 5$ $4 + y = 5$ $y = 1$	1
3	$2(3) + y = 5$ $6 + y = 5$ $y = -1$	-1
4	$2(4) + y = 5$ $8 + y = 5$ $y = -3$	-3
5	$2(5) + y = 5$ $10 + y = 5$ $y = -5$	-5

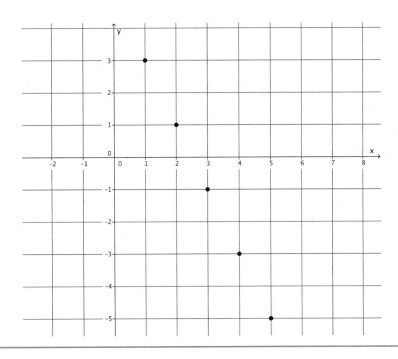

5. Find five solutions for the linear equation $3x - 5y = 15$, and plot the solutions as points on a coordinate plane.

Sample student work:

x	Linear equation: $3x - 5y = 15$	y
$\dfrac{20}{3}$	$3x - 5(1) = 15$ $3x - 5 = 15$ $3x - 5 + 5 = 15 + 5$ $3x = 20$ $\dfrac{3}{3}x = \dfrac{20}{3}$ $x = \dfrac{20}{3}$	1
$\dfrac{25}{3}$	$3x - 5(2) = 15$ $3x - 10 = 15$ $3x - 10 + 10 = 15 + 10$ $3x = 25$ $\dfrac{3}{3}x = \dfrac{25}{3}$ $x = \dfrac{25}{3}$	2
10	$3x - 5(3) = 15$ $3x - 15 = 15$ $3x - 15 + 15 = 15 + 15$ $3x = 30$ $x = 10$	3
$\dfrac{35}{3}$	$3x - 5(4) = 15$ $3x - 20 = 15$ $3x - 20 + 20 = 15 + 20$ $3x = 35$ $\dfrac{3}{3}x = \dfrac{35}{3}$ $x = \dfrac{35}{3}$	4
$\dfrac{40}{3}$	$3x - 5(5) = 15$ $3x - 25 = 15$ $3x - 25 + 25 = 15 + 25$ $3x = 40$ $\dfrac{3}{3}x = \dfrac{40}{3}$ $x = \dfrac{40}{3}$	5

Lesson 13: The Graph of a Linear Equation in Two Variables

Student Outcomes

- Students predict the shape of a graph of a linear equation by finding and plotting solutions on a coordinate plane.
- Students informally explain why the graph of a linear equation is not curved in terms of solutions to the given linear equation.

Classwork

Discussion (20 minutes)

- In the last lesson we saw that the solutions of a linear equation in two variables can be plotted on a coordinate plane as points. The collection of all points (x, y) in the coordinate plane so that each (x, y) is a solution of $ax + by = c$ is called the graph of $ax + by = c$.
- Do you think it is possible to plot *all* of the solutions of a linear equation on a coordinate plane?
  - *No, it's not possible. There are an infinite number of values we can use to fix one of the variables.*
- For that reason, we cannot draw the graph of a linear equation. What we can do is plot a few points of an equation and make predictions about what the graph should look like.
- Let's find five solutions to the linear equation $x + y = 6$ and plot the points on a coordinate plane. Name a solution.

As students provide solutions (samples provided below) organize them in an x-y table, as shown. It is most likely that students will give whole number solutions only. Accept them for now.

x	y
0	6
1	5
2	4
3	3
4	2

- Now let's plot these points of the graph of $x + y = 6$ on a coordinate plane.

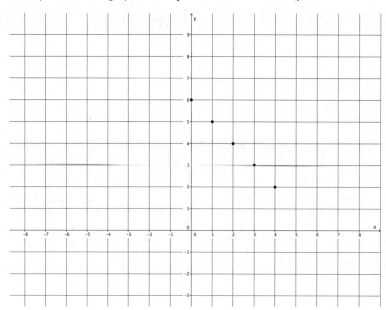

- Can you predict the shape of the graph of this linear equation based on just the five points we have so far?
  - *It looks like the points lie on a line.*
- Yes, at this point it looks like the graph of the equation is a line, but for all we know, there can be some curved parts between some of these points.

Draw curves between each of the points on the graph to show that the line could look similar to the graph below.

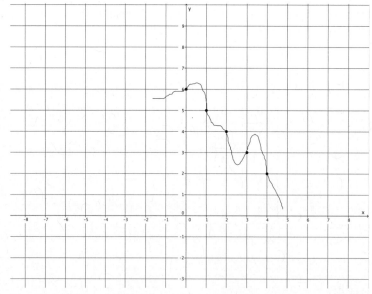

- The only thing we can do at this point is find more solutions that would show what the graph looks like between the existing points. That means we will have to look at some points with coordinates that are fractions. Name a solution that will plot as a point between the points we already have on the graph.

Add to the x-y table. Sample solutions provided below.

x	y
0	6
1	5
2	4
3	3
4	2
$\frac{1}{2}$	$5\frac{1}{2}$
$1\frac{1}{2}$	$4\frac{1}{2}$
$2\frac{1}{2}$	$3\frac{1}{2}$
$3\frac{1}{2}$	$2\frac{1}{2}$
$4\frac{1}{2}$	$1\frac{1}{2}$

- Now let's add these points of the graph of $x + y = 6$ on our coordinate plane.

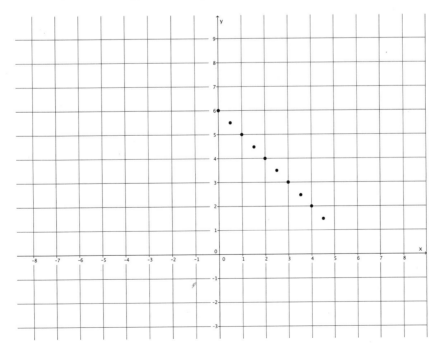

- Are you convinced that the graph of the linear equation $x + y = 6$ is a line? You shouldn't be! What if it looked like this.

Again, draw curves between each of the points on the graph to show what the graph could look like. Make sure to have curves in quadrants II and IV to illustrate the need to find points that fit (or don't fit) the pattern of the graph when x and y values are negative.

- Time to find more solutions. This time, we will need to come up with solutions where the x-value is negative or the y-value is negative.

Add to the x-y table. Sample solutions are provided below.

x	y
0	6
1	5
2	4
3	3
4	2
$\frac{1}{2}$	$5\frac{1}{2}$
$1\frac{1}{2}$	$4\frac{1}{2}$
$2\frac{1}{2}$	$3\frac{1}{2}$
$3\frac{1}{2}$	$2\frac{1}{2}$
$4\frac{1}{2}$	$1\frac{1}{2}$
-1	7
-2	8
-3	9
7	-1
8	-2

150

- Now we have 15 solutions to the equation $x + y = 6$. Are you convinced that the graph of this equation is a line?

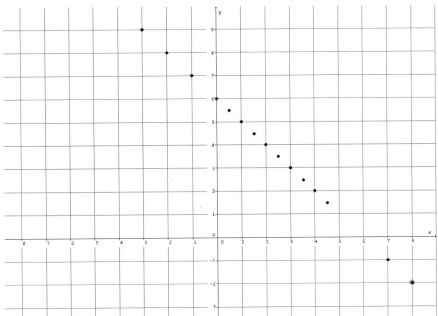

- □ *Students should say that they are still unsure, even though it looks like the graph is forming a line, there is a possibility for a curve between some of the existing points.*

- Based on the look of the graph, does the point $\left(\frac{17}{3}, \frac{1}{3}\right)$ belong to the graph of the linear equation $x + y = 6$? Why or why not?

- □ *It looks like $\left(\frac{17}{3}, \frac{1}{3}\right)$ should be on the graph of the linear equation because it looks like the point would follow the pattern of the rest of the points, i.e., be on the line.*

- Just by looking at the graph, we cannot be sure. We can predict that $\left(\frac{17}{3}, \frac{1}{3}\right)$ is on the graph of $x + y = 6$ because it looks like it should be. What can we do to find out for sure?

- □ *Since each point on the graph represents a solution to the equation, if $\frac{17}{3} + \frac{1}{3} = 6$, and it does, then we can say for sure that $\left(\frac{17}{3}, \frac{1}{3}\right)$ is a point on the graph of $x + y = 6$.*

- Just by looking at the graph, would you say that $\left(-2\frac{3}{7}, 4\right)$ is a point on the graph of $x + y = 6$?

- □ *Based on the graph, it doesn't look like the point $\left(-2\frac{3}{7}, 4\right)$ would be on the graph of $x + y = 6$.*

- How do you know that the graph doesn't curve down at that point? How can you be sure?

- □ *I would have to see if $\left(-2\frac{3}{7}, 4\right)$ is a solution to $x + y = 6$, which it is not because $-2\frac{3}{7} + 4 = 1\frac{4}{7}$, not 6. Therefore, the point $\left(-2\frac{3}{7}, 4\right)$ is not a solution to the equation.*

- At this point, we can predict that the graph of this linear equation is a line. Does that mean that the graph of every linear equation is a line? Might there be some linear equations that have curves in them? For now, our only method of proving or disproving our prediction is plotting solutions on a coordinate plane. The more we learn about linear equations, the better we will be able to answer the questions just asked.

COMMON CORE™   Lesson 13:   The Graph of a Linear Equation in Two Variables   151
            Date: 11/8/13

Exercises 1–6 (15 minutes)

Students will need graph paper to complete Exercises 1–2. Students work independently on Exercises 1–2 for the first 10 minutes. Then, they share their solutions with their partners, and plot more points on their graphs. As students work, verify through discussion that they are choosing a variety of rational numbers to get a good idea of what the graph of the linear equation will look like. Exercise 6 is an optional exercise as it challenges students to come up with an equation that does not graph as a line.

Exercises 1–6

1. Find at least 10 solutions to the linear equation $3x + y = -8$ and plot the points on a coordinate plane.

   Sample student work.

x	Linear Equation: $3x + y = -8$	y
1	$3(1) + y = -8$ $3 + y = -8$ $y = -11$	-11
$1\frac{1}{2}$	$3\left(1\frac{1}{2}\right) + y = -8$ $4\frac{1}{2} + y = -8$ $y = -12\frac{1}{2}$	$-12\frac{1}{2}$
2	$3(2) + y = -8$ $6 + y = -8$ $y = -14$	-14
3	$3(3) + y = -8$ $9 + y = -8$ $y = -17$	-17
$3\frac{1}{2}$	$3\left(3\frac{1}{2}\right) + y = -8$ $10\frac{1}{2} + y = -8$ $y = -18\frac{1}{2}$	$-18\frac{1}{2}$
4	$3(4) + y = -8$ $12 + y = -8$ $y = -20$	-20
-1	$3(-1) + y = -8$ $-3 + y = -8$ $y = -5$	-5
-2	$3(-2) + y = -8$ $-6 + y = -8$ $y = -2$	-2
-3	$3(-3) + y = -8$ $-9 + y = -8$ $y = 1$	1
-4	$3(-4) + y = -8$ $-12 + y = -8$ $y = 4$	4

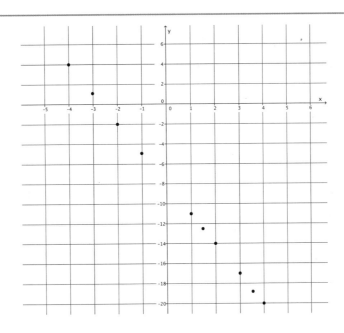

What shape is the graph of the linear equation taking?

The graph appears to be the shape of a line.

2. **Find at least 10 solutions to the linear equation** $x - 5y = 11$ **and plot the points on a coordinate plane.**

    Sample student work.

x	Linear Equation: $x - 5y = 11$	y
$13\frac{1}{2}$	$x - 5\left(\frac{1}{2}\right) = 11$ $x - 2\frac{1}{2} = 11$ $x = 13\frac{1}{2}$	$\frac{1}{2}$
16	$x - 5(1) = 11$ $x - 5 = 11$ $x = 16$	1
$18\frac{1}{2}$	$x - 5\left(1\frac{1}{2}\right) = 11$ $x - 7\frac{1}{2} = 11$ $x = 18\frac{1}{2}$	$1\frac{1}{2}$
21	$x - 5(2) = 11$ $x - 10 = 11$ $x = 21$	2

$23\frac{1}{2}$	$x - 5\left(2\frac{1}{2}\right) = 11$ $x - 12\frac{1}{2} = 11$ $x = 23\frac{1}{2}$	$2\frac{1}{2}$
26	$x - 5(3) = 11$ $x - 15 = 11$ $x = 26$	3
6	$x - 5(-1) = 11$ $x + 5 = 11$ $x = 6$	−1
1	$x - 5(-2) = 11$ $x + 10 = 11$ $x = 1$	−2
−4	$x - 5(-3) = 11$ $x + 15 = 11$ $x = -4$	−3
−9	$x - 5(-4) = 11$ $x + 20 = 11$ $x = -9$	−4

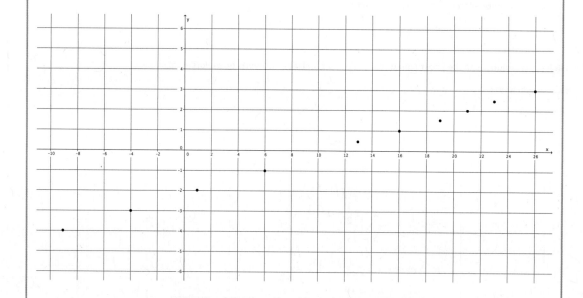

What shape is the graph of the linear equation taking?

The graph appears to be the shape of a line.

3.   Compare the solutions you found in Exercise 1 with a partner. Add their solutions to your graph.

Is the prediction you made about the shape of the graph still true? Explain.

Yes. With the additional points, the graph still appears to be the shape of a line.

4. Compare the solutions you found in Exercise 2 with a partner. Add their solutions to your graph.

    Is the prediction you made about the shape of the graph still true? Explain.

    Yes. With the additional points, the graph still appears to be the shape of a line.

5. Joey predicts that the graph of $-x + 2y = 3$ will look like the graph shown below. Do you agree? Explain why or why not.

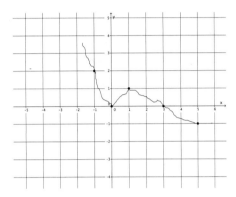

    Sample student work:

    No, I do not agree with Joey. The graph that Joey drew contains the point $(0, 0)$. If $(0, 0)$ is on the graph of the linear equation then it will be a solution to the equation; however, it is not. Therefore, the point cannot be on the graph of the equation which means Joey's prediction is incorrect.

6. We have looked at some equations that appear to be lines. Can you write an equation that has solutions that do not form a line? Try to come up with one and prove your assertion on the coordinate plane.

    Answers will vary. Any non-linear equation that students write will graph as something other than a line. For example, the graph of $y = x^2$ or the graph of $y = x^3$ will not be a line.

Closing (5 minutes)

Summarize, or ask students to summarize, the main points from the lesson:

-   All of the graphs of linear equations we have done so far appear to take the shape of a line.

-   We can show whether or not a point is on the graph of an equation by checking to see if it is a solution to the equation.

> **Lesson Summary**
>
> One way to determine if a given point is on the graph of a linear equation is by checking to see if it is a solution to the equation. At this point, all graphs of linear equations appear to be lines.

Exit Ticket (5 minutes)

Name _____ Date _____

Lesson 13: The Graph of a Linear Equation in Two Variables

Exit Ticket

1. Ethan found solutions to the linear equation $3x - y = 8$ and graphed them. What shape is the graph of the linear equation taking?

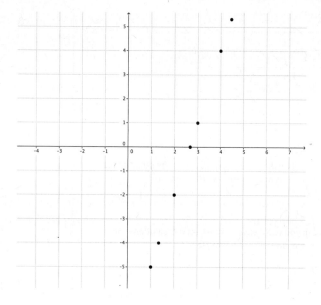

2. Could the following be the graph of $-x + 2y = 5$?

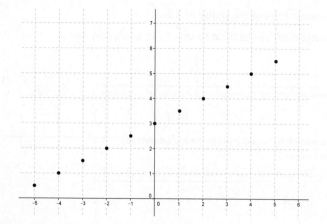

Exit Ticket Sample Solutions

1. Ethan found solutions to the linear equation $3x - y = 8$ and graphed them. What shape is the graph of the linear equation taking?

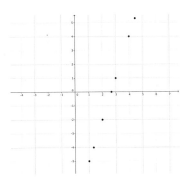

It appears to take the shape of a line.

2. Could the following be the graph of $-x + 2y = 5$?

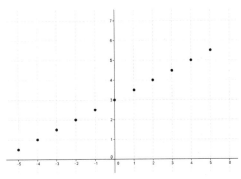

Sample student answer: Student may have chosen any point to make the claim that this is not the graph of the equation $-x + 2y = 5$.

Although the graph appears to be a line, the graph contains the point $(0, 3)$. The point $(0, 3)$ is not a solution to the linear equation; therefore, this is not the graph of $-x + 2y = 5$.

Note to teacher: Accept any point as not being a solution to the linear equation.

Problem Set Sample Solutions

In problem 1, students graph linear equations by plotting points that represent solutions. For that reason, they will need graph paper. Students informally explain why the graph of a linear equation is not curved by showing that a point on the curve is not a solution to the linear equation.

1. Find at least 10 solutions to the linear equation $\frac{1}{2}x + y = 5$ and plot the points on a coordinate plane.

   Sample student work:

x	Linear Equation: $\frac{1}{2}x + y = 5$	y
0	$\frac{1}{2}(0) + y = 5$ $0 + y = 5$ $y = 5$	5
1	$\frac{1}{2}(1) + y = 5$ $\frac{1}{2} + y = 5$ $y = 4\frac{1}{2}$	$4\frac{1}{2}$
$1\frac{1}{2}$	$\frac{1}{2}\left(1\frac{1}{2}\right) + y = 5$ $\frac{3}{4} + y = 5$ $y = 4\frac{1}{4}$	$4\frac{1}{4}$
2	$\frac{1}{2}(2) + y = 5$ $1 + y = 5$ $y = 4$	4
3	$\frac{1}{2}(3) + y = 5$ $1\frac{1}{2} + y = 5$ $y = 3\frac{1}{2}$	$3\frac{1}{2}$
-1	$\frac{1}{2}(-1) + y = 5$ $-\frac{1}{2} + y = 5$ $y = 5\frac{1}{2}$	$5\frac{1}{2}$
$-1\frac{1}{2}$	$\frac{1}{2}\left(-1\frac{1}{2}\right) + y = 5$ $-\frac{3}{4} + y = 5$ $y = 5\frac{3}{4}$	$5\frac{3}{4}$
-2	$\frac{1}{2}(-2) + y = 5$ $-1 + y = 5$ $y = 6$	6

-3	$\dfrac{1}{2}(-3) + y = 5$ $-\dfrac{3}{2} + y = 5$ $y = 6\dfrac{1}{2}$	$6\dfrac{1}{2}$
$-3\dfrac{1}{2}$	$\dfrac{1}{2}\left(-3\dfrac{1}{2}\right) + y = 5$ $-\dfrac{7}{4} + y = 5$ $y = 6\dfrac{3}{4}$	$6\dfrac{3}{4}$

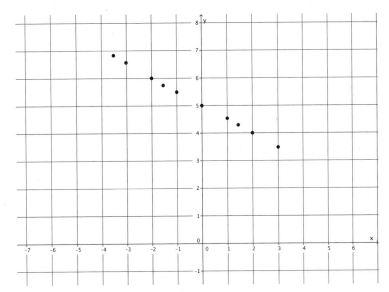

What shape is the graph of the linear equation taking?

The graph appears to be the shape of a line.

2.   Can the following be a graph of the equation $x - y = 0$? Explain.

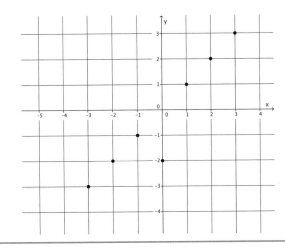

The graph shown contains the point $(0, -2)$. If $(0, -2)$ is on the graph of the linear equation then it will be a solution to the equation. It is not; therefore, the point cannot be on the graph of the equation, which means the graph shown cannot be the graph of the equation $x - y = 0$.

3. Can the following be a graph of the equation $x + 2y = 2$? Explain.

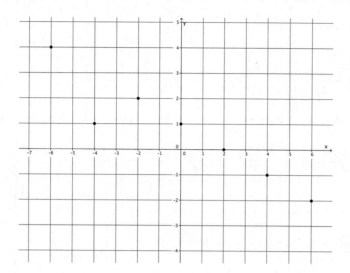

The graph shown contains the point $(-4, 1)$. If $(-4, 1)$ is on the graph of the linear equation then it will be a solution to the equation. It is not; therefore, the point cannot be on the graph of the equation which means the graph shown cannot be the graph of the equation $x + 2y = 2$.

4. Can the following be a graph of the equation $x - y = 7$? Explain.

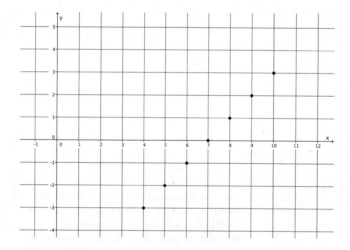

Yes, because each point on the graph represents a solution to the linear equation $x - y = 7$.

5.   Can the following be a graph of the equation $x + y = 2$? Explain.

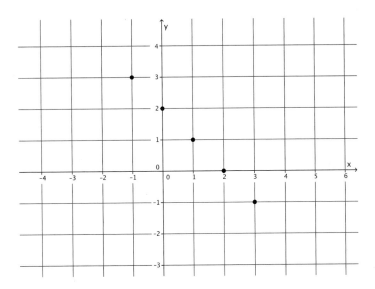

Yes, because each point on the graph represents a solution to the linear equation $x + y = 2$.

6.   Can the following be a graph of the equation $2x - y = 9$? Explain.

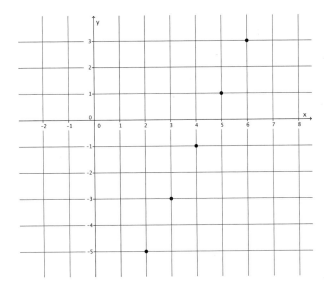

Yes, because each point on the graph represents a solution to the linear equation $2x - y = 9$.

7.   Can the following be a graph of the equation $x - y = 1$? Explain.

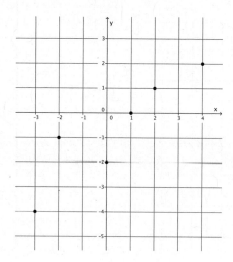

Sample student response:

The graph shown contains the point $(-2, -1)$. If $(-2, -1)$ is on the graph of the linear equation then it will be a solution to the equation. It is not; therefore, the point cannot be on the graph of the equation which means the graph shown cannot be the graph of the equation $x - y = 1$.

Lesson 14: Graph of a Linear Equation—Horizontal and Vertical Lines

Student Outcomes

- Students graph linear equations in standard form, $ax + by = c$ (a or $b = 0$), that produce a horizontal or a vertical line.

Lesson Notes

The goal of this lesson is for students to know that the graph of an equation in the form of $x = c$ or $y = c$, where c is a constant, is the graph of a vertical or horizontal line, respectively. In order to show this, we begin with linear equations in two variables, $ax + by = c$, where one of the coefficients of x or y is equal to zero. The reason behind this is that students know an ordered pair (x, y) is a point on a coordinate plane, as well as a solution to the equation $ax + by = c$. Frequently when students see an equation in the form of $x = c$ or $y = c$, they do not think of it as a point nor a line, just a number. To avoid this, the approach to graphs of horizontal and vertical lines is embedded with what students already know about points and solutions to linear equations in two variables. In this lesson, students begin by graphing and exploring the connection between $ax + by = c$ and $x = c$ in the first three exercises, and then a discussion follows to solidify the concept that the graph of the linear equation $x = c$ is a vertical line. Similar exercises precede the discussion for the graph of $y = c$ as a horizontal line.

Classwork

Exercises 1–3 (5 minutes)

Students complete Exercises 1–3 independently or in pairs in preparation for the discussion that follows. Students will need graph paper to complete the exercises.

Exercises 1–3

1.   Find at least 4 solutions to graph the linear equation $1x + 2y = 5$.

Lesson 14:   Graph of a Linear Equation—Horizontal and Vertical Lines
Date: 11/8/13

2.   Find at least 4 solutions to graph the linear equation $1x + 0y = 5$.

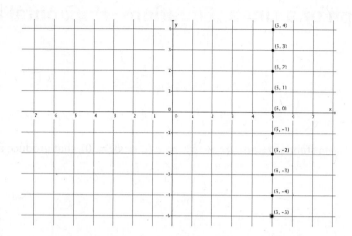

3.   What was different about the equations in Exercises 1 and 2? What effect did this change have on the graph?

In the first equation, the coefficient of y was 2. In the second equation, the coefficient of y was 0. The graph changed from being slanted to a vertical line.

Discussion (14 minutes)

▪   From Lesson 13, we can say that the graph of a linear equation in two variables looks like a line. We want to be able to prove that the graph is a line, not just predict. For that reason, we will begin with two special cases of linear equations in two variables.

    Given a linear equation in two variables $ax + by = c$, where a, b, and c are constants, we will look first at Case 1, where $a = 1$ and $b = 0$. (In the past we have said that $a, b \neq 0$). To do some investigating, let's say that $c = 5$. Then we have the following equation:

$$1 \cdot x + 0 \cdot y = 5$$

▪   For the linear equation $1 \cdot x + 0 \cdot y = 5$, we want to find solutions, (x, y) to plot as points on a coordinate plane. How have we found solutions in prior lessons?

   □   *We find solutions by picking a number for x or y, and then solve for the other variable. The numbers (x, y) are a solution to the equation.*

▪   What happens if we pick 7 for x? Explain.

   □   *If we pick 7 for x, then we get*

$$1 \cdot 7 + 0 \cdot y = 5$$
$$7 + 0 \cdot y = 5$$
$$0 \cdot y = -2$$
$$0 \neq -2$$

    If we replace x with 7, then we get an untrue statement. Therefore, $(7, y)$ is not a solution to this linear equation.

- What happens if we pick 7 for y? Explain.
  - *If we pick 7 for y, then we get*

$$1 \cdot x + 0 \cdot 7 = 5$$
$$x + 0 = 5$$
$$x = 5$$

If we replace y with 7, then we see that $x = 5$. Therefore, $(5, 7)$ is a solution to this linear equation.

- What happens if we pick -3 for y? Explain.
  - *If we pick -3 for y, then we get*

$$1 \cdot x + 0 \cdot (-3) = 5$$
$$x + 0 = 5$$
$$x = 5$$

If we replace y with -3, then we see that $x = 5$. Therefore, $(5, -3)$ is a solution to this linear equation.

- What happens if we pick $\frac{1}{2}$ for y? Explain.
  - *If we pick $\frac{1}{2}$ for y, then we get*

$$1 \cdot x + 0 \cdot \frac{1}{2} = 5$$
$$x + 0 = 5$$
$$x = 5$$

If we replace y with $\frac{1}{2}$, then we see that $x = 5$. Therefore, $\left(5, \frac{1}{2}\right)$ is a solution to this linear equation.

- What do you notice about the x-value each time we pick a number for y?
  - *Each time we pick a number for y, we keep getting $x = 5$.*
- Look at the equation again, can we show that x must always be equal to 5?
  - *Yes, if we transform the equation, we see that $x = 5$:*

$$1 \cdot x + 0 \cdot y = 5$$
$$x + 0 = 5$$
$$x = 5$$

- What does that mean for our y-values? Which number will produce a solution where $x = 5$?
  - *Our y-values can be any number. No matter which number we pick for y, the value for x will always be equal to 5.*
- Let's graph the solutions we found and a few more.

Add points to the graph as a result of student responses to "If $y = $ a number, then what value is x?" The graph should look something like what is shown below.

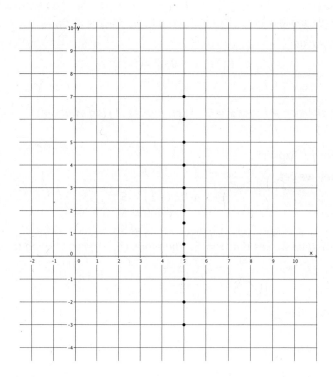

Focus in on one unit, between 2 and 3 for example, and explain that all of the fractional values for y between 2 and 3 will produce a solution where $x = 5$.

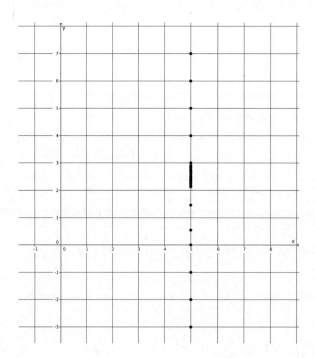

- If this process is repeated between all integers, then the result is the vertical line $x = 5$, as shown in blue.

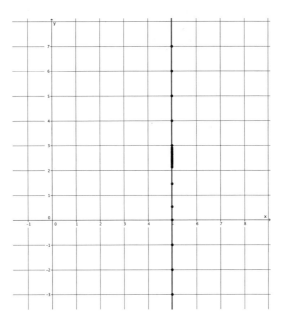

- The graph of the equation $ax + by = c$, where $a = 1, b = 0$, and $c = 5$, is the vertical line passing through point $(5, 0)$.
- The above situation is not unique. That is, in the equation $ax + by = c$, we chose the value for c to be 5. The same reasoning can be used for any value c. If we chose c to be 6, what do you think the graph would look like?

    ▫ *The graph would probably be a vertical line passing through the point $(6, 0)$.*

- If we chose c to be $-\frac{1}{2}$, what do you think the graph would look like?

    ▫ *The graph would probably be a vertical line passing through the point $\left(-\frac{1}{2}, 0\right)$.*

- Notice that the equation $1 \cdot x + 0 \cdot y = c$ is equivalent to $x = c$. Therefore, we can make the following conclusion in the form of a theorem:

Theorem: *The graph of $x = c$ is the vertical line passing through $(c, 0)$, where c is a constant.*

- To prove this theorem, we first want to show that the graph of $x = c$ will intersect the x-axis. To show that the graph of $x = c$ intersects the x-axis, we actually have to show that the graph of $x = c$ is not parallel to the x-axis because if it was parallel, it would not intersect the x-axis. Therefore, if we can show that $x = c$ is not parallel to the x-axis, then it must intersect it at some point. How do we know that the graph of $x = c$ is not parallel to the x-axis?

    ▫ *We know it's not parallel to the x-axis because it intersects the x-axis at $(c, 0)$.*

- Then the graph of $x = c$ must be parallel to the y-axis. This is because of how we define/set up the coordinate plane. The plane is comprised of horizontal lines parallel to the x-axis and vertical lines parallel to the y-axis. Since $x = c$ is not parallel to the x-axis, then it must be parallel to the y-axis.

- Now we need to show that $x = c$ is the graph of the only line that is parallel to the y-axis going through the point $(c, 0)$. How do we show that there is only one line parallel to the y-axis passing through a specific point?
    - *That goes back to what we learned about basic rigid motions. If we rotate a line around a center $180°$ (in this particular case we would rotate around the point $(2.5, 0)$), then we will get an image of the line parallel to the line itself. There exists only one line parallel to a given line that goes through a specific point.*
- For that reason, we know that the graph of $x = c$ is the vertical line that passes through $(c, 0)$.

Exercises 4–6 (3 minutes)

Students complete Exercises 4–6 independently. Students will need graph paper to complete the exercises.

4. Graph the linear equation $x = -2$.

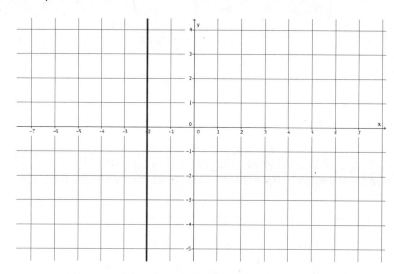

5. Graph the linear equation $x = 3$.

6. **What will the graph of $x = 0$ look like?**

    The graph of $x = 0$ will look like a vertical line that goes through the point $(0, 0)$. It will be the same as the y-axis.

Exercises 7–9 (5 minutes)

Students complete Exercises 7–9 independently or in pairs in preparation for the discussion that follows. Students will need graph paper to complete the exercises.

7. **Find at least 4 solutions to graph the linear equation $2x + 1y = 2$.**

    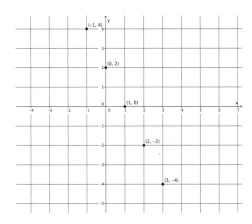

8. **Find at least 4 solutions to graph the linear equation $0x + 1y = 2$.**

    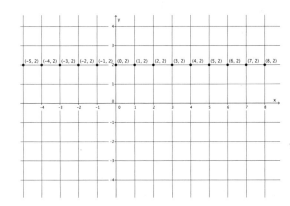

9. **What was different about the equations in Exercises 7 and 8? What effect did this change have on the graph?**

    In the first equation, the coefficient of x was 2. In the second equation, the coefficient of x was 0. The graph changed from being a slanted line to a horizontal line.

Discussion (8 minutes)

- Now for Case 2. We need to look at the graph of the linear equation in two variables $ax + by = c$, where $a = 0$ and $b = 1$, and c is a constant.

- Let's pick a number for c, as we did for Case 1. Let $c = 2$. Then we have the equation $0 \cdot x + 1 \cdot y = 2$.

- Now let's find a few solutions for this linear equation. What happens if we pick 7 for y? Explain.

  ▫ *If we pick 7 for y, then we get*

  $$0 \cdot x + 1 \cdot 7 = 2$$
  $$0 + 7 = 2$$
  $$7 \neq 2$$

  If we replace y with 7, then we get an untrue statement. Therefore, $(x, 7)$ is not a solution to this linear equation.

- If $x = 5$, what value does y have? Explain.

  ▫ *The value of y is 2 because*

  $$0 \cdot 5 + 1 \cdot y = 2$$
  $$0 + y = 2$$
  $$y = 2$$

  Therefore, $(5, 2)$ is a solution to the linear equation.

- If $x = -5$, what value does y have? Explain.

  ▫ *The value of y is 2 because*

  $$0 \cdot (-5) + 1 \cdot y = 2$$
  $$0 + y = 2$$
  $$y = 2$$

  Therefore, $(-5, 2)$ is a solution to the linear equation.

- If $x = \frac{1}{2}$, what value does y have? Explain.

  ▫ *The value of y is 2 because*

  $$0 \cdot \frac{1}{2} + 1 \cdot y = 2$$
  $$0 + y = 2$$
  $$y = 2$$

  Therefore, $\left(\frac{1}{2}, 2\right)$ is a solution to the linear equation.

- Do you see a similar pattern emerging for this linear equation? Explain.

  ▫ *Yes, no matter which value we pick for x the y-value is always 2. Therefore, the graph of $0 \cdot x + 1 \cdot y = 2$ is equivalent to $y = 2$.*

- What do you think the graph of $y = 2$ will look like?

  ▫ *Students may predict that the graph of $y = 2$ is the horizontal line that goes through the point $(0, 2)$.*

Lesson 14:	Graph of a Linear Equation—Horizontal and Vertical Lines
Date:	11/8/13

As before, place the solutions you found as points of a graph. Add points to the graph as a result of student responses to "If $x =$ a number, then what value is y?" The graph should look something like what is shown below.

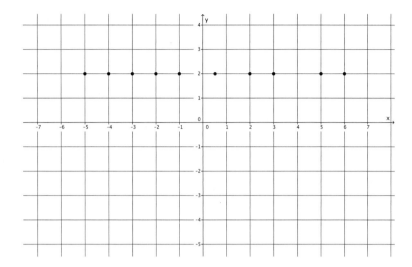

Again, focus in on one unit, between 5 and 6 for example, and explain that all of the fractional values for x between 5 and 6 will produce a solution where $y = 2$.

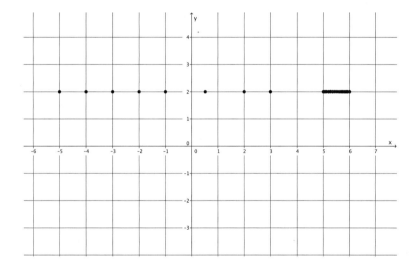

- If this process is repeated between all integers, then the result is the horizontal line $y = 2$, as shown in blue.

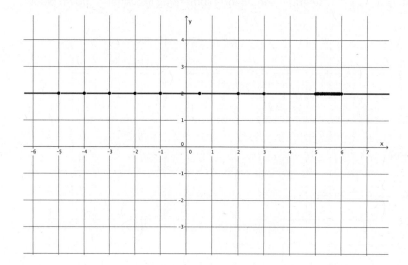

- The graph of the equation $ax + by = c$, where $a = 0$, $b = 1$, and $c = 2$ is the horizontal line passing through point $(0, 2)$.

- The above situation is not unique. As before in the equation $ax + by = c$, we chose the value for c to be 2. The same reasoning can be used for any value c. If we chose c to be 6, what do you think the graph would look like?

  □ *The graph would probably be a horizontal line passing through the point $(0, 6)$.*

- If we chose c to be $-\frac{1}{2}$, what do you think the graph would look like?

  □ *The graph would probably be a horizontal line passing through the point $\left(0, -\frac{1}{2}\right)$.*

- We can generalize this to a theorem:

Theorem: *The graph of $y = c$ is the horizontal line passing through the point $(0, c)$.*

- We can also say that there is only one line with the equation $y = c$ whose graph is parallel to the x-axis that goes through the point $(0, c)$.

- The proofs of these statements are similar to the proofs for vertical lines.

Exercises 10–12 (3 minutes)

Students complete Exercises 10–12 independently. Students will need graph paper to complete the exercises.

Exercises 10–12

10. Graph the linear equation $y = -2$.

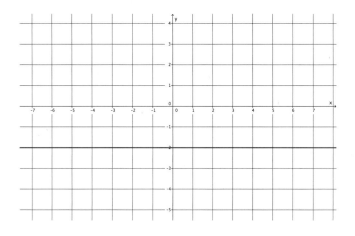

11. Graph the linear equation $y = 3$.

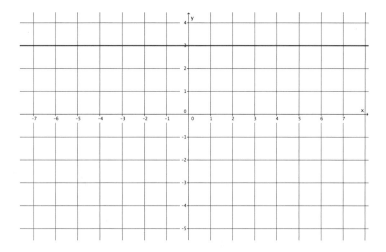

12. What will the graph of $y = 0$ look like?

The graph of $y = 0$ will look like a horizontal line that goes through the point $(0, 0)$. It will be the same as the x-axis.

Closing (3 minutes)

Summarize, or ask students to summarize, the main points from the lesson:

- The graph of the linear equation in two variables $ax + by = c$, where $a = 1$ and $b = 0$, is the graph of the equation $x = c$. The graph of $x = c$ is the vertical line that passes through the point $(c, 0)$.
- The graph of the linear equation in two variables $ax + by = c$, where $a = 0$ and $b = 1$, is the graph of the equation $y = c$. The graph of $y = c$ is the horizontal line that passes through the point $(0, c)$.

Lesson Summary

A linear equation in standard form, $ax + by = c$ where $a = 1$ and $b = 0$ is the graph of the equation $x = c$. The graph of $x = c$ is the vertical line passing through the point $(c, 0)$.

A linear equation in standard form, $ax + by = c$ where $a = 0$ and $b = 1$ is the graph of the equation $y = c$. The graph of $y = c$ is the horizontal line passing through the point $(0, c)$.

Exit Ticket (4 minutes)

Name _____   Date _____

Lesson 14: Graph of a Linear Equation—Horizontal and Vertical Lines

Exit Ticket

1. Graph the linear equation $ax + by = c$ where $a = 0$, $b = 1$, and $c = 1.5$.

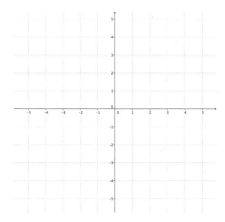

2. Graph the linear equation $ax + by = c$, where $a = 1$, $b = 0$, and $c = -\dfrac{5}{2}$.

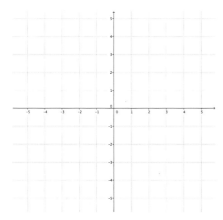

3. What linear equation represents the graph of the line that coincides with the x-axis?

4. What linear equation represents the graph of the line that coincides with the y-axis?

Exit Ticket Sample Solutions

1. Graph the linear equation $ax + by = c$, where $a = 0$, $b = 1$, and $c = 1.5$.

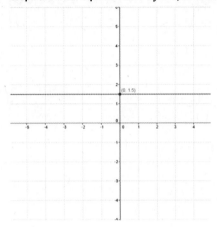

2. Graph the linear equation $ax + by = c$, where $a = 1$, $b = 0$, and $c = -\dfrac{5}{2}$.

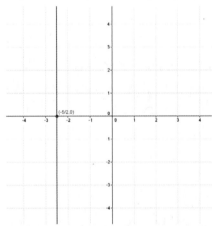

3. What linear equation represents the graph of the line that coincides with the x-axis?

   $y = 0$

4. What linear equation represents the graph of the line that coincides with the y-axis?

   $x = 0$

Problem Set Sample Solutions

Students will need graph paper to complete the Problem Set.

1. Graph the two variable linear equation $ax + by = c$ when $a = 0$, $y = 1$, and $c = -4$.

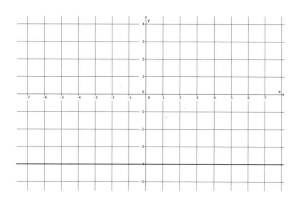

2. Graph the two variable linear equation $ax + by = c$ when $a = 1$, $y = 0$, and $c = 9$.

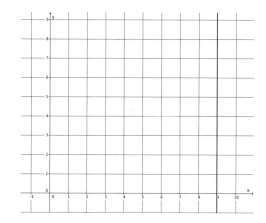

3. Graph the linear equation $y = 7$.

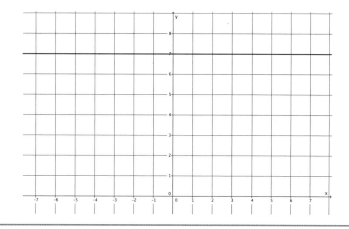

4.   Graph the linear equation $x = 1$.

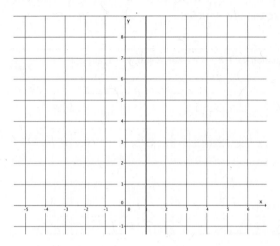

5.   Explain why the graph of a linear equation in the form of $y = c$ is the horizontal line, parallel to the x-axis passing through the point $(0, c)$.

The graph of $y = c$ passes through the point $(0, c)$, that means the graph of $y = c$ cannot be parallel to y-axis because the graph intersects it. For that reason, the graph of $y = c$ must be the horizontal line parallel to the x–axis.

6.   Explain why there is only one line with the equation $y = c$ that passes through the point $(0, c)$.

There can only be one line parallel to another that goes through a given point. Since the graph of $y = c$ is parallel to the x-axis and it goes through the point $(0, c)$, then it must be the only line that does. Therefore, there is only one line that is the graph of the equation $y = c$ that passes through $(0, c)$.

Name _____   Date _____

1. Write and solve each of the following linear equations.

    a. Ofelia has a certain amount of money. If she spends \$12, then she has $\frac{1}{5}$ of the original amount left. How much money did Ofelia have originally?

    b. Three consecutive integers have a sum of 234. What are the three integers?

    c. Gil is reading a book that has 276 pages. He has already read some of it last week. He plans to read 20 pages tomorrow. By then, he will be $\frac{2}{3}$ of the way through the book. How many pages did Gil read last week?

2. a. Without solving, identify which of the following equations has a unique solution, no solution, or infinitely many solutions.

$$3x + 5 = -2$$

$$6(x - 11) = 15 - 4x$$

$$12x + 9 = 8x + 1 + 4x$$

$$2(x - 3) = 10x - 6 - 8x$$

$$5x + 6 = 5x - 4$$

b. Solve the following equation for a number x. Verify that your solution is correct.

$$-15 = 8x + 1$$

c. Solve the following equation for a number x. Verify that your solution is correct.

$$7(2x + 5) = 4x - 9 - x$$

3. a. Parker paid $4.50 for three pounds of gummy candy. Assuming each pound of gummy candy costs the same amount, complete the table of values representing the cost of gummy candy in pounds.

Gummy Candy in pounds (x)	1	2	3	4	5	6	7	8	9
Cost (y)			$4.50						

   b. Graph the data on the coordinate plane.

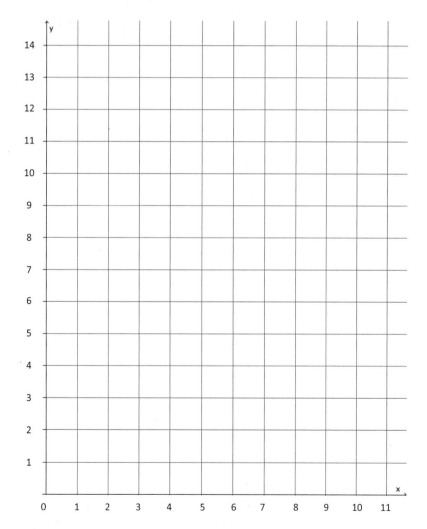

c.   On the same day, Parker's friend Peggy was charged $5 for $1\frac{1}{2}$ lb. of gummy candy. Explain in terms of the graph why this must be a mistake.

A Progression Toward Mastery					
Assessment Task Item		STEP 1 Missing or incorrect answer and little evidence of reasoning or application of mathematics to solve the problem.	STEP 2 Missing or incorrect answer but evidence of some reasoning or application of mathematics to solve the problem.	STEP 3 A correct answer with some evidence of reasoning or application of mathematics to solve the problem, <u>or</u> an incorrect answer with substantial evidence of solid reasoning or application of mathematics to solve the problem.	STEP 4 A correct answer supported by substantial evidence of solid reasoning or application of mathematics to solve the problem.
1	a 8.EE.C.7b	Student made no attempt to solve the problem or left the problem blank. Student may or may not have identified the variable.	Student did not set up an equation (i.e., guessed the answer). Student may or may not have identified the variable.	Student may or may not have set up correct equation. Student may or may not have identified the variable. Student may have made calculation errors.	Student identified the variable as "Let x be the amount of money Ofelia had" or something similar. <u>AND</u> Student set up a correct equation $x - 12 = \frac{1}{5}x$ or other equivalent version. <u>AND</u> Solved for the variable correctly, $x = 15$.
	b 8.EE.C.7b	Student made no attempt to solve the problem or left the problem blank. May or may not have identified the variables.	Student did not set up an equation and guessed the answer. Student may or may not have identified the variable. Student may have made calculation errors. Student may have only answered part of the question, like the first number is 77, and not given all three numbers.	Student attempted to set up an equation. Student may have set up an incorrect equation. Student may or may not have identified the variables. Student may have made calculation errors. Student may have only answered part of the question, like the first number is 77, and not given all three numbers.	Student identified the variable as "Let x be the first integer." <u>AND</u> Student set up a correct equation $3x + 3 = 234$ or other equivalent version. <u>AND</u> Student solved the equation correctly. Identified all three numbers correctly. The first number is 77, the second is 78, and the third is 79.
	c 8.EE.C.7b	Student made no attempt to solve the problem or left the problem blank. Student may or may not have identified the variable.	Student did not set up an equation and guessed the answer. Student may or may not have identified the variable.	Student attempted to set up an equation. Student may have set up an incorrect equation. Student may or may not have identified the variable.	Student identified the variable as "Let x be the number of pages Gil read last week" or something similar. <u>AND</u> Student set up a correct equation $x + 20 = 184$

					Student may have made calculation errors leading to an incorrect answer.	or other equivalent version. <u>AND</u> Student solved for the number of pages Gil read last week as 164 pages.
2	**a** **8.EE.C.7a**	Student made no attempt to determine the type of solution or left the problem blank. Student determined 0 of the solution types correctly. Student may have attempted to determine the solutions by solving.	Student determined 1–2 of the solution types correctly. Student may have attempted to determine the solutions by solving.	Student determined 3–5 of the solution types correctly. Student may have attempted to determine the solutions by solving.	Determined 5 of the solutions types correctly. Equations 1 and 2 have unique solutions, equation 3 has no solution, equation 4 has infinitely many solutions, and equation 5 has no solution. <u>AND</u> Student determined the solutions by observation only.
	b **8.EE.C.7b**	Student made no attempt to solve the problem or left the problem blank.	Student used properties of equality incorrectly, e.g., subtracted 1 from just one side of the equation, or divided by 8 on just one side of the equation, leading to an incorrect solution.	Student correctly used properties of rational numbers to solve the equation, but may have made a computational error leading to an incorrect solution. For example, student may have subtracted 1 from each side of the equation, but $-15 - 1$ led to an incorrect answer. Student may or may not have verified their answer.	Student correctly used properties of rational numbers to solve the equation (i.e., found $x = -2$). There is evidence that the student verified their solution.
	c **8.EE.C.7b**	Student made no attempt to solve the problem or left the problem blank.	Student used the distributive property incorrectly on both sides of the equation, e.g., $7(2x + 5) = 14x + 5$ or $4x - x = 4$, leading to an incorrect solution.	Student used the distributive property correctly on one or both sides of the equation, but made a computational error leading to an incorrect solution. Student may or may not have verified their answer.	Student used the distributive property correctly on both sides of the equation leading to a correct solution (i.e., $x = -4$). There is evidence that the student verified their solution.
3	**a** **8.EE.B.5**	Student made no attempt to complete the table or used completely random numbers in the blanks.	Student completed the table incorrectly, but only because of a simple computational error in finding the cost of one pound of candy, leading to all other parts being incorrect.	Student completed 6–7 parts of the table correctly. A computational error led to 1–2 parts being incorrect.	Student completed all 8 parts of the table correctly. (See table below for correct answers.)

Module 4:   Linear Equations
Date: 11/8/13

184

Gummy candy in pounds (x)	1	2	3	4	5	6	7	8	9
Cost (y)	$1.50	$3.00	$4.50	$.6.00	$7.50	$9.00	$10.50	$12.00	$13.50

	b 8.EE.B.5	Student made no attempt to put the data on the graph or points were put in randomly.	Student plotted data points on the graph, but may have misplaced a few points. <u>OR</u> Student may have inversed the data (i.e., plotted points according to (y, x) instead of (x, y)).	Student plotted 6–7 data points correctly according to the data in their table.	Student plotted all 8 data points correctly according to the data in their table.
	c 8.EE.B.5	Student left item blank.	Student may have performed a computation to prove the mistake. Little or no reference to the graph was made in the argument.	Student made a weak argument as to why $(1.5, 5)$ could not be correct. Student may have connected the dots on the graph to show $(1.5, 5)$ could not be correct.	Student made a convincing argument as to why the point $(1.5, 5)$ could not be correct. Student referenced the relationship being proportional and/or predicted that all points should fall into a line based on the existing pattern of points on the graph.

Name _____   Date _____

1. Transcribe and solve each of the following linear equations.

   a. Ofelia has a certain amount of money. If she spends 12 dollars, then she has $\frac{1}{5}$ of the original amount left. How much money did Ofelia have originally?

   LET x BE THE AMOUNT OF MONEY OFELIA HAD

   $$x - 12 = \frac{1}{5}x$$
   $$x - \frac{1}{5}x - 12 + 12 = \frac{1}{5}x - \frac{1}{5}x + 12$$
   $$\frac{4}{5}x = 12$$
   $$x = 12 \cdot \frac{5}{4} = \frac{60}{4}$$

   OFELIA HAD \$15.00 ORIGINALLY.

   b. Three consecutive integers have a sum of 234. What are the three integers?

   LET x BE THE FIRST INTEGER

   $$x + x+1 + x+2 = 234$$
   $$3x + 3 = 234$$
   $$3x + 3 - 3 = 234 - 3$$
   $$3x = 231$$
   $$x = 77$$

   THE INTEGERS ARE 77, 78, AND 79.

   c. Gil is reading a book that has 276 pages. He has already read some of it last week. He plans to read 20 pages tomorrow. By then, he will be $\frac{2}{3}$ of the way through the book. How many pages did Gil read last week?

   LET x BE THE NUMBER OF PAGES GIL READ LAST WEEK.

   $$x + 20 = \frac{2}{3}(276)$$
   $$x + 20 = 184$$
   $$x + 20 - 20 = 184 - 20$$
   $$x = 164$$

   GIL READ 164 PAGES LAST WEEK.

2.   a.   Without solving, identify which of the following equations has a unique solution, no solution, or infinitely many solutions.

$3x + 5 = -2$ UNIQUE

$6(x - 11) = 15 - 4x$ UNIQUE

$12x + 9 = 8x + 1 + 4x$ NO SOLUTION

$2(x - 3) = 10x - 6 - 8x$ INFINITELY MANY SOLUTIONS

$5x + 6 = 5x - 4$ NO SOLUTION

b.   Solve the following equation for a number x. Verify that your solution is correct.

$$-15 = 8x + 1$$
$$\underline{-1 \qquad\quad -1}$$
$$\frac{-16}{8} = \frac{8x}{8}$$
$$-2 = x$$

$-15 = 8(-2) + 1$
$-15 = -16 + 1$
$-15 = -15$

c.   Solve the following equation for a number x. Verify that your solution is correct.

$7(2x + 5) = 4x - 9 - x$
$14x + 35 = 4x - x - 9$
$14x + 35 = 3x - 9$
$14x - 3x + 35 = 3x - 3x - 9$
$11x + 35 = -9$
$11x + 35 - 35 = -9 - 35$
$11x = -44$
$x = -4$

$7(2(-4) + 5) = 4(-4) - 9 - (-4)$
$7(-8 + 5) = -16 - 9 + 4$
$7(-3) = -25 + 4$
$-21 = -21$

3. a.   Parker paid $4.50 for three pounds of gummy candy. Assuming each pound of gummy candy costs the same amount, complete the table of values representing the cost of gummy candy in pounds.

Gummy Candy in pounds (x)	1	2	3	4	5	6	7	8	9
Cost (y)	$1.50	$3.00	$4.50	$6.00	$7.50	$9.00	$10.50	$12.00	$13.50

b.   Graph the data on the coordinate plane.

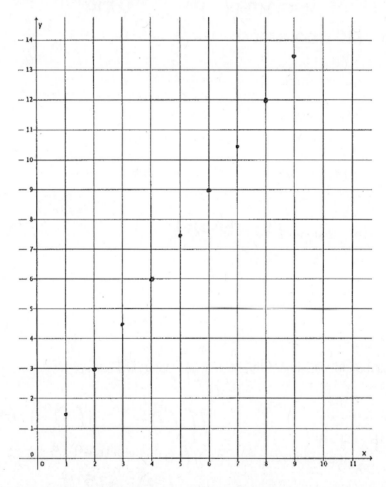

c.   On the same day, Parker's friend Peggy was charged $5 for one and a half pounds of gummy candy. Explain in terms of the graph why this must be a mistake.

EVEN THOUGH 1½ POUNDS OF CANDY ISN'T A POINT ON THE GRAPH, IT IS REASONABLE TO BELIEVE IT WILL FALL IN LINE WITH THE OTHER POINTS. THE COST OF 1½ POUNDS OF CANDY DOES NOT FIT THE PATTERN.

Topic C:

Slope and Equations of Lines

8.EE.B.5, 8.EE.B.6

Focus Standard:	8.EE.B.5	Graph proportional relationships, interpreting the unit rate as the slope of the graph. Compare two different proportional relationships represented in different ways.
	8.EE.B.6	Use similar triangles to explain why the slope m is the same between any two distinct points on a non-vertical line in the coordinate plane; derive the equation $y = mx$ for a line through the origin and the equation $y = mx + b$ of a line intercepting the vertical axis at b.
Instructional Days:	9	
Lesson 15:	The Slope of a Non-Vertical Line (P)[1]	
Lesson 16:	The Computation of the Slope of a Non-Vertical Line (S)	
Lesson 17:	The Line Joining Two Distinct Points of the Graph $y = mx + b$ has Slope m (S)	
Lesson 18:	There is Only One Line Passing through a Given Point with a Given Slope (P)	
Lesson 19:	The Graph of a Linear Equation in Two Variables is a Line (S)	
Lesson 20:	Every Line is a Graph of a Linear Equation (P)	
Lesson 21:	Some Facts about Graphs of a Linear Equation in Two Variables (P)	
Lesson 22:	Constant Rates Revisited (P)	
Lesson 23:	The Defining Equation of a Line (E)	

Topic C begins with students examining the slope of non-vertical lines. Students relate what they know about unit rate in terms of the slope of the graph of a line (**8.EE.B.5**). In Lesson 16, students learn the formula for computing slope between any two points. Students reason that any two points on the same line can be used to determine slope because of what they know about similar triangles (**8.EE.B.6**). In Lesson 17, students transform the standard form of an equation into slope-intercept form. Further, students learn that the slope of a line joining any two distinct points is the graph of a linear equation with slope, m. In Lesson 18, students investigate the concept of uniqueness of a line and recognize that if two lines have the same slope and a common point, the two lines are the same.

---

[1] Lesson Structure Key: **P**-Problem Set Lesson, **M**-Modeling Cycle Lesson, **E**-Exploration Lesson, **S**-Socratic Lesson

Lessons 19 and 20 prove to students that the graph of a linear equation is a line and that a line is a graph of a linear equation. In Lesson 21, students learn that the y-intercept is the location on the coordinate plane where the graph of a linear equation crosses the y-axis. Also in this lesson, students learn to write the equation of a line given the slope and a point. In Lesson 22, constant rate problems are revisited. Students learn that any constant rate problem can be described by a linear equation in two variables where the slope of the graph is the constant rate, i.e., rate of change. Lesson 22 also presents students with two proportional relationships expressed in different ways. Given a graph and an equation, students must use what they know about slope to determine which of the two has a greater rate of change. Lesson 23 introduces students to the symbolic representation of two linear equations that would graph as the same line.

COMMON CORE™   **Topic C:**   Slope and Equations of Lines
                    Date: 11/8/13   190

Lesson 15: The Slope of a Non-Vertical Line

Student Outcomes

- Students know slope is a number that describes the steepness or slant of a line.
- Students interpret the unit rate as the slope of a graph.

Lesson Notes

In Lesson 13, we made some predictions about what the graph of a linear equation would look like. In all cases, we predicted that the graph of a linear equation in two variables would be a line. In Lesson 14, we learned that the graph of the linear equation $x = c$ is the vertical line passing through the point $(c, 0)$ and the graph of the linear equation $y = c$ is the horizontal line passing through the point $(0, c)$.

We would like to prove that our predictions are true: That the graph of a linear equation in two variables is a line. Before we do, we need some tools:

1. We must define a number for each non-vertical line that can be used to measure the steepness or slant of the line. Once defined, this number will be called the *slope* of the line and is often referred to as the *rate of change*.

Rate of change is terminology that will be used in later lessons. In this first exposure to slope, it is referred to as steepness or slant of a line. In this lesson, students make observations about the steepness of a line. Further, students give directions about how to get from one point on the line to another point on the line. This leads students to the conclusion that the units in the directions have the same ratio. Students then compare ratios between graphs and describe lines as steeper or flatter.

2. We must show that *any* two points on a non-vertical line can be used to find the slope of the line.
3. We must show that the line joining two points on a graph of a linear equation of the form $= mx + b$ has the slope m.
4. We must show that there is only one line passing through a given point with a given slope.

These tools will be developed over the next few lessons. It is recommended that students are made aware of the four-part plan to achieve the goal of proving that the graph of a linear equation in two variables is a line as these parts are referenced in the next few lessons to help students make sense of the problem and persevere in solving it. In this lesson, we will look specifically at what is meant by the terms steepness and slant by defining the slope of a line. This lesson defines slope in the familiar context of unit rate; that is, slope is defined when the horizontal distance between two points is fixed at one. Defining slope this way solidifies the understanding that the unit rate is the slope of a graph. Further, students see that the number that describes slope is the distance between the y-coordinates leading to the general slope formula.

Opening (8 minutes)

To develop conceptual understanding of slope, have students complete the opening activity where they make informal observations about the steepness of lines. Model for students how to answer the questions with the first pair of graphs. Then have students work independently or in pairs to describe how to move from one point to another on a line in terms of units up or down and units right or left. Students also compare the ratios of their descriptions and relate the ratios to the steepness or flatness of the graph of the line.

Examine each pair of graphs and answer the questions that follow.

Example

Graph A

Graph B

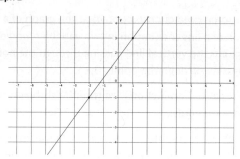

    a.   Which graph is steeper?

        It looks like Graph B is steeper.

    b.   Write directions that explain how to move from one point on the graph to the other for each of Graph A and Graph B.

        For Graph A, move 2 units up and 3 units right. For Graph B, move 4 units up and 3 units right.

    c.   Write the directions from part (b) as ratios, and then compare the ratios. How does this relate to which graph was steeper in part (a)?

        $\frac{2}{3} < \frac{4}{3}$ *Graph B was steeper and had the greater ratio.*

Pair 1:

Graph A

Graph B

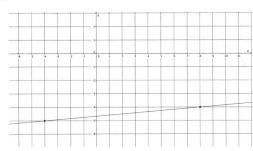

a.   Which graph is steeper?

It looks like Graph A is steeper.

b.   Write directions that explain how to move from one point on the graph to the other for each of Graph A and Graph B.

For Graph A, move 4 units up and 5 units right. For Graph B, move 1 unit up and 12 units right.

c.   Write the directions from part (b) as ratios, and then compare the ratios. How does this relate to which graph was steeper in part (a)?

$\dfrac{4}{5} > \dfrac{1}{12}$ *Graph A was steeper and had the greater ratio.*

Pair 2:

Graph A

Graph B

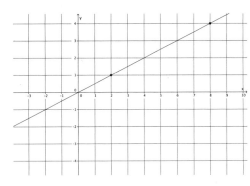

a.   Which graph is steeper?

It looks like Graph A is steeper.

b.   Write directions that explain how to move from one point on the graph to the other for each of Graph A and Graph B.

For Graph A, move 7 units up and 1 unit right. For Graph B, move 3 units up and 6 units right.

c.   Write the directions from part (b) as ratios, and then compare the ratios. How does this relate to which graph was steeper in part (a)?

$\dfrac{7}{1} > \dfrac{3}{6}$ *Graph A was steeper and had the greater ratio.*

Lesson 15:	The Slope of a Non-Vertical Line
Date:	11/8/13

193

Pair 3:

Graph A

Graph B

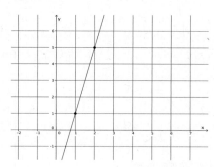

a.   Which graph is steeper?

It looks like Graph B is steeper.

b.   Write directions that explain how to move from one point on the graph to the other for each of Graph A and Graph B.

For Graph A, move 1 unit up and 5 units right. For Graph B, move 4 units up and 1 unit right.

c.   Write the directions from part (b) as ratios, and then compare the ratios. How does this relate to which graph was steeper in part (a)?

$\dfrac{1}{5} < \dfrac{4}{1}$ *Graph B was steeper and had the greater ratio.*

Pair 4:

Graph A

Graph B

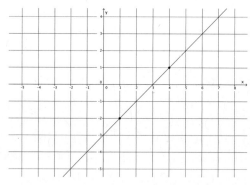

a.   Which graph is steeper?

They look about the same steepness.

b.   Write directions that explain how to move from one point on the graph to the other for each of Graph A and Graph B.

For Graph A, move 4 units up and 4 units right. For Graph B, move 3 units up and 3 units right.

c.   Write the directions from part (b) as ratios, and then compare the ratios. How does this relate to which graph was steeper in part (a)?

$\dfrac{4}{4} = \dfrac{3}{3}$ *The graphs have equal ratios, which may explain why they look like the same steepness.*

Classwork

Example 1 (2 minutes)

- Putting horizontal lines off to the side for a moment, there are two other types of non-vertical lines. Those that are *left-to-right inclining,* as in the graph of l_1, and those that are *left-to-right declining*, as in the graph of l_2, shown below.

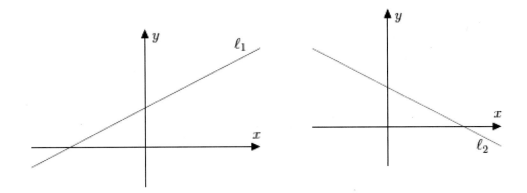

- We want to use a number to describe the amount of steepness or slant that each line has. The definition should be written in such a way that a horizontal line has a slope of 0, that is, no steepness and no slant.

- We begin by stating that lines that are *left-to-right inclining* are said to have a positive slope and lines that are *left-to-right declining* are said to have negative slope. We will discuss this more in a moment.

Example 2 (5 minutes)

- Now let's look more closely at finding the number that will be the slope of a line. Suppose a non-vertical line l is given in the coordinate plane. We let P be the point on line l that goes through the origin.

- Next, we locate a point Q, exactly one unit to the right of point P.

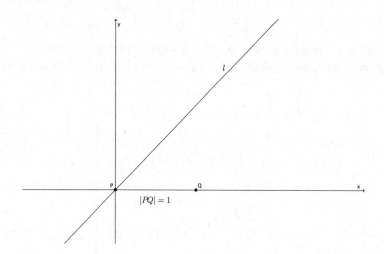

- Next, we draw a line, l_1, through point Q that is parallel to the y-axis. The point of intersection of line l and l_1 will be named point R.

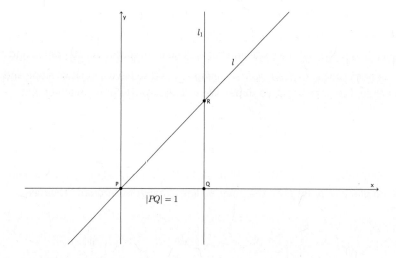

- Then the slope of line l is the number, m, associated with the y-coordinate of point R.

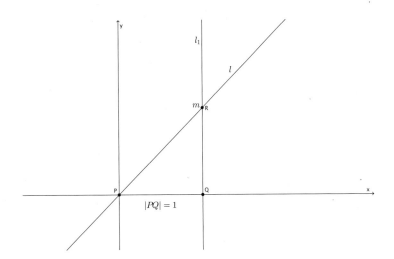

- The question remains, what is that number? Think of l_1 as a number line with point Q as zero, then however many units R is from Q is the number we are looking for, the slope m. Another way of thinking about this is through our basic rigid motion translation. We know that translation preserves lengths of segments. If we translate everything in the plane one unit to the left so that point Q maps onto the origin, then the segment QR will coincide with the y-axis and the y-coordinate of point R is the slope of the line.

Consider tracing the graph of the line and points P, Q, R onto a transparency. Demonstrate for students the translation along vector $\overrightarrow{QP}$ so that point Q is at the origin. Make clear that the translation moves point R to the y-axis, which is why the y-coordinate of point $R = (0, m)$ is the number that represents the slope of the line, m. This is how students would use the transparency, if needed, to complete the exercises in this lesson.

- Let's look at an example with real numbers. We have the same situation as just described. We have translated everything in the plane one unit to the left so that point Q maps onto the origin and the segment QR coincides with the y-axis. What is the slope of this line?

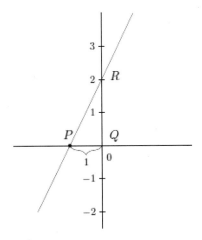

   □   *The slope of the line is 2, or $m = 2$.*

- This explains why the slope of lines that are *left-to-right inclining* are positive. When we consider the number line, the point R is at positive 2; hence this line has a positive slope.

Example 3 (4 minutes)

- Suppose a non-vertical line is given in the coordinate plane. As before, we mark a point P on the line and go one unit to the right of P and mark point Q.

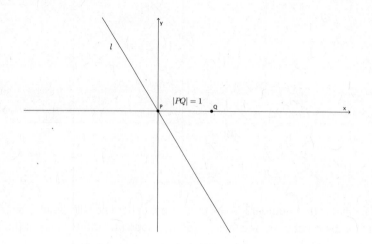

- Then we draw a line, l_1, through point Q that is parallel to the y-axis.

- We mark the intersection of lines l and l_1 as point R. Again, recall that we consider the line l_1 to be a vertical number line where point Q is at zero. Then the number associated with the y-coordinate of point R is the slope of the line.

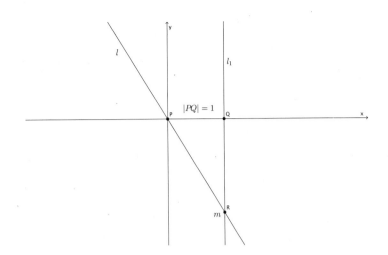

Again, consider tracing the graph of the line and points P, Q, R onto a transparency. Demonstrate for students the translation along vector $\overrightarrow{QP}$ so that point Q is at the origin. Make clear that the translation moves point R to the y-axis, which is why the y-coordinate of point $R = (0, m)$ is the number that represents the slope of the line, m. This is how students would use the transparency, if needed, to complete the exercises in this lesson.

- Let's look at this example with real numbers. We have the same situation as just described. We have translated everything in the plane one unit to the left so that point Q maps onto the origin and the segment QR coincides with the y-axis. What is the slope of this line?

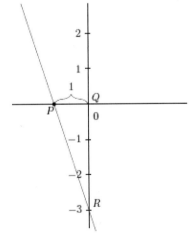

   □   *The slope of the line is -3, or $m = -3$.*

- This explains why the slope of lines that are *left-to-right declining* are negative. When we consider the number line, the point R is at negative 3; hence this line has a negative slope.

Example 4 (4 minutes)

- Now we have a line l that does not go through the origin of the graph.

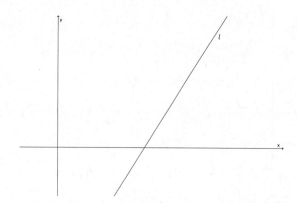

- Our process for finding slope changes only slightly. We will mark the point P at *any* location on the line l. Other than that, the work remains the same.

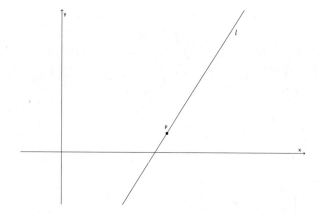

- We will go one unit to the right of P and mark point Q, then draw a line through Q parallel to the y-axis. We mark the intersection of lines l and l_1 point R. Again, recall that we consider the line l_1 to be a vertical number line where point Q is at zero. Then, the number associated with the y-coordinate of point R is the slope of the line.

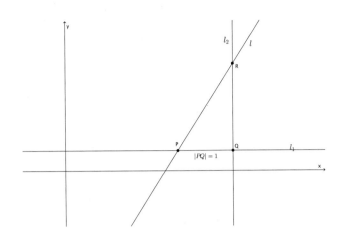

- Just as before, we translate so that point Q maps onto the origin and the segment QR coincides with the y-axis.

Again, consider tracing the graph of the line and points P, Q, R onto a transparency. Demonstrate for students the translation so that point Q is at the origin (along a vector from Q to the origin). Make clear that the translation moves point R to the y-axis, which is why the y-coordinate of point $R = (0, m)$ is the number that represents the slope of the line, m. This is how students would use the transparency, if needed, to complete the exercises in this lesson.

- What is the slope of this line?

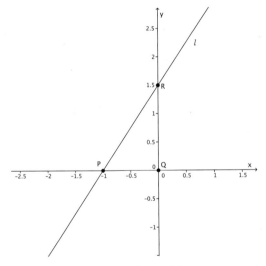

  □ *The slope of the line is 1.5; that is, $m = 1.5$.*

- In general, we describe slope as an integer or a fraction. Given that we know the y-coordinate of R is 1.5, how can we express that number as a fraction?

  □ *The slope of the line is $\frac{3}{2}$; that is, $m = \frac{3}{2}$.*

Exercises 1–6 (4 minutes)

Students complete Exercises 1–6 independently. The exercises are referenced in the discussion that follows.

Exercises 1–6

Use your transparency to find the slope of each line if needed.

1. What is the slope of this non-vertical line?

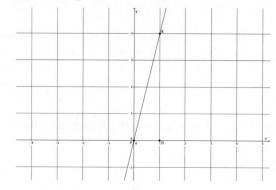

The slope of this line is 4, $m = 4$.

2. What is the slope of this non-vertical line?

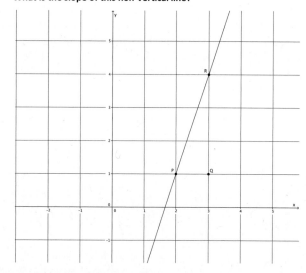

The slope of this line is 3, $m = 3$.

3. Which of the lines in Exercises 1 and 2 is steeper? Compare the slopes of each of the lines. Is there a relationship between steepness and slope?

The graph in Exercise 1 seems steeper. The slopes are 4 and 3. It seems like the greater the slope, the steeper the line.

---

4. What is the slope of this non-vertical line?

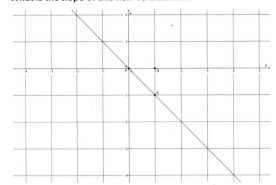

The slope of this line is -1, $m = -1$.

5. What is the slope of this non-vertical line?

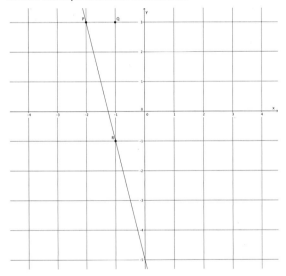

The slope of this line is -4, $m = -4$.

6. What is the slope of this non-vertical line?

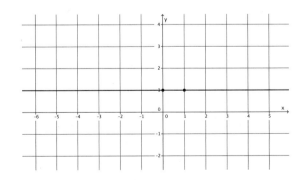

The slope of this line is 0, $m = 0$.

Discussion (6 minutes)

- When we began, we said that we wanted to define slope in a way so that a·horizontal line would have a slope of 0 because a horizontal line has no steepness or slant. What did you notice in Exercise 6?

  □ *The slope of the horizontal line was zero, like we wanted it to be.*

- In Exercise 3, you were asked to compare the steepness of the graphs of two lines and then compare their slopes. What did you notice?

  □ *The steeper the line, the greater the number that describes the slope. For example, Exercise 1 had the steeper line and the greater slope.*

- Does this same relationship exist for lines with negative slopes? Look specifically at Exercises 4 and 5.

Provide students a minute or two to look back at Exercises 4 and 5. They should draw the conclusion that the absolute value of the slopes of lines that are *left-to-right* declining will determine which is steeper. Use the points below to bring this fact to light.

  □ *A similar relationship exists. The line in Exercise 5 was steeper with a slope of −4. The line in Exercise 4 had a slope of −1. Based on our previous reasoning we'd say that because −1 > −4, that the line with a slope of −1 would have more steepness, but this is not the case.*

- We want to generalize the idea of steepness. When the slopes are positive we expect the line with greater steepness to have the greater slope. When the slopes are negative, it is actually the smaller number that has more steepness. Is there a way that we can compare the slopes so that our reasoning is consistent? That is, we want to say that a line is steeper than another when the number that describes the slope is larger than the other. How can we describe that mathematically, specifically when the slopes are negative?

  □ *We can compare just the absolute value of the slopes. That way, we can say that the steeper line will be the slope with the greater absolute value.*

Example 5 (4 minutes)

- Let's take another look at one of the proportional relationships that we graphed in Lesson 11. Here is the problem and the work that we did:

Pauline mows a lawn at a constant rate. Suppose she mowed a 35 square foot lawn in 2.5 minutes.

t (time in minutes)	Linear equation: $= \dfrac{35}{2.5} t$	(area in square feet)
0	$= \dfrac{35}{2.5}(0)$	0
1	$= \dfrac{35}{2.5}(1)$	$\dfrac{35}{2.5} = 14$
2	$= \dfrac{35}{2.5}(2)$	$\dfrac{70}{2.5} = 28$
3	$= \dfrac{35}{2.5}(3)$	$\dfrac{105}{2.5} = 42$
4	$= \dfrac{35}{2.5}(4)$	$\dfrac{140}{2.5} = 56$

Lesson 15:	The Slope of a Non-Vertical Line
Date:	11/8/13

204

Now if we assume that the points we plot on the coordinate plane make a line and the origin of the graph is point P, then we have

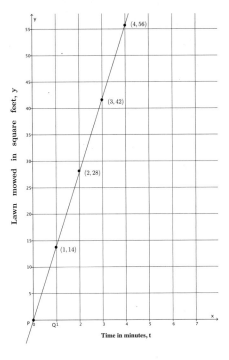

- What is the slope of this line? Explain.
  - *One unit to the right of point P is the point Q. That makes the point $(1, 14)$ the location of point R. Therefore the slope of this line is 14, $m = 14$.*
- What is the unit rate of mowing the lawn?
  - *Pauline's unit rate of mowing a lawn is 14 square feet per 1 minute.*
- When we graph proportional relationships, the unit rate is interpreted as the slope of the graph of the line, which is why slope is referred to as the rate of change.

Closing (3 minutes)

Summarize, or ask students to summarize, the main points from the lesson:

- We know that slope is a number that describes the steepness of a line.
- We know that lines that are left-to-right inclining have a positive slope and lines that are left-to-right declining have a negative slope.
- We can find the slope of a line by looking at the graph's unit rate.

Lesson 15:	The Slope of a Non-Vertical Line
Date:	11/8/13

Lesson Summary

Slope is a number that describes the steepness of a line. Slope is represented by the symbol m.

Lines that are left-to-right inclining have a positive slope, as shown below.

Lines that are left-to-right declining have a negative slope, as shown below.

Determine the slope of a line when the horizontal distance between points is fixed at 1 by translating point Q to the origin of the graph, and then identifying the y-coordinate of point R.

The slope of the line shown below is 2, or $m = 2$, because point R is at 2 on the y-axis.

Exit Ticket (3 minutes)

Name _____   Date _____

Lesson 15: The Slope of a Non-Vertical Line

Exit Ticket

1. What is the slope of this non-vertical line? Use your transparency if needed.

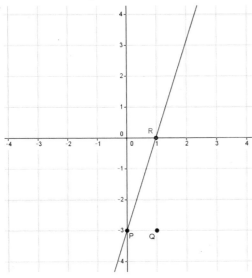

2. What is the slope of this non-vertical line? Use your transparency if needed.

Exit Ticket Sample Solutions

1. **What is the slope of this non-vertical line? Use your transparency if needed.**

The slope of the line is 3, $m = 3$.

2. **What is the slope of this non-vertical line? Use your transparency if needed.**

The slope of the line is -0.6 which is equal to $-\frac{3}{5}$, $m = -\frac{3}{5}$.

Problem Set Sample Solutions

Students practice identifying graphs of lines as having positive or negative slope. Students interpret the unit rate of a graph as the slope of the graph. The following solutions indicate an understanding of the objectives of this lesson:

1. **Does the graph of the line shown below have a positive or negative slope? Explain.**

The graph of this line has a negative slope. First of all it is left-to-right declining, which is an indication of negative slope. Also, if we were to mark a point P and a point Q one unit to the right of P, then draw a line parallel to the y-axis through Q, then the intersection of the two lines would be below Q, making the number that represents slope negative.

2. Does the graph of the line shown below have a positive or negative slope? Explain.

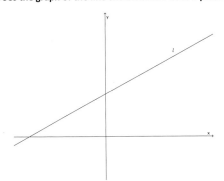

The graph of this line has a positive slope. First of all it is left-to-right inclining, which is an indication of positive slope. Also, if we were to mark a point P and a point Q one unit to the right of P, then draw a line parallel to the y-axis through Q, then the intersection of the two lines would be above Q, making the number that represents slope positive.

3. What is the slope of this non-vertical line? Use your transparency if needed.

The slope of this line is 1, $m = 1$.

4. What is the slope of this non-vertical line? Use your transparency if needed.

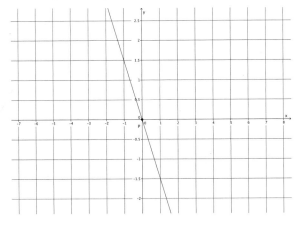

The slope of this line is $-\dfrac{3}{2}$, $m = -\dfrac{3}{2}$.

5.   What is the slope of this non-vertical line? Use your transparency if needed.

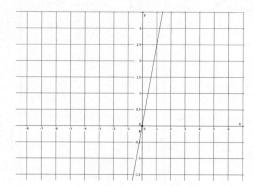

The slope of this line is $\dfrac{5}{2}$, $m = \dfrac{5}{2}$.

6.   What is the slope of this non-vertical line? Use your transparency if needed.

The slope of this line is 16, $m = 16$.

7.   What is the slope of this non-vertical line? Use your transparency if needed.

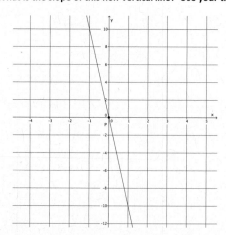

The slope of this line is -10, $m = -10$.

8. What is the slope of this non-vertical line? Use your transparency if needed.

The slope of this line is -5, $m = -5$.

9. What is the slope of this non-vertical line? Use your transparency if needed.

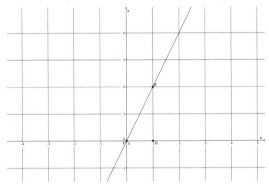

The slope of this line is 2, $m = 2$.

10. What is the slope of this non-vertical line? Use your transparency if needed.

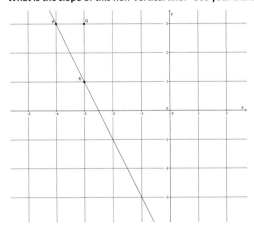

The slope of this line is -2, $m = -2$.

11. **What is the slope of this non-vertical line? Use your transparency if needed.**

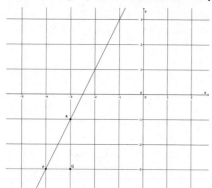

The slope of this line is 2, $m = 2$.

12. **What is the slope of this non-vertical line? Use your transparency if needed.**

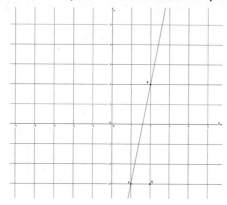

The slope of this line is 5, $m = 5$.

13. **What is the slope of this non-vertical line? Use your transparency if needed.**

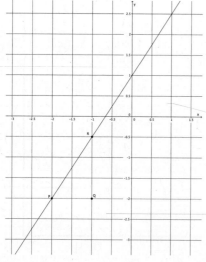

The slope of this line is $\frac{3}{2}$, $m = \frac{3}{2}$.

14. What is the slope of this non-vertical line? Use your transparency if needed.

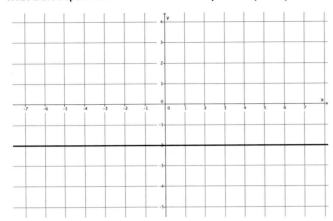

The slope of this line is 0, $m = 0$.

In Lesson 11, you did the work below involving constant rate problems. Use the table and the graphs provided to answer the questions that follow.

15. Suppose the volume of water that comes out in three minutes is 10.5 gallons.

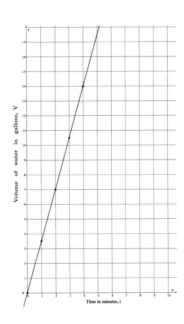

t (time in minutes)	Linear equation: $V = \dfrac{10.5}{3} t$	V (in gallons)
0	$V = \dfrac{10.5}{3}(0)$	0
1	$V = \dfrac{10.5}{3}(1)$	$\dfrac{10.5}{3} = 3.5$
2	$V = \dfrac{10.5}{3}(2)$	$\dfrac{21}{3} = 7$
3	$V = \dfrac{10.5}{3}(3)$	$\dfrac{31.5}{3} = 10.5$
4	$V = \dfrac{10.5}{3}(4)$	$\dfrac{42}{3} = 14$

a. How many gallons of water flow out of the faucet per minute, that is, what is the unit rate of water flow?

The unit rate of water flow is 3.5 *gallons per minute.*

b. Assume that the graph of the situation is a line, as shown in the graph. What is the slope of the line?

The slope of the line is 3.5, $m = 3.5$.

16. Emily paints at a constant rate. She can paint 32 square feet in five minutes.

t (time in minutes)	Linear equation: $A = \frac{32}{5}t$	A (area painted in square feet)
0	$A = \frac{32}{5}(0)$	0
1	$A = \frac{32}{5}(1)$	$\frac{32}{5} = 6.4$
2	$A = \frac{32}{5}(2)$	$\frac{64}{5} = 12.8$
3	$A = \frac{32}{5}(3)$	$\frac{96}{5} = 19.2$
4	$A = \frac{32}{5}(4)$	$\frac{128}{5} = 25.6$

a. How many square feet can Emily paint in one minute; that is, what is her unit rate of painting?

The unit rate at which Emily paints is 6.4 square feet per minute.

b. Assume that the graph of the situation is a line, as shown in the graph. What is the slope of the line?

The slope of the line is 6.4, $m = 6.4$.

17. A copy machine makes copies at a constant rate. The machine can make 80 copies in $2\frac{1}{2}$ minutes.

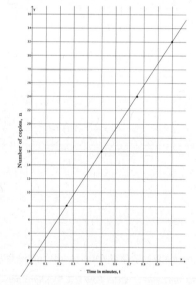

t (time in minutes)	Linear equation: $n = 32t$	n (number of copies)
0	$n = 32(0)$	0
0.25	$n = 32(0.25)$	8
0.5	$n = 32(0.5)$	16
0.75	$n = 32(0.75)$	24
1	$n = 32(1)$	32

a. How many copies can the machine make each minute; that is, what is the unit rate of the copy machine?

The unit rate of the copy machine is 32 copies per minute.

b. Assume that the graph of the situation is a line, as shown in the graph. What is the slope of the line?

The slope of the line is 32, $m = 32$.

Lesson 16: The Computation of the Slope of a Non-Vertical Line

Student Outcomes

- Students use similar triangles to explain why the slope m is the same between any two distinct points on a non-vertical line in the coordinate plane.
- Students use the slope formula to compute the slope of a non-vertical line.

Lesson Notes

Throughout the lesson, we use the phrase "rate of change" in addition to slope. The goal is for students to know that these are references to the same thing with respect to the graph of a line. At this point in students' learning, the phrases rate of change and slope are interchangeable, but it could be said that rate of change refers to constant rate problems where time is involved, i.e., rate of change over time. In Module 5, when students work with non-linear functions, they will learn that the rate of change is not always constant, as it is with linear equations and linear functions.

The points $P = (p_1, p_2)$ and $R = (r_1, r_2)$ are used throughout the lesson in order to make clear that we are looking at two distinct points. Using points P and R should decrease the chance of confusion compared to using the traditional (x_1, y_1) and (x_2, y_2). When considering what this this looks like in the formula, it should be clear that distinguishing the points by using different letters will clarify for students that we in fact have two distinct points. It is immediately recognizable that $m = \frac{r_2 - p_2}{p_1 - r_1}$ is written incorrectly compared to the traditional way of seeing the slope formula. Further, there should be less mixing up of the coordinates in the formula when it is presented with P and R.

There are several ways of representing the slope formula:

$$m = \frac{p_2 - r_2}{p_1 - r_1}, \quad m = \frac{r_2 - p_2}{r_1 - p_1}, \quad m = \frac{rise}{run}, \quad m = \frac{difference\ in\ y-values}{difference\ in\ x-values}$$

and each representation has merit. Please make clear to students throughout this and subsequent lessons that no matter how slope is represented, it should result in the same value for a given line.

Classwork

Example 1 (1 minute)

This example requires students to find the slope a line where the horizontal distance between two points with integer coordinates is fixed at 1.

Example 1

Using what you learned in the last lesson, determine the slope of the line with the following graph:

The slope of the line is 3.

Example 2 (1 minute)

This example requires students to find the slope a line where the horizontal distance between two points with integer coordinates is fixed at 1.

Example 2

Using what you learned in the last lesson, determine the slope of the line with the following graph:

The slope of this line is 2.

Example 3 (3 minutes)

This example requires students to find the slope a line where the horizontal distance can be fixed at one, but determining the slope will be difficult because it is not an integer. The point of this example is to make it clear to students that we will need to develop a strategy that will allow us to determine the slope of a line no matter what the horizontal distance is between the two points that are selected.

Example 3

What is different about this line compared to the last two examples?

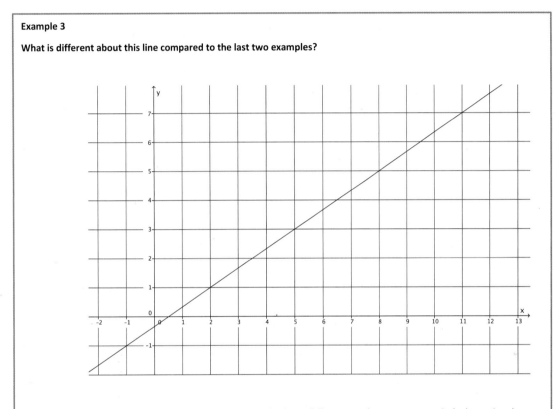

This time, if we choose two points on the line that have a horizontal distance at 1, we cannot precisely determine the slope of the line because the vertical change is not an integer. It is some fractional amount.

- Make a conjecture about how you could find the slope of this line.

Have students write their conjectures and share their ideas about how to find the slope of the line in this example; then continue with the discussion that follows.

Discussion (10 minutes)

- In the last lesson, we found a number that described the slope or rate of change of a line. In each case, we were looking at a special case of slope because the horizontal distance between the two points used to determine the slope, P and Q, was always 1. Since the horizontal distance was 1, the difference between the y- coordinates of points Q and R is equal to the slope or rate of change. For example, in the following graph we thought of point Q as zero on a vertical number line and noted how many units point R was from point Q.

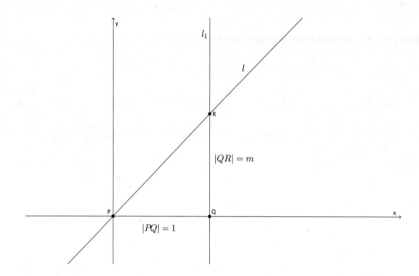

- Also in the last lesson we found that the unit rate of a problem was equal to the slope. Using that knowledge we can say that the slope or rate of change of a line $m = \dfrac{|QR|}{|PQ|}$.

- Now the task is to determine the rate of change of a non-vertical line when the distance between points P and Q is a number other than 1. We can use what we know already to guide our thinking.

■ Let's take a closer look at Example 2. There are several points on the line with integer coordinates that we could use to help us determine the slope of the line. Recall that we want to select points with integer coordinates because our calculation of slope will be simpler. In each case, from one point to the next we have a horizontal distance of 1 unit noted by the red segment and the difference in the y-values between the two points, which is a distance of 2, noted by the blue segments. When we compare the change in the y-values to the change in the x-values, we have a ratio $\frac{2}{1}$ which is equal to the slope of the line.

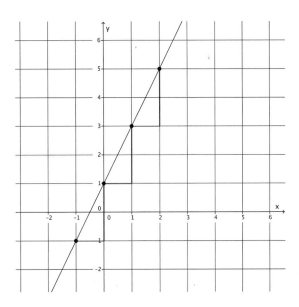

Each of the "slope triangles" shown have the ratio $\frac{2}{1}$. Using the same line, let's look at a different pair of "slope triangles".

- What is the ratio of the larger slope triangle?

    □   *The ratio of the larger slope triangle is $\frac{4}{2}$.*

- What do you notice about the ratio of the smaller slope triangle and the ratio of the larger slope triangle?

    □   *The ratios are equivalent $\frac{2}{1} = \frac{4}{2} = 2$.*

- We have worked with triangles before where the ratios of corresponding sides were equal. We called them similar triangles. Are the slope triangles in this diagram similar? How do you know?

    □   *Yes, the triangles are similar by the AA criterion. Each triangle has a right angle (at the intersection of the blue and red segments), and both triangles have a common angle (the angle formed by the red segment and the line itself).*

- When we have similar triangles we know that the ratios of corresponding side lengths must be equal. That is the reason that both of the slope triangles result in the same number for slope. Notice that we still got the correct number for the slope of the line even though the points chosen did not have a horizontal distance of 1. We now can find the slope of a line given any two points on the line. The horizontal distance between the points does not have to be 1.

Acknowledge any students that may have written or shared this strategy for finding slope from their work with Example 3.

- Now let's look again at Example 3. We did not have a strategy for finding slope before, but we do now. What do you think the slope of this line is? Explain.

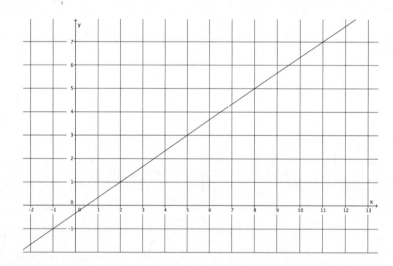

    □   *The slope of this line is $\frac{2}{3}$.*

Ask students to share their work and explanations with the class. Specifically have them show the slope triangle they used to determine the slope of the line.   Select several students to share their work, ideally students will pick different points and different slope triangles. Whether they do or not, have a discussion similar to the previous one that demonstrates that all slope triangles that could be drawn will be similar and that the ratios of corresponding sides are equal.

Lesson 16:   The Computation of the Slope of a Non-Vertical Line
Date: 11/8/13

Exercise (4 minutes)

Students complete the Exercise independently.

Exercise

Let's investigate concretely to see if the claim that we can find slope between any two points is true.

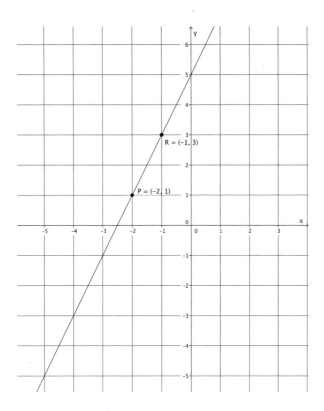

a. Select any two points on the line to label as P and R.

   Sample points selected on graph.

b. Identify the coordinates of points P and R.

   Sample points labeled on graph.

c. Find the slope of the line using as many different points as you can. Identify your points and show your work below.

   Points selected by students will vary, but the slope should always equal 2. Students could choose to use points $(0, 5)$, $(-1, 3)$, $(-2, 1)$, $(-3, -1)$, $(-4, -3)$, and $(-5, -5)$.

Lesson 16: The Computation of the Slope of a Non-Vertical Line
Date: 11/8/13

221

Discussion (10 minutes)

- We want to show that the slope of line l can be found using any two points P and R on the line.

- Let point $P = (p_1, p_2)$, where p_1 is the x-coordinate of point P and p_2 is the y-coordinate of point P. Also let point $Q = (q_1, q_2)$ and $R = (r_1, r_2)$.

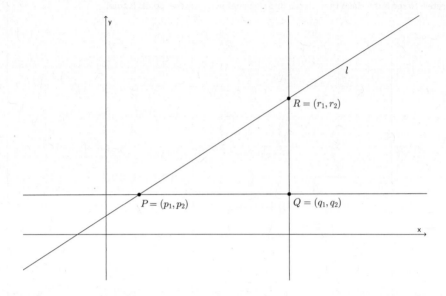

- Then we claim that the slope of line l is:

$$m = \frac{|QR|}{|PQ|}.$$

- From the last lesson, we found the length of segment QR by looking at the y-coordinate. Without having to translate, we can find the length of segment QR by finding the difference between the y-coordinates of points R and Q (vertical distance). Similarly, we can find the length of the segment PQ by finding the difference between the x-coordinates of P and Q (horizontal distance).

$$m = \frac{|QR|}{|PQ|} = \frac{(q_2 - r_2)}{(p_1 - q_1)}$$

- We can simplify this further by looking more closely at the coordinates of point Q. Consider the following concrete example:

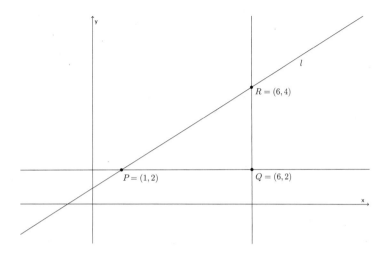

- What do you notice about the y-coordinates of points P and Q?
  - *The y-coordinates of points P and Q are the same, 2.*

- That means that $q_2 = p_2$. What do you notice about the x-coordinates of points R and Q?
  - *The x-coordinates of points R and Q are the same, 6.*

- That means that $q_1 = r_1$. Then by substitution:

$$m = \frac{|QR|}{|PQ|} = \frac{(q_2 - r_2)}{(p_1 - q_1)} = \frac{(p_2 - r_2)}{(p_1 - r_1)}$$

- Then we claim that the slope can be calculated regardless of the choice of points. Also, we have discovered something called "the slope formula". With the formula for slope, or rate of change, $m = \frac{(p_2 - r_2)}{(p_1 - r_1)}$, the slope of a line can be found using any two points P and R!

Ask students to translate the slope formula into words and provide them with the traditional ways of describing slope. For example, students may say the slope of a line is the "height of the slope triangle over the base of the slope triangle," or "the difference in the y-coordinates over the difference in the x-coordinates". Tell students that slope can be referred to as "rise over run" as well.

Discussion (3 minutes)

Show that the formula to calculate slope is true for horizontal lines.

- Suppose we are given a horizontal line. Based on our work in the last lesson, what do we expect the slope of this line to be?

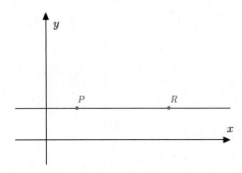

- □ *The slope should be zero because if we go one unit to the right of P, then identify the vertical difference between that point and point R, there is no difference. Therefore, the slope is zero.*

- As before, the coordinates of points P and R are represented as $P = (p_1, p_2)$ and $R = (r_1, r_2)$. Since this is a horizontal line, what do we know about the y-coordinates of each point?
   - □ *Horizontal lines are graphs of linear equations in the form of $y = c$, where the y-value does not change. Therefore, $p_2 = r_2$.*

- By the slope formula:

$$m = \frac{(p_2 - r_2)}{(p_1 - r_1)} = \frac{0}{p_1 - r_1} = 0$$

The slope of the horizontal line is zero, as expected, regardless of the value of the horizontal change.

Lesson 16:   The Computation of the Slope of a Non-Vertical Line
Date: 11/8/13

Discussion (7 minutes)

- Now for the general case. We want to show that we can choose any two points P and R to find the slope not just a point like R', where we have fixed the horizontal distance at 1. Consider the diagram below:

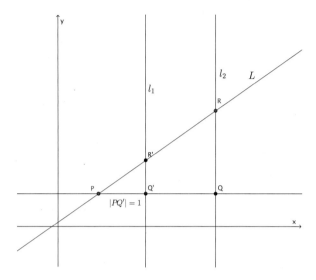

Now we have a situation where point Q is an unknown distance from point P. We know that if $\triangle PQ'R'$ is similar to $\triangle PQR$, then the ratio of the corresponding sides will be equal and the ratios are equal to the slope of the line L. Are $\triangle PQ'R'$ and $\triangle PQR$ similar? Explain.

- *Yes, the triangles are similar, i.e., $\triangle PQ'R' \sim \triangle PQR$. Both triangles have a common angle, $\angle RPQ$, and both triangles have a right angle, $\angle R'Q'P$ and $\angle RQP$. By the AA criterion, $\triangle PQ'R' \sim \triangle PQR$.*

Now what we want to do is find a way to express this information in a formula. Because we have similar triangles we know the following:

$$\frac{|R'Q'|}{|RQ|} = \frac{|PQ'|}{|PQ|} = \frac{|PR'|}{|PR|} = r$$

Based on our previous knowledge, we know that we know that $|R'Q'| = m$ and $|PQ'| = 1$. By substitution we have

$$\frac{m}{|RQ|} = \frac{1}{|PQ|}$$

which is equivalent to the following:

$$\frac{m}{1} = \frac{|RQ|}{|PQ|}$$

$$m = \frac{|RQ|}{|PQ|}$$

- We also know from our work earlier that $|RQ| = p_2 - r_2$ and $|PQ| = p_1 - r_1$. By substitution we have

$$m = \frac{p_2 - r_2}{p_1 - r_1}$$

The slope of a line can be computed using any two points!

Closing (3 minutes)

Summarize, or ask students to summarize, the main points from the lesson:

- We know that the slope of a line can be calculated using any two points on the line because of what we know about similar triangles.
- Slope is referred to as the difference in y-values compared to the difference in x-values, or as the height compared to the base of the slope triangle, or as rise over run.
- We know that the formula to calculate slope is $m = \frac{p_2 - r_2}{p_1 - r_1}$, where (p_1, p_2) and (r_1, r_2) are two points on the line.

Lesson Summary

The slope of a line can be calculated using *any* two points on the same line because the slope triangles formed are similar and corresponding sides will be equal in ratio.

The formula to calculate slope between points $P = (p_1, p_2)$ and $R = (r_1, r_2)$ is

$$m = \frac{p_2 - r_2}{p_1 - r_1}$$

The numerator in the formula is referred to as the difference in y-values and the denominator as the difference in x-values.

Exit Ticket (3 minutes)

	Lesson 16:	The Computation of the Slope of a Non-Vertical Line	
	Date:	11/8/13	226

Name _____   Date _____

Lesson 16: The Computation of the Slope of a Non-Vertical Line

Exit Ticket

1. Find the rate of change of the line by completing parts (a) and (b).

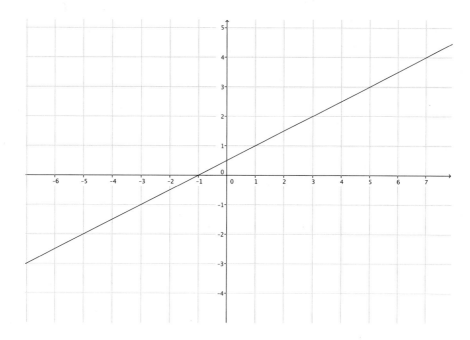

a.   Select any two points on the line to label as P and R. Name their coordinates.

b.   Compute the rate of change of the line.

Exit Ticket Sample Solutions

1. Find the rate of change of the line by completing parts (a) and (b).

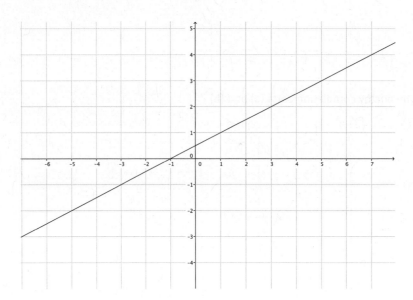

a. Select any two points on the line to label as P and R. Name their coordinates.

Sample student work. Other points on the graph may have been chosen.

$P = (-1, 0)$ *and* $R = (5, 3)$

b. Compute the rate of change of the line.

$$m = \frac{(p_2 \quad r_2)}{(p_1 - r_1)}$$
$$= \frac{0 - 3}{-1 - 5}$$
$$= \frac{-3}{-6}$$
$$= \frac{1}{2}$$

Problem Set Sample Solutions

Students practice finding slope between any two points on a line. Students also see that $m = \dfrac{p_2 - r_2}{p_1 - r_1}$ yields the same result as $m = \dfrac{r_2 - p_2}{r_1 - p_1}$.

1. Calculate the slope of the line using two different pairs of points.

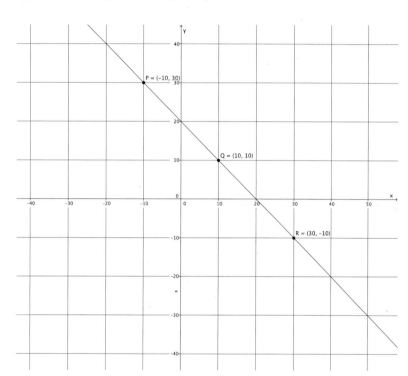

Sample student work:

$$m = \frac{p_2 - r_2}{p_1 - r_1}$$

$$= \frac{30 - (-10)}{-10 - 30}$$

$$= \frac{40}{-40}$$

$$= -\frac{1}{1}$$

$$= -1$$

$$m = \frac{q_2 - r_2}{q_1 - r_1}$$

$$= \frac{10 - (-10)}{10 - 30}$$

$$= \frac{20}{-20}$$

$$= -1$$

Lesson 16: The Computation of the Slope of a Non-Vertical Line
Date: 11/8/13

229

2.   Calculate the slope of the line using two different pairs of points.

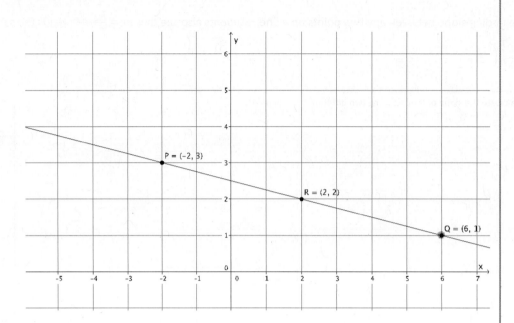

Sample student work:

$$m = \frac{p_2 - r_2}{p_1 - r_1}$$

$$= \frac{3 - 2}{-2 - 2}$$

$$= \frac{1}{-4}$$

$$= \frac{1}{4}$$

$$m = \frac{q_2 - r_2}{q_1 - r_1}$$

$$= \frac{1 - 2}{6 - 2}$$

$$= \frac{-1}{4}$$

$$= -\frac{1}{4}$$

3. Calculate the slope of the line using two different pairs of points.

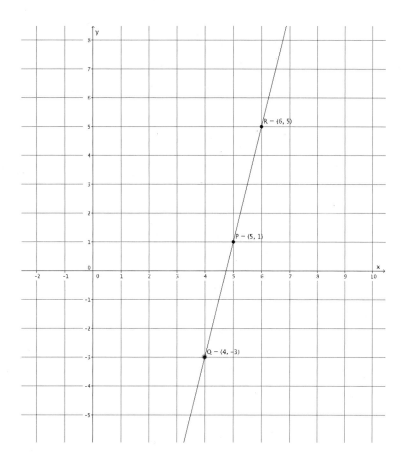

Sample student work:

$$m = \frac{p_2 - r_2}{p_1 - r_1}$$

$$= \frac{1 - 5}{5 - 6}$$

$$= \frac{-4}{-1}$$

$$= \frac{4}{1}$$

$$= 4$$

$$m = \frac{q_2 - r_2}{q_1 - r_1}$$

$$= \frac{-3 - 5}{4 - 6}$$

$$= \frac{-8}{-2}$$

$$= 4$$

Lesson 16:   The Computation of the Slope of a Non-Vertical Line
Date: 11/8/13

231

4.   **Calculate the slope of the line using two different pairs of points.**

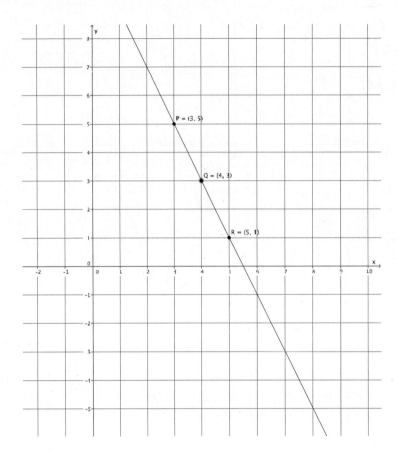

Sample student work:

$$m = \frac{p_2 - r_2}{p_1 - r_1}$$

$$= \frac{5 - 1}{3 - 5}$$

$$= \frac{4}{-2}$$

$$= -\frac{2}{1}$$

$$= -2$$

$$m = \frac{q_2 - r_2}{q_1 - r_1}$$

$$= \frac{3 - 1}{4 - 5}$$

$$= \frac{2}{-1}$$

$$= -2$$

Lesson 16:   The Computation of the Slope of a Non-Vertical Line
Date: 11/8/13

5. Calculate the slope of the line using two different pairs of points.

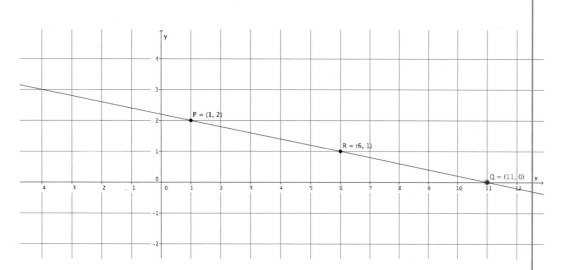

Sample student work:

$$m = \frac{p_2 - r_2}{p_1 - r_1}$$

$$= \frac{2 - 1}{1 - 6}$$

$$= \frac{1}{-5}$$

$$= -\frac{1}{5}$$

$$m = \frac{q_2 - r_2}{q_1 - r_1}$$

$$= \frac{0 - 1}{11 - 6}$$

$$= \frac{-1}{5}$$

$$= -\frac{1}{5}$$

6. Calculate the slope of the line using two different pairs of points.

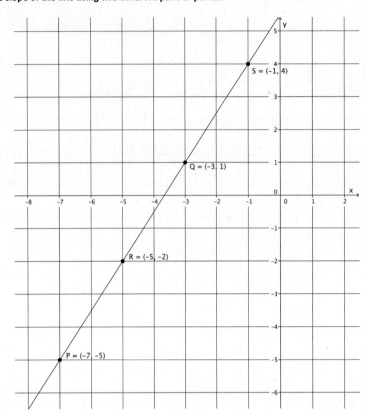

a. Select any two points on the line to compute the slope.

Sample student work:

$$m = \frac{p_2 - r_2}{p_1 - r_1}$$
$$= \frac{-5 - (-2)}{-7 - (-5)}$$
$$= \frac{-3}{-2}$$
$$= \frac{3}{2}$$

b. Select two different points on the line to calculate the slope.

Sample student work:

Let the two new points be $(-3, 1)$ *and* $(-1, 4)$.

$$m = \frac{q_2 - s_2}{q_1 - s_1}$$
$$= \frac{1 - 4}{-3 - (-1)}$$
$$= \frac{-3}{-2}$$
$$= \frac{3}{2}$$

c. **What do you notice about your answers in parts (a) and (b)? Explain.**

The slopes are equal in parts (a) and (b). This is true because of what we know about similar triangles, that is, the slope triangle that is drawn between the two points selected in part (a) is similar to the slope triangle that is drawn between the two points in part (b) by the AA criterion. Then because the corresponding sides of similar triangles are equal in ratio, the slopes are equal.

7. **Calculate the slope of the line in the graph below.**

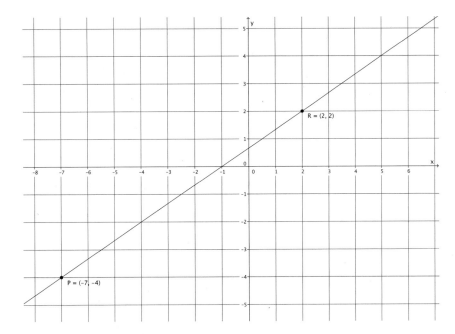

Sample student work:

$$m = \frac{p_2 - r_2}{p_1 - r_1}$$
$$= \frac{-4 - 2}{-7 - 2}$$
$$= \frac{-6}{-9}$$
$$= \frac{2}{3}$$

8. Your teacher tells you that a line goes through the points $\left(-6, \frac{1}{2}\right)$ and $(-4, 3)$. Calculate the slope of this line.

Sample student work:

$$m = \frac{p_2 - r_2}{p_1 - r_1}$$

$$= \frac{\frac{1}{2} - 3}{-6 - (-4)}$$

$$= \frac{-\frac{5}{2}}{-2}$$

$$= \frac{\frac{5}{2}}{2}$$

$$= \frac{5}{2} \div 2$$

$$= \frac{5}{2} \times \frac{1}{2}$$

$$= \frac{5}{4}$$

Do you think the slope will be the same if the order of the points is reversed? Verify by calculating the slope and explain your result.

The slope should be the same because we are joining the same two points.

$$m = \frac{p_2 - r_2}{p_1 - r_1}$$

$$= \frac{3 - \frac{1}{2}}{-4 - (-6)}$$

$$= \frac{\frac{5}{2}}{2}$$

$$= \frac{5}{4}$$

Since the slope of a line can be computed using any two points on the same line, it makes sense that it doesn't matter which point we name as P and which point we name as R.

9. Use the graph below to complete parts (a)–(c).

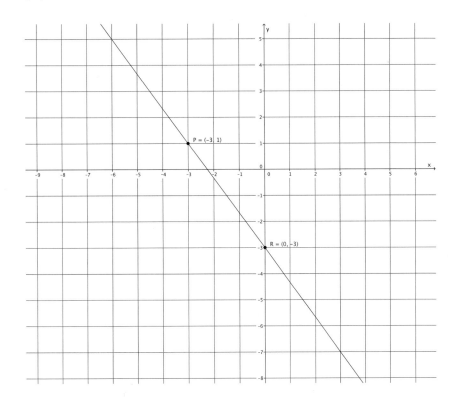

P = (–3, 1)

R = (0, –3)

a. Select any two points on the line to calculate the slope.

Sample student work:

$$m = \frac{p_2 - r_2}{p_1 - r_1}$$
$$= \frac{1 - (-3)}{-3 - 0}$$
$$= \frac{4}{-3}$$
$$= -\frac{4}{3}$$

b. Compute the slope again, this time reversing the order of the coordinates.

Sample student work:

$$m = \frac{(r_2 - p_2)}{(r_1 - p_1)}$$
$$= \frac{-3 - 1}{0 - (-3)}$$
$$= \frac{-4}{3}$$
$$= -\frac{4}{3}$$

c. What do you notice about the slopes you computed in parts (a) and (b)?

The slopes are equal.

d. Why do you think $m = \frac{(p_2 - r_2)}{(p_1 - r_1)} = \frac{(r_2 - p_2)}{(r_1 - p_1)}$?

If I multiply the first fraction by $\frac{-1}{-1}$, then I get the second fraction:

$$\frac{-1}{-1} \times \left(\frac{(p_2 - r_2)}{(p_1 - r_1)} \right) = \frac{(r_2 - p_2)}{(r_1 - p_1)}.$$

I can do the same thing to the second fraction to obtain the first:

$$\frac{-1}{-1} \times \left(\frac{(r_2 - p_2)}{(r_1 - p_1)} \right) = \frac{(p_2 - r_2)}{(p_1 - r_1)}.$$

Also, since I know that I can find the slope between any two points, it shouldn't matter which point I pick first.

10. Each of the lines in the lesson was non-vertical. Consider the slope of a non-vertical line, $x = 2$. Select two points on the line to calculate slope. Based on your answer, why do you think the topic of slope focuses only on non-vertical lines?

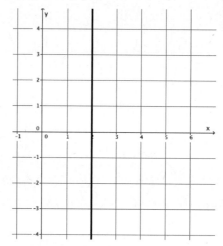

Students can use any points on the line $x = 2$ to determine that the slope is undefined, that is, the computation of slope using the formula leads to a fraction with zero as its denominator. Since the slope of a vertical line is undefined, there is no need to focus them.

11. Challenge: A certain line has a slope of $\frac{1}{2}$. Name two points that may be on the line.

Answers will vary. Accept any answers that have a difference in y-values equal to 1 and a difference of x-values equal to 2. Points $(6, 4)$ and $(4, 3)$ for example.

Lesson 17: The Line Joining Two Distinct Points of the

Graph $y = mx + b$ has Slope m

Student Outcomes

- Students show that the slope of a line joining any two distinct points of the graph of $y = mx + b$ has slope, m.
- Students transform the standard form of an equation into $y = -\frac{a}{b}x + \frac{c}{b}$.

Lesson Notes

In the previous lesson, we determined that slope can be calculated using any two points on the same line. In this lesson, we show that equations of the form $y = mx$ and $y = mx + b$ generate lines with slope m. Students need graph paper to complete some of the Exercises and Problem Set items.

Classwork

Exercises 1–3 (8 minutes)

Students work independently to complete Exercises 1–3.

Exercises

1. Find at least three solutions to the equation $y = 2x$, and graph the solutions as points on the coordinate plane. Connect the points to make a line. Find the slope of the line.

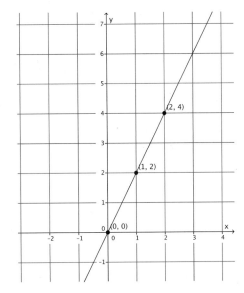

The slope of the line is 2, $m = 2$.

---

2. Find at least three solutions to the equation $y = 3x - 1$, and graph the solutions as points on the coordinate plane. Connect the points to make a line. Find the slope of the line.

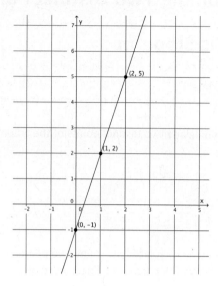

The slope of the line is 3, $m = 3$.

3. Find at least three solutions to the equation $y = 3x + 1$, and graph the solutions as points on the coordinate plane. Connect the points to make a line. Find the slope of the line.

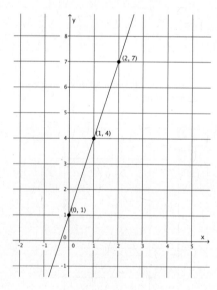

The slope of the line is 3, $m = 3$.

Discussion (12 minutes)

Recall the goal from Lesson 15: We want to prove that the graph of a linear equation is a line. To do so, we needed some tools, specifically two related to slope. Now that facts are known about slope, we will focus on showing that the line that joins two distinct points is a linear equation with slope m.

- We know from our previous work with slope that when the horizontal distance between two points is fixed at one, then the slope of the line is the difference in the y-coordinates. We also know that when the horizontal distance is not fixed at one, we can find the slope of the line using any two points because the ratio of corresponding sides of similar triangles will be equal. We can put these two facts together to prove that the graph of the line $y = mx$ has slope m. Consider the diagram below:

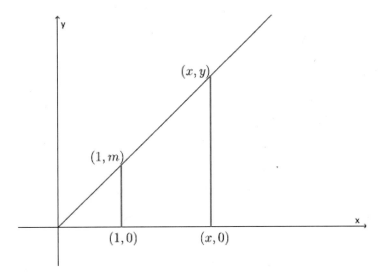

- Examine the diagram and think of how we could prove that $\dfrac{y}{m} = \dfrac{x}{1}$.

Provide students time to work independently, then time for them to discuss in pairs a possible proof of $\dfrac{y}{m} = \dfrac{x}{1}$. If necessary, use the four bullet points below to guide students' thinking.

- Do we have similar triangles? Explain.
  - *Yes. Each of the triangles has a common angle at the origin, and each triangle has a right angle. By the AA criterion these triangles are similar.*
- What is the slope of the line? Explain.
  - *The slope of the line is m. By our definition of slope and the information in the diagram, when the horizontal distance between two points is fixed at one, the slope is m.*
- Write the ratio of the corresponding sides. Then solve for y.
  - $\dfrac{y}{m} = \dfrac{x}{1}, \; y = mx$
- Therefore, the slope of the graph of $y = mx$ is m.

	Lesson 17:	The Line Joining Two Distinct Points of the Graph $y = mx + b$ has Slope m	241
	Date:	11/8/13	

Point students to their work in Exercise 1 where the graph of $y = 2x$ was a line with a slope of 2.

- We know that the graph of $y = mx$ has slope m, where m is a number. The y in the equation $y = mx$ is equal to the difference in y-coordinates as shown in the diagram below:

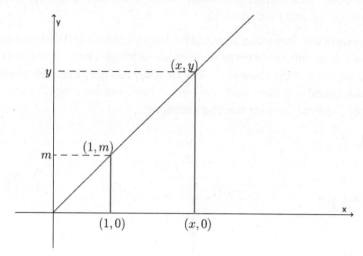

- Consider the diagram below. How does this compare to the graph of $y = mx$ that we just worked on?

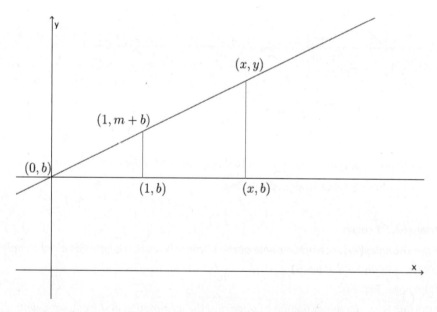

  □ *The graph is the same except for the fact that the line has been translated b units up the y-axis.*

- We want to write the ratio of corresponding sides of the slope triangles. We know the lengths of two sides of the smaller slope triangle; they are 1 and m. We also know one of the lengths of the larger slope triangle, x. What we need to do now is express the length of the larger slope triangle that corresponds to side m. When our line passed through the origin, the length was simply y, but that is not the case here. How can we express the length we need, noted in blue in the diagram below?

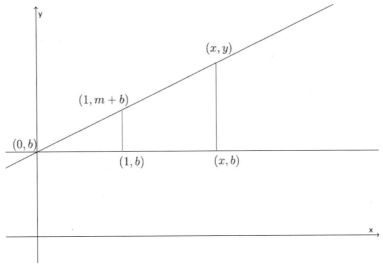

Provide students time to think and share in small groups. If necessary, show students the diagram below and ask them what the length of the dashed orange segment is. They should recognize that it is the length of b. Then ask them how they can use that information to determine the length of the blue segment.

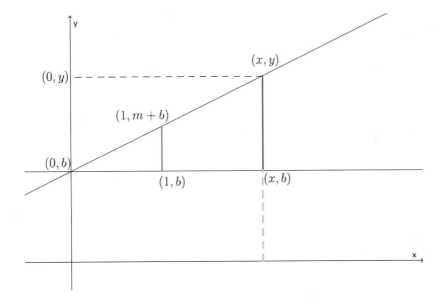

- *The length of the blue segment is $y - b$.*

- Now that we know the length of the blue segment, we can write ratios that represent the corresponding sides of the triangles:

$$\frac{m}{y-b} = \frac{1}{x}$$

Now we can solve for y:

$$mx = y - b$$

$$mx + b = y - b + b$$

$$mx + b = y$$

Therefore, the slope of an equation of the form $y = mx + b$ is m.

Point students to their work in Exercises 2 and 3 where the graph of $y = 3x - 1$ and $y = 3x + 1$ was a line with slope 3.

- We can show this algebraically using two distinct points on the graph of the line $y = 3x - 1$. Points $(1, 2)$ and $(2, 5)$ were on the graph of $y = 3x - 1$. Using the slope formula, we see that

$$m = \frac{5 - 2}{2 - 1}$$

$$= \frac{3}{1}$$

$$= 3$$

The next four bullet points generalize the slope between *any* two points of the graph of $y = 3x - 1$ is 3. This is an optional part of the discussion of slope between any two points. The last bullet point of this section should be shared with students as it orients them to our progress towards our ultimate goal: showing that the graph of a linear equation is a line.

- In general, let $P = (p_1, p_2)$ and $R = (r_1, r_2)$ be *any* two distinct points of the graph of $y = 3x - 1$. Recall what is known about points on a graph; it means that they are solutions to the equation. Since P is on the graph of $y = 3x - 1$, then

$$p_2 = 3p_1 - 1$$

Similarly, since R is on the graph of $y = 3x - 1$, then

$$r_2 = 3r_1 - 1$$

- By the slope formula, $m = \frac{p_2 - r_2}{p_1 - r_1}$, we can substitute the above values of p_2 and r_2 and use our properties of equality to simplify:

$$m = \frac{p_2 - r_2}{p_1 - r_1}$$

$$= \frac{(3p_1 - 1) - (3r_1 - 1)}{p_1 - r_1} \qquad \text{By substitution}$$

$$= \frac{3p_1 - 1 - 3r_1 + 1}{p_1 - r_1} \qquad \text{By taking the opposite of the terms in the second grouping}$$

$$= \frac{3p_1 - 3r_1}{p_1 - r_1} \qquad \text{By simplifying } (-1 + 1)$$

$$= \frac{3(p_1 - r_1)}{p_1 - r_1} \qquad \text{By the Distributive Property "collecting like terms"}$$

$$= 3 \qquad \text{By division, the number } p_1 - r_1 \text{ divided by itself}$$

- Thus we have shown that the line passing through points P and R has a slope of 3.
- To truly generalize our work, we need only replace 3 in the calculations with m and the -1 with b.

Make clear to students that we are still working toward our goal of proving that the graph of a linear equation is a line using the summary of work below.

- Our goal, ultimately, is to prove that the graph of a linear equation is a line. In Lesson 15, we said we have to develop the following tools:
    1. We must define a number for each non-vertical line that can be used to measure the "steepness" or "slant" of the line. Once defined, this number will be called the **slope** of the line and is often referred to as the "rate of change".
    2. We must show that *any* two points on a non-vertical line can be used to find the slope of the line.
    3. We must show that the line joining two points on a graph of a linear equation of the form $y = mx + b$ has the slope m.
    4. We must show that there is only one line passing through a given point with a given slope.

    At this point in our work, we just finished #3. Number 4, is the topic of the next lesson.

Discussion (5 minutes)

- When an equation is in the form $y = mx + b$, the slope m is easily identifiable compared to an equation in the form $ax + by = c$. Note that b in each of the equations is unique. That is, the number represented by b in the equation $y = mx + b$ is not necessarily the same as the number b in $ax + by = c$. For example, we will solve the equation $8x + 2y = 6$ for y. Our goal is to have y equal to an expression:

$$8x + 2y = 6$$

First we use our properties of equality to remove $8x$ from the left side of the equation

$$8x - 8x + 2y = 6 - 8x$$
$$2y = 6 - 8x$$

Now we divide both sides by 2

$$\frac{2y}{2} = \frac{6 - 8x}{2}$$
$$y = \frac{6}{2} - \frac{8x}{2}$$
$$y = 3 - 4x$$
$$y = -4x + 3$$

The slope of the graph of this equation is -4.

By convention (an agreed upon way of doing things) we place the term mx before the term b. This is a version of the standard form of a linear equation that is referred to as the "slope-intercept" form. It is called "slope-intercept" form because it makes clear the number that describes slope, i.e., m, and the y-intercept, which is something that will be discussed later. Also, notice the value of b is different in both forms of the equation.

Exercises 4–11 (11 minutes)

Students work independently or in pairs to identify the slope from an equation and to transform the standard form of an equation into slope-intercept form.

---

4. **The graph of the equation $y = 7x - 3$ has what slope?**

   The slope is 7.

5. **The graph of the equation $y = -\frac{3}{4}x - 3$ has what slope?**

   The slope is $-\frac{3}{4}$.

6. **You have $20 in savings at the bank. Each week, you add $2 to your savings. Let y represent the total amount of money you have saved at the end of x weeks. Write an equation to represent this situation and identify the slope of the equation. What does that number represent?**

   $y = 2x + 20$

   The slope is 2. It represents how much money is saved each week.

Lesson 17:   The Line Joining Two Distinct Points of the Graph $y = mx + b$ has
             Slope m
Date: 11/8/13

7. A friend is training for a marathon. She can run 4 miles in 28 minutes. Assume she runs at a constant rate. Write an equation to represent the total distance, y, your friend can run in x minutes. Identify the slope of the equation. What does that number represent?

$$\frac{y}{x} = \frac{4}{28}$$

$$y = \frac{4}{28}x$$

$$y = \frac{1}{7}x$$

The slope is $\frac{1}{7}$. It represents the rate at which my friend can run, one mile in seven minutes.

8. Four boxes of pencils cost $5. Write an equation that represents the total cost, y, for x boxes of pencils. What is the slope of the equation? What does that number represent?

$$y = \frac{5}{4}x$$

The slope is $\frac{5}{4}$. It represents the cost of one box of pencils, $1.25.

9. Solve the following equation for y: $9x - 3y = 15$, then identify the slope of the line.

$$9x - 3y = 15$$
$$9x - 9x - 3y = 15 - 9x$$
$$-3y = 15 - 9x$$
$$\frac{-3}{-3}y = \frac{15 - 9x}{-3}$$
$$y = \frac{15}{-3} - \frac{9x}{-3}$$
$$y = -5 + 3x$$
$$y = 3x - 5$$

The slope of the line is 3.

10. Solve the following equation for y: $5x + 9y = 6$, then identify the slope of the line.

$$5x + 9y = 8$$
$$5x - 5x + 9y = 8 - 5x$$
$$9y = 8 - 5x$$
$$\frac{9}{9}y = \frac{8 - 5x}{9}$$
$$y = \frac{8}{9} - \frac{5}{9}x$$
$$y = -\frac{5}{9}x + \frac{8}{9}$$

The slope of the line is $-\frac{5}{9}$.

11. Solve the following equation for y: $ax + by = c$, then identify the slope of the line.

$$ax + by = c$$
$$ax - ax + by = c - ax$$
$$by = c - ax$$
$$\frac{b}{b}y = \frac{c - ax}{b}$$
$$y = \frac{c}{b} - \frac{ax}{b}$$
$$y = \frac{c}{b} - \frac{a}{b}x$$
$$y = -\frac{a}{b}x + \frac{c}{b}$$

The slope of the line is $-\dfrac{a}{b}$.

Closing (4 minutes)

Summarize, or ask students to summarize, the main points from the lesson:

- We know that the line that joins any two distinct points of the graph $y = mx + b$ has slope m.
- We know how to identify the slope for any equation in the form $y = mx + b$.
- We know how to transform the standard form of a linear equation into another form to more easily identify the slope.

> **Lesson Summary**
>
> The line joining two distinct points of the graph of the linear equation $y = mx + b$ has slope m.
>
> The m of $y = mx + b$ is the number that describes the slope. For example, in the equation $y = -2x + 4$, the slope of the graph of the line is -2.

Exit Ticket (5 minutes)

Name _____   Date _____

Lesson 17: The Line Joining Two Distinct Points of the Graph $y = mx + b$ has Slope m

Exit Ticket

1. Solve the following equation for y: $35x - 7y = 49$.

2. What is the slope of the equation in problem 1?

3. Show, using similar triangles, why the graph of an equation of the form $y = mx$ is a line with slope m.

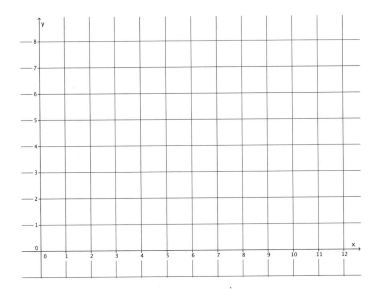

COMMON CORE | **Lesson 17:** The Line Joining Two Distinct Points of the Graph $y = mx + b$ has
| Slope m
| **Date:** 11/8/13

249

© 2013 Common Core, Inc. All rights reserved. **commoncore.org**

Exit Ticket Sample Solutions

1. Solve the following equation for y: $35x - 7y = 49$.

$$35x - 7y = 49$$
$$35x - 35x - 7y = 49 - 35x$$
$$-7y = 49 - 35x$$
$$\frac{-7}{-7}y = \frac{49}{-7} - \frac{35}{-7}x$$
$$y = -7 - (-5x)$$
$$y = 5x - 7$$

2. What is the slope of the equation in problem 1?

    The slope of $y = 5x - 7$ is 5.

3. Show, using similar triangles, why the graph of an equation of the form $y = mx$ is a line with slope m.

    Solutions will vary. Sample solution is shown below.

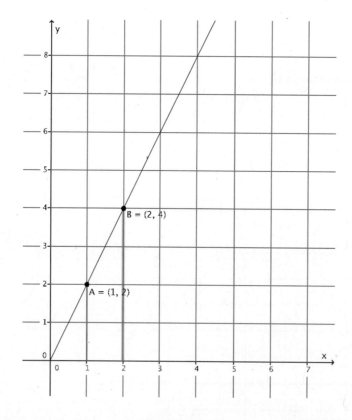

The line shown has slope 2. When we compare the corresponding side lengths of the similar triangles we have the ratios $\frac{2}{1} = \frac{4}{2} = 2$. In general, the ratios would be $\frac{x}{1} = \frac{y}{m}$, equivalently $y = mx$, which is a line with slope m.

Problem Set Sample Solutions

Students practice transforming equations from standard form into slope-intercept form and showing that the line joining two distinct points of the graph $y = mx + b$ has slope m. Students graph the equation and informally note the y-intercept.

---

1. Solve the following equation for y: $-4x + 8y = 24$.

$$-4x + 8y = 24$$
$$-4x + 4x + 8y = 24 + 4x$$
$$8y = 24 + 4x$$
$$\frac{8}{8}y = \frac{24}{8} + \frac{4}{8}x$$
$$y = 3 + \frac{1}{2}x$$
$$y = \frac{1}{2}x + 3$$

a. Based on your transformed equation, what is the slope of the linear equation $-4x + 8y = 24$?

The slope is $\frac{1}{2}$.

b. Complete the table to find solutions to the linear equation.

x	Transformed linear equation: $y = \frac{1}{2}x + 3$	y
-2	$y = \frac{1}{2}(-2) + 3$ $= -1 + 3$ $= 2$	2
0	$y = \frac{1}{2}(0) + 3$ $= 0 + 3$ $= 3$	3
2	$y = \frac{1}{2}(2) + 3$ $= 1 + 3$ $= 4$	4
4	$y = \frac{1}{2}(4) + 3$ $= 2 + 3$ $= 5$	5

---

c.   Graph the points on the coordinate plane.

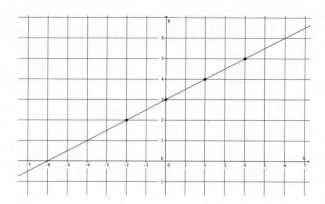

d.   Find the slope between any two points.

Using points $(0, 3)$ *and* $(2, 4)$:

$$m = \frac{4 - 3}{2 - 0}$$

$$= \frac{1}{2}$$

e.   The slope you found in part (d) should be equal to the slope you noted in part (a). If so, connect the points to make the line that is the graph of an equation of the form $y = mx + b$ that has slope m.

f.   Note the location (ordered pair) that describes where the line intersects the y-axis.

$(0, 3)$ is the location where the line intersects the y-axis.

2.   Solve the following equation for y: $9x + 3y = 21$.

$$9x + 3y = 21$$

$$9x - 9x + 3y = 21 - 9x$$

$$3y = 21 - 9x$$

$$\frac{3}{3}y = \frac{21}{3} - \frac{9}{3}x$$

$$y = 7 - 3x$$

$$y = -3x + 7$$

a.   Based on your transformed equation, what is the slope of the linear equation $9x + 3y = 21$?

The slope is -3.

b.   Complete the table to find solutions to the linear equation.

x	Transformed linear equation: $y = -3x + 7$	y
-1	$y = -3(-1) + 7$ $= 3 + 7$ $= 10$	10
0	$y = -3(0) + 7$ $= 0 + 7$ $= 7$	7
1	$y = -3(1) + 7$ $= -3 + 7$ $= 4$	4
2	$y = -3(2) + 7$ $= -6 + 7$ $= 1$	1

c.   Graph the points on the coordinate plane.

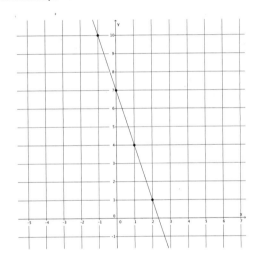

d.   Find the slope between any two points.

Using points $(1, 4)$ *and* $(2, 1)$:

$$m = \frac{4 - 1}{1 - 2}$$
$$= \frac{3}{-1}$$
$$= -3$$

e.   The slope you found in part (d) should be equal to the slope you noted in part (a). If so, connect the points to make the line that is the graph of an equation of the form $y = mx + b$ that has slope m.

f.   Note the location (ordered pair) that describes where the line intersects the y-axis.

$(0, 7)$ is the location where the line intersects the y-axis.

3.   Solve the following equation for y: $2x + 3y = -6$.

$$2x + 3y = -6$$
$$2x - 2x + 3y = -6 - 2x$$
$$3y = -6 - 2x$$
$$\frac{3}{3}y = \frac{-6}{3} - \frac{2}{3}x$$
$$y = -2 - \frac{2}{3}x$$
$$y = -\frac{2}{3}x - 2$$

a.   Based on your transformed equation, what is the slope of the linear equation $2x + 3y = -6$?

The slope is $-\frac{2}{3}$.

b.   Complete the table to find solutions to the linear equation.

x	Transformed linear equation: $y = -\frac{2}{3}x - 2$	y
-6	$y = -\frac{2}{3}(-6) - 2$ $= 4 - 2$ $= 2$	2
-3	$y = -\frac{2}{3}(-3) - 2$ $= 2 - 2$ $= 0$	0
0	$y = -\frac{2}{3}(0) - 2$ $= 0 - 2$ $= -2$	-2
3	$y = -\frac{2}{3}(3) - 2$ $= -2 - 2$ $= -4$	-4

c.   Graph the points on the coordinate plane.

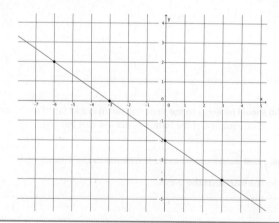

    d.   **Find the slope between any two points.**

        Using points $(-6, 2)$ *and* $(3, -4)$:

$$m = \frac{2 - (-4)}{-6 - 3}$$
$$= \frac{6}{-9}$$
$$= -\frac{2}{3}$$

    e.   **The slope you found in part (d) should be equal to the slope you noted in part (a). If so, connect the points to make the line that is the graph of an equation of the form $y = mx + b$ that has slope m.**

    f.   **Note the location (ordered pair) that describes where the line intersects the y-axis.**

        $(0, -2)$ is the location where the line intersects the y-axis.

4.   **Solve the following equation for y: $5x - y = 4$.**

$$5x - y = 4$$
$$5x - 5x - y = 4 - 5x$$
$$-y = 4 - 5x$$
$$y = -4 + 5x$$
$$y = 5x - 4$$

    a.   **Based on your transformed equation, what is the slope of the linear equation $5x - y = 4$?**

        The slope is 5.

    b.   **Complete the table to find solutions to the linear equation.**

x	Transformed linear equation: $y = 5x - 4$	y
-1	$y = 5(-1) - 4$ $= -5 - 4$ $= -9$	-9
0	$y = 5(0) - 4$ $= 0 - 4$ $= -4$	-4
1	$y = 5(1) - 4$ $= 5 - 4$ $= 1$	1
2	$y = 5(2) - 4$ $= 10 - 4$ $= 6$	6

c.   Graph the points on the coordinate plane.

d.   **Find the slope between any two points.**

Using points $(0, -4)$ *and* $(1, 1)$*:*

$$m = \frac{-4 - 1}{0 - 1}$$
$$= \frac{-5}{-1}$$
$$= 5$$

e.   The slope you found in part (d) should be equal to the slope you noted in part (a). If so, connect the points to make the line that is the graph of an equation of the form $y = mx + b$ that has slope m.

f.   Note the location (ordered pair) that describes where the line intersects the y-axis.

$(0, -4)$ *is the location where the line intersects the* y*-axis.*

Lesson 18: There is Only One Line Passing Through a Given Point with a Given Slope

Student Outcomes

- Students graph equations in the form of $y = mx + b$ using information about slope and y-intercept.
- Students know that if they have two straight lines with the same slope and a common point that the lines are the same.

Lesson Notes

The Opening Exercise requires students to examine part (f) from the problem set of Lesson 17. Each part (f) requires students to identify the point where the graph of the line intersects the y-axis. Knowing that this point represents the y-intercept and that it is the point $(0, b)$ in the equation $y = mx + b$ is integral for the content in the lesson.

To keep consistent, throughout the lesson students form the slope triangle with points P, Q, and R. Since slope has been defined in terms of lengths of sides of similar triangles, there is notation and verbiage about numbers in terms of distances. As you work through the examples, make clear that the lengths of the slope triangle are positive distances, but that does not necessarily mean that the slope must be positive (see Example 2). Remind students that graphs of lines with positive slopes are *left-to-right inclining* and graphs of lines with negative slopes are *left-to-right declining*.

Coordinate planes are provided for students in the exercises of this lesson, but they will need graph paper to complete the Problem Set.

Classwork

Opening Exercise (5 minutes)

Examine each of the graphs and their equations below. Identify the coordinates of the point where the line intersects the y-axis. Describe the relationship between the point and the equation $y = mx + b$.

a. $y = \frac{1}{2}x + 3$

b. $y = -3x + 7$

c. $y = -\frac{2}{3}x - 2$

d. $y = 5x - 4$

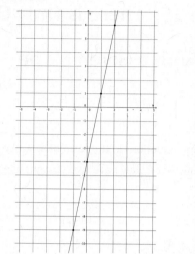

MP.8

Points noted in graphs above where the line intersects the y-axis:

a. $y = \frac{1}{2}x + 3$, $(0, 3)$

b. $y = -3x + 7$, $(0, 7)$

c. $y = -\frac{2}{3}x - 2$, $(0, -2)$

d. $y = 5x - 4$, $(0, -4)$

In each equation, the number b was the y-coordinate of the point where the line intersected the y-axis.

Discussion (5 minutes)

- In the last lesson, we transformed the standard form of a linear equation $ax + by = c$, into what was referred to as the slope-intercept form $y = mx + b$. We know that the slope is represented by m, but we did not discuss the meaning of b. In the Opening Exercise you were asked to note the location (ordered pair) that describes where the line intersected the y-axis.

- What do you notice about the value of b in relation to the point where the graph of the equation intersected the y-axis?

MP.7

  □ *The value of b was the same number as the y-coordinate of each location.*

- When a linear equation is in the form $y = mx + b$, it is known as the slope-intercept form because this form provides information about the slope, m, and y-intercept, $(0, b)$ of the graph. The y-intercept is defined as the location on the graph where a line intersects the y-axis.

- In this lesson, we develop the last tool that we need in order to prove that the graph of a linear equation in two variables $ax + by = c$, where a, b, and c are constants is a straight line. We will show that if two straight lines have the same slope and pass through the same point, then they are the same line.

MP.3

- Since an equation of the form $y = mx + b$ provides information about both the y-intercept and slope, we will use this equation to graph lines.

- Recall that we began discussing slope graphically, $m = \frac{|QR|}{|PQ|}$:

Lesson 18: There is Only One Line Passing Through a Given Point with a Given Slope

Date: 11/8/13

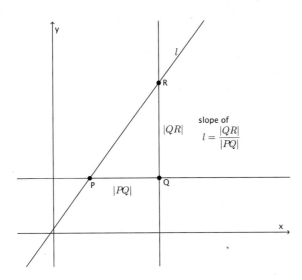

Example 1 (6 minutes)

Graph equation in the form of $y = mx + b$.

Example 1

Graph the equation $y = \frac{2}{3}x + 1$. **Name the slope and** y**-intercept.**

The slope, $m = \frac{2}{3}$ **and the** y**-intercept is** $(0, 1)$**.**

- ▪ To graph the equation, we must begin with the known point. In this case the y-intercept. We cannot begin with the slope because the slope describes the rate of change between two points. That means we need a point to begin with. On a graph, we plot the point $(0, 1)$.

Next, we use the slope to find the second point. The slope tells us exactly how many units to go to the right to find point Q, and then how many vertical units we need to go from Q to find point R. How many units will we go to the right in order to find point Q? How do you know?

> ▫ *We need to go 3 units to the right of point P to find Q. We go 3 units because $|PQ| = 3$.*

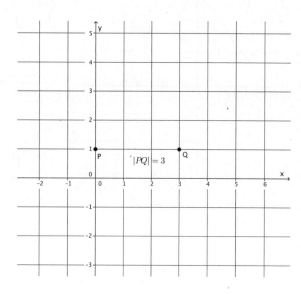

- How many vertical units from point Q must we go to find point R? How do you know?
  - ▫ *We need to go 2 units from point Q to find R. We go 2 units because $|QR| = 2$.*
- Will we go up from point Q or down from point Q to find point R? How do you know?
  - ▫ *We need to go up because the slope is positive. That means that the line will be left-to-right inclining.*

▪ Since we know that the line joining two distinct points of the form $y = mx + b$ has slope m, and we specifically constructed points P and R with the slope in mind, we can join the points with a line.

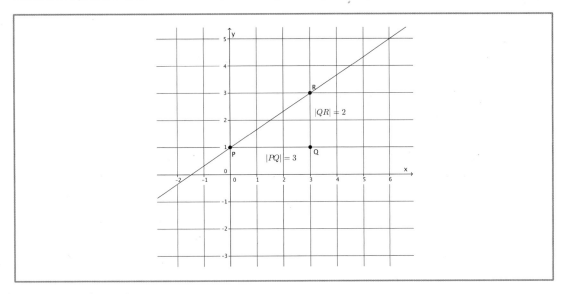

Example 2 (4 minutes)

Graph equation in the form of $y = mx + b$.

Example 2

Graph the equation $y = -\dfrac{3}{4}x - 2$. **Name the slope and y-intercept.**

The slope, $m = -\dfrac{3}{4}$ and the y-intercept is $(0, -2)$.

▪ How do we begin?

　□ *We must begin by putting a known point on the graph, $(0, -2)$.*

- How many units will we go to the right in order to find point Q? How do you know?
  - *We need to go 4 units to the right of point P to find Q. We go 4 units because $|PQ| = 4$.*

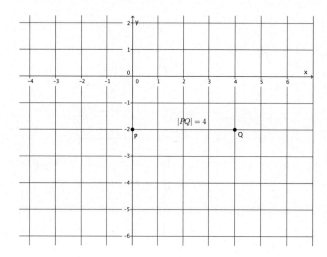

- How many units from point Q must we go to find point R? How do you know?
  - *We need to go 3 units from point Q to find R. We go 3 units because $|QR| = 3$.*
- Will we go up from point Q or down from point Q to find R? How do you know?
  - *We need to go down from point Q to point R because the slope is negative. That means that the line will be left-to-right declining.*

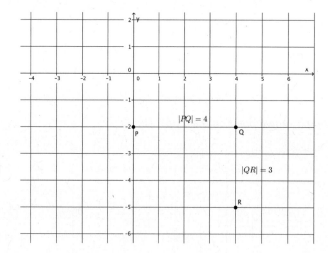

- Now we draw the line through the points P and R.

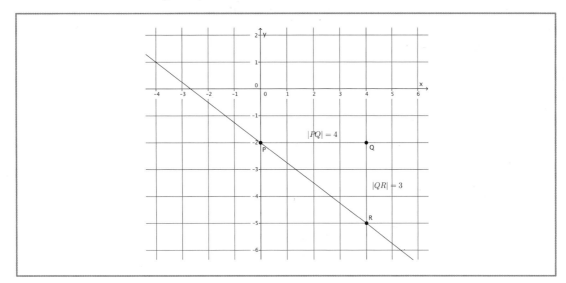

Example 3 (4 minutes)

Graph equation in the form of $y = mx + b$.

- Graph the equation $y = 4x - 7$. Name the slope and y-intercept.
  - *The slope, $m = 4$ and the y-intercept is $(0, -7)$.*
- How do we begin?
  - *We must begin by putting a known point on the graph, $(0, -7)$.*

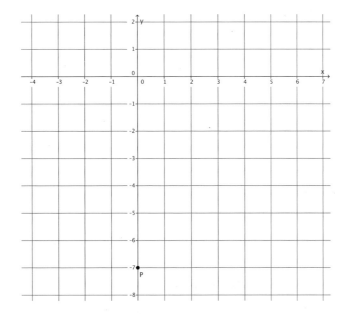

	Lesson 18:	There is Only One Line Passing Through a Given Point with a Given Slope
	Date:	11/8/13

263

- Notice this time that the slope is the integer 4. In the last two examples, our slopes have been in the form of a fraction so that we can use the information in the numerator and denominator to determine the lengths of $|PQ|$ and $|QR|$. If $m = \frac{|QR|}{|PQ|} = 4$, then what fraction can we use to represent slope to help us graph?

  □ *The number 4 is equivalent to the fraction $\frac{4}{1}$.*

- How many units will we go to the right in order to find point Q? How do you know?

  □ *We need to go 1 unit to the right of point P to find Q. We go 1 unit because $|PQ| = 1$.*

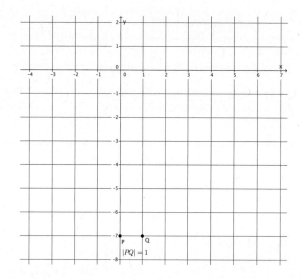

- How many vertical units from point Q must we go to find point R? How do you know?

  □ *We need to go 4 units from point Q to find R. We go 4 units because $|QR| = 4$.*

- Will we go up from point Q or down from point Q to find R? How do you know?

  □ *We need to go up from point Q to point R because the slope is positive. That means that the line will be left-to-right inclining.*

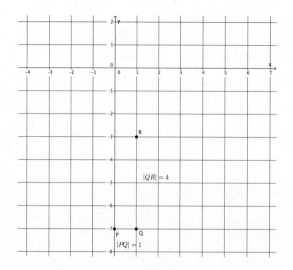

There is Only One Line Passing Through a Given Point with a Given Slope
11/8/13

▪ Now we join the points P and R to make the line.

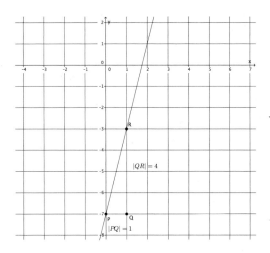

Exercises 1–4 (9 minutes)

Students complete Exercises 1–4 individually or in pairs.

Exercises 1–4

1. Graph the equation $y = \frac{5}{2}x - 4$.

    a. **Name the slope and the y-intercept.**

    The slope is $m = \frac{5}{2}$ and the y-intercept is $(0, -4)$.

    b. **Graph the known point, then use the slope to find a second point before drawing the line.**

    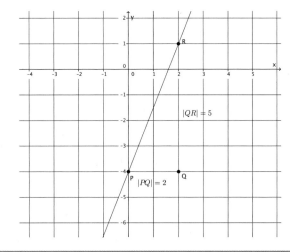

COMMON CORE™

Lesson 18:	There is Only One Line Passing Through a Given Point with a Given Slope
Date:	11/8/13

265

© 2013 Common Core, Inc. All rights reserved. **commoncore.org**

2. Graph the equation $y = -3x + 6$.

    a. Name the slope and the y-intercept.

        The slope is $m = -3$ and the y-intercept is $(0, 6)$.

    b. Graph the known point, then use the slope to find a second point before drawing the line.

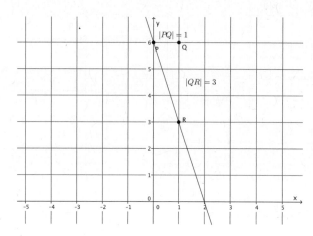

3. The equation $y = 1x + 0$ can be simplified to $y = x$. Graph the equation $y = x$.

    a. Name the slope and the y-intercept.

        The slope is $m = 1$ and the y-intercept is $(0, 0)$.

    b. Graph the known point, then use the slope to find a second point before drawing the line.

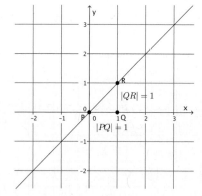

4.   Graph the point $(0, 2)$.

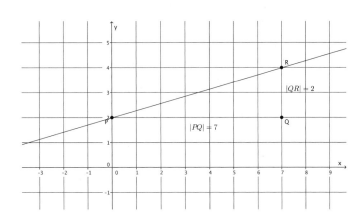

a.   Find another point on the graph using the slope, $m = \frac{2}{7}$.

b.   Connect the points to make the line.

c.   Draw a different line that goes through the point $(0, 2)$ with slope $m = \frac{2}{7}$. What do you notice?

Only one line can be drawn through the given point with the given slope.

Discussion (8 minutes)

The following proof is optional. An exercise, below the discussion, can be used as an alternative.

- Now we must show that if two straight lines have the same slope and pass through the same point, then they are the same line, which is what you observed in Exercise 4.

- We let l and l' be two lines with the same slope m passing through the same point P. Since m is a number, m could be positive, negative, or equal to zero. For this proof, we will let $m > 0$. Since $m > 0$, both lines l and l' are left-to-right inclining.

- Since we are trying to show that l and l' are the same line, let's assume that they are not and prove that our assumption is false.

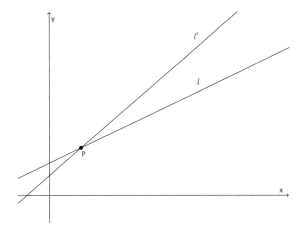

- Using our first understanding of slope, we will pick a point Q one unit to the right of point P. Then draw a line parallel to the y-axis going through point Q, as shown.

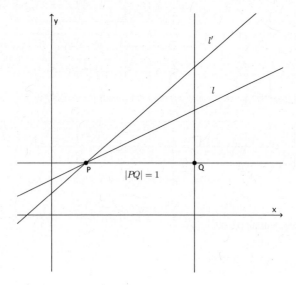

- Now we label the point of intersection of the line we just drew and line l and l' as R and R', respectively.

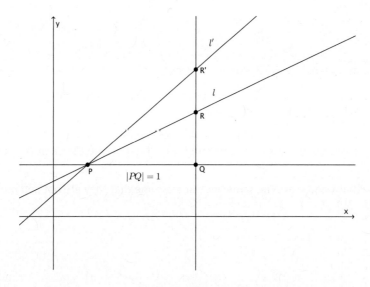

- By definition of slope, the length $|QR|$ is the slope of line l and the length of $|QR'|$ is the slope of line l'. What do we know about the slopes of lines l and l'?

  □ *The slopes are the same.*

- Then what do we know about the lengths $|QR|$ and $|QR'|$?

  □ *They must be equal.*

- For that reason points R and R' must coincide. This means lines l and l' are the same line, not as we originally drew them. Therefore, there is just one line passing through a given point with a given slope.

	Lesson 18:	There is Only One Line Passing Through a Given Point with a Given
		Slope
	Date:	11/8/13

Exercises 5–6 (8 minutes)

Students complete Exercises 5–6 individually or in pairs.

Exercises 5–6

5. A bank put 10 into a savings account when you opened the account. Eight weeks later you have a total of 24.
Assume you saved the same amount every week.

   a. If y is the total amount of money in the savings account and x represents the number of weeks, write an
equation in the form $y = mx + b$ that describes the situation.

   $$24 = m(8) + 10$$
   $$14 = 8m$$
   $$\frac{14}{8} = m$$
   $$\frac{7}{4} = m$$
   $$y = \frac{7}{4}x + 10$$

   b. Identify the slope and the y-intercept. What do these numbers represent?

   The slope is $\frac{7}{4}$ and the y-intercept is $(0, 10)$. The y-intercept represents the amount of money the bank gave

   me, in the amount of 10. The slope represents the amount of money I save each week, $\frac{7}{4} = \$1.75$.

   c. Graph the equation on a coordinate plane.

   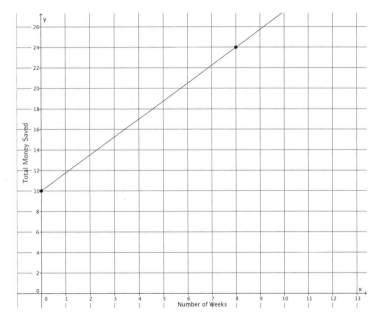

   d. Could any other line represent this situation? For example, could a line through point $(0, 10)$ with slope $\frac{7}{5}$
represent the amount of money you save each week? Explain.

   No, a line through point $(0, 10)$ with slope $\frac{7}{5}$ cannot represent this situation. That line would show that at
   the end of the 8 weeks I would have 21.20, but I was told that I would have 24 by the end of the 8 weeks.

---

6.   A group of friends are on a road trip. So far they have driven 120 miles. They continue their trip and drive at a constant rate of 50 miles per hour.

a.   Let y represent the total distance traveled in x hours. Write an equation to represent the total number of miles driven in x hours.

$$y = 50x + 120$$

b.   Identify the slope and the y-intercept. What do these numbers represent?

The slope is 50 and represents the rate of driving. The y-intercept is 120 and represents the number of miles they had already driven before driving at the given constant rate.

c.   Graph the equation on a coordinate plane.

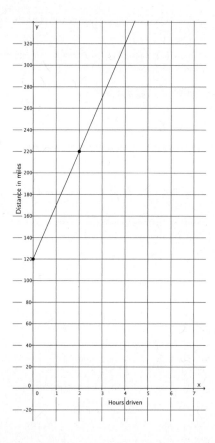

d.   Could any other line represent this situation? For example, could a line through point $(0, 120)$ with slope 75 represent the total distance the friends drive? Explain.

No, a line through point $(0, 120)$ with a slope of 75 could not represent this situation. That line would show that after an hour the friends traveled a total distance of 195 miles. According to the information given, the friends would only have traveled 170 miles after one hour.

Closing (4 minutes)

Summarize, or ask students to summarize, the main points from the lesson:

- We know that in the equation $y = mx + b$, $(0, b)$ is the location where the graph of the line intersects the y-axis.
- We know how to graph a line using a point, namely the y-intercept, and the slope.
- We know that there is only one line with a given slope passing through a given point.

Lesson Summary

The equation $y = mx + b$ is in slope-intercept form. The number m represents the slope of the graph and the point $(0, b)$ is the location where the graph of the line intersects the y-axis.

To graph a line from the slope-intercept form of a linear equation, begin with the known point, $(0, b)$, then use the slope to find a second point. Connect the points to graph the equation.

There is only one line passing through a given point with a given slope.

Exit Ticket (4 minutes)

Name _____   Date _____

Lesson 18: There is Only One Line Passing Through a Given Point with a Given Slope

Exit Ticket

Mrs. Hodson said that the graphs of the equations below are incorrect. Find the student's errors and correctly graph the equations.

1. Student graph of $y = \frac{1}{2}x + 4$.

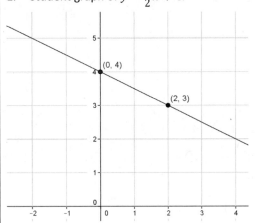

Error:

Correct graph of equation:

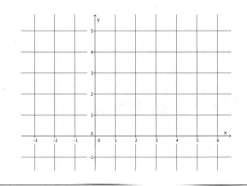

2. Student graph of $y = -\frac{3}{5}x - 1$.

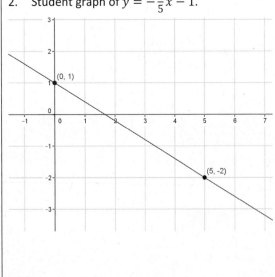

Error:

Correct graph of equation:

Exit Ticket Sample Solutions

Mrs. Hodson said that the graphs of the equations below are incorrect. Find the student's errors and correctly graph the equations.

1. Student graph of the equation $y = \frac{1}{2}x + 4$.

Error: *The student should have gone up 1 unit when finding $|QR|$ since the slope is positive.*

Correct graph of equation:

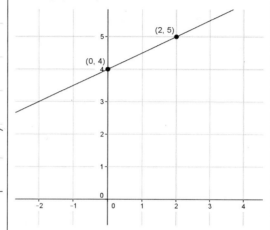

2. Student graph of the equation $y = -\frac{3}{5}x - 1$.

Error: *The student did not find the y intercept correctly. It should be the point $(0, -1)$.*

Correct graph of equation:

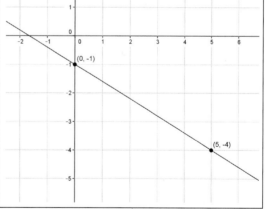

COMMON CORE™

Lesson 18:

Date:

There is Only One Line Passing Through a Given Point with a Given Slope

11/8/13

273

Problem Set Sample Solutions

Students practice graphing equations using y-intercept and slope. Students need graph paper to complete the problem set. Optional problem 11 has students show that there is only one line passing through a point with a given negative slope.

1. Graph the equation $y = \frac{4}{5}x - 5$.

 a. Name the slope and the y-intercept.

  The slope is $m = \frac{4}{5}$ and the y-intercept is $(0, -5)$.

 b. Graph the known point, and then use the slope to find a second point before drawing the line.

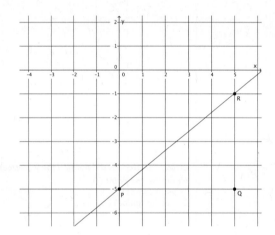

2. Graph the equation $y = x + 3$.

 a. Name the slope and the y-intercept.

  The slope is $m = 1$ and the y-intercept is $(0, 3)$.

 b. Graph the known point, and then use the slope to find a second point before drawing the line.

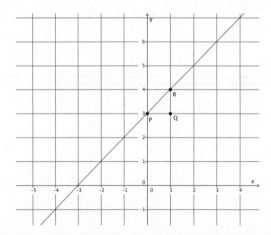

COMMON CORE™ Lesson 18: There is Only One Line Passing Through a Given Point with a Given Slope 274

Date: 11/8/13

3.   Graph the equation $y = -\frac{4}{3}x + 4$.

a.   Name the slope and the y-intercept.

The slope is $m = -\frac{4}{3}$ and the y-intercept is $(0,\ 4)$.

b.   Graph the known point, and then use the slope to find a second point before drawing the line.

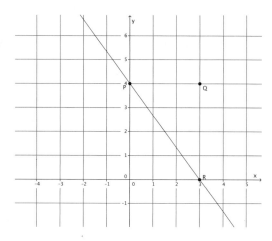

4.   Graph the equation $y = \frac{5}{2}x$.

a.   Name the slope and the y-intercept.

The slope is $m = \frac{5}{2}$ and the y-intercept is $(0,0)$.

b.   Graph the known point, and then use the slope to find a second point before drawing the line.

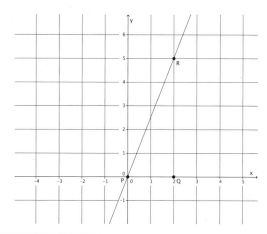

5. Graph the equation $y = 2x - 6$.

    a. Name the slope and the y-intercept.

      The slope is $m = 2$ and the y-intercept is $(0, -6)$.

    b. Graph the known point, and then use the slope to find a second point before drawing the line.

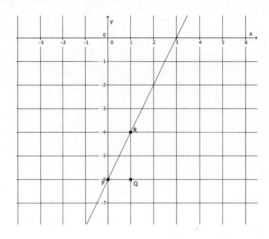

6. Graph the equation $y = -5x + 9$.

    a. Name the slope and the y-intercept.

      The slope is $m = -5$ and the y-intercept is $(0, 9)$.

    b. Graph the known point, and then use the slope to find a second point before drawing the line.

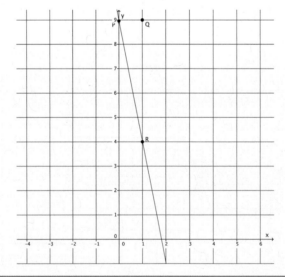

COMMON CORE™

Lesson 18:   There is Only One Line Passing Through a Given Point with a Given
          Slope
Date: 11/8/13

276

7.   Graph the equation $y = \frac{1}{3}x + 1$.

   a.   Name the slope and the y-intercept.

   The slope is $m = \frac{1}{3}$ and the y-intercept is $(0, 1)$.

   b.   Graph the known point, and then use the slope to find a second point before drawing the line.

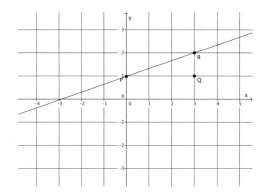

8.   Graph the equation $5x + 4y = 8$. (Hint: transform the equation so that it is of the form $y = mx + b$.)

   a.   Name the slope and the y-intercept.

$$5x + 4y = 8$$
$$5x - 5x + 4y = 8 - 5x$$
$$4y = 8 - 5x$$
$$\frac{4}{4}y = \frac{8}{4} - \frac{5}{4}x$$
$$y = 2 - \frac{5}{4}x$$
$$y = -\frac{5}{4}x + 2$$

   The slope is $m = -\frac{5}{4}$ and the y-intercept is $(0, 2)$.

   b.   Graph the known point, and then use the slope to find a second point before drawing the line.

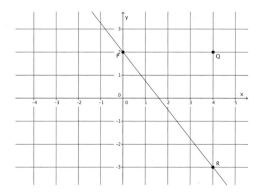

9.   Graph the equation $-2x + 5y = 30$.

a.   Name the slope and the y-intercept.

$$-2x + 5y = 30$$
$$2x + 2x + 5y = 30 + 2x$$
$$5y = 30 + 2x$$
$$\frac{5}{5}y = \frac{30}{5} + \frac{2}{5}x$$
$$y = 6 + \frac{2}{5}x$$
$$y = \frac{2}{5}x + 6$$

The slope is $m = \frac{2}{5}$ and the y-intercept is $(0, 6)$.

b.   Graph the known point, and then use the slope to find a second point before drawing the line.

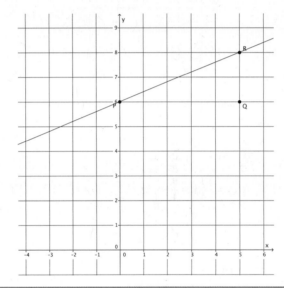

COMMON
CORE™

Lesson 18:   There is Only One Line Passing Through a Given Point with a Given
Slope
Date: 11/8/13

278

10. Let l and l' be two lines with the same slope m passing through the same point P. Show that there is only one line with a slope m, where $m < 0$, passing through the given point P. Draw a diagram if needed.

First assume that there are two different lines l and l' with the same negative slope passing through P. From point P, I mark a point Q one unit to the right. Then I draw a line parallel to the y-axis through point Q. The intersection of this line and line l and l' are noted with points R and R'. By definition of slope, the lengths $|QR|$ and $|QR'|$ represent the slopes of lines l and l', respectively. We are given that the lines have the same slope, which means that lengths $|QR|$ and $|QR'|$ are equal. Since that is true, then points R and R' coincide and so do lines l and l'. Therefore, our assumption that they are different lines is false; l and l' must be the same line. Therefore, there is only one line with slope m passing through the given point P.

Lesson 19: The Graph of a Linear Equation in Two Variables is a Line

Student Outcomes

- Students prove that any point on the graph of $y = mx + b$ is on a line l and that any point on a line l is a point on the graph of $y = mx + b$.
- Students graph linear equations on the coordinate plane.

Lesson Notes

Included in this and the next several lessons are an analytical approach to understanding linear equations and their graphs. Though the analytical understandings are not *required* for Grade 8 students, it is of tremendous value for students to understand the proofs of common assertions about lines. For that reason, these lessons are structured to offer extensions (i.e., the proofs) in cases where the students are ready, and also to provide alternate activities that deepen conceptual understanding. The theorems are presented to students and, based on the readiness of each class, the teacher can choose to discuss the proof of the theorem or have students explore the theorem experimentally by completing the exercises of the alternate activity.

This lesson is the result of many lessons leading up to this one. In previous lessons, it was stated that there were four things that needed to be proved about lines before we could state, definitively, that the graph of a linear equation in two variables is in fact a line.

1. We must define a number for each non-vertical line that can be used to measure the "steepness" or "slant" of the line. Once defined, this number will be called the *slope* of the line and is often referred to as the "rate of change".

2. We must show that *any* two points on a non-vertical line can be used to find the slope of the line.

3. We must show that the line joining two points on the graph of a linear equation of the form $y = mx + b$ has slope m.

4. We must show that there is only one line passing through a given point with a given slope.

This lesson is the conclusion of that work, and it is an important result for students to observe. There are two options for the first part of the lesson. You may choose to use the formal proof in the first discussion beginning on page 281 and Exercise 1 beginning on page 283. This lesson path skips Exercises 2–5 and resumes the lesson with Example 1 on page 291. The other option is to skip the Discussion and Exercise 1 on the first five pages, having students examine several equations in the form of $ax + by = c$, create their graphs, and informally conclude that the graphs of equations of this type always result in lines. The alternate activity begins on page 285 of this lesson with Exercises 2–8. Following these exercises is Example 1 on page 291 and Exercises 9–11 where students learn how to graph a linear equation using intercepts. Students need graph paper to complete the Exercises and the Problem Set.

Classwork

Discussion (15 minutes)

Now that all of the necessary tools have been developed, we are ready to show that the graph of a linear equation in two variables in the form $y = mx + b$, where b is always a constant, is a non-vertical line.

- To prove that the graph of a linear equation is a line, we need to show the following:

  (1) *any* point on the graph of $y = mx + b$ is a point on a line l, and

  (2) *any* point on the line l is a point on the graph of $y = mx + b$.

- Why do we need to show both (1) and (2)? Consider the following: Let P and Q be two distinct points on the graph of $y = mx + b$. Let l be the line passing through points P and Q. Also, let the graph of $y = mx + b$ be the collection of red segments denoted by G, as shown.

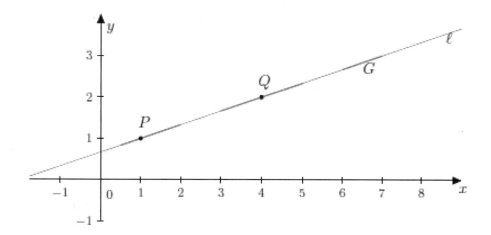

If G is the collection of red segments, as shown, then (1) is true, but (2) is not. Therefore, if we can show that both (1) and (2) are true, then we know that the graph of $y = mx + b$ is exactly the same as the graph of line l.

- Let's look at a specific case before proving (1) and (2) in general. Show that the graph of $y = 2x + 3$ is a non-vertical line.

- We need two points that we know are on the graph of $y = 2x + 3$. Are points $(0, 3)$ and $(4, 11)$ solutions to the equation $y = 2x + 3$? Explain.

  □ *Yes, because $3 = 2(0) + 3$ and $11 = 2(4) + 3$ are true statements.*

- Let line l pass through the points $P = (0, 3)$ and $Q = (1, 5)$. By our work in Lesson 17, we know that an equation in the form of $y = mx + b$ has slope m. Then, the slope of $y = 2x + 3$ is 2 and therefore the slope of line l is 2. We claim that the graph of $y = 2x + 3$ is the line l.

Lesson 19:	The Graph of a Linear Equation in Two Variables is a Line
Date:	11/8/13

281

MP.2

- Now we will show that *any* point on the graph of $y = 2x + 3$ is on line l. Let R be any point on the graph of $y = 2x + 3$ (other than points P and Q because if $R = P$ or if $R = Q$ there would be nothing to prove; we already showed that they are solutions to the equation $y = 2x + 3$). Let l' be the line passing through points P and R, as shown.

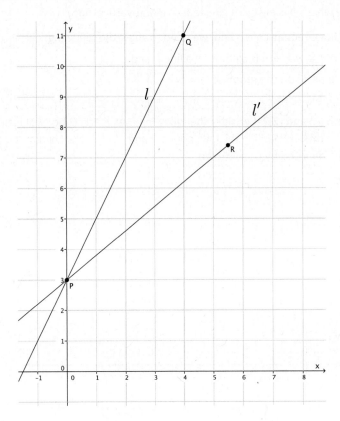

- We need to show that line l' has a slope of 2. We have done this before in Lesson 16. Since P and R are on the graph of $y = 2x + 3$, then the coordinates of $P = (p_1, 2p_1 + 3)$ and $R = (r_1, 2r_1 + 3)$. We also know the following:

$$\text{slope of } l' = \frac{(2p_1 + 3) - (2r_1 + 3)}{p_1 - r_1}$$

$$= \frac{2p_1 - 2r_1}{p_1 - r_1}$$

$$= \frac{2(p_1 - r_1)}{p_1 - r_1}$$

$$= 2$$

- Now that we know the slope of l' is 2, what can we say about lines l and l'? Hint: What do we know about lines that have the same slope and pass through the same point?

  □ *Lines l and l' must be the same line. There can be only one line with a slope of 2 that passes through a given point, in this case P.*

- Therefore, point R must be on line l and the proof that any point on the graph of $y = 2x + 3$ is on line l is finished.

- Now we must show that *any* point on l is on the graph of $y = 2x + 3$. Let S be *any* point on l (except for P and Q for the same reason as before). Using $S = (s_1, s_2)$ and $P = (0, 3)$ in the slope formula, we get the following:

$$\text{slope of } l = \frac{s_2 - 3}{s_1 - 0}$$

We know the slope of l is 2.

$$2 = \frac{s_2 - 3}{s_1 - 0}$$
$$2(s_1 - 0) = s_2 - 3$$
$$2s_1 = s_2 - 3$$
$$2s_1 + 3 = s_2 - 3 + 3$$
$$2s_1 + 3 = s_2$$

The equation above shows that point $S = (s_1, s_2)$ is a solution to the equation $y = 2x + 3$ and must be on the graph of $y = 2x + 3$.

- We have just shown that any point R on the graph of $y = 2x + 3$ is on line l and any point S on line l is on the graph of $y = 2x + 3$. Therefore, the proof is complete.

Exercise 1 (10 minutes)

Students work in pairs or small groups to prove the theorem in general. This is an optional exercise and related directly to the optional discussion above. If you chose the alternative path for this lesson, then this exercise should not be assigned.

Exercise 1

Theorem: The graph of a linear equation $y = mx + b$ is a non-vertical line with slope m and passing through $(0, b)$, where b is a constant.

1. Prove the theorem by completing parts (a)–(c). Given two distinct points, P and Q, on the graph of $y = mx + b$ and let l be the line passing through P and Q. You must show:

   (1) any point on the graph of $y = mx + b$ is on line l, and

   (2) any point on the line l is on the graph of $y = mx + b$.

---

a. Proof of (1): Let R be any point on the graph of $y = mx + b$. Show that R is on l. Begin by assuming it is not. Assume the graph looks like the diagram below where R is on l'.

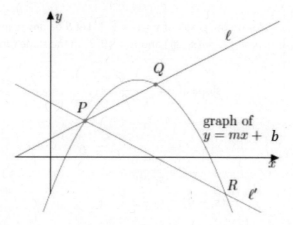

What is the slope of line l?

Since the points P and Q are on the graph of $y = mx + b$, then we know that the slope of the line passing through those points must have slope m. Therefore, line l has slope m.

What is the slope of line l'?

We know that point R is on the graph of $y = mx + b$. Then the coordinates of point $R = (r_1, mr_1 + b)$ because R is a solution to $y = mx + b$ and $r_2 = mr_1 + b$. Similarly, the coordinates of $P = (p_1, mp_2 + b)$. Then,

$$\begin{aligned} slope\ of\ l' &= \frac{(mp_2 + b) - (mr_2 + b)}{p_1 - r_1} \\ &= \frac{mp_2 + b - mr_2 - b}{p_1 - r_1} \\ &= \frac{mp_2 - mr_2}{p_1 - r_1} \\ &= \frac{m(p_2 - r_2)}{p_1 - r_1} \\ &= m \end{aligned}$$

What can you conclude about lines l and l'? Explain.

Lines l and l' are the same line. Both lines go through point P and have slope m. There can be only one line with a given slope going through a given point; therefore, line $l = l'$.

b.   **Proof of (2): Let S be any point on line l, as shown.**

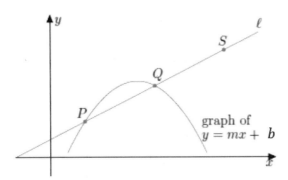

Show that S is a solution to $y = mx + b$. Hint: Use the point $(0, b)$.

Point S is on line l. Let $S = (s_1, s_2)$. Then,

$$\text{slope of } l = \frac{s_2 - b}{s_1 - 0}$$

We know the slope of l is m; therefore,

$$m = \frac{s_2 - b}{s_1 - 0}$$

$$m(s_1 - 0) = s_2 - b$$

$$ms_1 = s_2 - b$$

$$ms_1 + b = s_2 - b + b$$

$$ms_1 + b = s_2$$

$$s_2 = ms_1 + b$$

which shows S is a solution to $y = mx + b$.

c.   **Now that you have shown that any point on the graph of $y = mx + b$ is on line l (part a), and any point on line l is on the graph of $y = mx + b$ (part b), what can you conclude about the graphs of linear equations?**

The graph of a linear equation is a line.

Exercises 2–8 (25 minutes)

These exercises should be completed in place of the Discussion and Exercise 1 above. Students need graph paper to complete the following exercises. This is the alternate activity that was described in the Lesson Notes. For these exercises, students graph a linear equation and informally verify that any point on the graph of the equation is on the line and that any point on the line is a point on the graph of the equation. Exercises 6–8 ask students to draw these conclusions based on their work in Exercises 2–5. Consider having a class discussion based on Exercises 6–8, where students share their conclusions. End the discussion by making it clear that the graph of a linear equation is a line. Then proceed with Example 1 and Exercises 9–11.

2. Use $x = 4$ and $x = -4$ to find two solutions to the equation $x + 2y = 6$. Plot the solutions as points on the coordinate plane and connect the points to make a line.

The solutions are $(4, 1)$ and $(-4, 5)$.

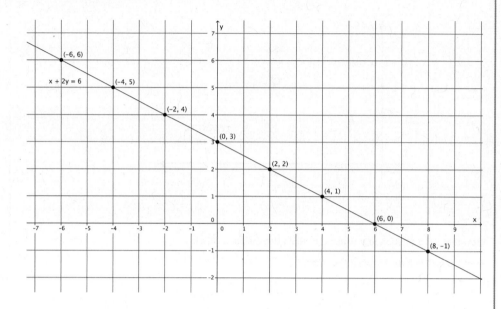

a. Identify two other points on the line with integer coordinates. Verify that they are solutions to the equation $x + 2y = 6$.

Choice of points and verifications will vary. Several possibilities are noted in the graph above.

b. When $x = 1$, what is the value of y? Does this solution appear to be a point on the line?

$$1 + 2y = 6$$
$$2y = 5$$
$$y = \frac{5}{2}$$

Yes, $\left(1, \frac{5}{2}\right)$ does appear to be a point on the line.

c. When $x = -3$, what is the value of y? Does this solution appear to be a point on the line?

$$-3 + 2y = 6$$
$$2y = 9$$
$$y = \frac{9}{2}$$

Yes, $\left(-3, \frac{9}{2}\right)$ does appear to be a point on the line.

d. Is the point $(3, 2)$ on the line?

No, $(3, 2)$ is not a point on the line.

Lesson 19: The Graph of a Linear Equation in Two Variables is a Line
Date: 11/8/13

e.   Is the point $(3, 2)$ a solution to the linear equation $x + 2y = 6$?

No, $(3, 2)$ is not a solution to $x + 2y = 6$ because

$$3 + 2(2) = 6$$
$$3 + 4 = 6$$
$$7 \neq 6$$

3.   Use $x = 4$ and $x = 1$ to find two solutions to the equation $3x - y = 9$. Plot the solutions as points on the coordinate plane and connect the points to make a line.

The solutions are $(4, 3)$ and $(1, -6)$.

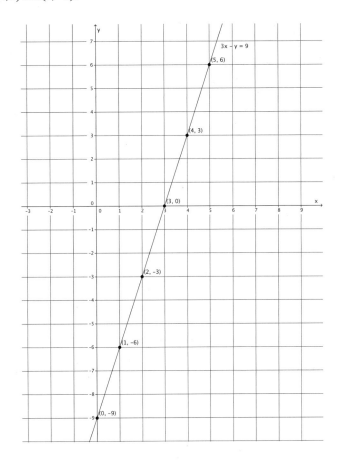

a.   Identify two other points on the line with integer coordinates. Verify that they are solutions to the equation $3x - y = 9$.

Choice of points and verifications will vary. Several possibilities are noted in the graph above.

b.   When $x = 4.5$, what is the value of y? Does this solution appear to be a point on the line?

$$3(4.5) - y = 9$$
$$13.5 - y = 9$$
$$-y = -4.5$$
$$y = 4.5$$

Yes, $(4.5, 4.5)$ does appear to be a point on the line.

c. When $x = \frac{1}{2}$, what is the value of y? Does this solution appear to be a point on the line?

$$3\left(\frac{1}{2}\right) - y = 9$$
$$\frac{3}{2} - y = 9$$
$$-y = 7.5$$
$$y = -7.5$$

Yes, $\left(\frac{1}{2}, -7.5\right)$ does appear to be a point on the line.

d. Is the point $(2, 4)$ on the line?

No, $(2, 4)$ is not a point on the line.

e. Is the point $(2, 4)$ a solution to the linear equation $3x - y = 9$?

No, $(2, 4)$ is not a solution to $3x - y = 9$ because

$$3(2) - 4 = 9$$
$$6 - 4 = 9$$
$$2 \neq 9$$

4. Use $x = 3$ and $x = -3$ to find two solutions to the equation $2x + 3y = 12$. Plot the solutions as points on the coordinate plane and connect the points to make a line.

The solutions are $(-3, 6)$ and $(3, 2)$.

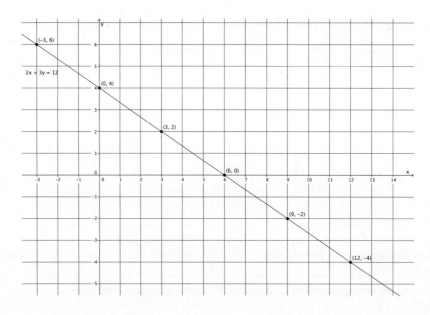

a. Identify two other points on the line with integer coordinates. Verify that they are solutions to the equation $2x + 3y = 12$.

Choice of points and verifications will vary. Several possibilities are noted in the graph above.

b.   When $x = 2$, what is the value of y? Does this solution appear to be a point on the line?

$$2(2) + 3y = 12$$
$$4 + 3y = 12$$
$$3y = 8$$
$$y = \frac{8}{3}$$

Yes, $\left(2, \frac{8}{3}\right)$ *does appear to be a point on the line.*

c.   When $x = -2$, what is the value of y? Does this solution appear to be a point on the line?

$$2(-2) + 3y = 12$$
$$-4 + 3y = 12$$
$$3y = 16$$
$$y = \frac{16}{3}$$

Yes, $\left(-2, \frac{16}{3}\right)$ *does appear to be a point on the line.*

d.   Is the point $(8, -3)$ on the line?

No, $(8, -3)$ *is not a point on the line.*

e.   Is the point $(8, -3)$ a solution to the linear equation $2x + 3y = 12$?

No, $(8, -3)$ *is not a solution to* $2x + 3y = 12$ *because*

$$2(8) + 3(-3) = 12$$
$$16 - 9 = 12$$
$$7 \neq 12$$

5.   Use $x = 4$ and $x = -4$ to find two solutions to the equation $x - 2y = 8$. Plot the solutions as points on the coordinate plane and connect the points to make a line.

The solutions are $(4, -2)$ *and* $(-4, -6)$.

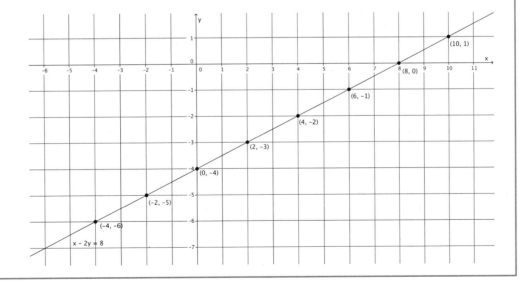

a. Identify two other points on the line with integer coordinates. Verify that they are solutions to the equation $x - 2y = 8$.

Choice of points and verifications will vary. Several possibilities are noted in the graph above.

b. When $x = 7$, what is the value of y? Does this solution appear to be a point on the line?

$$7 - 2y = 8$$
$$-2y = 1$$
$$y = -\frac{1}{2}$$

Yes, $\left(7, -\frac{1}{2}\right)$ does appear to be a point on the line.

c. When $x = -3$, what is the value of y? Does this solution appear to be a point on the line?

$$-3 - 2y = 8$$
$$-2y = 11$$
$$y = -\frac{11}{2}$$

Yes, $\left(-3, -\frac{11}{2}\right)$ does appear to be a point on the line.

d. Is the point $(-2, -3)$ on the line?

No, $(-2, -3)$ is not a point on the line.

e. Is the point $(-2, -3)$ a solution to the linear equation $x - 2y = 8$?

No, $(-2, -3)$ is not a solution to $x - 2y = 8$ because

$$-2 - 2(-3) = 8$$
$$-2 + 6 = 8$$
$$4 \neq 8$$

6. Based on your work in Exercises 2–5, what conclusions can you draw about the points on a line and solutions to a linear equation?

It appears that all points on the line represent a solution to the equation. That is, any point identified on the line is a solution to the linear equation.

MP.8

7. Based on your work in Exercises 2–5, will a point that is not a solution to a linear equation be a point on the graph of a linear equation? Explain.

No, each time we were given a point off the line in part (d), we verified that it was not a solution to the equation in part (e). For that reason, I would expect that all points not on the line would not be a solution to the equation.

8. Based on your work in Exercises 2–5, what conclusions can you draw about the graph of a linear equation?

The graph of a linear equation is a line.

Example 1 (4 minutes)

- Now that we know that the graph of a linear equation in two variables is a line and that there is only one line that can pass through two points, then we can easily graph equations using intercepts.

- We already know that the y-intercept is the location on the graph of a line where the line intersects the y-axis. The point of intersection will have coordinates $(0, y)$. Similarly, the x-intercept is the location on the graph of a line where the line intersects the x-axis. The point of intersection will have coordinates $(x, 0)$.

- To graph using intercepts, simply replace the symbols x and y with zero, one at a time, and solve.

- Graph the equation: $2x + 3y = 9$.

  Replace x with zero and solve for y to determine the y-intercept:

  $$2(0) + 3y = 9$$
  $$3y = 9$$
  $$y = 3$$

  The y-intercept is at $(0, 3)$.

  Replace y with zero and solve for x to determine the x-intercept:

  $$2x + 3(0) = 9$$
  $$2x = 9$$
  $$x = \frac{9}{2}$$

  The x-intercept is at $\left(\frac{9}{2}, 0\right)$.

- Now that we know the intercepts, we can place those two points on the graph and connect them to graph the linear equation $2x + 3y = 9$:

- Graphing using intercepts is an efficient way of graphing linear equations that are in standard form. Graphing using the slope and y-intercept is the most efficient way of graphing linear equations that are in slope-intercept form. Creating a table and finding solutions is another way we have learned how to graph linear equations. All three methods work, but some methods will save time depending on the form of the equation.

Exercise 9–11 (5 minutes)

9. **Graph the equation $-3x + 8y = 24$ using intercepts.**

$$-3x + 8y = 24$$
$$-3(0) + 8y = 24$$
$$8y = 24$$
$$y = 3$$

The y-intercept is $(0, 3)$.

$$-3x + 8y = 24$$
$$-3x + 8(0) = 24$$
$$-3x = 24$$
$$x = -8$$

The x-intercept is $(-8, 0)$.

10. **Graph the equation $x - 6y = 15$ using intercepts.**

$$x - 6y = 15$$
$$0 - 6y = 15$$
$$-6y = 15$$
$$y = -\frac{15}{6}$$
$$y = -\frac{5}{2}$$

The y-intercept Is $\left(0, -\frac{5}{2}\right)$.

$$x - 6y = 15$$
$$x - 6(0) = 15$$
$$x = 15$$

The x-intercept is $(15, 0)$.

11. Graph the equation $4x + 3y = 21$ using intercepts.

$$4x + 3y = 21$$
$$4(0) + 3y = 21$$
$$3y = 21$$
$$y = 7$$

The y-intercept is $(0, 7)$.

$$4x + 3y = 21$$
$$4x + 3(0) = 21$$
$$4x = 21$$
$$x = \frac{21}{4}$$

The x-intercept is $\left(\frac{21}{4}, 0\right)$.

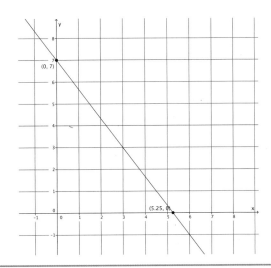

Closing (5 minutes)

Summarize, or ask students to summarize, the main points from the lesson:

- We know that to prove the graph of a linear equation is a line we have to show that any point on the graph of the equation is on the line, and any point on the line is on the graph of the equation.

- We can use what we know about slope and the fact that there is only one line with a given slope that goes through a given point, to prove that the graph of a linear equation is a line.

- We have another method for graphing linear equations: using intercepts.

Lesson Summary

The graph of a linear equation is a line. A linear equation can be graphed using two-points: the x-intercept and the y-intercept.

Example:

Graph the equation: $2x + 3y = 9$.

Replace x with zero and solve for y to determine the y-intercept:

$$2(0) + 3y = 9$$
$$3y = 9$$
$$y = 3$$

The y-intercept is at $(0, 3)$.

Replace y with zero and solve for x to determine the x-intercept:

$$2x + 3(0) = 9$$
$$2x = 9$$
$$x = \frac{9}{2}$$

The x-intercept is at $\left(\frac{9}{2}, 0\right)$.

Exit Ticket (5 minutes)

Name _____   Date _____

Lesson 19: The Graph of a Linear Equation in Two Variables is a Line

Exit Ticket

1. Graph the equation $y = \frac{5}{4}x - 10$ using the y-intercept and slope.

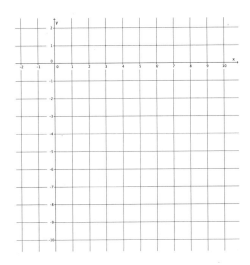

2. Graph the equation $5x - 4y = 40$ using intercepts.

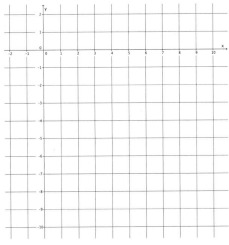

3. What can you conclude about the equations $y = \frac{5}{4}x - 10$ and $5x - 4y = 40$?

Exit Ticket Sample Solutions

1. Graph the equation $y = \frac{5}{4}x - 10$ using the y-intercept and slope.

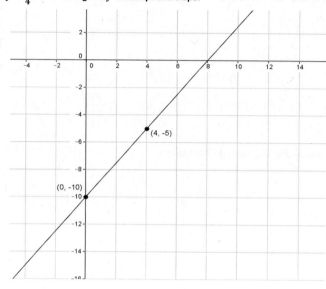

2. Graph the equation $5x - 4y = 40$ using intercepts.

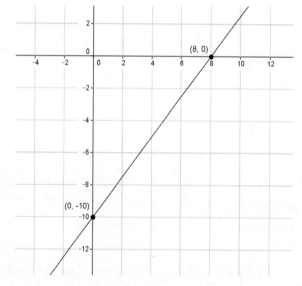

3. What can you conclude about the equations $y = \frac{5}{4}x - 10$ and $5x - 4y = 40$?

    Since the points $(0, -10)$, $(4, -5)$, and $(8, 0)$ are common to both graphs, then the lines must be the same. There is only one line that can pass through two points. If you transform the equation $y = \frac{5}{4}x - 10$ so that it is in standard form, it is the equation $5x - 4y = 40$.

Problem Set Sample Solutions

Now that students know the graph of a linear equation is a line, students practice graphing linear equations in two variables using an appropriate method.   Students need graph paper to complete the Problem Set.

1.   **Graph the equation:** $y = -6x + 12$.

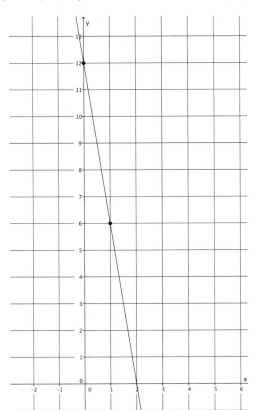

2.   **Graph the equation:** $9x + 3y = 18$.

$$9(0) + 3y = 18$$
$$3y = 18$$
$$y = 6$$

The y-intercept is $(0, 6)$.

$$9x + 3(0) = 18$$
$$9x = 18$$
$$x = 2$$

The x-intercept is $(2, 0)$.

3. **Graph the equation:** $y = 4x + 2$.

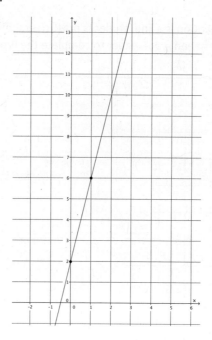

4. **Graph the equation:** $y = -\frac{5}{7}x + 4$.

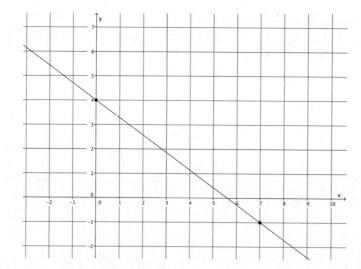

5. **Graph the equation:**

$$\frac{3}{4}x + y = 8.$$

$$\frac{3}{4}(0) + y = 8$$
$$y = 8$$

The y-intercept is $(0, 8)$.

$$\frac{3}{4}x + 0 = 8$$
$$\frac{3}{4}x = 8$$
$$x = \frac{32}{3}$$

The x-intercept is $\left(\frac{32}{3}, 0\right)$.

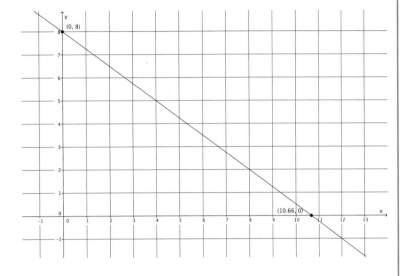

6. **Graph the equation:** $2x - 4y = 12$.

$$2(0) - 4y = 12$$
$$-4y = 12$$
$$y = -3$$

The y-intercept is $(0, -3)$.

$$2x - 4(0) = 12$$
$$2x = 12$$
$$x = 6$$

The x-intercept is $(6, 0)$.

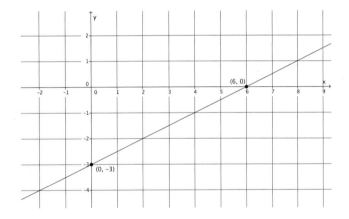

7. **Graph the equation:** $y = 3$. **What is the slope of the graph of this line?**

The slope of this line is zero.

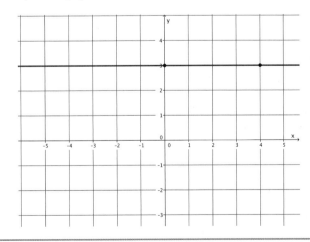

8.   Graph the equation: $x = -4$. What is the slope of the graph of this line?

The slope of this line is undefined.

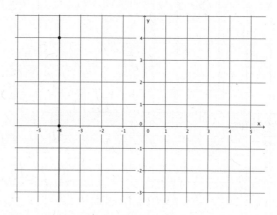

9.   Is the graph of $4x + 5y = \frac{3}{7}$ a line? Explain.

Yes, the graph of $4x + 5y = \frac{3}{7}$ is a line because it is a linear equation comprised of linear expressions on both side of the equal sign.

10. Is the graph of $6x^2 - 2y = 7$ a line? Explain.

Maybe. The equation $6x^2 - 2y = 7$ is not a linear equation because the expression on the left side of the equal sign is not a linear expression. If this were a linear equation, then I would be sure that it graphs as a line, but because it is not, I'm not sure what the graph of this equation would look like.

Lesson 20: Every Line is a Graph of a Linear Equation

Student Outcomes

- Students know that any non-vertical line is the graph of a linear equation in the form of $y = mx + b$, where b is a constant.
- Students write the equation that represents the graph of a line.

Lesson Notes

The proof that every line is the graph of a linear equation in the first discussion below is optional. If you choose to use the Discussion below, you will need to skip the Opening Exercise that begins on page 302 and resume the lesson with Example 1 on page 303. Complete all other examples and exercises that follow. As an alternative to the discussion below, you may choose to complete the opening activity by showing a graph of a line on the coordinate plane and having students attempt to name the equation of the line. Two graphs are provided for your use beginning on page 302. Have students write their equations and strategies for determining the equation of the line; then lead the discussion described on page 302. Once the Opening Exercise is complete, work through Example 1 on page 303 and the remaining examples and exercises in the lesson. Revisit the equations and strategies students developed by having them critique their reasoning in comparison to the work in the example; then continuing with the remainder of the lesson.

Classwork

Discussion (10 minutes)

- Now that we are confident that the graph of every linear equation is a line, can we say that every line is the graph of a linear equation? We can say yes with respect to vertical and horizontal lines, recall $x = c$ and $y = c$. But what about other non-vertical lines?
- We must prove that any non-vertical (and non-horizontal) line is a graph of a linear equation in the form of $y = mx + b$, where $m \neq 0$ and b are constants.
- Let l be any non-vertical (and non-horizontal) line. Suppose the slope of the line is m and that the line intersects the y-axis at point $Q = (0, b)$.
- First, we show that any point on the line l is a point on the graph of the linear equation $y = mx + b$.
- Let $P = (x, y)$ be any point on line l. We need to show that P is a solution to $y = mx + b$. Think about how we did this in the last lesson. What should we do?

  □ *Use the points P and Q in the slope formula:*

  $$m = \frac{y - b}{x - 0}$$
  $$mx = y - b$$
  $$mx + b = y - b + b$$
  $$mx + b = y$$

That shows that point P is a point on the graph of $y = mx + b$. Point Q is also on the graph of $y = mx + b$ because $b = m \cdot 0 + b$. Therefore, any point on the line l is a point on the graph of the linear equation $y = mx + b$.

P.3

- Now, we want to show that any point on the graph of $y = mx + b$ is on l.

- Let R be any point on the graph of the linear equation $y = mx + b$. We know that the graph of $y = mx + b$ is a line with slope m. Let's call this line l'. We know that Q is on l' because $b = m \cdot 0 + b$. Therefore, l' is a line with slope m that passes through point Q. But l is a line with slope m that passes through point Q. What does that mean about lines l and l'?

  - *The lines l and l' are the same line because there is only one line with a given slope that can go through a given point.*

- Therefore, R is a point on l.

- Now we can be certain that every line is a graph of a linear equation.

MP.3

Opening (10 minutes)

Show students Graph 1 below and challenge them to write the equation for the line. Provide students time to work independently, then in pairs. Lead a discussion where students share their strategies for developing the equation of the line. Ask students how they knew their equations were correct, i.e., did they verify that the points with integer coordinates were solutions to the equation they wrote? Ask students what kind of equation they wrote: linear or non-linear. Ask students if they were given another line, could they write an equation for it using their strategy. Show them Graph 2 and, again, ask them to write the equation of the line. Verify that they wrote the correct equation, and conclude the discussion by stating that every line is the graph of a linear equation.

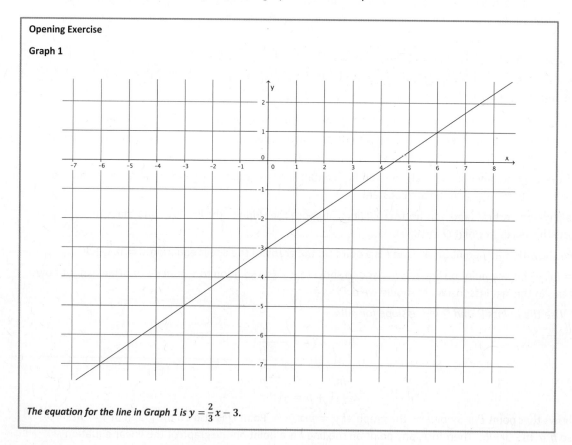

Opening Exercise

Graph 1

The equation for the line in Graph 1 is $y = \frac{2}{3}x - 3$.

Graph 2

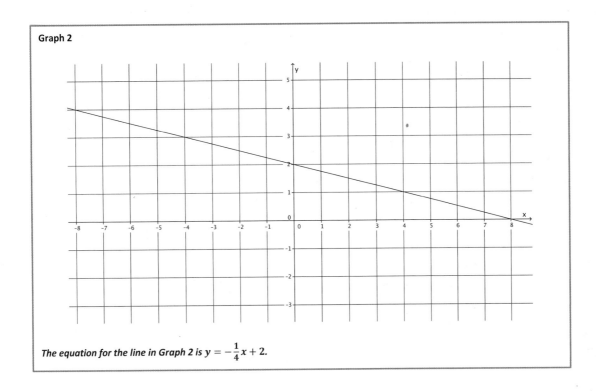

The equation for the line in Graph 2 is $y = -\frac{1}{4}x + 2$.

Example 1 (5 minutes)

- Given the graph of a line, we want to be able to write the equation that represents it.

- Which form of a linear equation do you think will be most valuable for this task, the standard form $ax + by = c$ or slope-intercept form $y = mx + b$?

  □ *The slope-intercept form because we can easily identify the slope and y-intercept from both the equation and the graph.*

- Write the equation that represents the graph of the line shown below:

- First, identify the y-intercept.
  - *The line intersects the y-axis at* $(0, 4)$.
- Now we must use what we know about slope to determine the slope of the line. Recall the following:

$$m = \frac{|QR|}{|PQ|}$$

  The point P is represents our y-intercept. Let's locate a point R on the line with integer coordinates.
  - *We can use the point* $(5, 2)$ *or* $(-5, 6)$.
- We can use either point. For this example, let's use $(5, 2)$.

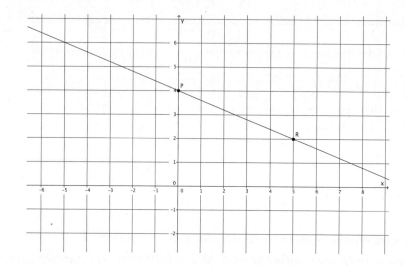

- Now we can locate point Q. It must be to the right of point P and be on a line parallel to the y-axis that goes through point R. What is the location of Q?
  - *Point Q must be* $(5, 4)$.
- What fraction represents the slope of this line?

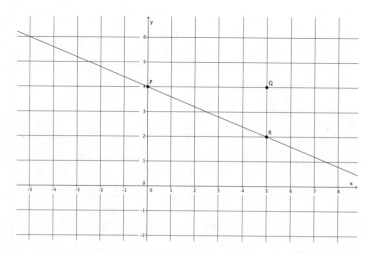

  - *The slope* $m = -\frac{2}{5}$.

| Lesson 20:   Every Line is a Graph of a Linear Equation
                                        | Date: 11/8/13

- The slope of the line is $m = -\frac{2}{5}$ and the y-intercept is $(0, 4)$. What must the equation of the line be?

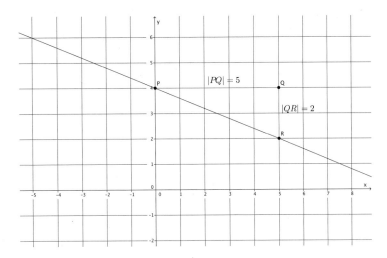

  □   *The line is the graph of $y = -\frac{2}{5}x + 4$.*

Example 2 (5 minutes)

- What is the y-intercept of the line?

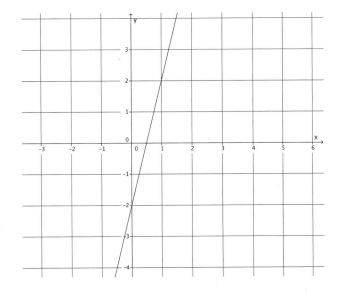

  □   *The y-intercept is $(0, -2)$.*

- Select another point, R, on the line with integer coordinates.

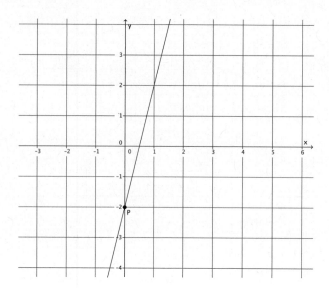

    ▫ *Let R be the point located at $(1, 2)$.*

- Now place point Q and find the slope of the line.

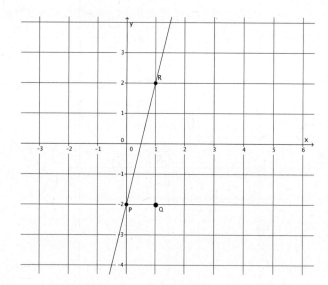

    ▫ *The slope of the line is $m = 4$.*

- Write the equation for the line.

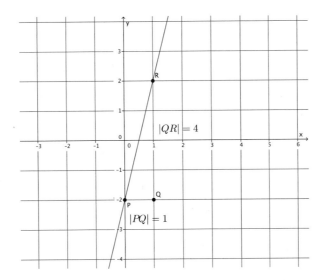

- *The line is the graph of $y = 4x - 2$.*

Example 3 (5 minutes)

- What is the y-intercept of the line? Notice the units on the coordinate plane have increased.

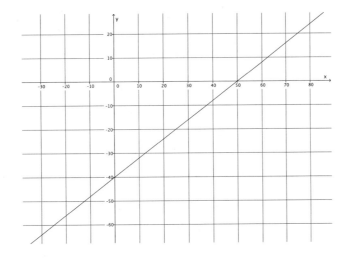

- *The y-intercept is $(0, -40)$.*

- Select another point, R, on the line with integer coordinates.

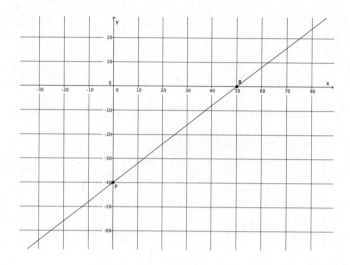

     □   *Let $R = (50, 0)$.*

- Now place point Q and find the slope of the line.

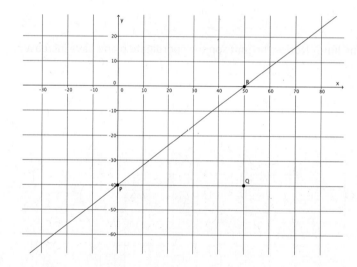

     □   *The slope of the line is $m = \dfrac{40}{50} = \dfrac{4}{5}$.*

- Write the equation for the line.

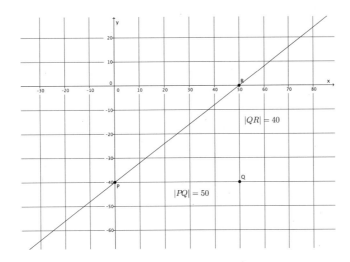

- *The line is the graph of $y = \frac{4}{5}x - 40$.*

- The last thing we will do to this linear equation is rewrite it in standard form $ax + by = c$ where a, b, and c are integers and a is not negative. That means we must multiply the entire equation by a number that will turn $\frac{4}{5}$ into an integer. What number should we multiply by?

  - $\frac{4}{5}(5) = 4$.

- We multiply the entire equation by 5:

$$\left(y = \frac{4}{5}x - 40\right)5$$
$$5y = 4x - 200$$
$$-4x + 5y = 4x - 4x - 200$$
$$-4x + 5y = -200$$
$$-1(-4x + 5y = -200)$$
$$4x - 5y = 200$$

The standard form of the linear equation is $4x - 5y = 200$.

Exercises 1–6 (10 minutes)

Students complete Exercises 1–6 independently.

Exercises

1. Write the equation that represents the line shown.

   $y = 3x + 2$

   Use the properties of equality to change the equation from slope intercept form, $y = mx + b$, to standard form, $ax + by = c$, where a, b, and c are integers and a is not negative.

   $$y = 3x + 2$$
   $$-3x + y = 3x - 3x + 2$$
   $$-3x + y = 2$$
   $$-1(-3x + y = 2)$$
   $$3x - y = -2$$

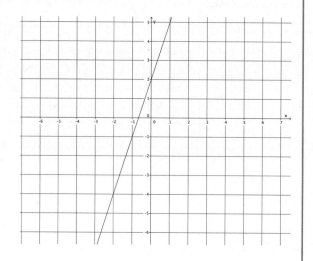

2. Write the equation that represents the line shown.

   $$y = -\frac{2}{3}x - 1$$

   Use the properties of equality to change the equation from slope intercept form, $y = mx + b$, to standard form, $ax + by = c$, where a, b, and c are integers and a is not negative.

   $$y = -\frac{2}{3}x - 1$$
   $$\left(y = -\frac{2}{3}x - 1\right)3$$
   $$3y = -2x - 3$$
   $$2x + 3y = -2x + 2x - 3$$
   $$2x + 3y = -3$$

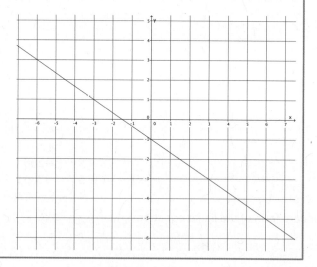

COMMON CORE | Lesson 20:   Every Line is a Graph of a Linear Equation
              | Date: 11/8/13

310

3.   Write the equation that represents the line shown.

$$y = -\frac{1}{5}x - 4$$

Use the properties of equality to change the equation from slope intercept form, $y = mx + b$, to standard form, $ax + by = c$, where a, b, and c are integers and a is not negative.

$$y = -\frac{1}{5}x - 4$$

$$\left(y = -\frac{1}{5}x - 4\right)5$$

$$5y = -x - 20$$

$$x + 5y = -x + x - 20$$

$$x + 5y = -20$$

$$x + 5y = -20$$

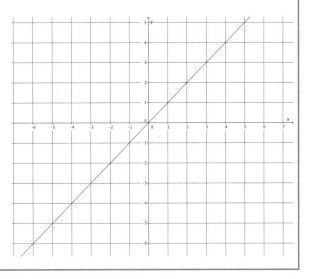

4.   Write the equation that represents the line shown.

$$y = x$$

Use the properties of equality to change the equation from slope intercept form, $y = mx + b$, to standard form, $ax + by = c$, where a, b, and c are integers and a is not negative.

$$y = x$$

$$-x + y = x - x$$

$$-x + y = 0$$

$$-1(-x + y = 0)$$

$$x - y = 0$$

COMMON CORE™

| Lesson 20: | Every Line is a Graph of a Linear Equation |
| Date: | 11/8/13 |

5. Write the equation that represents the line shown.

$$y = \frac{1}{4}x + 5$$

Use the properties of equality to change the equation from slope intercept form, $y = mx + b$, to standard form, $ax + by = c$, where a, b, and c are integers and a is not negative.

$$y = \frac{1}{4}x + 5$$

$$\left(y = \frac{1}{4}x + 5\right)4$$

$$4y = x + 20$$

$$-x + 4y = x - x + 20$$

$$-x + 4y = 20$$

$$-1(-x + 4y = 20)$$

$$x - 4y = -20$$

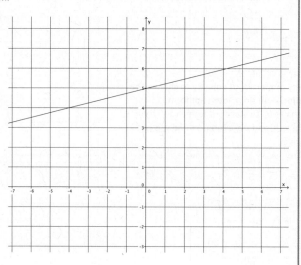

6. Write the equation that represents the line shown.

$$y = -\frac{8}{5}x - 7$$

Use the properties of equality to change the equation from slope intercept form, $y = mx + b$, to standard form, $ax + by = c$, where a, b, and c are integers and a is not negative.

$$y = -\frac{8}{5}x - 7$$

$$\left(y = -\frac{8}{5}x - 7\right)5$$

$$5y = -8x - 35$$

$$8x + 5y = -8x + 8x - 35$$

$$8x + 5y = -35$$

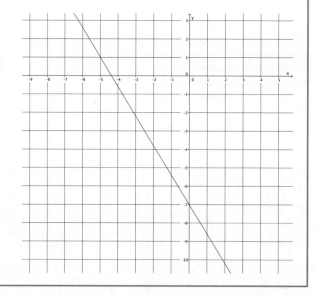

Closing (5 minutes)

Summarize, or ask students to summarize, the main points from the lesson:

- We know that every line is a graph of a linear equation.
- We know how to use the y-intercept and the slope of a line to write the equation that represents the graph of a line.

Lesson Summary

Write the equation of a line by determining the y-intercept, $(0, b)$ and the slope, m, and replacing the numbers b and m into the equation $y = mx + b$.

Example:

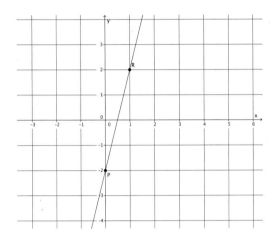

The y-intercept of this graph is $(0, -2)$.

The slope of this graph is $m = \frac{4}{1} = 4$.

The equation that represents the graph of this line is $y = 4x - 2$.

Exit Ticket (5 minutes)

Lesson 20:	Every Line is a Graph of a Linear Equation
Date:	11/8/13

313

Name _____   Date _____

Lesson 20: Every Line is a Graph of a Linear Equation

Exit Ticket

1. Write an equation in slope intercept form that represents the line shown.

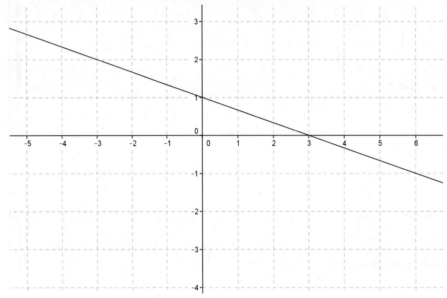

2. Use the properties of equality to change the equation you wrote for problem 1 from slope intercept form, $y = mx + b$, to standard form, $ax + by = c$, where a, b, and c are integers and a is not negative.

3. Write an equation in slope intercept form that represents the line shown.

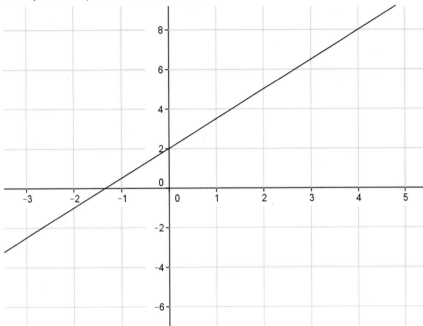

4. Use the properties of equality to change the equation you wrote for problem 3 from slope intercept form, $y = mx + b$, to standard form, $ax + by = c$, where a, b, and c are integers and a is not negative.

Exit Ticket Sample Solutions

1. Write an equation in slope intercept form that represents the line shown.

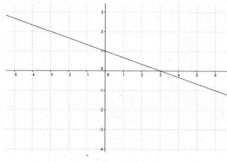

$$y = -\frac{1}{3}x + 1$$

2. Use the properties of equality to change the equation you wrote for problem 1 from slope intercept form, $y = mx + b$, to standard form, $ax + by = c$, where a, b, and c are integers and a is not negative.

$$y = -\frac{1}{3}x + 1$$
$$\left(y = -\frac{1}{3}x + 1\right)3$$
$$3y = -x + 3$$
$$x + 3y = -x + x + 3$$
$$x + 3y = 3$$

3. Write an equation in slope intercept form that represents the line shown.

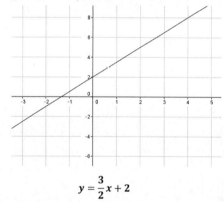

$$y = \frac{3}{2}x + 2$$

4. Use the properties of equality to change the equation you wrote for problem 3 from slope intercept form, $y = mx + b$, to standard form, $ax + by = c$, where a, b, and c are integers and a is not negative.

$$y = \frac{3}{2}x + 2$$
$$\left(y = \frac{3}{2}x + 2\right)2$$
$$2y = 3x + 4$$
$$-3x + 2y = 3x - 3x + 4$$
$$-3x + 2y = 4$$
$$-1(-3x + 2y = 4)$$
$$3x - 2y = -4$$

Lesson 20:   Every Line is a Graph of a Linear Equation
Date: 11/8/13

316

Problem Set Sample Solutions

Students practice writing equations for lines.

1. **Write the equation that represents the line shown.**

    $$y = -\frac{2}{3}x - 4$$

    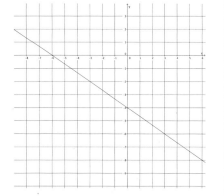

    Use the properties of equality to change the equation from slope intercept form, $y = mx + b$, to standard form, $ax + by = c$, where a, b, and c are integers and a is not negative.

    $$y = -\frac{2}{3}x - 4$$
    $$\left(y = -\frac{2}{3}x - 4\right)3$$
    $$3y = -2x - 12$$
    $$2x + 3y = -2x + 2x - 12$$
    $$2x + 3y = -12$$

2. **Write the equation that represents the line shown.**

    $$y = 8x + 1$$

    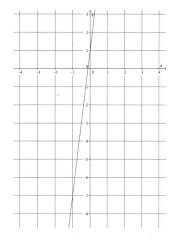

    Use the properties of equality to change the equation from slope intercept form, $y = mx + b$, to standard form, $ax + by = c$, where a, b, and c are integers and a is not negative.

    $$y = 8x + 1$$
    $$-8x + y = 8x - 8x + 1$$
    $$-8x + y = 1$$
    $$-1(-8x + y = 1)$$
    $$8x - y = -1$$

3. Write the equation that represents the line shown.

$$y = \frac{1}{2}x - 4$$

Use the properties of equality to change the equation from slope intercept form, $y = mx + b$, to standard form, $ax + by = c$, where a, b, and c are integers and a is not negative.

$$y = \frac{1}{2}x - 4$$
$$\left(y = \frac{1}{2}x - 4\right)2$$
$$2y = x - 8$$
$$-x + 2y = x - x - 8$$
$$-x + 2y = -8$$
$$-1(-x + 2y = -8)$$
$$x - 2y = 8$$

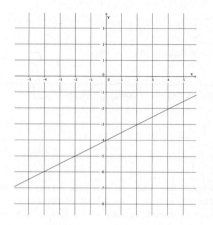

4. Write the equation that represents the line shown.

$$y = -9x - 8$$

Use the properties of equality to change the equation from slope intercept form, $y = mx + b$, to standard form, $ax + by = c$, where a, b, and c are integers and a is not negative.

$$y = -9x - 8$$
$$9x + y = -9x + 9x - 8$$
$$9x + y = -8$$

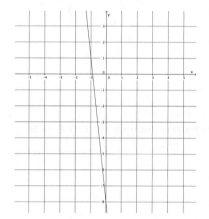

5. Write the equation that represents the line shown.

$$y = 2x - 14$$

Use the properties of equality to change the equation from slope intercept form, $y = mx + b$, to standard form, $ax + by = c$, where a, b, and c are integers and a is not negative.

$$y = 2x - 14$$
$$-2x + y = 2x - 2x - 14$$
$$-2x + y = -14$$
$$-1(-2x + y = -14)$$
$$2x - y = 14$$

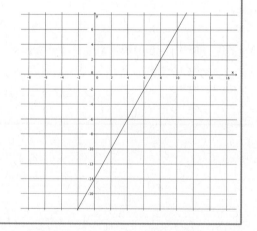

6. Write the equation that represents the line shown.

$$y = -5x + 45$$

Use the properties of equality to change the equation from slope intercept form, $y = mx + b$, to standard form, $ax + by = c$, where a, b, and c are integers and a is not negative.

$$y = -5x + 45$$
$$5x + y = -5x + 5x + 45$$
$$5x + y = 45$$

Lesson 21: Some Facts about Graphs of Linear Equations in Two Variables

Student Outcomes

- Students write the equation of a line given two points or the slope and a point on the line.
- Students know the traditional forms of the slope formula and slope-intercept equation.

Classwork

Example 1 (10 minutes)

Students determine the equation of a line from a graph by using information about slope and a point.

- Let a line l be given in the coordinate plane. Our goal is to find the equation that represents the graph of line l. Can we use information about the slope and intercept to write the equation of the line, like we did in the last lesson?

MP.1

Provide students time to attempt to write the equation of the line. Ask students to share their equations and explanations. Consider having the class vote on whose explanation/equation they think is correct.

Example 1

Let a line l be given in the coordinate plane. What linear equation is the graph of line?

Scaffolding:

If necessary, include another point, as done in Lesson 15, to help students determine the slope of the line.

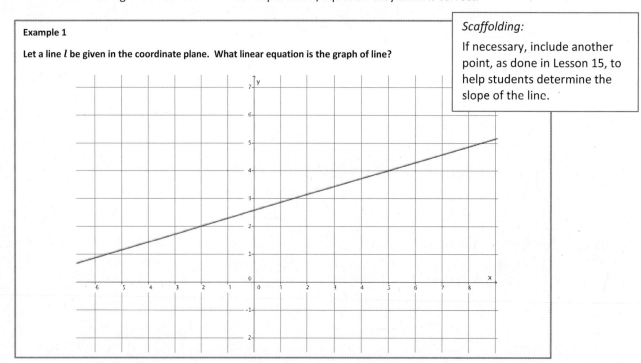

- *We can pick two points to determine the slope, but the precise location of the y-intercept cannot be determined from the graph.*

- Calculate the slope of the line.

  - *Using points, $(-2, 2)$ and $(5, 4)$, the slope of the line is*

  $$m = \frac{2 - 4}{-2 - 5}$$
  $$= \frac{-2}{-7}$$
  $$= \frac{2}{7}$$

- Now we need to determine the y-intercept of the line. We know that it is a point with coordinates $(0, b)$ and we know that the line that goes through points $(-2, 2)$ and $(5, 4)$ and has slope $m = \frac{2}{7}$. Using this information, we can determine the coordinates of the y-intercept and the value of b that we need in order to write the equation of the line.

- Recall what it means for a point to be on a line; the point is a solution to the equation. In the equation $y = mx + b$, (x, y), is a solution and m is the slope. Can we find the value of b? Explain.

  - *Yes, we can substitute one of the points and the slope into the equation and solve for b.*

- Do you think it matters which point we choose to substitute into the equation? That is, will we get a different equation if we use the point $(-2, 2)$ compared to $(5, 4)$?

  - *No, because there can be only one line with a given slope that goes through a point.*

- Verify this claim by using $m = \frac{2}{7}$ and $(-2, 2)$ to find the equation of the line, then using $m = \frac{2}{7}$ and $(5, 4)$ to see if the result is the same equation.

  - *Sample student work:*

  $$2 = \frac{2}{7}(-2) + b$$
  $$2 = -\frac{4}{7} + b$$
  $$2 + \frac{4}{7} = -\frac{4}{7} + \frac{4}{7} + b$$
  $$\frac{18}{7} = b$$

  $$4 = \frac{2}{7}(5) + b$$
  $$4 = \frac{10}{7} + b$$
  $$4 - \frac{10}{7} = \frac{10}{7} - \frac{10}{7} + b$$
  $$\frac{18}{7} = b$$

  The y-intercept is at $\left(0, \frac{18}{7}\right)$ and the equation of the line is $y = \frac{2}{7}x + \frac{18}{7}$.

COMMON CORE

Lesson 21:	Some Facts about Graphs of Linear Equations in Two Variables
Date:	11/8/13

- The equation of the line is:

$$y = \frac{2}{7}x + \frac{18}{7}$$

Write it in standard form:

  □ *Sample student work:*

$$\left(y = \frac{2}{7}x + \frac{18}{7}\right)7$$

$$7y = 2x + 18$$

$$-2x + 7y = 2x - 2x + 18$$

$$-2x + 7y = 18$$

$$-1(-2x + 7y = 18)$$

$$2x - 7y = -18$$

Example 2 (5 minutes)

Students determine the equation of a line from a graph by using information about slope and a point.

- Let a line l be given in the coordinate plane. What information do we need to write the equation of the line?

  □ *We need to know the slope, so we must identify two points we can use to calculate the slope. Then we can use the slope and a point to determine the equation of the line.*

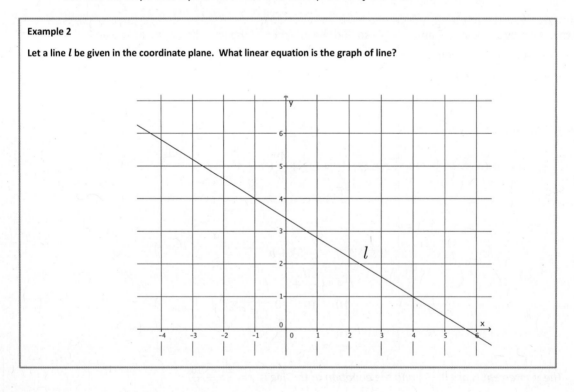

Example 2

Let a line l be given in the coordinate plane. What linear equation is the graph of line?

- ▫ *Using points, $(-1, 4)$ and $(4, 1)$, the slope of the line is*

$$m = \frac{4 - 1}{-1 - 4}$$

$$= \frac{3}{-5}$$

$$= -\frac{3}{5}$$

- ▪ Now to determine the y-intercept of the line.

  - ▫ *Sample student work:*

$$4 = \left(-\frac{3}{5}\right)(-1) + b$$

$$4 = \frac{3}{5} + b$$

$$4 - \frac{3}{5} = \frac{3}{5} - \frac{3}{5} + b$$

$$\frac{17}{5} = b$$

The y-intercept is at $\left(0, \frac{17}{5}\right)$.

- ▪ Now that we know the slope, $m = -\frac{3}{5}$ and the y-intercept, $\left(0, \frac{17}{5}\right)$, write the equation of the line l in slope-intercept form.

  - ▫ $y = -\frac{3}{5}x + \frac{17}{5}$

- ▪ Transform the equation so that it is written in standard form.

  - ▫ *Sample student work:*

$$y = -\frac{3}{5}x + \frac{17}{5}$$

$$\left(y = -\frac{3}{5}x + \frac{17}{5}\right)5$$

$$5y = -3x + 17$$

$$3x + 5y = -3x + 3x + 17$$

$$3x + 5y = 17$$

Example 3 (5 minutes)

Students determine the equation of a line from a graph by using information about slope and a point.

- Let a line l be given in the coordinate plane. Assume the y-axis intervals are units of one (like the visible x-axis). What information do we need to write the equation of the line?

  - *We need to know the slope, so we must identify two points we can use to calculate the slope. Then we can use the slope and a point to determine the equation of the line.*

Example 3

Let a line l be given in the coordinate plane. What linear equation is the graph of line?

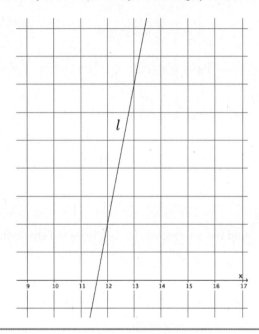

  - *Using points, $(12, 2)$ and $(13, 7)$, the slope of the line is*

$$m = \frac{2 - 7}{12 - 13}$$
$$= \frac{-5}{-1}$$
$$= 5$$

- Now to determine the y-intercept of the line and write the equation of the line in slope-intercept form.

  - *Sample student work:*

$$2 = 5(12) + b$$
$$2 = 60 + b$$
$$b = -58$$

The y-intercept is at $(0, -58)$ and the equation of the line is $y = 5x - 58$.

- Now that we know the slope, $m = 5$ and the y-intercept, $(0, -58)$, write the equation of the line l in standard form.

  □ *Sample student work:*

  $$y = 5x - 58$$
  $$-5x + y = 5x - 5x - 58$$
  $$-5x + y = -58$$
  $$-1(-5x + y = -58)$$
  $$5x - y = 58$$

Example 4 (3 minutes)

Students determine the equation of a line from a graph by using information about slope and a point.

- Let a line l be given in the coordinate plane. Write the equation for this line.

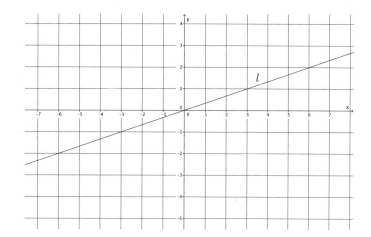

  □ *Using points, $(3, 1)$ and $(-3, -1)$, the slope of the line is*

  $$m = \frac{-1 - 1}{-3 - 3}$$
  $$= \frac{-2}{-6}$$
  $$= \frac{1}{3}$$

  The y-intercept is at $(0, 0)$ and the equation of the line is $y = \frac{1}{3}x$.

- The y-intercept is the origin of the graph. What value does b have when this occurs?

  □ *When the line goes through the origin the value of b is zero.*

- All linear equations that go through the origin have the form $y = mx + 0$ or simply $y = mx$. We have done a lot of work with equations in this form. Which do you remember?

  □ *All problems that describe proportional relationships have equations of this form.*

 CORE™ | **Lesson 21:** Some Facts about Graphs of Linear Equations in Two Variables
Date: 11/8/13

325

Concept Development (5 minutes)

- The following are some facts about graphs of linear equations in two variables.

- Let (x_1, y_1) and (x_2, y_2) be the coordinates of two distinct points on the graph of a line l. We find the slope of the line by:

$$m = \frac{y_2 - y_1}{x_2 - x_1}$$

Where this version of the slope formula, using coordinates of x and y instead of p and r, is a commonly accepted version.

- As soon as you multiply the slope by the denominator of the fraction above you get the following equation:

$$m(x_2 - x_1) = y_2 - y_1$$

This form of an equation is referred to as the point-slope form of a linear equation. As you can see, it doesn't convey any more information than the slope formula. It is just another way to look at it.

- Given a known (x, y), then the equation is written as

$$m(x - x_1) = (y - y_1)$$

- The following is the slope-intercept form of a line:

$$y = mx + b$$

In this equation, m is slope and $(0, b)$ is the y-intercept.

- What information must you have in order to write the equation of a line?

  □ *We need two points or one point and slope.*

- The names and symbols used are not nearly as important as your understanding of the concepts. Basically, if you can remember a few simple facts about lines, namely the slope formula and the fact that slope is the same between any two points on a line, you can derive the equation of any line.

Exercises 1–5 (7 minutes)

Students complete Exercises 1–5 independently.

Exercises 1–5

1. Write the equation for the line l shown in the graph.

    Using the points $(-1, -3)$ and $(2, -2)$, the slope of the line is

$$m = \frac{-3 - (-2)}{-1 - 2}$$
$$= \frac{-1}{-3}$$
$$= \frac{1}{3}$$
$$-2 = \frac{1}{3}(2) + b$$
$$-2 = \frac{2}{3} + b$$
$$-2 - \frac{2}{3} = \frac{2}{3} - \frac{2}{3} + b$$
$$-\frac{8}{3} = b$$

The equation of the line is $y = \frac{1}{3}x - \frac{8}{3}$.

	Lesson 21:	Some Facts about Graphs of Linear Equations in Two Variables		326
	Date:	11/8/13		

2.   Write the equation for the line l shown in the graph.

Using the points $(-3, 7)$ and $(2, 8)$, the slope of the line is

$$m = \frac{7 - 8}{-3 - 2}$$
$$= \frac{-1}{-5}$$
$$= \frac{1}{5}$$
$$8 = \frac{1}{5}(2) + b$$
$$8 = \frac{2}{5} + b$$
$$8 - \frac{2}{5} = \frac{2}{5} - \frac{2}{5} + b$$
$$\frac{38}{5} = b$$

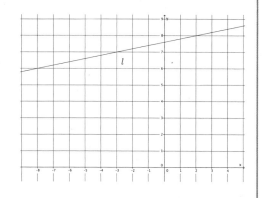

The equation of the line is $y = \frac{1}{5}x + \frac{38}{5}$.

3.   Determine the equation of the line that goes through points $(-4, 5)$ and $(2, 3)$.

The slope of the line is

$$m = \frac{5 - 3}{-4 - 2}$$
$$= \frac{2}{-6}$$
$$= -\frac{1}{3}$$

The y-intercept of the line is

$$3 = -\frac{1}{3}(2) + b$$
$$3 = -\frac{2}{3} + b$$
$$\frac{11}{3} = b$$

The equation of the line is $y = -\frac{1}{3}x + \frac{11}{3}$.

4.   Write the equation for the line l shown in the graph.

Using the points $(-7, 2)$ and $(-6, -2)$, the slope of the line is

$$m = \frac{2 - (-2)}{-7 - (-6)}$$
$$= \frac{4}{-1}$$
$$= -4$$
$$-2 = -4(-6) + b$$
$$-2 = 24 + b$$
$$-26 = b$$

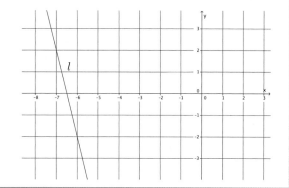

The equation of the line is $y = -4x - 26$.

5. A line goes through the point $(8, 3)$ and has slope $m = 4$. Write the equation that represents the line.

$$3 = 4(8) + b$$
$$3 = 32 + b$$
$$-29 = b$$

The equation of the line is $y = 4x - 29$.

Closing (5 minutes)

Summarize, or ask students to summarize, the main points from the lesson:

- We know how to write an equation for a line from a graph, even if the line does not intersect the y-axis at integer coordinates.
- We know how to write the equation for a line given two points or one point and the slope of the line.
- We know other versions of the formulas and equations that we have been using related to linear equations.

Lesson Summary

Let (x_1, y_1) and (x_2, y_2) be the coordinates of two distinct points on the graph of a line l. We find the slope of the line by:

$$m = \frac{y_2 - y_1}{x_2 - x_1}$$

Where this version of the slope formula, using coordinates of x and y instead of p and r, is a commonly accepted version.

As soon as you multiply the slope by the denominator of the fraction above you get the following equation:

$$m(x_2 - x_1) = y_2 - y_1$$

This form of an equation is referred to as the point-slope form of a linear equation.

Given a known (x, y), then the equation is written as

$$m(x - x_1) = (y - y_1)$$

The following is slope-intercept form of a line:

$$y = mx + b$$

In this equation, m is slope and $(0, b)$ is the y-intercept.

To write the equation of a line you must have two points, one point and slope, or a graph of the line.

Exit Ticket (5 minutes)

Name _____   Date _____

Lesson 21: Some Facts about Graphs of Linear Equations in Two Variables

Exit Ticket

1.   Write the equation for the line l shown in the graph below.

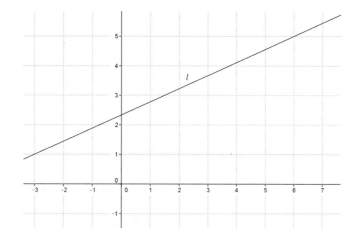

2.   A line goes through the point $(5, -7)$ and has slope $m = -3$. Write the equation that represents the line.

Exit Ticket Sample Solutions

Note that some students may write equations in standard form.

---

1. Write the equation for the line l shown in the graph below.

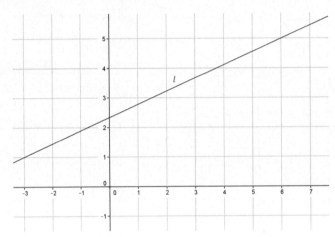

Using the points $(-3, 1)$ and $(6, 5)$, the slope of the line is

$$m = \frac{5-1}{6-(-3)}$$
$$m = \frac{4}{9}$$
$$5 = \frac{4}{9}(6) + b$$
$$5 = \frac{8}{3} + b$$
$$5 - \frac{8}{3} = \frac{8}{3} - \frac{8}{3} + b$$
$$\frac{7}{3} = b$$

The equation of the line is $y = \frac{4}{9}x + \frac{7}{3}$.

2. A line goes through the point $(5, -7)$ and has slope $m = -3$. Write the equation that represents the line.

$$-7 = -3(5) + b$$
$$-7 = -15 + b$$
$$8 = b$$

The equation of the line is $y = -3x + 8$.

Problem Set Sample Solutions

Students practice writing equations from graphs of lines. Students write the equation of a line given only the slope and a point.

1. **Write the equation for the line l shown in the graph.**

   Using the points $(-3, 2)$ and $(2, -2)$, the slope of the line is

   $$m = \frac{2 - (-2)}{-3 - 2}$$
   $$= \frac{4}{-5}$$
   $$= -\frac{4}{5}$$
   $$2 = \left(-\frac{4}{5}\right)(-3) + b$$
   $$2 = \frac{12}{5} + b$$
   $$2 - \frac{12}{5} = \frac{12}{5} - \frac{12}{5} + b$$
   $$-\frac{2}{5} = b$$

   The equation of the line is $y = -\frac{4}{5}x - \frac{2}{5}$.

2. **Write the equation for the line l shown in the graph.**

   Using the points $(-6, 2)$ and $(-5, 5)$, the slope of the line is

   $$m = \frac{2 - 5}{-6 - (-5)}$$
   $$= \frac{-3}{-1}$$
   $$= 3$$
   $$5 = 3(-5) + b$$
   $$5 = -15 + b$$
   $$20 = b$$

   The equation of the line is $y = 3x + 20$.

   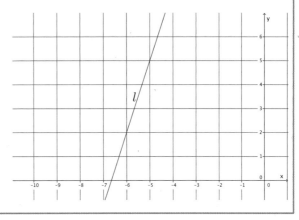

3. Write the equation for the line l shown in the graph.

    Using the points $(-3, 1)$ and $(2, 2)$, the slope of the line is

    $$m = \frac{1 - 2}{-3 - 2}$$
    $$= \frac{-1}{-5}$$
    $$= \frac{1}{5}$$
    $$2 = \frac{1}{5}(2) + b$$
    $$2 = \frac{2}{5} + b$$
    $$2 - \frac{2}{5} = \frac{2}{5} - \frac{2}{5} + b$$
    $$\frac{8}{5} = b$$

    The equation of the line is $y = \frac{1}{5}x + \frac{8}{5}$.

4. Triangle $\triangle ABC$ is made up line segments formed from the intersection of lines L_{AB}, L_{BC}, and L_{AC}. Write the equations that represents the lines that make up the triangle.

    $A = (-3, -3), B = (3, 2), C = (5, -2)$

    The equation of L_{AB}:

    The slope of L_{AB} is
    $$m = \frac{-3 - 2}{-3 - 3}$$
    $$= \frac{-5}{-6}$$
    $$= \frac{5}{6}$$
    $$2 = \frac{5}{6}(3) + b$$
    $$2 = \frac{5}{2} + b$$
    $$2 - \frac{5}{2} = \frac{5}{2} - \frac{5}{2} + b$$
    $$-\frac{1}{2} = b$$

    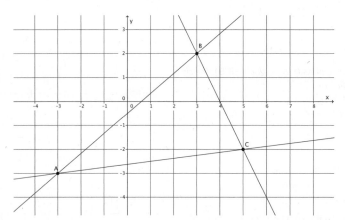

    The equation of L_{AB} is $y = \frac{5}{6}x - \frac{1}{2}$.

    The slope of L_{BC}:
    $$m = \frac{2 - (-2)}{3 - 5}$$
    $$= \frac{4}{-2}$$
    $$= -2$$
    $$2 = -2(3) + b$$
    $$2 = -6 + b$$
    $$8 = b$$

    The equation of L_{BC} is $y = -2x + 8$.

    The slope of L_{AC}:
    $$m = \frac{-3 - (-2)}{-3 - 5}$$
    $$= \frac{-1}{-8}$$
    $$= \frac{1}{8}$$
    $$-2 = \frac{1}{8}(5) + b$$
    $$-2 = \frac{5}{8} + b$$
    $$-2 - \frac{5}{8} = \frac{5}{8} - \frac{5}{8} + b$$
    $$-\frac{21}{8} = b$$

    The equation of L_{AC} is $y = \frac{1}{8}x - \frac{21}{8}$.

5.   Write the equation for the line that goes through point $(-10, 8)$ with slope $m = 6$.

$$8 = 6(-10) + b$$
$$8 = -60 + b$$
$$68 = b$$

The equation of the line is $y = 6x + 68$.

6.   Write the equation for the line that goes through point $(12, 15)$ with slope $m = -2$.

$$15 = -2(12) + b$$
$$15 = -24 + b$$
$$39 = b$$

The equation of the line is $y = -2x + 39$.

7.   Write the equation for the line that goes through point $(1, 1)$ with slope $m = -9$.

$$1 = -9(1) + b$$
$$1 = -9 + b$$
$$10 = b$$

The equation of the line is $y = -9x + 10$.

8.   Determine the equation of the line that goes through points $(1, 1)$ and $(3, 7)$.

The slope of the line is

$$m = \frac{1 - 7}{1 - 3}$$
$$= \frac{-6}{-2}$$
$$= 3$$

The y-intercept of the line is

$$7 = 3(3) + b$$
$$7 = 9 + b$$
$$-2 = b$$

The equation of the line is $y = 3x - 2$.

Lesson 22: Constant Rates Revisited

Student Outcomes

- Students know that any constant rate problem can be described by a linear equation in two variables where the slope of the graph is the constant rate.
- Students compare two different proportional relationships represented by graphs, equations, and tables to determine which has a greater rate of change.

Classwork

Example 1 (8 minutes)

- Recall our definition of constant rate: If the average speed of motion over any time interval is equal to the same constant, then we say the motion has constant speed.
- Erika set her stopwatch to zero and switched it on at the beginning of her walk. She walks at a constant speed of 3 miles per hour. Work in pairs to express this situation as an equation, table of values, and a graph.

> **Scaffolding:**
> You may need to review the definition of average speed as well: Average speed is the distance (or area, pages typed, etc.) divided by the time interval spent moving that distance (or painting the given area, or typing a specific number of pages, etc.)

Provide students time to analyze the situation and represent it in the requested forms. If necessary, provide support to students with the next few bullet points. Once students have finished working resume the work on the example (bullets below the graph).

- Suppose Erika walked a distance of y miles in x hours. Then her average speed in the time interval from 0 to x hours is $\frac{y}{x}$. Since Erika walks at a constant speed of 3 miles per hour, we can express her motion as $\frac{y}{x} = 3$.

- Solve the equation for y.

  □ $\frac{y}{x} = 3$
     $y = 3x$

- We can use the equation to develop a table of values where x is the number of hours Erika walks and y is the distance she walks in miles. Complete the table for the given x-values.

x	y
0	0
1	3
2	6
3	9

Lesson 22:	Constant Rates Revisited
Date:	11/8/13

- In terms of x and y, $y = 3x$ is a linear equation in two variables. Its graph is a line.

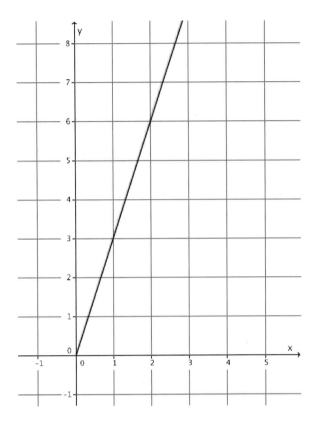

- What is the meaning of the 3 in the equation $y = 3x$?
    - *The 3 is the slope of the line. It represents the rate at which Erika walks.*

- We can prove that her motion is constant, i.e., she walks at a constant speed, by showing that the slope is 3 over any time interval that she walks:

    Assume Erika walks y_1 miles in the time interval from 0 to x_1, and she walks y_2 miles in the time interval from 0 to x_2.

    Her average distance between time interval x_1 and x_2 = $\frac{y_2 - y_1}{x_2 - x_1}$

    We know that $y = 3x$; therefore, $y_2 = 3x_2$ and $y_1 = 3x_1$. Then by substitution we have

$$= \frac{3x_2 - 3x_1}{x_2 - x_1}$$

$$= \frac{3(x_2 - x_1)}{x_2 - x_1}$$

$$= 3$$

Scaffolding:

Explain that we are looking at the distance traveled between times x_1 and x_2; therefore, we must subtract the distances traveled to represent the total distance traveled in $x_2 - x_1$. Concrete numbers and a diagram like the following may be useful as well:

	3 miles		12 miles
0	1 hour		4 hours

$$\text{Average speed of walking over interval from 1 hour to 4 hours} = \frac{distance\ traveled\ in\ time\ interv}{time\ of\ interval}$$

$$= \frac{12 - 3}{4 - 1}$$

$$= \frac{9}{3}$$

$$= 3$$

- Therefore, Erika's average speed in the time interval between x_1 and x_2 is 3 mph. Since x_1 and x_2 can be any two times, then the average speed she walks over any time interval is 3 mph and we have confirmed that she walks at a constant speed of 3 mph. We can also show that her motion is constant by looking at the slope between different points on the graph:

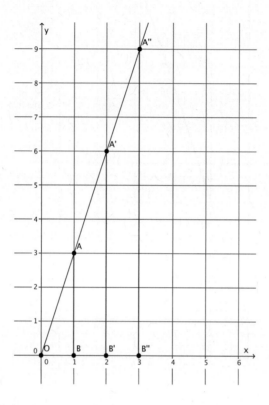

- Are triangles $\triangle AOB$, $\triangle A'OB'$, and $\triangle A''OB''$ similar?
  - *Yes, because each triangle has a common angle, $\angle AOB$ and a right angle. By the AA criterion the triangles are similar.*

- We used similar triangles before to show that the slope of a line would be the same between any two points. Since we have similar triangles, we can conclude that the rate at which Erika walks is constant because the ratio of the corresponding sides will be equal to a constant, i.e., the scale factor of dilation. For example, when we compare the ratio of corresponding sides for triangles $\triangle A'OB'$ and $\triangle A''OB''$ we see that

$$\frac{9}{6} = \frac{3}{2}$$

Make clear to students that the ratio of corresponding sides will not be equal to the slope of the line; rather, the ratios will be equal to one another and the scale factor of dilation.

- Or we could compare the ratio of corresponding side lengths for triangles $\triangle AOB$ and $\triangle A'OB'$:

$$\frac{6}{3} = \frac{2}{1}$$

- Again, because the ratio of corresponding sides are equal, we know that the rate at which Erika walks is constant.

    Lesson 22:   Constant Rates Revisited
Date: 11/8/13   336

Example 2 (5 minutes)

- A faucet leaks at a constant rate of 7 gallons per hour. Suppose y gallons leak in x hours from 6:00 a.m. Express the situation as a linear equation in two variables.

- If we say the leak began at 6:00 a.m. and the total number of gallons leaked over the time interval from 6:00 a.m. to x hours is y, then we know the average rate of the leak is $\frac{y}{x}$.

- Since we know that the faucet leaks at a constant rate, then we can write the linear equation in two variables as $\frac{y}{x} = 7$, which can then be transformed to $y = 7x$.

- Again, take note of the fact that the number that represents slope in the equation is the same as the constant rate of water leaking.

- Another faucet leaks at a constant rate and the table below shows the number of gallons y, that leak in x hours.

Hours (x)	Gallons (y)
2	13
4	26
7	45.5
10	65

- How can we determine the rate at which this faucet leaks?
  - *If these were points on a graph, we could find the slope between them.*

- Using what you know about slope, determine the rate the faucet leaks.
  - *Sample student work:*

$$m = \frac{26 - 13}{4 - 2}$$
$$= \frac{13}{2}$$
$$= 6.5$$

- The number of gallons that leak from each faucet is dependent on the amount of time the faucet leaks. The information provided for each faucet's rate of change, i.e., slope allows us to answer a question, such as the following: Which faucet has the worse leak? That is, which faucet leaks more water over a given time interval?
  - *The first faucet has the worse leak because the rate is greater, 7 compared to 6.5.*

Example 3 (4 minutes)

▪ The graph below represents the constant rate at which Train A travels.

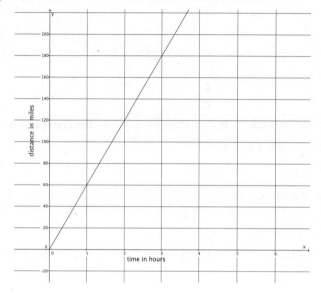

▪ What is the constant rate of travel for Train A?

   □ *We know that the constant rate of travel is the same as the slope. On the graph, we can see that the train is traveling 60 miles every hour. That means that the slope of the line is 60.*

▪ Train B travels at a constant rate. The train travels at an average rate of 95 miles every one and a half hours. We want to know which train is traveling at a greater speed. Let's begin by writing a linear equation that represents the constant rate of Train B. If y represents the total distance traveled over any time period x, then

$$\frac{95}{1.5} = \frac{y}{x}$$

$$y = \frac{95}{1.5}x$$
$$y = 63\frac{1}{3}x$$

▪ Which train is traveling at a greater speed? Explain.

Provide students time to talk to their partners about how to determine which train is traveling at a greater speed.

   □ *Train B is traveling at a greater speed. The graph provided the information about the constant rate of Train A, that is, Train A travels at a constant rate of 60 miles per hour. The given rate for Train B, the slope of the graph for Train B, is equal to $63\frac{1}{3}$. Since $63\frac{1}{3} > 60$, Train B is traveling at a greater speed.*

▪ Why do you think the strategy of comparing each rate of change allows us to determine which train is travelling at a greater speed?

   □ *The distance that each train travels is proportional to the amount of time the train travels. Therefore, if we can describe the rate of change as a number, i.e. slope, and compare the numbers, we can determine which train travels at a greater speed.*

Lesson 22:	Constant Rates Revisited
Date:	11/8/13

338

Example 4 (5 minutes)

▪ The graph below represents the constant rate at which Kristina can paint.

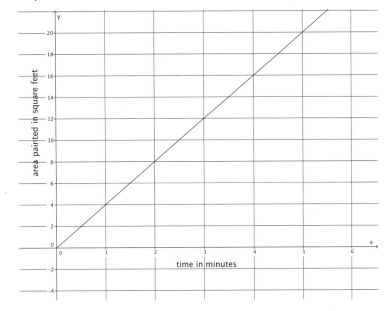

▪ Her sister Tracee paints at an average rate of 45 square feet in 12 minutes. Assuming Tracee paints at a constant rate, determine which sister paints faster.

Provide students time to determine the linear equation that represents Tracee's constant rate and then discuss with their partner who is the faster painter.

      □ *If we let y represent the total area Tracee paints in x minutes, then her constant rate is*

$$\frac{45}{12} = \frac{y}{x}$$

$$\frac{45}{12}x = y$$

We need to compare the slope of the line for Kristina with the slope of the equation for Tracee. The slope of the line is 4 and the slope in the equation that represents Tracee's rate is $\frac{45}{12}$. Since $4 > \frac{45}{12}$, Kristina paints at a faster rate.

▪ How does the slope provide the information we need to answer the question about which sister paints faster?

      □ *The slope describes the rate of change for proportional relationships. If we know which rate of change is greater, then we can determine which sister paints faster.*

Example 5 (5 minutes)

▪ The graph below represents the constant rate of watts of energy produced from a single solar panel produced by Company A.

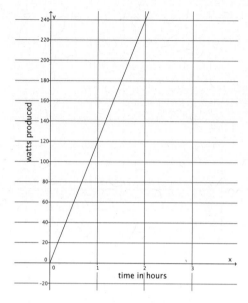

▪ Company B offers a solar panel that produces energy at an average rate of 325 watts in 2.6 hours. Assuming solar panels produce energy at a constant rate, determine which company produces more efficient solar panels (solar panels that produce more energy per hour).

Provide students time to work with their partners to answer the question.

□ *If we let y represent the energy produced by a solar panel made by Company B in x minutes, then the constant rate is*

$$\frac{325}{2.6} = \frac{y}{x}$$

$$\frac{325}{2.6}x = y$$

$$125x = y$$

We need to compare the slope of the line for Company A with the slope in the equation that represents the rate for Company B. The slope of the line representing Company A is 120, and the slope of the line representing Company B is equal to 125. Since 125 > 120, Company B produces the more efficient solar panel.

Exercises 1–5 (10 minutes)

Students work in pairs or small groups to complete Exercises 1–5. Discuss Exercise 5 as it generalizes a strategy for comparing proportional relationships.

Exercises

1.   Peter paints a wall at a constant rate of 2 square-feet per minute. Assume he paints an area y, in square feet after x minutes.

   a.   Express this situation as a linear equation in two variables.

   $$\frac{y}{x} = \frac{2}{1}$$
   $$y = 2x$$

   b.   Graph the linear equation.

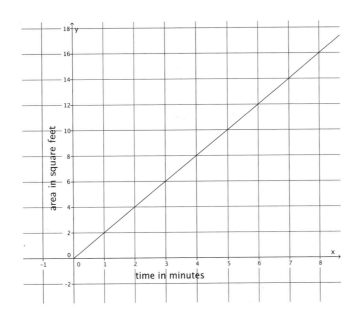

   c.   Using the graph or the equation, determine the total area he paints after 8 minutes, $1\frac{1}{2}$ hours, and 2 hours. Note that the units are in minutes and *hours*.

   In 8 minutes, he paints **16** *square feet.*

   In $1\frac{1}{2}$ *hours, he paints*

   $$y = 2(90)$$
   $$= 180$$

   180 *square feet.*

   In 2 hours, he paints

   $$y = 2(120)$$
   $$= 240$$

   240 *square feet.*

	Lesson 22:	Constant Rates Revisited
	Date:	11/8/13

341

2. The graph below represents Nathan's constant rate of walking.

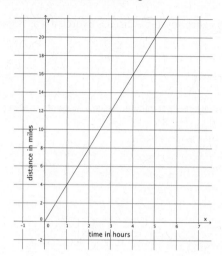

a. Nicole just finished a 5 mile walkathon. It took her 1.4 hours. Assume she walks at a constant rate. Let y represent the distance Nicole walks in x hours. Describe Nicole's walking at a constant rate as a linear equation in two variables.

$$\frac{y}{x} = \frac{5}{1.4}$$
$$y = \frac{25}{7}x$$

b. Who walks at a greater speed? Explain.

Nathan walks at a greater speed. The slope of the graph for Nathan is 4, and the slope or rate for Nicole is $\frac{25}{7}$. When you compare the slopes, you see that $4 > \frac{25}{7}$.

3. a. Susan can type 4 pages of text in 10 minutes. Assuming she types at a constant rate, write the linear equation that represents the situation.

Let y represent the total number of pages Susan can type in x minutes. We can write $\frac{y}{x} = \frac{4}{10}$ and $y = \frac{2}{5}x$.

b. The table of values below represents the number of pages that Anne can type, y, in x minutes. Assume she types at a constant rate.

Minutes (x)	Pages Typed (y)
3	2
5	$\frac{10}{3}$
8	$\frac{16}{3}$
10	$\frac{20}{3}$

Who types faster? Explain.

Anne types faster. Using the table we can determine the slope that represents Anne's constant rate of typing is $\frac{2}{3}$. The slope or rate for Nicole is $\frac{2}{5}$. When you compare the slopes you see that $\frac{2}{3} > \frac{2}{5}$.

4. a. Phil can build 3 birdhouses in 5 days. Assuming he builds birdhouses at a constant rate, write the linear equation that represents the situation.

Let y represent the total number of birdhouses Phil can build in x days. We can write $\frac{y}{x} = \frac{3}{5}$ and $y = \frac{3}{5}x$.

 b. The graph represents Karl's constant rate of building the same kind of birdhouses. Who builds birdhouses faster? Explain.

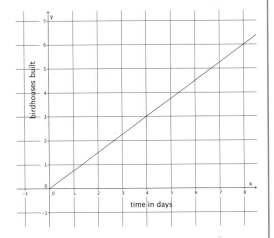

Karl can build birdhouses faster. The slope of the graph for Karl is $\frac{3}{4}$, and the slope or rate of change for Phil is $\frac{3}{5}$. When you compare the slopes, $\frac{3}{4} > \frac{3}{5}$.

5. Explain your general strategy for comparing proportional relationships.

When comparing proportional relationships we look specifically at the rate of change for each situation. The relationship with the greater rate of change will end up producing more, painting a greater area, or walking faster when compared to the same amount of time with the other proportional relationship.

Closing (4 minutes)

Summarize, or ask students to summarize, the main points from the lesson:

- We know how to write a constant rate problem as a linear equation in two variables.
- We know that in order to determine who has a greater speed (or is faster at completing a task), we need only to compare the slopes (rates of change) that apply to two situations. Whichever has the greater slope has the greater rate. We can determine rate (slope) from an equation, a graph, or a table.

Lesson Summary

Problems involving constant rate can be expressed as linear equations in two variables.

When given information about two proportional relationships, determine which is less or greater by comparing their slopes (rates of change).

Exit Ticket (4 minutes)

Name _____   Date _____

Lesson 22: Constant Rates Revisited

1. Water flows out of Pipe A at a constant rate. Pipe A can fill 3 buckets of the same size in 14 minutes.

    a.   Write a linear equation that represents the situation.

The graph below represents the rate at which Pipe B can fill the same sized buckets.

    b.   Which pipe fills buckets faster? Explain.

Exit Ticket Sample Solutions

---

1.   Water flows out of Pipe A at a constant rate. Pipe A can fill 3 buckets of the same size in 14 minutes.

a.   Write a linear equation that represents the situation.

Let y represent the total number of buckets that Pipe A can fill in x minutes. We can write $\frac{y}{x} = \frac{3}{14}$ *and*

$y = \frac{3}{14}x.$

The graph below represents the rate at which Pipe B can fill the same sized buckets.

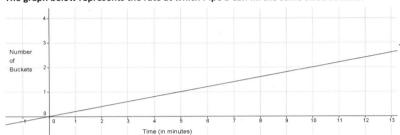

b.   Which pipe fills buckets faster? Explain.

Pipe A fills the same sized buckets faster than Pipe B. The slope of the graph for Pipe B is $\frac{1}{5}$*, the slope or rate*

for Pipe A is $\frac{3}{14}$*. When you compare the slopes you see that* $\frac{3}{14} > \frac{1}{5}$*.*

Problem Set Sample Solutions

Students practice writing constant rate problems as linear equations in two variables. Students determine which of two proportional relationships is greater.

---

1.   a.   Train A can travel a distance of 500 miles in 8 hours. Assuming the train travels at a constant rate, write the linear equation that represents the situation.

Let y represent the total number of miles Train A travels in x minutes. We can write $\frac{y}{x} = \frac{500}{8}$ *and* $y = \frac{125}{2}x.$

b.   The graph represents the constant rate of travel for Train B.

Which train is faster? Explain.

Train B is faster than Train A. The slope or rate for Train A is $\frac{125}{2}$*, and the slope of the line for Train B is* $\frac{200}{3}$*. When you compare the slopes,* $\frac{200}{3} > \frac{125}{2}$*.*

---

2. a. Natalie can paint 40 square feet in 9 minutes. Assuming she paints at a constant rate, write the linear equation that represents the situation.

Let y represent the total square feet Natalie can paint in x minutes. We can write $\frac{y}{x} = \frac{40}{9}$ and $y = \frac{40}{9}x$.

b. The table of values below represents Steven's constant rate of painting.

Minutes (x)	Area Painted (y)
3	10
5	$\frac{50}{3}$
6	20
8	$\frac{80}{3}$

Who paints faster? Explain.

Natalie paints faster. Using the table of values I can find the slope that represents Steven's constant rate of painting: $\frac{10}{3}$. The slope or rate for Natalie is $\frac{40}{9}$. When you compare the slopes you see that $\frac{40}{9} > \frac{10}{3}$.

3. a. Bianca can run 5 miles in 41 minutes. Assuming she runs at a constant rate, write the linear equation that represents the situation.

Let y represent the total number of miles Bianca can run in x minutes. We can write $\frac{y}{x} = \frac{5}{41}$ and $y = \frac{5}{41}x$.

b. The graph below represents Cynthia's constant rate of running.

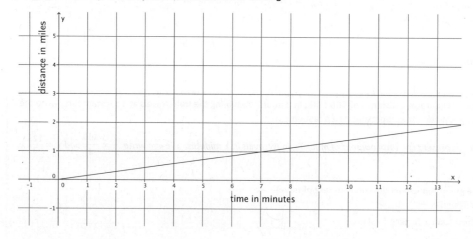

Who runs faster? Explain.

Cynthia runs faster. The slope of the graph for Cynthia is $\frac{1}{7}$, and the slope or rate for Nicole is $\frac{5}{41}$. When you compare the slopes you see that $\frac{1}{7} > \frac{5}{41}$.

4.   a.   Geoff can mow an entire lawn of 450 square feet in 30 minutes. Assuming he mows at a constant rate, write the linear equation that represents the situation.

Let y represent the total number of square feet Geoff can mow in x minutes. We can write $\frac{y}{x} = \frac{450}{30}$ *and* $y = 15x.$

b.   The graph represents Mark's constant rate of mowing a lawn.

Who mows faster? Explain.

Geoff mows faster. The slope of the graph for Mark is $\frac{14}{2} = 7$, *and the slope or rate for Geoff is* $\frac{450}{30} = 15.$ *When you compare the slopes you see that* $15 > 7.$

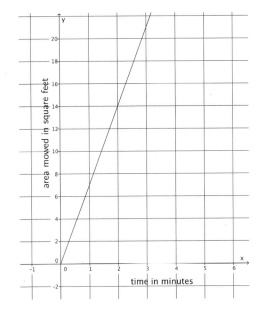

5.   a.   Juan can walk to school, a distance of 0.75 miles, in 8 minutes. Assuming he walks at a constant rate, write the linear equation that represents the situation.

Let y represent the total distance in miles that Juan can walk in x minutes. We can write $\frac{y}{x} = \frac{0.75}{8}$ *and* $y = \frac{3}{32}x.$

b.   The graph below represents Lena's constant rate of walking.

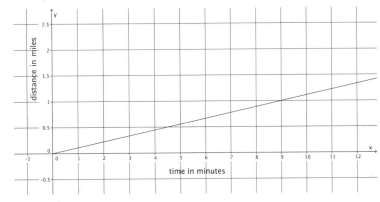

Who walks faster? Explain.

Lena walks faster. The slope of the graph for Lena is $\frac{1}{9}$, *and the slope of the equation for Juan is* $\frac{0.75}{8}$ *or* $\frac{3}{32}.$ *When you compare the slopes you see that* $\frac{1}{9} > \frac{3}{32}.$

Lesson 23: The Defining Equation of a Line

Student Outcomes

- Students know that two equations in the form of $ax + by = c$ and $a'x + b'y = c'$ graph as the same line when $\dfrac{a'}{a} = \dfrac{b'}{b} = \dfrac{c'}{c}$ and at least one of a or b is nonzero.

- Students know that the graph of a linear equation $ax + by = c$, where a, b, and c are constants and at least one of a or b is nonzero, is the line defined by the equation $ax + by = c$.

Lesson Notes

Following the Exploratory Challenge is a discussion that presents a theorem about the defining equation of a line (page 351) and then a proof of the theorem. The proof of the theorem is optional. The discussion can end with the theorem and in place of the proof, students can complete Exercises 4–8 beginning on page 353. Whether you choose to discuss the proof or have students complete Exercises 4–8, it is important that students understand that two equations that are written differently can be the same and their graph will be the same line. This reasoning becomes important when you consider systems of linear equations. In order to make sense of "infinitely many solutions" to a system of linear equations, students must know that equations that might appear different can have the same graph and represent the same line. Further, students should be able to recognize when two equations define the same line without having to graph each equation, which is the goal of this lesson. Students need graph paper to complete the Exploratory Challenge.

Classwork

Exploratory Challenge/Exercises 1–3 (20 minutes)

Students need graph paper to complete the Exercises in the Exploratory Challenge. Students complete Exercises 1–3 in pairs or small groups.

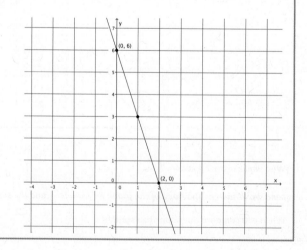

Exploratory Challenge/Exercises 1–3

1. Graph the equation $9x + 3y = 18$ using intercepts. Then answer parts (a)–(f) that follow.

$$9(0) + 3y = 18$$
$$3y = 18$$
$$y = 6$$

The y-intercept is $(0, 6)$.

$$9x + 3(0) = 18$$
$$9x = 18$$
$$x = 2$$

The x-intercept is $(2, 0)$.

Lesson 23:	The Defining Equation of a Line
Date:	11/8/13

a.   Graph the equation $y = -3x + 6$ on the same coordinate plane.

b.   What do you notice about the graphs of $9x + 3y = 18$ and $y = -3x + 6$? Why do you think this is so?

The graphs of the equations produce the same line. Both equations go through the same two points so they are the same line.

c.   Rewrite $y = -3x + 6$ in standard form.

$$y = -3x + 6$$
$$3x + y = 6$$

d.   Identify the constants, a, b, c of the equation in standard form from part (c).

$a = 3, b = 1, and \, c = 6.$

e.   Identify the constants of the equation $9x + 3y = 18$. Note them as $a', b',$ and c'.

$a' = 9, b' = 3, and \, c' = 18$

f.   What do you notice about $\dfrac{a'}{a}, \dfrac{b'}{b},$ and $\dfrac{c'}{c}$?

$$\frac{a'}{a} = \frac{9}{3} = 3, \qquad \frac{b'}{b} = \frac{3}{1} = 3, \quad and \quad \frac{c'}{c} = \frac{18}{6} = 3$$

Each fraction is equal to the number 3.

2.   Graph the equation $y = \frac{1}{2}x + 3$ using the y-intercept and the slope. Then answer parts (a)–(f) that follow.

a.   Graph the equation $4x - 8y = -24$ using intercepts on the same coordinate plane.

$$4(0) - 8y = -24$$
$$-8y = -24$$
$$y = 3$$

The y-intercept is $(0, 3)$.

$$4x - 8(0) = -24$$
$$4x = -24$$
$$x = -6$$

The x-intercept is $(-6, 0)$.

b.   What do you notice about the graphs of $y = \frac{1}{2}x + 3$ and $4x - 8y = -24$? Why do you think this is so?

The graphs of the equations produce the same line. Both equations go through the same two points, so they are the same line.

c. Rewrite $y = \frac{1}{2}x + 3$ in standard form.

$$y = \frac{1}{2}x + 3$$
$$\left(y = \frac{1}{2}x + 3\right)2$$
$$2y = x + 6$$
$$-x + 2y = 6$$
$$-1(-x + 2y = 6)$$
$$x - 2y = -6$$

d. Identify the constants, a, b, c of the equation in standard form from part (c).

$a = 1, b = -2$, and $c = -6$.

e. Identify the constants of the equation $4x - 8y = -24$. Note them as $a', b',$ and c'.

$a' = 4, b' = -8$, and $c' = -24$

f. What do you notice about $\frac{a'}{a}, \frac{b'}{b},$ and $\frac{c'}{c}$?

$$\frac{a'}{a} = \frac{4}{1} = 4, \qquad \frac{b'}{b} = \frac{-8}{-2} = 4, \qquad and \quad \frac{c'}{c} = \frac{-24}{-6} = 4$$

Each fraction is equal to the number 4.

3. The equations $y = \frac{2}{3}x - 4$ and $6x - 9y = 36$ graph as the same line.

a. Rewrite $y = \frac{2}{3}x - 4$ in standard form.

$$y = \frac{2}{3}x - 4$$
$$\left(y = \frac{2}{3}x - 4\right)3$$
$$3y = 2x - 12$$
$$-2x + 3y = -12$$
$$-1(-2x + 3y = -12)$$
$$2x - 3y = 12$$

b. Identify the constants, $a, b, c,$ of the equation in standard form from part (a).

$a = 2, b = -3$, and $c = 12$.

c. Identify the constants of the equation $6x - 9y = 36$. Note them as $a', b',$ and c'.

$a' = 6, b' = -9$, and $c' = 36$

d. What do you notice about $\frac{a'}{a}, \frac{b'}{b},$ and $\frac{c'}{c}$?

$$\frac{a'}{a} = \frac{6}{2} = 3, \qquad \frac{b'}{b} = \frac{-9}{-3} = 3, \qquad and \quad \frac{c'}{c} = \frac{36}{12} = 3$$

Each fraction is equal to the number 3.

---

e.   You should have noticed that each fraction was equal to the same constant. Multiply that constant by the standard form of the equation from part (a). What do you notice?

$$2x - 3y = 12$$
$$3(2x - 3y = 12)$$
$$6x - 9y = 36$$

After multiplying the equation from part (a) by 3, I noticed that it is the exact same equation that was given.

Discussion (15 minutes)

Following the statement of the theorem is an optional proof of the theorem. Below the proof are Exercises 4–8 (beginning on page 353) that can be completed instead of the proof.

- What did you notice about the equations you graphed in each of the Exercises 1–3?
  - □ *In each case, the equations graphed as the same line.*

- What you observed in Exercises 1–3 can be summarized in the following theorem:

Theorem. *Suppose a, b, c, a', b', and c' are constants,* where at least one of a or b is nonzero, and one of a' or b' is nonzero .

(1) *If there is a non-zero number s, so that $a' = sa$, $b' = sb$, and $c' = sc$, then the graphs of the equations $ax + by = c$ and $a'x + b'y = c'$ are the same line.*

(2) *If the graphs of the equations $ax + by = c$ and $a'x + b'y = c'$ are the same line, then there exists a nonzero number s so that $a' = sa$, $b' = sb$, and $c' = sc$.*

The optional part of the discussion begins here.

- We want to show that (1) is true. We need to show that the equations $ax + by = c$ and $a'x + b'y = c'$ are the same. What information are we given in (1) that will be useful in showing that the two equations are the same?
  - □ *We are given that $a' = sa$, $b' = sb$, and $c' = sc$. We can use substitution in the equation $a'x + b'y = c'$ since we know what a', b', and c' are equal to.*

- Then by substitution, we have

$$a'x + b'y = c'$$
$$sax + sby = sc$$

By the distributive property

$$s(ax + by) = sc$$

Divide both sides of the equation by s

$$ax + by = c$$

Which is what we wanted $a'x + b'y = c'$ to be equal to. Therefore, we have proved (1).

- ▪ To prove (2), we will assume that $a, b \neq 0$, that is, we are not dealing with horizontal or vertical lines. Proving (2) will require us to rewrite the given equations, $ax + by = c$ and $a'x + b'y = c'$, in slope-intercept form. Rewrite the equations.

  - □ $ax + by = c$

$$by = -ax + c$$
$$\frac{b}{b}y = -\frac{a}{b}x + \frac{c}{b}$$
$$y = -\frac{a}{b}x + \frac{c}{b}$$

  - □ $a'x + b'y = c'$

$$b'y = -a'x + c'$$
$$\frac{b'}{b'}y = -\frac{a'}{b'}x + \frac{c'}{b'}$$
$$y = -\frac{a'}{b'}x + \frac{c'}{b'}$$

- ▪ We will refer to $y = -\frac{a}{b}x + \frac{c}{b}$ as (A) and $y = -\frac{a'}{b'}x + \frac{c'}{b'}$ as (B).

- ▪ What are the slopes of (A) and (B)?

  - □ *The slope of (A) is $-\frac{a}{b}$ and the slope of (B) is $-\frac{a'}{b'}$.*

- ▪ Since we know that the two lines are the same, we know the slopes must be the same.

$$-\frac{a}{b} = -\frac{a'}{b'}$$

and when we multiply both sides of the equation by (-1), we have

$$\frac{a}{b} = \frac{a'}{b'}$$

By using the multiplication property of equality we can rewrite $\frac{a}{b} = \frac{a'}{b'}$ as

$$\frac{a'}{a} = \frac{b'}{b}$$

Notice that this proportion is equivalent to the original form.

> **Scaffolding:**
>
> Students may need to see the intermediate steps in the rewriting of $\frac{a}{b} = \frac{a'}{b'}$ as $\frac{a'}{a} = \frac{b'}{b}$.

- ▪ What are the y-intercepts of $y = -\frac{a}{b}x + \frac{c}{b}$ (A) and $y = -\frac{a'}{b'}x + \frac{c'}{b'}$ (B)?

  - □ *The y-intercept of (A) is $\frac{c}{b}$, and the y-intercept of (B) is $\frac{c'}{b'}$.*

- Because we know that the two lines are the same, the y-intercepts will be the same.

$$\frac{c}{b} = \frac{c'}{b'}$$

We can rewrite the proportion.

$$\frac{c'}{c} = \frac{b'}{b}$$

Using the transitive property and the fact that $\frac{a'}{a} = \frac{b'}{b}$ and $\frac{c'}{c} = \frac{b'}{b}$, we can make the following statement:

$$\frac{a'}{a} = \frac{b'}{b} = \frac{c'}{c}$$

Therefore, all three ratios are equal to the same number. Let this number be s.

$$\frac{a'}{a} = s, \frac{b'}{b} = s, \frac{c'}{c} = s$$

We can rewrite this to state that $a' = sa$, $b' = sb$, and $c' = sc$. Therefore, (2) is proved.

- When two equations are the same, i.e., they graph as the same line, we say that any one of those equations is the *defining equation* of the line.

Exercises 4–8 (15 minutes)

Students complete Exercises 4–8 independently or in pairs. Consider having students share the equations they write for each exercise while others in the class verify which equations graph as the same line.

Exercises 4–8

4. Write three equations that would graph as the same line as the equation $3x + 2y = 7$.

   Answers will vary. Verify that students have multiplied a, b, and c by the same constant when they write the new equation.

5. Write three equations that would graph as the same line as the equation $x - 9y = \frac{3}{4}$.

   Answers will vary. Verify that students have multiplied a, b, and c by the same constant when they write the new equation.

6. Write three equations that would graph as the same line as the equation $-9x + 5y = -4$.

   Answers will vary. Verify that students have multiplied a, b, and c by the same constant when they write the new equation.

---

7. Write at least two equations in the form $ax + by = c$ that would graph as the line shown below.

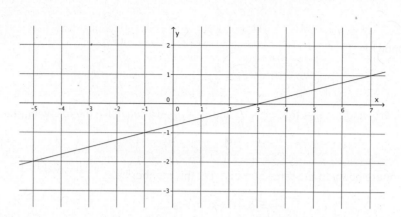

Answers will vary. Verify that students have the equation $-x + 4y = -3$ in some form.

8. Write at least two equations in the form $ax + by = c$ that would graph as the line shown below.

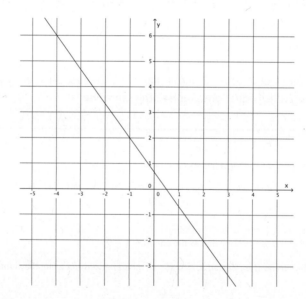

Answers will vary. Verify that students have the equation $4x + 3y = 2$ in some form.

Closing (5 minutes)

Summarize, or ask students to summarize, the main points from the lesson:

- We know that when two equations graph as the same line it is because they are the same equation in different forms.

- We know that even if the equations that graph as the same line look different (i.e., different constants or different forms) that any one of those equations can be referred to as the defining equation of the line.

Lesson Summary

Two equations that graph as the same line are said to define the same line. Two equations that define the same line are the same equation, just in different forms. The equations may look different (different constants, different coefficients, or different forms).

When two equations are written in standard form, $ax + by = c$ and $a'x + b'y = c'$, they define the same line when $\dfrac{a'}{a} = \dfrac{b'}{b} = \dfrac{c'}{c}$ is true.

Exit Ticket (5 minutes)

Name _____   Date _____

Lesson 23: The Defining Equation of a Line

Exit Ticket

1.   Do the equations $-16x + 12y = 33$ and $-4x + 3y = 8$ graph as the same line? Why or why not?

2.   Given the equation $3x - y = 11$, write another equation that will graph as the same line. Explain why.

Exit Ticket Sample Solutions

1. Do the equations $-16x + 12y = 33$ and $-4x + 3y = 8$ graph as the same line? Why or why not?

    No, in the first equation $a = -16$, $b = 12$, and $c = 33$, and in the second equation $a' = -4$, $b' = 3$, and $c' = 8$. Then,

    $$\frac{a'}{a} = \frac{-4}{-16} = \frac{1}{4}, \qquad \frac{b'}{b} = \frac{3}{12} = \frac{1}{4},$$

    $$but \quad \frac{c'}{c} = \frac{8}{33} = \frac{8}{33}.$$

    Since each fraction does not equal the same number, then they do not graph to the same line.

2. Given the equation $3x - y = 11$, write another equation that will graph as the same line. Explain why.

    Answers will vary. Verify that the student has written an equation that defines the same line by showing that the fractions $\frac{a'}{a} = \frac{b'}{b} = \frac{c'}{c} = s$, where s is some constant.

Problem Set Sample Solutions

Students practice identifying pairs of equations as the defining equation of a line or two distinct lines.

1. Do the equations $x + y = -2$ and $3x + 3y = -6$ define the same line? Explain.

    Yes, these equations define the same line. When you compare the constants from each equation you get:

    $$\frac{a'}{a} = \frac{3}{1} = 3, \qquad \frac{b'}{b} = \frac{3}{1} = 3, \qquad and \qquad \frac{c'}{c} = \frac{-6}{-2} = 3$$

    When I multiply the first equation by 3, I get the second equation:

    $$(x + y = -2)3$$
    $$3x + 3y = -6$$

    Therefore, these equations define the same line.

2. Do the equations $y = -\frac{5}{4}x + 2$ and $10x + 8y = 16$ define the same line? Explain.

    Yes, these equations define the same line. When you rewrite the first equation in standard form you get:

    $$y = -\frac{5}{4}x + 2$$
    $$\left(y = -\frac{5}{4}x + 2\right)4$$
    $$4y = -5x + 8$$
    $$5x + 4y = 8$$

    When you compare the constants from each equation you get:

    $$\frac{a'}{a} = \frac{10}{5} = 2, \qquad \frac{b'}{b} = \frac{8}{4} = 2, \qquad and \qquad \frac{c'}{c} = \frac{16}{8} = 2$$

    When I multiply the first equation by 2, I get the second equation:

    $$(5x + 4y = 8)2$$
    $$10x + 8y = 16$$

    Therefore, these equations define the same line.

3. Write an equation that would define the same line as $7x - 2y = 5$.

    Answers will vary. Verify that the student has written an equation that defines the same line by showing that the fractions $\dfrac{a'}{a} = \dfrac{b'}{b} = \dfrac{c'}{c} = s$, where s is some constant.

4. Challenge: Show that if the two lines given by $ax + by = c$ and $a'x + b'y = c'$ are the same when $b = 0$ (vertical lines), then there exists a non-zero number s, so that $a' = sa$, $b' = sb$, and $c' = sc$.

    When $b = 0$, then the equations are $ax = c$ and $a'x = c'$. We can rewrite the equations as $x = \dfrac{c}{a}$ and $x = \dfrac{c'}{a'}$. Because the equations graph as the same line, then we know that

    $$\frac{c}{a} = \frac{c'}{a'}$$

    and we can rewrite those fractions as

    $$\frac{a'}{a} = \frac{c'}{c}$$

    These fractions are equal to the same number. Let that number be s. Then $\dfrac{a'}{a} = s$ and $\dfrac{c'}{c} = s$, and therefore, $a' = sa$ and $c' = sc$, as desired.

5. Challenge: Show that if the two lines given by $ax + by = c$ and $a'x + b'y = c'$ are the same when $a = 0$ (horizontal lines), then there exists a non-zero number s, so that $a' = sa$, $b' = sb$, and $c' = sc$.

    When $a = 0$, then the equations are $by = c$ and $b'y = c'$. We can rewrite the equations as $y = \dfrac{c}{b}$ and $y = \dfrac{c'}{b'}$. Because the equations graph as the same line, then we know that their slopes are the same.

    $$\frac{c}{b} = \frac{c'}{b'}$$

    We can rewrite the proportion.

    $$\frac{b'}{b} = \frac{c'}{c}$$

    These fractions are equal to the same number. Let that number be s. Then $\dfrac{b'}{b} = s$ and $\dfrac{c'}{c} = s$. Therefore, $b' = sb$ and $c' = sc$.

Topic D:

Systems of Linear Equations and Their Solutions

8.EE.B.5, 8.EE.C.8

Focus Standards:	8.EE.B.5	Graph proportional relationships, interpreting the unit rate as the slope of the graph. Compare two different proportional relationships represented in different ways.
	8.EE.C.8	Analyze and solve pairs of simultaneous linear equations.
		a. Understand that solutions to a system of two linear equations in two variables correspond to points of intersection of their graphs, because points of intersection satisfy both equations simultaneously.
		b. Solve systems of two linear equations in two variables algebraically, and estimate solutions by graphing the equations. Solve simple cases by inspection. *For example, 3x + 2y = 5 and 3x + 2y = 6 have no solution because 3x + 2y cannot simultaneously be 5 and 6.*
		c. Solve real-world and mathematical problems leading to two linear equations in two variables. *For example, given coordinates for two pairs of points, determine whether the line through the first pair of points intersects the line through the second pair.*

Instructional Days: 7

[1] Lesson Structure Key: **P**-Problem Set Lesson, **M**-Modeling Cycle Lesson, **E**-Exploration Lesson, **S**-Socratic Lesson

Topic D introduces students to systems of linear equations by comparing distance-time graphs to determine which of two objects has greater speed (**8.EE.B.5**, **8.EE.C.8c**). Lessons 25–27 expose students to the possibilities for solutions of a system of linear equations. In Lesson 25, students graph two linear equations on a coordinate plane and identify the point of intersection of the two lines as the solution to the system (**8.EE.C.8a**). Next, students look at systems of equations that graph as parallel lines (**8.EE.C.8b**). In Lesson 26, students learn that a system can have no solutions because parallel lines do not have a point of intersection (**8.EE.C.8b**). Lesson 27 continues this thinking with respect to systems that have infinitely many solutions (**8.EE.C.8b**). In Lesson 28, students learn how to solve a system of equations using computational methods like elimination and substitution (**8.EE.C.8b**). In Lesson 29, students must use all of the skills of the module to transcribe written statements into a system of linear equations, find the solution(s) if it exists, and then verify that it is correct. Lesson 30 is an application of what students have learned about linear equations. Students develop a linear equation that represents the conversion between temperatures in Celsius to temperatures in Fahrenheit.

Lesson 24: Introduction to Simultaneous Equations

Student Outcomes

- Students know that a system of linear equations, also known as simultaneous equations, is when two or more equations are involved in the same problem and work must be completed on them simultaneously. Students also learn the notation for simultaneous equations.

- Students compare the graphs that comprise a system of linear equations, in the context of constant rates, to answer questions about time and distance.

Lesson Notes

In the Opening Exercise students complete Exercises 1–3 as an introduction to simultaneous linear equations in a familiar context. Example 1 demonstrates what happens to the graph of a line when there is change in the circumstances involving time with constant rate problems. It is in preparation for the examples that follow. It is not necessary that Example 1 be shown to students, but it is provided as a scaffold. If Example 1 is used, consider skipping Example 3.

Classwork

Opening Exercises 1–3 (5 minutes)

Students complete the opening activity in pairs. Once students are finished, continue with the discussion about systems of linear equations.

Opening Exercises 1–3

1. Derek scored 30 points in the basketball game he played and not once did he go to the free throw line. That means that Derek scored two point shots and three point shots. List as many combinations of two and three pointers as you can that would total 30 points.

Number of Two-Pointers	Number of Three-Pointers
15	0
0	10
12	2
9	4
6	6
3	8

Write an equation to describe the data.

Let x represent the number of 2 pointers and y represent the number of 3 pointers.

$30 = 2x + 3y$

Lesson 24:	Introduction to Simultaneous Equations	
Date:	11/8/13	

2. Derek tells you that the number of two-point shots that he made is five more than the number of three-point shots. How many combinations can you come up with that fit this scenario? (Don't worry about the total number of points.)

Number of Two-Pointers	Number of Three-Pointers
6	1
7	2
8	3
9	4
10	5
11	6

Write an equation to describe the data.

Let x represent the number of two-pointers and y represent the number of three-pointers.

$x = 5 + y$

3. Which pair of numbers from your table in Exercise 2 would show Derek's actual score of 30 points?

The pair 9 and 4 would show Derek's actual score of 30 points.

Discussion (5 minutes)

- There are situations where we need to work with two linear equations simultaneously. Hence, the phrase *simultaneous linear equations*. Sometimes a pair of linear equations is referred to as a *system of linear equations*.

- The situation with Derek can be represented as a system of linear equations:

  Let x represent the number of two-pointers and y represent the number of three-pointers, then

$$\begin{cases} 2x + 3y = 30 \\ x = 5 + y \end{cases}$$

- The notation for simultaneous linear equations let's us know that we are looking for the ordered pair (x, y) that makes both equations true. That point is called the solution to the system.

- Just like equations in one variable, some systems of equations have exactly one solution, no solution, or infinitely many solutions. This is a topic for later lessons.

- Ultimately our goal is to determine the exact location on the coordinate plane where the graphs of the two linear equations intersect, giving us the ordered pair (x, y) that is the solution to the system of equations. This too is a topic for a later lesson.

Lesson 24:   Introduction to Simultaneous Equations
Date: 11/8/13

- We can graph both equations on the same coordinate plane:

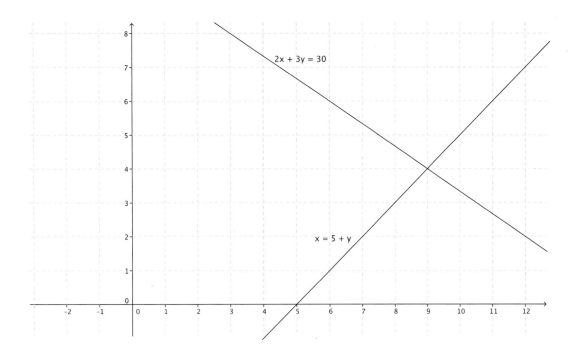

- Because we are graphing two distinct lines on the same graph, we identify the lines in some manner. In this case, by the equations.

- Note the point of intersection. Does it satisfy both equations in the system?
    - *The point of intersection of the two lines is $(9, 4)$.*

$$2(9) + 3(4) = 30$$

$$18 + 12 = 30$$

$$30 = 30$$

$$9 = 4 + 5$$

$$9 = 9$$

Yes, $x = 9$ and $y = 4$ satisfies both equations of the system.

- Therefore, Derek made 9 two-point shots and 4 three-point shots.

Example 1 (6 minutes)

- Pia types at a constant rate of 3 pages every 15 minutes. Suppose she types y pages in x minutes. Pia's constant rate can be expressed as the linear equation $y = \frac{1}{5}x$.

- We can complete a table to make sure that our graph is correct:

Number of Minutes (x)	Pages Typed (y)
0	0
5	1
10	2
15	3
20	4
25	5

- Here is the graph that represents Pia's constant rate of typing.

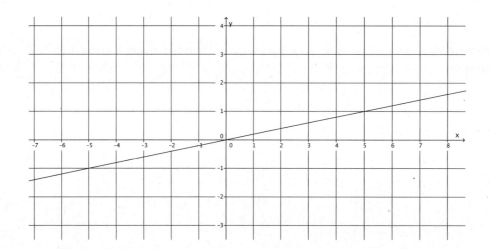

- Pia typically begins work at 8:00 a.m. every day. On our graph, her start time is reflected as the origin of the graph $(0, 0)$, that is, zero minutes worked and zero pages typed. For some reason, she started working 5 minutes earlier today. How can we reflect her extra time working today on our graph?

  □ *The x-axis represents the time worked so we need to do something on the x-axis to reflect the additional 5 minutes of work.*

- If we translate the graph of $y = \frac{1}{5}x$ to the right 5 units to reflect the "additional" 5 minutes of work, then we have

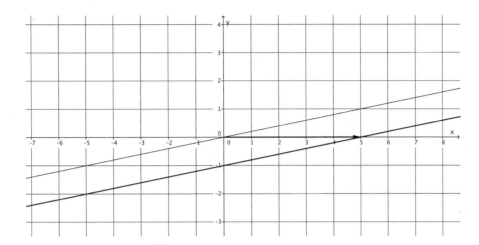

- Does a translation of 5 units to the right reflect her working an additional 5 minutes?
  - *No, it makes it look like she got nothing done the first 5 minutes she was at work.*

- Let's see what happens when we translate 5 units to the left.

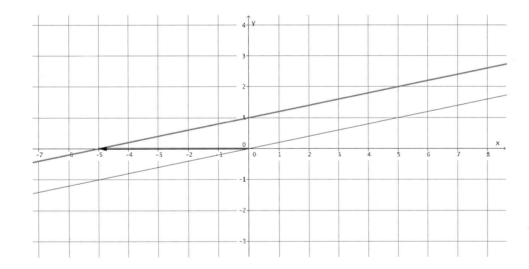

- Does a translation of 5 units to the left reflect her working an additional 5 minutes?
  - *Yes, it shows that she was able to type 1 page by the time she normally begins work.*

- What is the equation that represents the graph of the translated line?
  - *The equation that represents the graph of the red line is $y = \frac{1}{5}x + 1$.*

- Note again, that even though the graph has been translated, the slope of the line is still equal to the constant rate of typing.

- When you factor out $\frac{1}{5}$ from $\frac{1}{5}x + 1$, we can better see the "additional" 5 minutes of work time:

  $y = \frac{1}{5}(x + 5)$. Pia typed for an additional 5 minutes so it makes sense that we are adding 5 to the number of minutes, x that she types. However, on the graph, we translated 5 units to the left of zero. How can we make sense of that?

  - *Since her normal start time was 8:00, then 5 minutes before 8:00 is 5 minutes less than 8:00, which means we would need to go to the left of 8:00, in this case the origin of the graph, to mark her start time.*

- If Pia started work 20 minutes early, what equation would represent the number of pages she could type in x minutes?

  - *The equation that represents the graph of the red line is $y = \frac{1}{5}(x + 20)$.*

Example 2 (10 minutes)

- Now we will look at an example of a situation that requires simultaneous linear equations.

  Sandy and Charlie walk at constant speeds. Sandy walks from their school to the train station in 15 minutes and Charlie walks the same distance in 10 minutes. Charlie starts 4 minutes after Sandy left the school. Can Charlie catch up to Sandy? The distance between the school and the station is 2 miles.

- What is Sandy's average speed in 15 minutes? Explain.

  - *Sandy's average speed in 15 minutes is $\frac{2}{15}$ miles per minute because she walks 2 miles in 15 minutes.*

- Since we know Sandy walks at a constant speed, then her constant speed is $\frac{2}{15}$ miles per minute.

MP.2

- What is Charlie's average speed in 10 minutes? Explain.

  - *Charlie's average speed in 10 minutes is $\frac{2}{10}$ miles per minute, which is the same as $\frac{1}{5}$ miles per minute because he walks 1 mile in 5 minutes.*

- Since we know Charlie walks at a constant speed, then his constant speed is $\frac{1}{5}$ miles per minute.

- Suppose the distance walked by Charlie in x minutes is y miles. Then we can write a linear equation to represent Charlie's motion:

$$\frac{y}{x} = \frac{1}{5}$$
$$y = \frac{1}{5}x$$

- Let's put some information about Charlie's walk in a table:

Number of Minutes (x)	Miles Walked (y)
0	0
5	1
10	2
15	3
20	4
25	5

- At x minutes, Sandy has walked 4 minutes longer than Charlie. Then the distance that Sandy walked in $x + 4$ minutes is y miles. Then the linear equation that represents Sandy's motion is:

$$\frac{y}{x+4} = \frac{2}{15}$$

$$y = \frac{2}{15}(x + 4)$$

$$y = \frac{2}{15}x + \frac{8}{15}$$

Let's put some information about Sandy's walk in a table:

Number of Minutes (x)	Miles Walked (y)
0	$\dfrac{8}{15}$
5	$\dfrac{18}{15} = 1\dfrac{3}{15} = 1\dfrac{1}{5}$
10	$\dfrac{28}{15} = 1\dfrac{13}{15}$
15	$\dfrac{38}{15} = 2\dfrac{8}{15}$
20	$\dfrac{48}{15} = 3\dfrac{3}{15} = 3\dfrac{1}{5}$
25	$\dfrac{58}{15} = 3\dfrac{13}{15}$

- Now let's graph each linear equation on a coordinate plane.

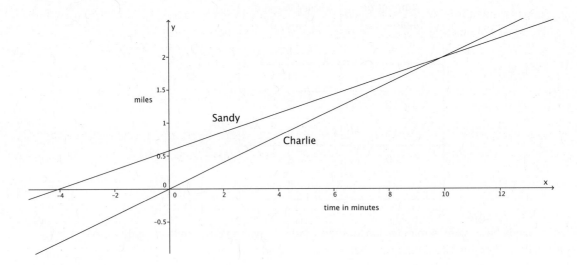

- A couple of comments about our graph:

  - The y-intercept of the graph of Sandy shows exactly the distance she has walked at the moment that Charlie starts walking. Notice that the x-intercept of the graph of Sandy shows that she starts walking 4 minutes before Charlie.

  - Since the y-axis represents the distance traveled, then the point of intersection of the graphs of the two lines represents the moment they have both walked the same distance.

- Recall the original question that was asked, can Charlie catch up to Sandy? Keep in mind that the train station is 2 miles from the school.

  - *It looks like the lines intersect at a point between 1.5 and 2 miles; therefore, the answer is yes, Charlie can catch up to Sandy.*

- At approximately what point do the graphs of the lines intersect?

  - *The lines intersect at approximately $(10, 1.8)$.*

- A couple of comments about our equations, $y = \frac{1}{5}x$ and $y = \frac{2}{15}x + \frac{8}{15}$:

  - Notice that x (the representation of time) is the same in both equations.

  - Notice that we are interested in finding out when $y = y$, that is, when the distance traveled by both Sandy and Charlie is the same (that's when Charlie catches up to Sandy).

  - We write the pair of simultaneous linear equations as

$$\begin{cases} y = \frac{2}{15}x + \frac{8}{15} \\ y = \frac{1}{5}x \end{cases}$$

Lesson 24: Introduction to Simultaneous Equations
Date: 11/8/13

368

Example 3 (6 minutes)

- Randi and Craig ride their bikes at constant speeds. It takes Randi 25 minutes to bike 4 miles. Craig can bike 4 miles in 32 minutes. If Randi gives Craig a 20 minute head start, about how long will it take Randi to catch up to Craig?

- We want to express the information about Randi and Craig in terms of a system of linear equations. Write the linear equations that represent their constant speeds.

  - *Randi's average speed in 25 minutes is $\frac{4}{25}$ miles per minute. Since Randi bikes at a constant speed, if we let y be the distance Randi travels in x minutes, then the linear equation that represents her motion is*

$$\frac{y}{x} = \frac{4}{25}$$
$$y = \frac{4}{25}x$$

  - *Craig's average speed in 32 minutes is $\frac{4}{32}$ miles per minute, which is equivalent to $\frac{1}{8}$ miles per minute. Since Craig bikes at a constant speed, if we let y be the distance Craig travels in x minutes, then the linear equation that represent his motion is*

$$\frac{y}{x} = \frac{1}{8}$$
$$y = \frac{1}{8}x$$

- We want to account for the head start that Craig is getting. Since Craig gets a head start of 20 minutes, then we need to add that time to his total number of minutes traveled at his constant rate:

$$y = \frac{1}{8}(x + 20)$$
$$y = \frac{1}{8}x + \frac{20}{8}$$
$$y = \frac{1}{8}x + \frac{5}{2}$$

- The system of linear equations that represents this situation is

$$\begin{cases} y = \frac{1}{8}x + \frac{5}{2} \\ y = \frac{4}{25}x \end{cases}$$

■   Now we can graph the system of equations on a coordinate plane.

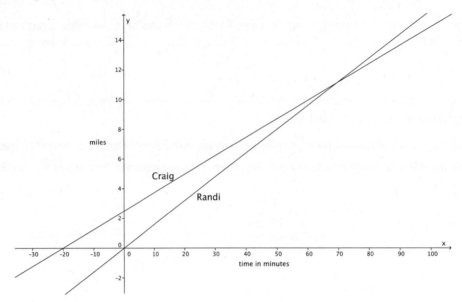

Notice again that the y-intercept of Craig's graph shows the distance that Craig was able to travel at the moment Randi began biking. Also notice that the x-intercept of Craig's graph shows us that he started biking 20 minutes before Randi.

■   Now to answer the question: About how long will it take Randi to catch up to Craig? We can give two answers, one in terms of time and the other in terms of distance. What are those answers?

    □   *It will take Randi about* 70 *minutes or about* 11 *miles to catch up to Craig.*

■   At approximately what point do the graphs of the lines intersect?

    □   *The lines intersect at approximately* $(70, 11)$.

Exercises 4–5 (10 minutes)

Students complete Exercises 4–5 individually or in pairs.

Exercises

4.   Efrain and Fernie are on a road trip. Each of them drives at a constant speed. Efrain is a safe driver and travels 45 miles per hour for the entire trip. Fernie is not such a safe driver. He drives 70 miles per hour throughout the trip. Fernie and Efrain left from the same location, but Efrain left at 8:00 a.m. and Fernie left at 11:00 a.m. Assuming they take the same route, will Fernie ever catch up to Efrain? If so, approximately when?

   a.   Write the linear equation that represents Efrain's constant speed. Make sure to include in your equation the extra time that Efrain was able to travel.

   Efrain's average speed over one hour is $\dfrac{45}{1}$ *miles per hour, which is the same as* 45 *miles per hour. If y represents the distance he travels in x hours, then we have* $\dfrac{y}{x} = 45$ *and the linear equation* $y = 45x$. *To account for his additional 5 hours of driving time that Efrain gets, we write the equation*

   $$y = 45(x + 3)$$
   $$y = 45x + 135$$

---

b.   Write the linear equation that represents Fernie's constant speed.

Fernie's average speed over one hour is $\frac{70}{1}$ miles per hour, which is the same as 70 miles per hour. If y represents the distance he travels in x hours, then we have $\frac{y}{x} = 70$ and the linear equation $y = 70x$.

c.   Write the system of linear equations that represents this situation.

$$\begin{cases} y = 45x + 135 \\ y = 70x \end{cases}$$

d.   Sketch the graph.

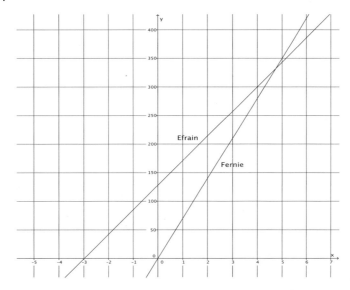

e.   Will Fernie ever catch up to Efrain? If so, approximately when?

Yes, Fernie will catch up to Efrain after about $4\frac{1}{2}$ hours of driving or after traveling about 325 miles.

f.   At approximately what point do the graphs of the lines intersect?

The lines intersect at approximately $(4.5, 325)$.

5.   Jessica and Karl run at constant speeds. Jessica can run 3 miles in 15 minutes. Karl can run 2 miles in 8 minutes. They decide to race each other. As soon as the race begins, Karl realizes that he did not tie his shoes properly and takes 1 minute to fix them.

     a.   Write the linear equation that represents Jessica's constant speed. Make sure to include in your equation the extra time that Jessica was able to run.

Jessica's average speed over 15 minutes is $\frac{3}{15}$ miles per minute, which is equivalent to $\frac{1}{5}$ miles per minute. If y represents the distance she runs in x minutes, then we have $\frac{y}{x} = \frac{1}{5}$ and the linear equation $y = \frac{1}{5}x$. To account for her additional 1 minute of running that Jessica gets, we write the equation

$$y = \frac{1}{5}(x + 1)$$
$$y = \frac{1}{5}x + \frac{1}{5}$$

b.   Write the linear equation that represents Karl's constant speed.

Karl's average speed over 8 minutes is $\frac{2}{8}$ miles per minute, which is the same as $\frac{1}{4}$ miles per minute. If y represents the distance he runs in x minutes, then we have $\frac{y}{x} = \frac{1}{4}$ and the linear equation $y = \frac{1}{4}x$.

c.   Write the system of linear equations that represents this situation.

$$\begin{cases} y = \dfrac{1}{5}x + \dfrac{1}{5} \\ y = \dfrac{1}{4}x \end{cases}$$

d.   Sketch the graph.

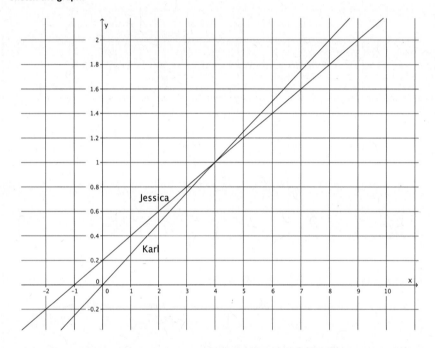

e.   Use the graph to answer the questions below.

i.   If Jessica and Karl raced for 2 miles. Who would win? Explain.

If the race were 2 miles, then Karl would win. It only takes Karl 8 minutes to run 2 miles, but it takes Jessica 9 minutes to run the distance of 2 miles.

ii.   If the winner of the race was the person who got to a distance of $\frac{1}{2}$ mile first, who would the winner be? Explain.

At $\frac{1}{2}$ miles, Jessica would be the winner. She would reach the distance of $\frac{1}{2}$ miles between 1 and 2 minutes, but Karl wouldn't get there until about 2 minutes have passed.

iii.   At approximately what point would Jessica and Karl be tied? Explain.

Jessica and Karl would be tied after about 4 minutes or a distance of 1 mile. That is where the graphs of the lines intersect.

Closing (4 minutes)

Summarize, or ask students to summarize, the main points from the lesson:

- We know that some situations require two linear equations. In those cases, we have what is called a system of linear equations or simultaneous linear equations.

- The solution to a system of linear equations, similar to a linear equation, is all of the points that make the equations true.

- We can recognize a system of equations by the notation used, for example: $\begin{cases} y = \frac{1}{8}x + \frac{5}{2} \\ y = \frac{4}{25}x \end{cases}$.

Lesson Summary

Simultaneous linear equations, or a system of linear equations, is when two or more linear equations are involved in the same problem. Simultaneous linear equations are graphed on the same coordinate plane.

The solution to a system of linear equations is the set of all points that make the equations of the system true. If given two equations in the system, the solution(s) must make both equations true.

Systems of linear equations are identified by the notation used, for example: $\begin{cases} y = \frac{1}{8}x + \frac{5}{2} \\ y = \frac{4}{25}x \end{cases}$.

Exit Ticket (5 minutes)

Name _____   Date _____

Lesson 24: Introduction to Simultaneous Equations

Exit Ticket

1. Darnell and Hector ride their bikes at constant speeds. Darnell leaves Hector's house to bike home. He can bike the 8 miles in 32 minutes. Five minutes after Darnell leaves, Hector realizes that Darnell left his phone. Hector rides to catch up. He can ride to Darnell's house in 24 minutes. Assuming they bike the same path, will Hector catch up to Darnell before he gets home?

    a. Write the linear equation that represents Darnell's constant speed.

    b. Write the linear equation that represents Hector's constant speed. Make sure to take into account that Hector left after Darnell.

    c. Write the system of linear equations that represents this situation.

d.   Sketch the graph.

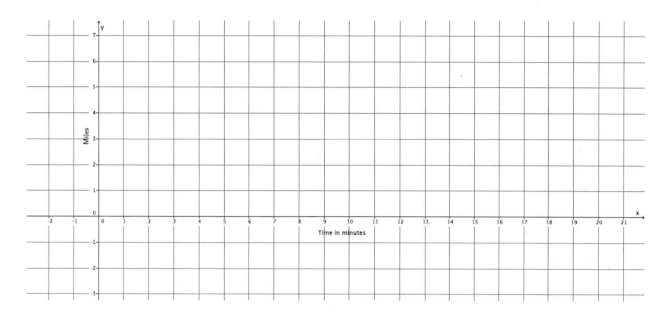

e.   Will Hector catch up to Darnell before he gets home? If so, approximately when?

f.   At approximately what point do the graphs of the lines intersect?

Exit Ticket Sample Solutions

1. Darnell and Hector ride their bikes at constant speeds. Darnell leaves Hector's house to bike home. He can bike the 8 miles in 32 minutes. Five minutes after Darnell leaves, Hector realizes that Darnell left his phone. Hector rides to catch up. He can ride to Darnell's house in 24 minutes. Assuming they bike the same path, will Hector catch up to Darnell before he gets home?

   a. Write the linear equation that represents Darnell's constant speed.

   Darnell's average speed over 32 minutes is $\frac{1}{4}$ miles per minute. If y represents the distance he bikes in x minutes, then the linear equations is $y = \frac{1}{4}x$.

   b. Write the linear equation that represents Hector's constant speed. Make sure to take into account that Hector left after Darnell.

   Hector's average speed over 24 minutes is $\frac{1}{3}$ miles per minute. If y represents the distance he bikes in x minutes, then the linear equation is $y = \frac{1}{3}x$. To account for the extra time Darnell has to bike, we write the equation

   $$y = \frac{1}{3}(x - 5)$$
   $$y = \frac{1}{3}x - \frac{5}{3}$$

   c. Write the system of linear equations that represents this situation.

   $$\begin{cases} y = \frac{1}{4}x \\ y = \frac{1}{3}x - \frac{5}{3} \end{cases}$$

   d. Sketch the graph.

   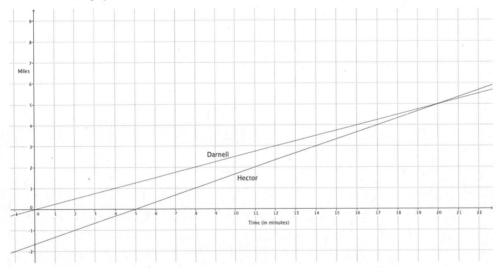

   e. Will Hector catch up to Darnell before he gets home? If so, approximately when?

   Hector will catch up 20 minutes after Darnell left his house (or 15 minutes of biking by Hector) or approximately 5 miles.

   f. At approximately what point do the graphs of the lines intersect?

   The lines intersect at approximately $(20, 5)$.

Lesson 24:	Introduction to Simultaneous Equations
Date:	11/8/13

Problem Set Sample Solutions

1. Jeremy and Gerardo run at constant speeds. Jeremy can run 1 mile in 8 minutes and Gerardo can run 3 miles in 33 minutes. Jeremy started running 10 minutes after Gerardo. Assuming they run the same path, when will Jeremy catch up to Gerardo?

   a. Write the linear equation that represents Jeremy's constant speed.

   Jeremy's average speed over 8 minutes is $\frac{1}{8}$ miles per minute. If y represents the distance he runs in x minutes, then we have $\frac{y}{x} = \frac{1}{8}$ and the linear equation $y = \frac{1}{8}x$.

   b. Write the linear equation that represents Gerardo's constant speed. Make sure to include in your equation the extra time that Gerardo was able to run.

   Gerardo's average speed over 33 minutes is $\frac{3}{33}$ miles per minute, which is the same as $\frac{1}{11}$ miles per minute. If y represents the distance he runs in x minutes, then we have $\frac{y}{x} = \frac{1}{11}$ and the linear equation $y = \frac{1}{11}x$. To account for the extra time that Gerardo gets to run, we write the equation

   $$y = \frac{1}{11}(x + 10)$$
   $$y = \frac{1}{11}x + \frac{10}{11}$$

   c. Write the system of linear equations that represents this situation.

   $$\begin{cases} y = \frac{1}{8}x \\ y = \frac{1}{11}x + \frac{10}{11} \end{cases}$$

   d. Sketch the graph.

   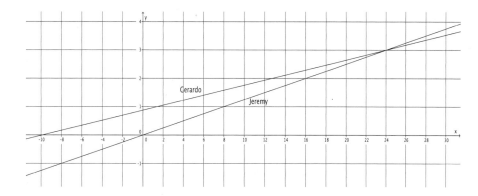

   e. Will Jeremy ever catch up to Gerardo? If so, approximately when?

   Yes, Jeremy will catch up to Gerardo after about 24 minutes or about 3 miles.

   f. At approximately what point do the graphs of the lines intersect?

   The lines intersect at approximately $(24, 3)$.

Lesson 24: Introduction to Simultaneous Equations
Date: 11/8/13

377

2. Two cars drive from town A to town B at constant speeds. The blue car travels 25 miles per hour and the red car travels 60 miles per hour. The blue car leaves at 9:30 a.m. and the red car leaves at noon. The distance between the two towns is 150 miles. Who will get there first? Write and graph the system of linear equations that represents this situation.

The linear equation that represents the blue car is $y = 25(x + 2.5)$, which is the same as $y = 25x + 62.5$. The linear equation that represents the red car is $y = 60x$. The system of linear equations that represents this situation is

$$\begin{cases} y = 25x + 62.5 \\ y = 60x \end{cases}$$

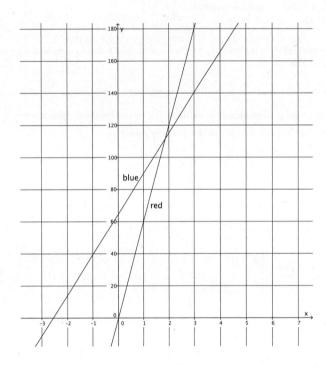

The red car will get to town B first.

a. At approximately what point do the graphs of the lines intersect?

The lines intersect at approximately $(1.8, 110)$.

Lesson 25: Geometric Interpretation of the Solutions of a Linear System

Student Outcomes

- Students graph two equations and find the point of intersection.
- Students identify the point of intersection of the two lines as the solution to the system.
- Students verify by computation that the point of intersection is a solution to each of the equations in the system.

Lesson Notes

In the last lesson students were introduced to the concept of simultaneous equations. Students compared the graphs of two different equations and found the point of intersection. Students estimated the coordinates of the point of intersection of the lines in order to answer questions about the context related to time and distance. In this lesson, students first graph systems of linear equations and find the precise point of intersection. Then, students verify that the ordered pair that is the intersection of the two lines is a solution to *each* equation in the system. Finally, students informally verify that there can be only one point of intersection of two distinct lines in the system by checking to see if another point that is a solution to one equation is a solution to both equations.

Students need graph paper to complete the problem set.

Classwork

Exercises 1–5 (25 minutes)

Students work independently on Exercises 1–5.

Exercises

1. Graph the linear system on a coordinate plane: $\begin{cases} 2y + x = 12 \\ y = \dfrac{5}{6}x - 2 \end{cases}$

   For the equation $2y + x = 12$:

   $$2y + 0 = 12$$
   $$2y = 12$$
   $$y = 6$$

   The y-intercept is $(0, 6)$.

   $$2(0) + x = 12$$
   $$x = 12$$
   $$x = 12$$

   The x-intercept is $(12, 0)$.

   For the equation $y = \dfrac{5}{6}x - 2$:

   The slope is $\dfrac{5}{6}$, and the y-intercept is $(0, -2)$.

	Lesson 25:	Geometric Interpretation of the Solutions of a Linear System	
	Date:	11/8/13	379

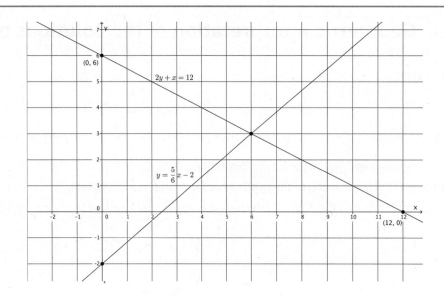

a.   Name the ordered pair where the graphs of the two linear equations intersect.

$$(6, 3)$$

b.   Verify that the ordered pair named in (a) is a solution to $2y + x = 12$.

$$2(3) + 6 = 12$$
$$6 + 6 = 12$$
$$12 = 12$$

The left and right sides of the equation are equal.

c.   Verify that the ordered pair named in (a) is a solution to $y = \frac{5}{6}x - 2$.

$$3 = \frac{5}{6}(6) - 2$$
$$3 = 5 - 2$$
$$3 = 3$$

The left and right sides of the equation are equal.

d.   Could the point $(4, 4)$ be a solution to the system of linear equations? That is, would $(4, 4)$ make both equations true? Why or why not?

No. The graphs of the equations represent all of the possible solutions to the given equations. The point $(4, 4)$ is a solution to the equation $2y + x = 12$ because it is on the graph of that equation. However, the point $(4, 4)$ is not on the graph of the equation $y = \frac{5}{6}x - 2$. Therefore, $(4, 4)$ cannot be a solution to the system of equations.

2. Graph the linear system on a coordinate plane: $\begin{cases} x + y = -2 \\ y = 4x + 3 \end{cases}$

For the equation $x + y = -2$:

$$0 + y = -2$$
$$y = -2$$
The y-intercept is $(0, -2)$.

$$x + 0 = -2$$
$$x = -2$$

The x-intercept is $(-2, 0)$.

For the equation $y = 4x + 3$:

The slope is $\frac{4}{1}$, and the y-intercept is $(0, 3)$.

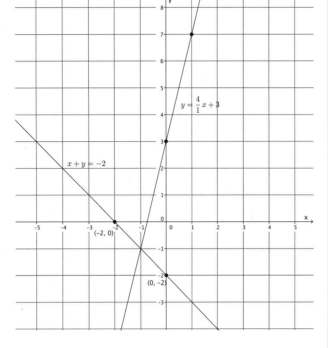

a. Name the ordered pair where the graphs of the two linear equations intersect.

$$(-1, -1)$$

b. Verify that the ordered pair named in (a) is a solution to $x + y = -2$.

$$-1 + (-1) = -2$$
$$-2 = -2$$

The left and right sides of the equation are equal.

c. Verify that the ordered pair named in (a) is a solution to $y = 4x + 3$.

$$-1 = 4(-1) + 3$$
$$-1 = -4 + 3$$
$$-1 = -1$$

The left and right sides of the equation are equal.

d. Could the point $(-4, 2)$ be a solution to the system of linear equations? That is, would $(-4, 2)$ make both equations true? Why or why not?

No. The graphs of the equations represent all of the possible solutions to the given equations. The point $(-4, 2)$ is a solution to the equation $x + y = -2$ because it is on the graph of that equation. However, the point $(-4, 2)$ is not on the graph of the equation $y = 4x + 3$. Therefore, $(-4, 2)$ cannot be a solution to the system of equations.

3. Graph the linear system on a coordinate plane: $\begin{cases} 3x + y = -3 \\ -2x + y = 2 \end{cases}$

For the equation $3x + y = -3$:

$$3(0) + y = -3$$
$$y = -3$$

The y-intercept is $(0, -3)$.

$$3x + 0 = -3$$
$$3x = -3$$
$$x = -1$$

The x-intercept is $(-1, 0)$.

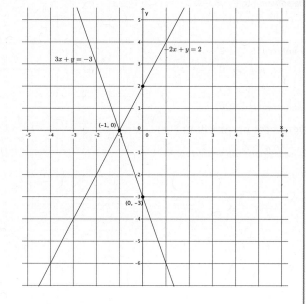

For the equation $-2x + y = 2$:

$$-2(0) + y = 2$$
$$y = 2$$

The y-intercept is $(0, 2)$.

$$-2x + 0 = 2$$
$$-2x = 2$$
$$x = -1$$

The x-intercept is $(-1, 0)$.

a. Name the ordered pair where the graphs of the two linear equations intersect.

$$(-1, 0)$$

b. Verify that the ordered pair named in (a) is a solution to $3x + y = -3$.

$$3(-1) + 0 = -3$$
$$-3 = -3$$

The left and right sides of the equation are equal.

c. Verify that the ordered pair named in (a) is a solution to $-2x + y = 2$.

$$-2(-1) + 0 = 2$$
$$2 = 2$$

The left and right sides of the equation are equal.

d. Could the point $(1, 4)$ be a solution to the system of linear equations? That is, would $(1, 4)$ make both equations true? Why or why not?

No. The graphs of the equations represent all of the possible solutions to the given equations. The point $(1, 4)$ is a solution to the equation $-2x + y = 2$ because it is on the graph of that equation. However, the point $(1, 4)$ is not on the graph of the equation $3x + y = -3$. Therefore, $(1, 4)$ cannot be a solution to the system of equations.

4.   **Graph the linear system on a coordinate plane:** $\begin{cases} 2x - 3y = 18 \\ 2x + y = 2 \end{cases}$

For the equation $2x - 3y = 18$:

$$2(0) - 3y = 18$$
$$-3y = 18$$
$$y = -6$$

The y-intercept is $(0, -6)$.

$$2x - 3(0) = 18$$
$$2x = 18$$
$$x = 9$$

The x-intercept is $(9, 0)$.

For the equation $2x + y = 2$:

$$2(0) + y = 2$$
$$y = 2$$

The y-intercept is $(0, 2)$.

$$2x + 0 = 2$$
$$2x = 2$$
$$x = 1$$

The x-intercept is $(1, 0)$.

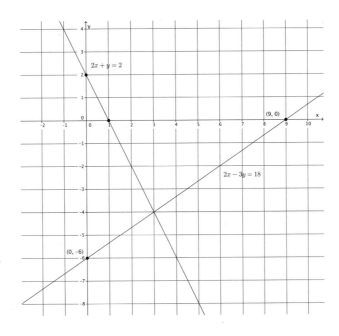

a.   **Name the ordered pair where the graphs of the two linear equations intersect.**

$$(3, -4)$$

b.   Verify that the ordered pair named in (a) is a solution to $2x - 3y = 18$.

$$2(3) - 3(-4) = 18$$
$$6 + 12 = 18$$
$$18 = 18$$

The left and right sides of the equation are equal.

c.   Verify that the ordered pair named in (a) is a solution to $2x + y = 2$.

$$2(3) + (-4) = 2$$
$$6 - 4 = 2$$
$$2 = 2$$

The left and right sides of the equation are equal.

d.   Could the point $(3, -1)$ be a solution to the system of linear equations? That is, would $(3, -1)$ make both equations true? Why or why not?

No. The graphs of the equations represent all of the possible solutions to the given equations. The point $(3, -1)$ is not on the graph of either line; therefore, it is not a solution to the system of linear equations.

5.   Graph the linear system on a coordinate plane: $\begin{cases} y - x = 3 \\ y = -4x - 2 \end{cases}$

For the equation $y - x = 3$:

$$y - 0 = 3$$
$$y = 3$$

The y-intercept is $(0, 3)$.

$$0 - x = 3$$
$$-x = 3$$
$$x = -3$$

The x-intercept is $(-3, 0)$.

For the equation $y = -4x - 2$:

The slope is $-\dfrac{4}{1}$, and the y-intercept is $(0, -2)$.

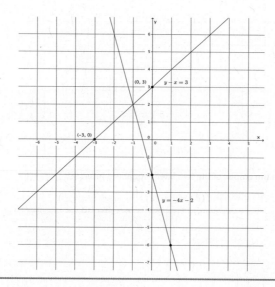

a.   Name the ordered pair where the graphs of the two linear equations intersect.

$$(-1, 2)$$

b.   Verify that the ordered pair named in (a) is a solution to $y - x = 3$.

$$2 - (-1) = 3$$
$$3 = 3$$

The left and right sides of the equation are equal.

c.   Verify that the ordered pair named in (a) is a solution to $y = -4x - 2$.

$$2 = -4(-1) - 2$$
$$2 = 4 - 2$$
$$2 = 2$$

The left and right sides of the equation are equal.

d.   Could the point $(-2, 6)$ be a solution to the system of linear equations? That is, would $(-2, 6)$ make both equations true? Why or why not?

No. The graphs of the equations represent all of the possible solutions to the given equations. The point $(-2, 6)$ is a solution to the equation $y = -4x - 2$ because it is on the graph of that equation. However, the point $(-2, 6)$ is not on the graph of the equation $y - x = 3$. Therefore, $(-2, 6)$ cannot be a solution to the system of equations.

Discussion (10 minutes)

The formal proof shown below is optional. The discussion can be modified by first asking students the questions in the first two bullet points, then having them make conjectures about why there is just one solution to the system of equations.

- How many points of intersection of the two lines were there?
  - *There was only one point of intersection for each pair of lines.*
- Was your answer to part (d) in Exercises 1–5 ever "yes"? Explain.
  - *No, the answer was always "no." Each time, the point given was either a solution to just one of the equations, or it was not a solution to either equation.*
- So far, what you have observed strongly suggests that the solution of a system of linear equations is the point of intersection of two distinct lines. Let's show that this observation is true.

Theorem. Let

$$\begin{cases} a_1 x + b_1 y = c_1 \\ a_2 x + b_2 y = c_2 \end{cases}$$

be a system of linear equations, where $a_1, b_1, c_1, a_2, b_2,$ and c_2 are constants. At least one of a_1, b_1 is not equal to zero, and at least one of a_2, b_2 is not equal to zero. Let l_1 and l_2 be the lines defined by $a_1 x + b_1 y = c_1$ and $a_2 x + b_2 y = c_2$, respectively. Then, the solution of the system is exactly the point of intersection of l_1 and l_2.

Lesson 25:   Geometric Interpretation of the Solutions of a Linear System
Date: 11/8/13

- To prove the theorem, we have to show two things.
  (1) Any point that lies in the intersection of the two lines is a solution of the system.
  (2) Any solution of the system lies in the intersection of the two lines.
- We begin by showing that (1) is true. To show that (1) is true, use the definition of a solution. What does it mean to be a solution to an equation?
  - *A solution is the ordered pair of numbers that makes an equation true. A solution is also a point on the graph of a linear equation.*
- Suppose (x_0, y_0) is the point of intersection of l_1 and l_2. Since the point (x_0, y_0) is on l_1, it means that it is a solution to $a_1 x + b_1 y = c_1$. Similarly, since the point (x_0, y_0) is on l_2, it means that it is a solution to $a_2 x + b_2 y = c_2$. Therefore, since the point (x_0, y_0) is a solution to each linear equation, it is a solution to the system of linear equations, and the proof of (1) is complete.
- To prove (2), use the definition of a solution again. Suppose (x_0, y_0) is a solution to the system. Then, the point (x_0, y_0) is a solution to $a_1 x + b_1 y = c_1$, and therefore, lies on l_1. Similarly, the point (x_0, y_0) is a solution to $a_2 x + b_2 y = c_2$, and therefore, lies on l_2. Since there can be only one point shared by two distinct lines, then (x_0, y_0) must be the point of intersection of l_1 and l_2. This completes the proof of (2).
- Therefore, given a system of two distinct linear equations, there can be only one point of intersection, which means there is just one solution to the system.

Exercise 6 (3 minutes)

This exercise is optional. It requires students to write two different systems for a given solution. The exercise can be completed independently or in pairs.

> 6. **Write two different systems of equations with $(1, -2)$ as the solution.**
>
> *Answers will vary. Two sample solutions are provided:*
>
> $\begin{cases} 3x + y = 1 \\ 2x - 3y = 8 \end{cases}$ *and* $\begin{cases} -x + 3y = -7 \\ 9x - 4y = 17 \end{cases}$

Closing (5 minutes)

Summarize, or ask students to summarize, the main points from the lesson:

- We know how to graph a system of linear equations and find the point of intersection of the lines.
- We know that the point of intersection represents the solution to the system of linear equations.
- We know that two distinct lines will intersect at only one point; therefore, the point of intersection is an ordered pair of numbers that makes both equations in the system true.

	Lesson 25:	Geometric Interpretation of the Solutions of a Linear System
	Date:	11/8/13

386

Lesson Summary

When a system of linear equations is graphed, the point of intersection of the lines of the graph represents the solution to the system. Two distinct lines intersect at most at one point. The coordinates of that point (x, y) represent values that make both equations of the system true.

Example: The system $\begin{cases} x + y = 3 \\ x - y = 5 \end{cases}$ graphs as shown below.

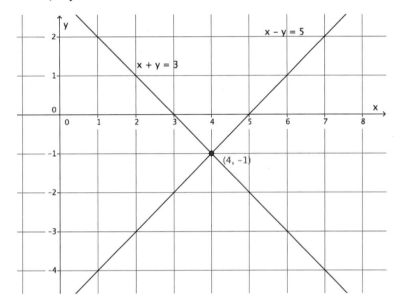

The graphs of the lines intersect at $(4, -1)$. That means the equations in the system are true when $x = 4$ and $y = -1$:

$$x + y = 3$$
$$4 + (-1) = 3$$
$$3 = 3$$

$$x - y = 5$$
$$4 - (-1) = 5$$
$$5 = 5$$

Exit Ticket (5 minutes)

Name _____   Date _____

Lesson 25: Geometric Interpretation of the Solutions of a Linear System

Exit Ticket

1. Graph the linear system on a coordinate plane: $\begin{cases} 2x - y = -1 \\ y = 5x - 5 \end{cases}$.

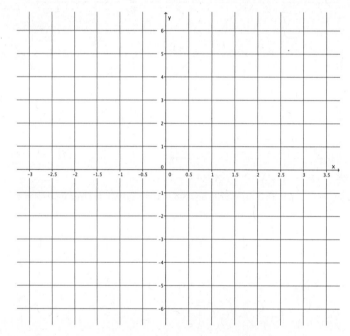

a. Name the ordered pair where the graphs of the two linear equations intersect.

b. Verify that the ordered pair named in (a) is a solution to $2x - y = -1$.

c. Verify that the ordered pair named in (a) is a solution to $y = 5x - 5$.

Exit Ticket Sample Solutions

1. Graph the linear system on a coordinate plane: $\begin{cases} 2x - y = -1 \\ y = 5x - 5 \end{cases}$

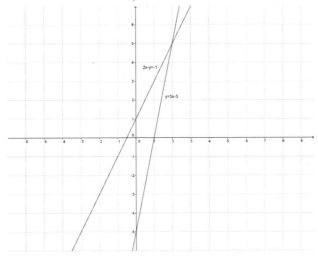

a. Name the ordered pair where the graphs of the two linear equations intersect.

$$(2, 5)$$

b. Verify that the ordered pair named in (a) is a solution to $2x - y = -1$.

$$2(2) - 5 = -1$$
$$4 - 5 = -1$$
$$-1 = -1$$

The left and right sides of the equation are equal.

c. Verify that the ordered pair named in (a) is a solution to $y = 5x - 5$.

$$5 = 5(2) - 5$$
$$5 = 10 - 5$$
$$5 = 5$$

The left and right sides of the equation are equal.

Problem Set Sample Solutions

1. Graph the linear system on a coordinate plane:
    $$\begin{cases} y = \frac{1}{3}x + 1 \\ y = -3x + 11 \end{cases}$$

    For the equation $y = \frac{1}{3}x + 1$:

    The slope is $\frac{1}{3}$, and the y-intercept is $(0, 1)$.

    For the equation $y = -3x + 11$:

    The slope is $-\frac{3}{1}$, and the y-intercept is $(0, 11)$.

    a. Name the ordered pair where the graphs of the two linear equations intersect.

        $(3, 2)$

    b. Verify that the ordered pair named in (a) is a solution to $y = \frac{1}{3}x + 1$.

        $$2 = \frac{1}{3}(3) + 1$$
        $$2 = 1 + 1$$
        $$2 = 2$$

        The left and right sides of the equation are equal.

    c. Verify that the ordered pair named in (a) is a solution to $y = -3x + 11$.

        $$2 = -3(3) + 11$$
        $$2 = -9 + 11$$
        $$2 = 2$$

        The left and right sides of the equation are equal.

2. Graph the linear system on a coordinate plane: $\begin{cases} y = \frac{1}{2}x + 4 \\ x + 4y = 4 \end{cases}$

    For the equation $y = \frac{1}{2}x + 4$:

    The slope is $\frac{1}{2}$, and the y-intercept is $(0, 4)$.

    For the equation $x + 4y = 4$:

    $$0 + 4y = 4$$
    $$4y = 4$$
    $$y = 1$$

    The y-intercept is $(0, 1)$.

    $$x + 4(0) = 4$$
    $$x = 4$$

    The x-intercept is $(4, 0)$.

    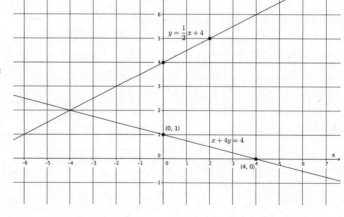

a.   Name the ordered pair where the graphs of the two linear equations intersect.

$(-4, 2)$

b.   Verify that the ordered pair named in (a) is a solution to $y = \frac{1}{2}x + 4$.

$$2 = \frac{1}{2}(-4) + 4$$
$$2 = -2 + 4$$
$$2 = 2$$

The left and right sides of the equation are equal.

c.   Verify that the ordered pair named in (a) is a solution to $x + 4y = 4$.

$$-4 + 4(2) = 4$$
$$-4 + 8 = 4$$
$$4 = 4$$

The left and right sides of the equation are equal.

3.   Graph the linear system on a coordinate plane: $\begin{cases} y = 2 \\ x + 2y = 10 \end{cases}$

For the equation $x + 2y = 10$:

$$0 + 2y = 10$$
$$2y = 10$$
$$y = 5$$

The y-intercept is $(0, 5)$.

$$x + 2(0) = 10$$
$$x = 10$$

The x-intercept is $(10, 0)$.

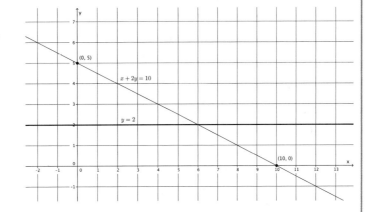

a.   Name the ordered pair where the graphs of the two linear equations intersect.

$(6, 2)$

b.   Verify that the ordered pair named in (a) is a solution to $y = 2$.

$$2 = 2$$

The left and right sides of the equation are equal.

c.   Verify that the ordered pair named in (a) is a solution to $x + 2y = 10$.

$$6 + 2(2) = 10$$
$$6 + 4 = 10$$
$$10 = 10$$

The left and right sides of the equation are equal.

4. Graph the linear system on a coordinate plane: $\begin{cases} -2x + 3y = 18 \\ 2x + 3y = 6 \end{cases}$

For the equation $-2x + 3y = 18$:

$$-2(0) + 3y = 18$$
$$3y = 18$$
$$y = 6$$

The y-intercept is $(0, 6)$.

$$-2x + 3(0) = 18$$
$$-2x = 18$$
$$x = -9$$

The x-intercept is $(-9, 0)$.

For the equation $2x + 3y = 6$:

$$2(0) + 3y = 6$$
$$3y = 6$$
$$y = 2$$

The y-intercept is $(0, 2)$.

$$2x + 3(0) = 6$$
$$2x = 6$$
$$x = 3$$

The x-intercept is $(3, 0)$.

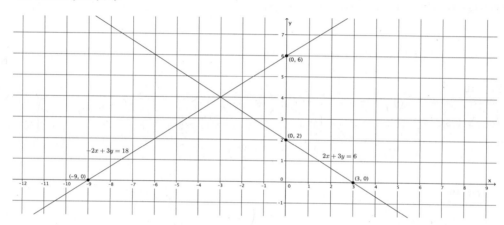

a. Name the ordered pair where the graphs of the two linear equations intersect.

$(-3, 4)$

b. Verify that the ordered pair named in (a) is a solution to $-2x + 3y = 18$.

$$-2(-3) + 3(4) = 18$$
$$6 + 12 = 18$$
$$18 = 18$$

The left and right sides of the equation are equal.

c. Verify that the ordered pair named in (a) is a solution to $2x + 3y = 6$.

$$2(-3) + 3(4) = 6$$
$$-6 + 12 = 6$$
$$6 = 6$$

The left and right sides of the equation are equal.

5.   Graph the linear system on a coordinate plane: $\begin{cases} x + 2y = 2 \\ y = \frac{2}{3}x - 6 \end{cases}$

For the equation $x + 2y = 2$:

$$0 + 2y = 2$$
$$2y = 2$$
$$y = 1$$

The y-intercept is $(0, 1)$.

$$x + 2(0) = 2$$
$$x = 2$$

The x-intercept is $(2, 0)$.

For the equation $y = \frac{2}{3}x - 6$:

The slope is $\frac{2}{3}$, and the y-intercept is $(0, -6)$.

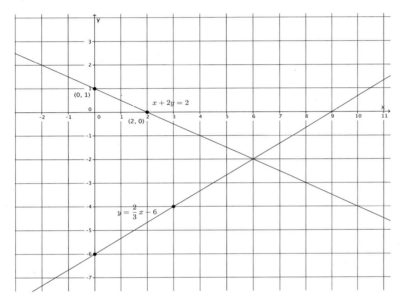

a.   Name the ordered pair where the graphs of the two linear equations intersect.

$$(6, -2)$$

b.   Verify that the ordered pair named in (a) is a solution to $x + 2y = 2$.

$$6 + 2(-2) = 2$$
$$6 - 4 = 2$$
$$2 = 2$$

The left and right sides of the equation are equal.

c.   Verify that the ordered pair named in (a) is a solution to $y = \frac{2}{3}x - 6$.

$$-2 = \frac{2}{3}(6) - 6$$
$$-2 = 4 - 6$$
$$-2 = -2$$

The left and right sides of the equation are equal.

6.   Without graphing, name the ordered pair where the graphs of the two linear equations intersect.

$$\begin{cases} x = 2 \\ y = -3 \end{cases}$$

$$(2, -3)$$

Lesson 26: Characterization of Parallel Lines

Student Outcomes

- Students know that when a system of linear equations has no solution, i.e., no point of intersection of the lines, then the lines are parallel.

Lesson Notes

The discussion that begins on page 398 is an optional proof of the theorem about parallel lines. You can choose to discuss the proof with students or have students complete Exercises 4–10.

Classwork

Exercises 1–3 (10 minutes)

Students complete Exercises 1–3 independently. Once students are finished, debrief their work using the questions in the discussion that follows the exercises.

Exercises

1. Graph the system: $\begin{cases} y = \dfrac{2}{3}x + 4 \\ y = \dfrac{4}{6}x - 3 \end{cases}$.

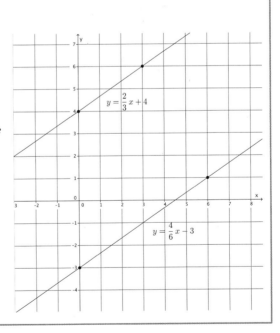

a. Identify the slope of each equation. What do you notice?

The slope of the first equation is $\dfrac{2}{3}$, and the slope of the second equation is $\dfrac{4}{6}$. The slopes are equivalent.

b. Identify the y-intercept of each equation. Are the y-intercepts the same or different?

The y-intercepts are $(0, 4)$ and $(0, -3)$. The y-intercepts are different.

2.   Graph the system: $\begin{cases} y = -\frac{5}{4}x + 7 \\ y = -\frac{5}{4}x + 2 \end{cases}$.

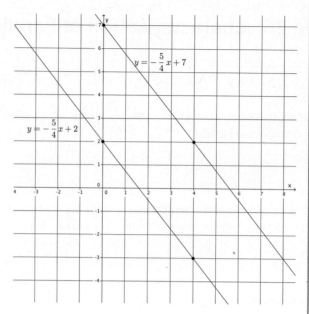

    a.   Identify the slope of each equation. What do you notice?

       The slope of both equations is $-\frac{5}{4}$. The slopes are equal.

    b.   Identify the y-intercept of each equation. Are the y-intercepts the same or different?

       The y-intercepts are $(0, 7)$ and $(0, 2)$. The y-intercepts are different.

3.   Graph the system: $\begin{cases} y = 2x - 5 \\ y = 2x - 1 \end{cases}$.

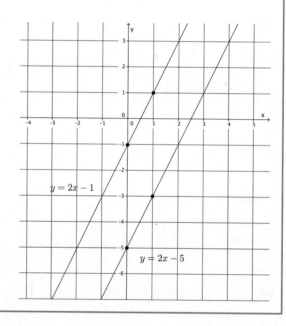

    a.   Identify the slope of each equation. What do you notice?

       The slope of both equations is 2. The slopes are equal.

    b.   Identify the y-intercept of each equation. Are the y-intercepts the same or different?

       The y-intercepts are $(0, -5)$ and $(0, -1)$. The y-intercepts are different.

Discussion (10 minutes)

MP.3
&
MP.8

- What did you notice about each of the systems you graphed in Exercises 1–3?
    - *For each exercise, the lines graphed as parallel lines.*
- What did you notice about the slopes in each system?
    - *Each time, the linear equations of the system had the same slope.*
- What did you notice about the y-intercepts of the equations in each system?
    - *In each case, the y-intercepts were different.*

- If the equations had the same y-intercept and the same slope, what would we know about the graphs of the lines?
  - *There is only one line that can go through a given point with a given slope. If the equations had the same slope and y-intercept, they would graph as the same line.*
- For that reason, when we discuss lines with the same slope, we must make sure to identify them as distinct lines.
- Write a summary of the conclusions you have reached by completing Exercises 1–3.

Provide time for students to write their conclusions. Share the theorem with them, and have students compare the conclusions that they reached to the statements in the theorem.

- What you observed in Exercises 1–3 can be captured in the following theorem.

Theorem.
(1) Two distinct, non-vertical lines in the plane are parallel if they have the same slope.
(2) If two distinct, non-vertical lines have the same slope, then they are parallel.

- Suppose you have a pair of parallel lines on a coordinate plane. In how many places will those lines intersect?
  - *By definition, parallel lines never intersect.*
- Suppose you are given a system of linear equations that graph as parallel lines. How many solutions will the system have?
  - *Based on work in the previous lesson, students learned that the solution to a system of equations is represented by the ordered pair that is the location where the lines intersect. Since parallel lines do not intersect, then a system containing linear equations that graph as parallel lines will have no solution.*
- What we want to find out is how to recognize when the lines defined by the equations are parallel. Then, we would know immediately that we have a system with no solution as long as the lines are unique.
- A system can easily be recognized as having no solutions when it is in the form of $\begin{cases} x = 2 \\ x = -7 \end{cases}$ or $\begin{cases} y = 6 \\ y = 15 \end{cases}$. Why is that so?
  - *Because the system $\begin{cases} x = 2 \\ x = -7 \end{cases}$ graphs as two vertical lines. All vertical lines are parallel to the y-axis, and therefore, are parallel to one another. Similarly, the system $\begin{cases} y = 6 \\ y = 15 \end{cases}$ graphs as two horizontal lines. All horizontal lines are parallel to the x-axis, and therefore, are parallel to one another.*
- We want to be able to recognize when we have a system of parallel lines that are not vertical or horizontal. What characteristics did each pair of equations have?
  - *Each pair of equations had the same slope, but different y-intercepts.*

Discussion (15 minutes)

The following discussion is proof of the theorem about parallel lines. Having this discussion with students is <u>optional</u>. Instead, you may have students complete Exercises 4–10 beginning on page 401.

- We begin by proving (1). Recall that when we were shown that the slope between any two points would be equal to the same constant, m, we used what we knew about similar triangles. We will do something similar to prove (1).

- Suppose we have two non-vertical and non-horizontal parallel lines l_1 and l_2 in the coordinate plane. Assume that the y-intercept of l_1 is greater than the y-intercept of l_2. (We could assume the opposite is true; it doesn't make a difference with respect to the proof. We just want to say something clearly so our diagram will make sense.) Let's also assume that these lines are left-to-right inclining, i.e., positive slope.

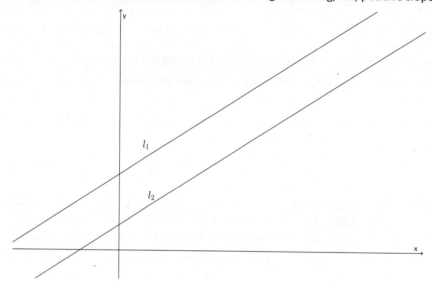

- Pick a point $P = (p_1, p_2)$ on l_1 and draw a vertical line from P so that it intersects l_2 at point Q and the x-axis at point R. From points Q and R, draw horizontal lines so that they intersect lines l_1 and l_2 at points S and T, respectively.

- By construction, $\angle PQS$ and $\angle QRT$ are right angles. How do we know for sure?

  □   *We drew a vertical line from point P. Therefore, the vertical line is parallel to the y-axis and perpendicular to the x-axis. Therefore, $\angle QRT = 90°$. Since we also drew horizontal lines, we know they are parallel. The vertical line through P is then a transversal that intersects parallel lines, which means corresponding angles are congruent. Since $\angle QRT$ corresponds to $\angle PQS$, then $\angle PQS = 90°$.*

- We want to show that $\triangle PQS \sim \triangle QRT$, which means we need another pair of equal angles in order to use the AA criterion. Do we have another pair of equal angles? Explain.

  □   *Yes. We know that lines l_1 and l_2 are parallel. Still using the vertical line through P as the transversal, corresponding angles $\angle TQR = \angle SPQ$. Therefore, $\triangle PQS \sim \triangle QRT$.*

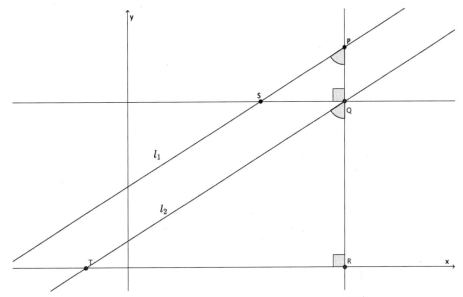

- To better see what we are doing, we will translate $\triangle PQS$ along vector $\overrightarrow{QR}$ as shown.

- By definition of dilation, we know that:

$$\frac{|P'Q'|}{|QR|} = \frac{|Q'S'|}{|RT|}.$$

Equivalently, by the multiplication property of equality:

$$\frac{|P'Q'|}{|Q'S'|} = \frac{|QR|}{|RT|}.$$

Because translation preserves lengths of segments, we know that $|P'Q'| = |PQ|$ and $|Q'S'| = |QS|$, so we have

$$\frac{|PQ|}{|QS|} = \frac{|QR|}{|RT|}.$$

By definition of slope, $\dfrac{|PQ|}{|QS|}$ is the slope of l_1 and $\dfrac{|QR|}{|RT|}$ is the slope of l_2. Therefore, the slopes of l_1 and l_2 are equal and (1) is proved.

- To prove (2), use the same construction as we did for (1). The difference this time is that we know we have side lengths that are equal in ratio because we are given that the slopes are the same, so we are trying to prove that the lines l_1 and l_2 are parallel. Since we don't know the lines are parallel, we also don't know that $\angle TQR = \angle SPQ$, but we do know that $\angle PQS$ and $\angle QRT$ are right angles.

- Then again, we translate △ PQS along vector $\overrightarrow{QR}$ as shown.

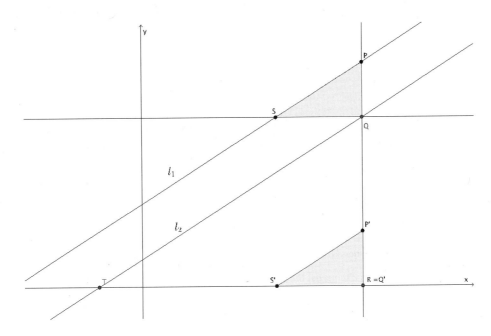

- Since the corresponding sides are equal in ratio to the scale factor $\dfrac{|P'Q'|}{|QR|} = \dfrac{|Q'S'|}{|RT|}$ and share a common angle $\angle P'RS'$, by the Fundamental Theorem of Similarity, we know that the lines containing $P'S'$ and QT are parallel. Since the line containing $P'S'$ is a translation of line PS, and translations preserve angle measures, then we know that line PS is parallel to line QT. Since the line containing PS is l_1 and the line containing QT is line l_2, then we can conclude that $l_1 \parallel l_2$. This finishes the proof of the theorem.

Exercises 4–10 (15 minutes)

Students complete Exercises 4–10 independently. Once students are finished, debrief their work using the questions in the discussion that follows the exercises.

4. Write a system of equations that has no solution.

   Answers will vary. Verify that the system that has been written has equations that have the same slope and unique y-intercepts. Sample student solution: $\begin{cases} y = \frac{3}{4}x + 1 \\ y = \frac{3}{4}x - 2 \end{cases}$.

5. Write a system of equations that has $(2, 1)$ as a solution.

   Answers will vary. Verify that students have written a system where $(2, 1)$ is a solution to each equation. Sample student solution: $\begin{cases} 5x + y = 11 \\ y = \frac{1}{2}x \end{cases}$.

6. How can you tell if a system of equations has a solution or not?

If the slopes of the equations are different, the lines will intersect at some point, and there will be a solution to the system. If the slopes of the equations are the same, and the y-intercepts are different, then the equations will graph as parallel lines, which means the system will not have a solution.

7. Does the system of linear equations shown below have a solution? Explain.

$$\begin{cases} 6x - 2y = 5 \\ 4x - 3y = 5 \end{cases}$$

Yes, this system does have a solution. The slope of the first equation is 3, and the slope of the second equation is $\frac{4}{3}$. Since the slopes are different, these equations will graph as non-parallel lines, which means they will intersect at some point.

8. Does the system of linear equations shown below have a solution? Explain.

$$\begin{cases} -2x + 8y = 14 \\ x = 4y + 1 \end{cases}$$

No, this system does not have a solution. The slope of the first equation is $\frac{2}{8} = \frac{1}{4}$, and the slope of the second equation is $\frac{1}{4}$. Since the slopes are the same, but the lines are distinct, these equations will graph as parallel lines. Parallel lines never intersect, which means this system has no solution.

9. Does the system of linear equations shown below have a solution? Explain.

$$\begin{cases} 12x + 3y = -2 \\ 4x + y = 7 \end{cases}$$

No, this system does not have a solution. The slope of the first equation is $-\frac{12}{3} = -4$, and the slope of the second equation is -4. Since the slopes are the same but the lines are distinct, these equations will graph as parallel lines. Parallel lines never intersect, which means this system has no solution.

10. Genny babysits for two different families. One family pays her $6 each hour and a bonus of $20 at the end of the night. The other family pays her $3 every half hour and a bonus of $25 dollars at the end of the night. Write and solve the system of equations that represents this situation. At what number of hours do the two families pay the same for babysitting service from Genny?

Let y represent the total amount Genny is paid for babysitting x hours. The first family pays $y = 6x + 20$. Since the other family pays by the half hour, $3 \cdot 2$ would represent the amount Genny is paid each hour. So, the other family pays $y = (3 \cdot 2)x + 25$, which is the same as $y = 6x + 25$. The system is

$$\begin{cases} y = 6x + 20 \\ y = 6x + 25 \end{cases}$$

Since the equations in the system have the same slope and different y-intercepts, there will not be a point of intersection. That means that there will not be a number of hours for when Genny is paid the same amount by both families. The second family will always pay her $5 more than the first family.

Closing (5 minutes)

Summarize, or ask students to summarize, the main points from the lesson:

- We know that systems of vertical lines will have no solution because all vertical lines are parallel to the y-axis, and therefore, are parallel to one another. Similarly, systems of horizontal lines will have no solution because all horizontal lines are parallel to the x-axis, and therefore, are parallel to one another.

- We know that if a system contains linear equations with graphs of distinct lines that have the same slope, then the graphs of the lines are parallel and, therefore, the system has no solution.

Lesson Summary

By definition, parallel lines do not intersect; therefore, a system of linear equations that graph as parallel lines will have no solution.

Parallel lines have the same slope, but no common point. Verify that lines are parallel by comparing their slopes and their y-intercepts.

Exit Ticket (5 minutes)

Name _____   Date _____

Lesson 26: Characterization of Parallel Lines

Exit Ticket

Does each system of linear equations have a solution? Explain your answer.

1. $\begin{cases} y = \frac{5}{4}x - 3 \\ y + 2 = \frac{5}{4}x \end{cases}$

2. $\begin{cases} y = \frac{2}{3}x - 5 \\ 4x - 8y = 11 \end{cases}$

3. $\begin{cases} \frac{1}{3}x + y = 8 \\ x + 3y = 12 \end{cases}$

Exit Ticket Sample Solutions

Does each system of linear equations have a solution? Explain your answer.

1. $\begin{cases} y = \dfrac{5}{4}x - 3 \\ y + 2 = \dfrac{5}{4}x \end{cases}$

   No, this system does not have a solution. The slope of the first equation is $\dfrac{5}{4}$, and the slope of the second equation is $\dfrac{5}{4}$. Since the slopes are the same, and they are distinct lines, these equations will graph as parallel lines; since parallel lines never intersect, this system has no solution.

2. $\begin{cases} y = \dfrac{2}{3}x - 5 \\ 4x - 8y = 11 \end{cases}$

   Yes, this system does have a solution. The slope of the first equation is $\dfrac{2}{3}$, and the slope of the second equation is $\dfrac{1}{2}$. Since the slopes are different, these equations will graph as non-parallel lines, which means they will intersect at some point.

3. $\begin{cases} \dfrac{1}{3}x + y = 8 \\ x + 3y = 12 \end{cases}$

   No, this system does not have a solution. The slope of the first equation is $-\dfrac{1}{3}$, and the slope of the second equation is $-\dfrac{1}{3}$. Since the slopes are the same, and they are distinct lines, these equations will graph as parallel lines; since parallel lines never intersect, this system has no solution.

Problem Set Sample Solutions

Answer problems 1–5 without graphing the equations.

1. Does the system of linear equations shown below have a solution? Explain.

   $$\begin{cases} 2x + 5y = 9 \\ -4x - 10y = 4 \end{cases}$$

   No, this system does not have a solution. The slope of the first equation is $-\dfrac{2}{5}$, and the slope of the second equation is $-\dfrac{4}{10}$, which is equivalent to $-\dfrac{2}{5}$. Since the slopes are the same, but the lines are distinct, these equations will graph as parallel lines. Parallel lines never intersect, which means this system has no solution.

2. Does the system of linear equations shown below have a solution? Explain.

   $$\begin{cases} \dfrac{3}{4}x - 3 = y \\ 4x - 3y = 5 \end{cases}$$

   Yes, this system does have a solution. The slope of the first equation is $\dfrac{3}{4}$, and the slope of the second equation is $\dfrac{4}{3}$. Since the slopes are different, these equations will graph as non-parallel lines, which means they will intersect at some point.

3.   Does the system of linear equations shown below have a solution? Explain.

$$\begin{cases} x + 7y = 8 \\ 7x - y = -2 \end{cases}$$

Yes, this system does have a solution. The slope of the first equation is $-\frac{1}{7}$, and the slope of the second equation is 7. Since the slopes are different, these equations will graph as non-parallel lines, which means they will intersect at some point.

4.   Does the system of linear equations shown below have a solution? Explain.

$$\begin{cases} y = 5x + 12 \\ 10x - 2y = 1 \end{cases}$$

No, this system does not have a solution. The slope of the first equation is 5, and the slope of the second equation is $\frac{10}{2}$, which is equivalent to 5. Since the slopes are the same but the lines are distinct, these equations will graph as parallel lines. Parallel lines never intersect, which means this system has no solution.

5.   Does the system of linear equations shown below have a solution? Explain.

$$\begin{cases} y = \frac{5}{3}x + 15 \\ 5x - 3y = 6 \end{cases}$$

No, this system does not have a solution. The slope of the first equation is $\frac{5}{3}$, and the slope of the second equation is $\frac{5}{3}$. Since the slopes are the same, but the lines are distinct, these equations will graph as parallel lines. Parallel lines never intersect, which means this system has no solution.

6.   Given the graph of a system of linear equations below, is there a solution to the system that we cannot see on this portion of the coordinate plane? That is, will the lines intersect somewhere on the plane not represented in the picture? Explain.

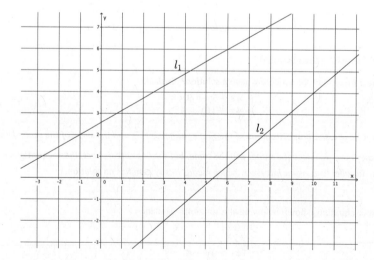

The slope of l_1 is $\frac{4}{7}$, and the slope of l_2 is $\frac{6}{7}$. Since the slopes are different, these equations will graph as non-parallel lines, which means they will intersect at some point. Therefore, the system of linear equations that represents the graph will have a solution.

7. Given the graph of a system of linear equations below, is there a solution to the system that we cannot see on this portion of the coordinate plane? That is, will the lines intersect somewhere on the plane not represented in the picture? Explain.

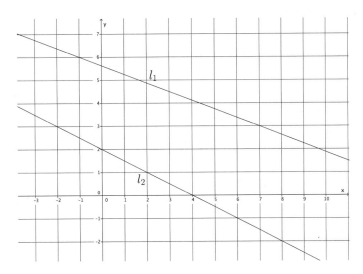

The slope of l_1 is $-\frac{3}{8}$, and the slope of l_2 is $-\frac{1}{2}$. Since the slopes are different, these equations will graph as non-parallel lines, which means they will intersect at some point. Therefore, the system of linear equations that represents the graph will have a solution.

8. Given the graph of a system of linear equations below, is there a solution to the system that we cannot see on this portion of the coordinate plane? That is, will the lines intersect somewhere on the plane not represented in the picture? Explain.

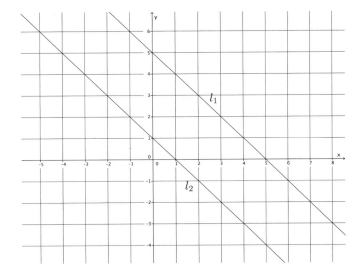

The slope of l_1 is -1, and the slope of l_2 is -1. Since the slopes are the same, these equations will graph as parallel lines, which means they will not intersect, and the system of linear equations that represents the graph will have no solution.

9. Given the graph of a system of linear equations below, is there a solution to the system that we cannot see on this portion of the coordinate plane? That is, will the lines intersect somewhere on the plane not represented in the picture? Explain.

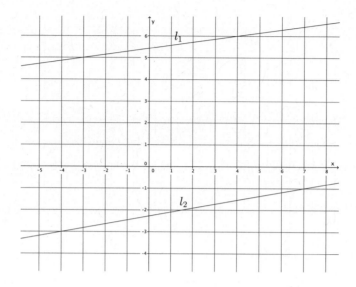

The slope of l_1 is $\frac{1}{7}$, and the slope of l_2 is $\frac{2}{11}$. Since the slopes are different, these equations will graph as non-parallel lines, which means they will intersect at some point. Therefore, the system of linear equations that represents the graph will have a solution.

10. Given the graph of a system of linear equations below, is there a solution to the system that we cannot see on this portion of the coordinate plane? That is, will the lines intersect somewhere on the plane not represented in the picture? Explain.

Lines l_1 and l_2 are horizontal lines. That means that they are both parallel to the x-axis, and therefore, are parallel to one another. Therefore, the system of linear equations that represents the graph will have no solution.

Lesson 27: Nature of Solutions of a System of Linear Equations

Student Outcomes

- Students know that since two equations in the form $ax + by = c$ and $a'x + b'y = c'$ graph as the same line when $\dfrac{a'}{a} = \dfrac{b'}{b} = \dfrac{c'}{c}$, then the system of linear equations has infinitely many solutions.
- Students know a strategy for solving a system of linear equations algebraically.

Classwork

Exercises 1–3 (5 minutes)

Students complete Exercises 1–3 independently in preparation for the discussion that follows about infinitely many solutions.

Exercises 1–3

Determine the nature of the solution to each system of linear equations.

1. $\begin{cases} 3x + 4y = 5 \\ y = -\dfrac{3}{4}x + 1 \end{cases}$

   The slopes of these two distinct equations are the same, which means they graph as parallel lines. Therefore, this system will have no solutions.

2. $\begin{cases} 7x + 2y = -4 \\ x - y = 5 \end{cases}$

   The slopes of these two equations are unique. That means they graph as distinct lines and will intersect at one point. Therefore, this system has one solution.

3. $\begin{cases} 9x + 6y = 3 \\ 3x + 2y = 1 \end{cases}$

   These equations graph as the same line because they have the same slope and the same y-intercept.

Discussion (7 minutes)

Ask students to summarize the nature of the solutions for each of the Exercises 1–3. Students should be able to state clearly what they observed in Exercise 1 and Exercise 2 as stated in (1) and (2) below.

- So far, our work with systems of linear equations has taught us that:
    (1) If the lines defined by the equations in the system are parallel, then the system has no solutions.
    (2) If the lines defined by the equations in the system are not parallel, then the system has exactly one solution, and it is the point of intersection of the two lines.

Have students discuss their "solution" to Exercise 3. Ask students what they noticed, if anything, about the equations in Exercise 3. If necessary, show that the first equation can be obtained from the second equation by multiplying each term by 3. Then, the equations are exactly the same. Proceed with the second example below, along with the discussion points that follow.

- We now know there is a third possibility with respect to systems of equations. Consider the following system of linear equations:
$$\begin{cases} 3x + 2y = 5 \\ 6x + 4y = 10 \end{cases}$$
    What do you notice about the constants a, b, and c of the first equation, compared to the constants a', b' and c' of the second equation?

MP.2
    □ *When you compare $\dfrac{a'}{a} = \dfrac{b'}{b} = \dfrac{c'}{c}$, they are equal to the same constant* 2.

- If you multiplied each term of the first equation by the constant 2, what is the result?
    □ *Sample student work:*
$$2(3x + 2y = 5)$$
$$6x + 4y = 10$$
    When you multiply each term of the first equation by the constant 2, the result is the second equation.

- What does this mean about the graphs of the equations in the system?
    □ *It means that the equations define the same line. That is, they graph as the same line.*

- When two equations define the same line, it means that every solution to one equation is also a solution to the other equation. Since we can find an infinite number of solutions to any linear equation in two variables, systems that are comprised of equations that define the same line have infinitely many solutions.

Provide students with time to verify the fact that the system, $\begin{cases} 3x + 2y = 5 \\ 6x + 4y = 10 \end{cases}$, has infinitely many solutions. Instruct them to find at least two solutions to the first equation, and then show that the same ordered pairs satisfy the second equation as well.

    □ *Sample student work:*
$$\begin{cases} 3x + 2y = 5 \\ 6x + 4y = 10 \end{cases}$$

Two solutions to $3x + 2y = 5$ are $(1,1)$ and $(3, -2)$. Replacing the solutions in the second equation results in the true equations:

$$6(1) + 4(1) = 10$$
$$6 + 4 = 10$$
$$10 = 10$$

and

$$6(3) + 4(-2) = 10$$
$$18 - 8 = 10$$
$$10 = 10$$

- Therefore, the nature of the solutions of a system of linear equations is one of three possibilities: one solution, no solution, or infinitely many solutions. A system will have one solution when the equations graph as distinct lines with different slopes. A system will have no solution when the equations have the same slope and different y-intercepts, which produces a graph of parallel lines. A system will have infinitely many solutions when the equations define the same line; these equations will have the same slope and same y-intercept, producing the same line.

Example 1 (7 minutes)

In this example, students realize that graphing a system of equations will yield a solution, but the precise coordinates of the solution cannot be determined from the graph.

- The following is the graph of the system $\begin{cases} y = 3x + 5 \\ y = 8x + 3 \end{cases}$.

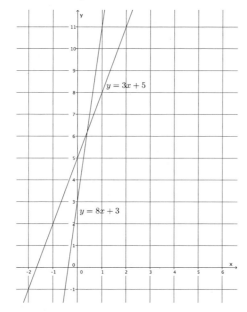

- Though the equations were easy to graph, it is not easy to identify the solution to the system because the intersection of the lines does not have integer coordinates. Estimate the solution, based on the graph.

    □ *The solution looks like it could be $\left(\frac{1}{3}, 6\right)$.*

- When we need a precise answer, we must use an alternative strategy for solving systems of linear equations.

Understanding the substitution method requires an understanding of the transitive property. One accessible way to introduce this to students at this level is through symbolic puzzles; one possible example follows.

If ! = $$ and $$ = &, is it true that ! = &? Why or why not? Allow students time to think about the symbol puzzle and share their thoughts with the class. Then, continue with the points below.

- When two linear expressions are equal to the same number, then the expressions are equal to each other, just like ! = & because both ! and & are equal to $$. Look at the system of equations given in this example:

$$\begin{cases} y = 3x + 5 \\ y = 8x + 3 \end{cases}$$

  How is this like our puzzle about !, $$, and &?

  - *Both of the equations in the system are equal to y; therefore, $3x + 5$ must be equal to $8x + 3$.*

- The equation $3x + 5 = 8x + 3$ is a linear equation in one variable. Solve it for x.

  - *Sample student work:*

$$3x + 5 = 8x + 3$$
$$2 = 5x$$
$$\frac{2}{5} = x$$

- Keep in mind that we are trying to identify the point of intersection of the lines, that is, the solution that is common to both equations. What we have just found is the x-coordinate of that solution, $\frac{2}{5}$, and we must now determine the y-coordinate. To do so, we can substitute the value of x into either of the two equations of the system to determine the value for y.

$$y = 3\left(\frac{2}{5}\right) + 5$$
$$y = \frac{6}{5} + 5$$
$$y = \frac{31}{5}$$

- Verify that we would get the same value for y using the second equation.

  - *Sample student work:*

$$y = 8\left(\frac{2}{5}\right) + 3$$
$$y = \frac{16}{5} + 3$$
$$y = \frac{31}{5}$$

- The solution to the system is $\left(\frac{2}{5}, \frac{31}{5}\right)$. Look at the graph. Does it look like this could be the solution?

  - *Yes, the coordinates look correct, and they are close to our estimated solution.*

- Our estimation was close to the actual answer, but not as precise as when we solved the system algebraically.

Example 2 (4 minutes)

- Does the system $\begin{cases} y = 7x - 2 \\ 2y - 4x = 10 \end{cases}$ have a solution?

    □ *Yes, the slopes are different, which means they are not parallel and not the same line.*

- Now that we know that the system has a solution, we will solve it without graphing.

- Notice that in this example we do not have two linear expressions equal to the same number. However, we do know what y is; it is equal to the expressions $7x - 2$. Therefore, we can substitute the expression that y is equal to in the second equation. Since $y = 7x - 2$, then:

$$2y - 4x = 10$$
$$2(7x - 2) - 4x = 10$$
$$14x - 4 - 4x = 10$$
$$10x - 4 = 10$$
$$10x = 14$$
$$x = \frac{14}{10}$$
$$x = \frac{7}{5}$$

- What does $x = \frac{7}{5}$ represent?

    □ *It represents the x-coordinate of the point of intersection of the graphs of the lines, or the solution to the system.*

- How can we determine the y-coordinate of the solution to the system?

    □ *Since we know the x-coordinate of the solution, we can substitute the value of x into either equation to determine the value of the y-coordinate.*

- Determine the y-coordinate of the solution to the system.

    □ *Sample student work:*

$$y = 7\left(\frac{7}{5}\right) - 2$$
$$y = \frac{49}{5} - 2$$
$$y = \frac{39}{5}$$

- The solution to this system is $\left(\frac{7}{5}, \frac{39}{5}\right)$. What does the solution represent?

    □ *The solution is the point of intersection of the graphs of the lines of the system. It is a solution that makes both equations of the system true.*

	Lesson 27:	Nature of Solutions of a System of Linear Equations
	Date:	11/8/13

Example 3 (8 minutes)

- Does the system $\begin{cases} 4y = 26x + 4 \\ y = 11x - 1 \end{cases}$ have a solution?

  □ *Yes, the slopes are different, which means they are not parallel and not the same line.*

- Solve this system using substitution; since we know what y is equal to, we can replace that value with the expression $11x - 1$ in the first equation.

  □ *Sample student work:*

$$\begin{cases} 4y = 26x + 4 \\ y = 11x - 1 \end{cases}$$
$$4(11x - 1) = 26x + 4$$
$$44x - 4 = 26x + 4$$
$$44x - 26x - 4 = 26x - 26x + 4$$
$$18x - 4 = 4$$
$$18x - 4 + 4 = 4 + 4$$
$$18x = 8$$
$$x = \frac{8}{18}$$
$$x = \frac{4}{9}$$

$$y = 11\left(\frac{4}{9}\right) - 1$$
$$y = \frac{44}{9} - 1$$
$$y = \frac{35}{9}$$

The solution to the system is $\left(\frac{4}{9}, \frac{35}{9}\right)$.

- There is another option for solving this equation. We could multiply the second equation by 4. Then, we would have two linear equations equal to $4y$ that could then be written as a single equation, as in Example 1. Or, we could multiply the first equation by $\frac{1}{4}$. Then, we would have two linear equations equal to y that could be written as a single equation, as in Example 1, again.

- For this system, let's multiply the second equation by 4. Then, we have:

$$4(y = 11x - 1)$$
$$4y = 44x - 4$$

Lesson 27:   Nature of Solutions of a System of Linear Equations
Date: 11/8/13

- Now, the system can be written as $\begin{cases} 4y = 26x + 4 \\ 4y = 44x - 4 \end{cases}$, and we can write the two linear expressions $26x + 4$ and $44x - 4$ as equal to one another. Solve the system.

    □ *Sample student work:*

$$26x + 4 = 44x - 4$$
$$4 = 18x - 4$$
$$8 = 18x$$
$$\frac{8}{18} = x$$
$$\frac{4}{9} = x$$

$$y = 11\left(\frac{4}{9}\right) - 1$$
$$y = \frac{44}{9} - 1$$
$$y = \frac{35}{9}$$

The solution to the system is $\left(\frac{4}{9}, \frac{35}{9}\right)$.

- Compare the solution we got algebraically to the graph of the system of linear equations:

We can see that our answer is correct because it looks like the lines intersect at $\left(\frac{4}{9}, \frac{35}{9}\right)$.

Exercises 4–7 (7 minutes)

Students complete Exercises 4–7 independently.

Exercises 4–7

Determine the nature of the solution to each system of linear equations. If the system has a solution, find it algebraically; then, verify that your solution is correct by graphing.

4. $\begin{cases} 3x + 3y = -21 \\ x + y = -7 \end{cases}$

   These equations define the same line. Therefore, this system will have infinitely many solutions.

5. $\begin{cases} y = \dfrac{3}{2}x - 1 \\ 3y = x + 2 \end{cases}$

   The slopes of these two equations are unique. That means they graph as distinct lines and will intersect at one point. Therefore, this system has one solution.

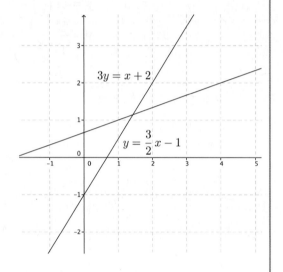

$$3\left(y = \frac{3}{2}x - 1\right)$$

$$3y = \frac{9}{2}x - 3$$

$$x + 2 = \frac{9}{2}x - 3$$

$$2 = \frac{7}{2}x - 3$$

$$5 = \frac{7}{2}x$$

$$\frac{10}{7} = x$$

$$y = \frac{3}{2}\left(\frac{10}{7}\right) - 1$$

$$y = \frac{15}{7} - 1$$

$$y = \frac{8}{7}$$

The solution is $\left(\dfrac{10}{7}, \dfrac{8}{7}\right)$.

COMMON CORE

Lesson 27: Nature of Solutions of a System of Linear Equations
Date: 11/8/13

6. $\begin{cases} x = 12y - 4 \\ x = 9y + 7 \end{cases}$

The slopes of these two equations are unique. That means they graph as distinct lines and will intersect at one point. Therefore, this system has one solution.

$$12y - 4 = 9y + 7$$
$$3y - 4 = 7$$
$$3y = 11$$
$$y = \frac{11}{3}$$

$$x = 9\left(\frac{11}{3}\right) + 7$$
$$x = 33 + 7$$
$$x = 40$$

The solution is $\left(40, \frac{11}{3}\right)$.

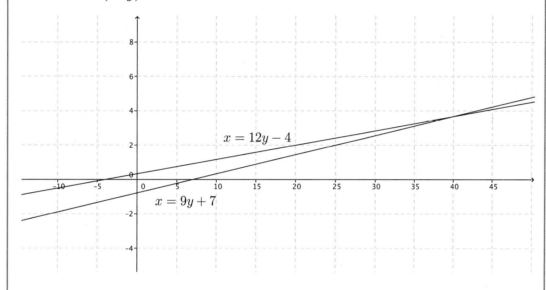

7. Write a system of equations with $(4, -5)$ as its solution.

Answers will vary. Verify that students have written a system of equations where $(4, -5)$ is a solution to each equation in the system. Sample solution: $\begin{cases} y = x - 9 \\ x + y = -1 \end{cases}$

Closing (3 minutes)

Summarize, or ask students to summarize, the main points from the lesson:

- A system can have one solution, no solution, or infinitely many solutions. It will have one solution when the lines are distinct and their slopes are different; it will have no solution when the equations graph as distinct lines with the same slope; it will have infinitely many solutions when the equations define the same line.

- We learned a method for solving a system of linear equations algebraically. It requires us to write linear expressions equal to one another and substitution.

Lesson Summary

A system of linear equations can have a unique solution, no solutions, or infinitely many solutions.

Systems with a unique solution will be comprised of linear equations that have different slopes that graph as distinct lines, intersecting at only one point.

Systems with no solution will be comprised of linear equations that have the same slope that graph as parallel lines (no intersection).

Systems with infinitely many solutions will be comprised of linear equations that have the same slope and y-intercept that graph as the same line. When equations graph as the same line, every solution to one equation will also be a solution to the other equation.

A system of linear equations can be solved using a substitution method. That is, if two expressions are equal to the same value, then they can be written equal to one another.

Example:

$$\begin{cases} y = 5x - 8 \\ y = 6x + 3 \end{cases}$$

Since both equations in the system are equal to y, we can write the equation, $5x - 8 = 6x + 3$, and use it to solve for x and then the system.

Example:

$$\begin{cases} 3x = 4y + 2 \\ x = y + 5 \end{cases}$$

In this example, you can multiply each term of the equation $x = y + 5$ by 3 to produce the equivalent equation $3x = 3y + 15$. Now, as is the previous example, since both equations equal $3x$ we can write $4y + 2 = 3y + 15$, and use this equation to solve for y and then the system.

Exit Ticket (4 minutes)

Name _____   Date _____

Lesson 27: Nature of Solutions of a System of Linear Equations

Exit Ticket

Determine the nature of the solution to each system of linear equations. If the system has a solution, then find it without graphing.

1. $\begin{cases} y = \frac{1}{2}x + \frac{5}{2} \\ x - 2y = 7 \end{cases}$

2. $\begin{cases} y = \frac{2}{3}x + 4 \\ 2y + \frac{1}{2}x = 2 \end{cases}$

3. $\begin{cases} y = 3x - 2 \\ -3x + y = -2 \end{cases}$

Exit Ticket Sample Solutions

Determine the nature of the solution to each system of linear equations. If the system has a solution, then find it without graphing.

1. $\begin{cases} y = \frac{1}{2}x + \frac{5}{2} \\ x - 2y = 7 \end{cases}$

The slopes of these two equations are the same, and the y-intercepts are different, which means they graph as parallel lines. Therefore, this system will have no solutions.

2. $\begin{cases} y = \frac{2}{3}x + 4 \\ 2y + \frac{1}{2}x = 2 \end{cases}$

The slopes of these two equations are unique. That means they graph as distinct lines and will intersect at one point. Therefore, this system has one solution.

$$2\left(\frac{2}{3}x + 4\right) + \frac{1}{2}x = 2$$

$$\frac{4}{3}x + 8 + \frac{1}{2}x = 2$$

$$\frac{11}{6}x + 8 = 2$$

$$\frac{11}{6}x = -6$$

$$x = -\frac{36}{11}$$

$$y = \frac{2}{3}\left(-\frac{36}{11}\right) + 4$$

$$y = -\frac{24}{11} + 4$$

$$y = \frac{20}{11}$$

The solution is $\left(-\frac{36}{11}, \frac{20}{11}\right)$.

3. $\begin{cases} y = 3x - 2 \\ -3x + y = -2 \end{cases}$

These equations define the same line. Therefore, this system will have infinitely many solutions.

Problem Set Sample Solutions

Students practice determining the nature of solutions of a system of linear equations and finding the solution for systems that have one.

Determine the nature of the solution to each system of linear equations. If the system has a solution, find it algebraically; then, verify that your solution is correct by graphing.

1. $\begin{cases} y = \frac{3}{7}x - 8 \\ 3x - 7y = 1 \end{cases}$

   The slopes of these two equations are the same, which means they graph as parallel lines. Therefore, this system will have no solutions.

2. $\begin{cases} 2x - 5 = y \\ -3x - 1 = 2y \end{cases}$

   $$(2x - 5 = y)2$$

   $$4x - 10 = 2y$$

   $$\begin{cases} 4x - 10 = 2y \\ -3x - 1 = 2y \end{cases}$$

   $$4x - 10 = -3x - 1$$

   $$7x - 10 = -1$$

   $$7x = 9$$

   $$x = \frac{9}{7}$$

   $$y = 2\left(\frac{9}{7}\right) - 5$$

   $$y = \frac{18}{7} - 5$$

   $$y = -\frac{17}{7}$$

   The solution is $\left(\frac{9}{7}, -\frac{19}{7}\right)$.

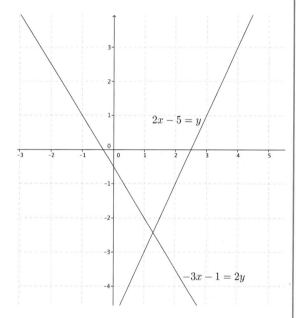

---

3. $\begin{cases} x = 6y + 7 \\ x = 10y + 2 \end{cases}$

$$6y + 7 = 10y + 2$$
$$7 = 4y + 2$$
$$5 = 4y$$
$$\frac{5}{4} = y$$
$$x = 6\left(\frac{5}{4}\right) + 7$$
$$x = \frac{15}{2} + 7$$
$$x = \frac{29}{2}$$

The solution is $\left(\frac{29}{2}, \frac{5}{4}\right)$.

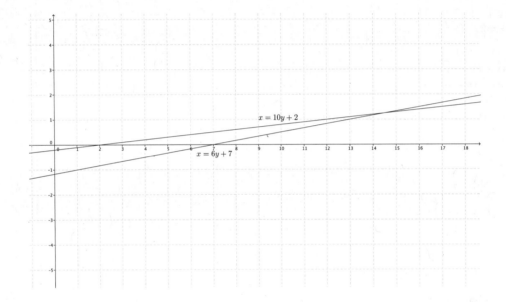

4. $\begin{cases} 5y = \frac{15}{4}x + 25 \\ y = \frac{3}{4}x + 5 \end{cases}$

These equations define the same line. Therefore, this system will have infinitely many solutions.

5. $\begin{cases} x + 9 = y \\ x = 4y - 6 \end{cases}$

$$4y - 6 + 9 = y$$
$$4y + 3 = y$$
$$3 = -3y$$
$$-1 = y$$

$$x + 9 = -1$$
$$x = -10$$

The solution is $(-10, -1)$.

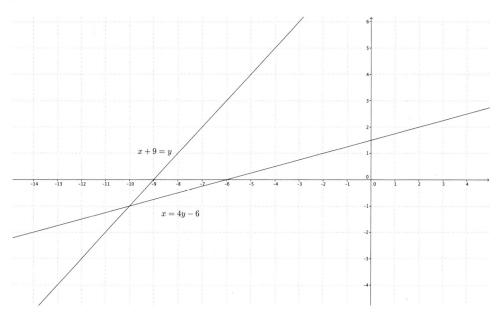

$x + 9 = y$

$x = 4y - 6$

6. $\begin{cases} 3y = 5x - 15 \\ 3y = 13x - 2 \end{cases}$

$$5x - 15 = 13x - 2$$
$$-15 = 8x - 2$$
$$-13 = 8x$$
$$-\frac{13}{8} = x$$
$$3y = 5\left(-\frac{13}{8}\right) - 15$$
$$3y = -\frac{65}{8} - 15$$
$$3y = -\frac{185}{8}$$
$$y = -\frac{185}{24}$$

The solution is $\left(-\frac{13}{8}, -\frac{185}{24}\right)$.

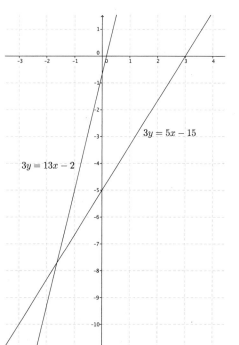

$3y = 5x - 15$

$3y = 13x - 2$

COMMON CORE™   **Lesson 27:**   Nature of Solutions of a System of Linear Equations
               Date: 11/8/13

7. $\begin{cases} 6x - 7y = \frac{1}{2} \\ 12x - 14y = 1 \end{cases}$

   These equations define the same line. Therefore, this system will have infinitely many solutions.

8. $\begin{cases} 5x - 2y = 6 \\ -10x + 4y = -14 \end{cases}$

   The slopes of these two equations are the same, which means they graph as parallel lines. Therefore, this system will have no solutions.

9. $\begin{cases} y = \frac{3}{2}x - 6 \\ 2y = 7 - 4x \end{cases}$

   $$2\left(y = \frac{3}{2}x - 6\right)$$
   $$2y = 3x - 12$$
   $$\begin{cases} 2y = 3x - 12 \\ 2y = 7 - 4x \end{cases}$$
   $$3x - 12 = 7 - 4x$$
   $$7x - 12 = 7$$
   $$7x = 19$$
   $$x = \frac{19}{7}$$
   $$y = \frac{3}{2}\left(\frac{19}{7}\right) - 6$$
   $$y = \frac{57}{14} - 6$$
   $$y = -\frac{27}{14}$$

   The solution is $\left(\frac{19}{7}, -\frac{27}{14}\right)$.

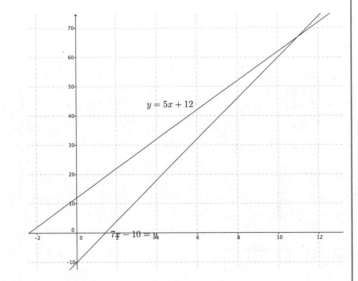

10. $\begin{cases} 7x - 10 = y \\ y = 5x + 12 \end{cases}$

    $$7x - 10 = 5x + 12$$
    $$2x - 10 = 12$$
    $$2x = 22$$
    $$x = 11$$
    $$y = 5(11) + 12$$
    $$y = 55 + 12$$
    $$y = 67$$

    The solution is $(11, 67)$.

11. Write a system of linear equations with $(-3, 9)$ as its solution.

    Answers will vary. Verify that students have written a system of equations where $(-3, 9)$ is a solution to each equation in the system. Sample solution: $\begin{cases} y = x + 12 \\ x + y = 6 \end{cases}$

Lesson 28: Another Computational Method of Solving a Linear System

Student Outcomes

- Students learn the elimination method for solving a system of linear equations.
- Students use properties of rational numbers to find a solution to a system, if it exists, through computation using substitution and elimination methods.

Lesson Notes

Throughout the lesson, students are asked to verify that their solution to a system is correct by graphing the system and comparing the point of intersection to their solution. For that reason, provide graph paper for student use for both Exercises and the Problem Set. Graphs should be provided during the presentation of the Examples so that you can discuss with students whether or not their estimated point of intersection verifies their solution.

Classwork

Discussion (5 minutes)

- In the last lesson, we saw that if a system of linear equations has a solution, it can be found without graphing. In each case, the first step was to eliminate one of the variables.

- Describe how you would solve this system algebraically: $\begin{cases} y = 3x + 5 \\ y = 8x + 3 \end{cases}$

  □ *Since both equations were equal to y, we could write $3x + 5 = 8x + 3$, thereby eliminating the y from the system.*

- Describe how you would solve this system algebraically: $\begin{cases} y = 7x - 2 \\ 2y - 4x = 10 \end{cases}$

  □ *We can substitute $7x - 2$ for y in the second equation, i.e., $2(7x - 2) - 4x = 10$, thereby eliminating the y again.*

- Describe how you would solve this system algebraically: $\begin{cases} x = 6y + 7 \\ x = 10y + 2 \end{cases}$

  □ *Since both equations are equal to x, we could write $6y + 7 = 10y + 2$, thereby eliminating the x.*

- In this lesson, we will learn a method for solving systems that requires us to eliminate one of the variables, but in a different way from the last lesson.

Example 1 (8 minutes)

> **Example 1**
>
> Use what you noticed about adding equivalent expressions to solve the following system by elimination:
> $$\begin{cases} 6x - 5y = 21 \\ 2x + 5y = -5 \end{cases}$$

Show students the three examples of adding integer equations together. Ask students to verbalize what they notice in the examples and to generalize what they observe. The goal is for students to see that we can add equivalent expressions and still have an equivalence.

Example 1: If $2 + 5 = 7$ and $1 + 9 = 10$, does $2 + 5 + 1 + 9 = 7 + 10$?

Example 2: If $1 + 5 = 6$ and $7 - 2 = 5$, does $1 + 5 + 7 - 2 = 6 + 5$?

Example 3: If $-3 + 11 = 8$ and $2 + 1 = 3$, does $-3 + 11 + 2 + 1 = 8 + 3$?

- Use what you noticed about adding equivalent expressions to solve the following system by elimination:

$$\begin{cases} 6x - 5y = 21 \\ 2x + 5y = -5 \end{cases}$$

MP.1

Provide students with time to attempt to solve the system by adding the equations together. Have students share their work with the class. If necessary, use the points below to support students.

- Notice that terms $-5y$ and $5y$ are opposites; that is, they have a sum of zero when added. If we were to add the equations in the system, the y would be eliminated.

$$6x - 5y + 2x + 5y = 21 + (-5)$$
$$6x + 2x - 5y + 5y = 16$$
$$8x = 16$$
$$x = 2$$

- Just as before, now that we know what x is, we can substitute it into either equation to determine the value of y.

$$2(2) + 5y = -5$$
$$4 + 5y = -5$$
$$5y = -9$$
$$y = -\frac{9}{5}$$

The solution to the system is $\left(2, -\frac{9}{5}\right)$.

- We can verify our solution by graphing the system:

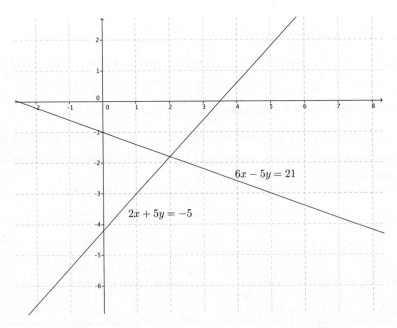

Example 2 (5 minutes)

> **Example 2**
>
> Solve the following system by elimination:
> $$\begin{cases} -2x + 7y = 5 \\ 4x - 2y = 14 \end{cases}$$

- We will solve the following system by elimination:
$$\begin{cases} -2x + 7y = 5 \\ 4x - 2y = 14 \end{cases}$$

- In this example it is not as obvious which variable to eliminate. It will become obvious as soon as we multiply the first equation by 2:
$$2(-2x + 7y = 5)$$
$$-4x + 14y = 10$$

Now we have the system $\begin{cases} -4x + 14y = 10 \\ 4x - 2y = 14 \end{cases}$, and it is clear that when we add $-4x + 4x$, the x will be eliminated. Add the equations of this system together and determine the solution to the system.

- *Sample student work:*

$$-4x + 14y + 4x - 2y = 10 + 12 \qquad\qquad 4x - 2(2) = 14$$
$$14y - 2y = 24 \qquad\qquad\qquad\qquad 4x - 4 = 14$$
$$12y = 24 \qquad\qquad\qquad\qquad\qquad 4x = 18$$
$$y = 2 \qquad\qquad\qquad\qquad\qquad\quad x = \frac{18}{4}$$
$$x = \frac{9}{2}$$

The solution to the system is $\left(\frac{9}{2}, 2\right)$.

- We can verify our solution by graphing the system:

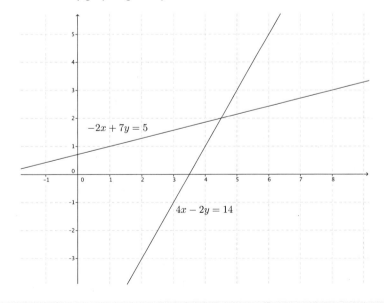

Example 3 (5 minutes)

Example 3

Solve the following system by elimination:

$$\begin{cases} 7x - 5y = -2 \\ 3x - 3y = 7 \end{cases}$$

- We will solve the following system by elimination:

$$\begin{cases} 7x - 5y = -2 \\ 3x - 3y = 7 \end{cases}$$

Provide time for students to solve this system on their own before discussing it as a class.

- In this case, it is even less obvious which variable to eliminate. On these occasions, we need to rewrite both equations. We multiply the first equation by -3 and the second equation by 7.

$$-3(7x - 5y = -2)$$

$$-21x + 15y = 6$$

$$7(3x - 3y = 7)$$

$$21x - 21y = 49$$

Now we have the system $\begin{cases} -21x + 15y = 6 \\ 21x - 21y = 49 \end{cases}$, and it is obvious that the x can be eliminated.

- Look at the system again:

$$\begin{cases} 7x - 5y = -2 \\ 3x - 3y = 7 \end{cases}$$

What would we do if we wanted to eliminate the y from the system?

  - *We could multiply the first equation by 3 and the second equation by -5.*

Students may say to multiply the first equation by -3 and the second equation by 5. Whichever answer is given first, ask if the second is also a possibility. Students should answer, "yes."

Exercises 1–3 (8 minutes)

Students complete Exercises 1–3 independently.

Exercises

Each of the following systems has a solution. Determine the solution to the system by eliminating one of the variables. Verify the solution using the graph of the system.

1. $\begin{cases} 6x - 7y = -10 \\ 3x + 7y = -8 \end{cases}$

$$6x - 7y + 3x + 7y = -10 + (-8)$$
$$9x = -18$$
$$x = -2$$
$$3(-2) + 7y = -8$$
$$-6 + 7y = -8$$
$$7y = -2$$
$$y = -\frac{2}{7}$$

The solution is $\left(-2, -\frac{2}{7}\right)$.

Lesson 28:   Another Computational Method of Solving a Linear System
Date: 11/8/13

2. $\begin{cases} x - 4y = 7 \\ 5x + 9y = 6 \end{cases}$

$$-5(x - 4y = 7)$$
$$-5x + 20y = -35$$

$\begin{cases} -5x + 20y = -35 \\ 5x + 9y = 6 \end{cases}$

$$-5x + 20y + 5x + 9y = -35 + 6$$
$$29y = -29$$
$$y = -1$$

$$x - 4(-1) = 7$$
$$x + 4 = 7$$
$$x = 3$$

The solution is $(3, -1)$.

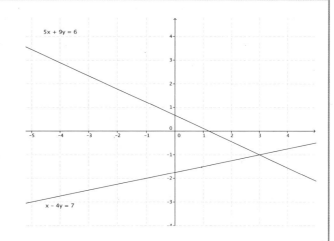

3. $\begin{cases} 2x - 3y = -5 \\ 3x + 5y = 1 \end{cases}$

$$-3(2x - 3y = -5)$$
$$-6x + 9y = 15$$
$$2(3x + 5y = 1)$$
$$6x + 10y = 2$$

$\begin{cases} -6x + 9y = 15 \\ 6x + 10y = 2 \end{cases}$

$$-6x + 9y + 6x + 10y = 15 + 2$$
$$19y = 17$$
$$y = \frac{17}{19}$$

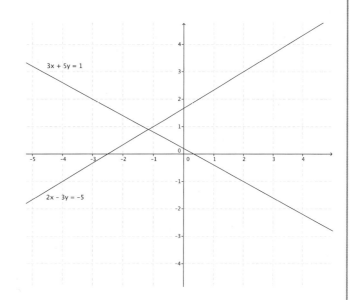

$$2x - 3\left(\frac{17}{19}\right) = -5$$

$$2x - \frac{51}{19} = -5$$

$$2x = -5 + \frac{51}{19}$$

$$2x = -\frac{44}{19}$$

$$x = -\frac{44}{38}$$

$$x = -\frac{22}{19}$$

The solution is $\left(-\frac{22}{19}, \frac{17}{19}\right)$.

Discussion (6 minutes)

- Systems of linear equations can be solved by graphing, substitution (as was shown in the last lesson), or elimination (as was shown in this lesson). Some systems can be solved more efficiently by elimination, while others by substitution. Which method do you think would be most efficient for the following system? Explain.

$$\begin{cases} y = 5x - 19 \\ 3x + 11 = y \end{cases}$$

  - *Substitution would be the most efficient method. Since each equation is equal to y, it would be easiest to write the expressions $5x - 19$ and $3x + 11$ equal to one another; then, solve for y.*

- What method would you use for the following system? Explain.

$$\begin{cases} 2x - 9y = 7 \\ x + 9y = 5 \end{cases}$$

  - *Elimination would be the most efficient method because the terms $-9y + 9y$, when added, would eliminate the y from the equation.*

- What method would you use for the following system? Explain.

$$\begin{cases} 4x - 3y = -8 \\ x + 7y = 4 \end{cases}$$

  - *Elimination would likely be the most efficient method because we could multiply the second equation by -4 to eliminate the x from the equation.*

- What method would you use for the following system? Explain.

$$\begin{cases} x + y = -3 \\ 6x + 6y = 6 \end{cases}$$

  - *Accept any reasonable answer students provide; then, remind them that the most efficient use of time is to check to see if the system has a solution at all. Since the slopes of the graphs of these lines are parallel, this system has no solution.*

Closing (4 minutes)

Summarize, or ask students to summarize, the main points from the lesson:

- We know how to solve a system by eliminating one of the variables. In some cases, you will have to multiply one or both of the given equations by a constant in order to eliminate a variable.
- We know that some systems are solved more efficiently by elimination than by other methods.

Lesson 28:   Another Computational Method of Solving a Linear System
Date: 11/8/13

Lesson Summary

Systems of linear equations can be solved by eliminating one of the variables from the system. One way to eliminate a variable is by setting both equations equal to the same variable, then writing the expressions equal to one another.

Example: Solve the system $\begin{cases} y = 3x - 4 \\ y = 2x + 1 \end{cases}$

Since both equation of the system are equal to y, then we can write and solve the equation:

$$3x - 4 = 2x + 1$$

Another way to eliminate a variable is by multiplying each term of an equation by the same constant to make an equivalent equation. Then use the equivalent equation to eliminate one of the variables and solve the system.

Example: Solve the system $\begin{cases} 2x + y = 8 \\ x + y = 10 \end{cases}$

Multiply the second equation by -2 to eliminate the x:

$$-2(x + y = 10)$$
$$-2x - 2y = -20$$

Now we have the system $\begin{cases} 2x + y = 8 \\ -2x - 2y = -20 \end{cases}$

When the equations are added together, the x is eliminated:

$$2x + y - 2x - 2y = 8 + (-20)$$
$$y - 2y = 8 + (-20)$$

Once a solution has been found, verify the solution graphically or by substitution.

Exit Ticket (4 minutes)

The graphs have been provided in the Exit Ticket in order to allow students to check their solution within the four minutes allotted.

Name _____   Date _____

Lesson 28: Another Computational Method of Solving a Linear System

Exit Ticket

Determine the solution, if it exists, for each system of linear equations. Verify your solution on the coordinate plane.

1. $\begin{cases} y = 3x - 5 \\ y = -3x + 7 \end{cases}$

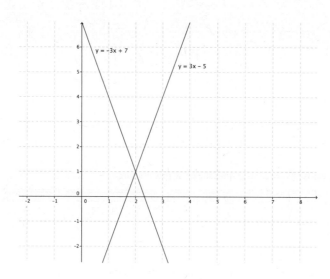

2. $\begin{cases} y = -4x + 6 \\ 2x - y = 11 \end{cases}$

Exit Ticket Sample Solutions

Determine the solution, if it exists, for each system of linear equations. Verify your solution on the coordinate plane.

1. $\begin{cases} y = 3x - 5 \\ y = -3x + 7 \end{cases}$

$$3x - 5 = -3x + 7$$
$$6x = 12$$
$$x = 2$$

$$y = 3(2) - 5$$
$$y = 6 - 5$$
$$y = 1$$

The solution is $(2, 1)$.

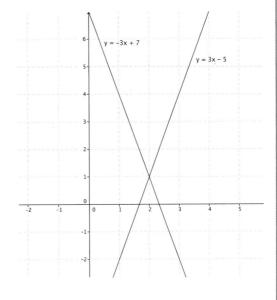

2. $\begin{cases} y = -4x + 6 \\ 2x - y = 11 \end{cases}$

$$2x - (-4x + 6) = 11$$
$$2x + 4x - 6 = 11$$
$$6x = 17$$
$$x = \frac{17}{6}$$

$$y = -4\left(\frac{17}{6}\right) + 6$$
$$y = -\frac{34}{3} + 6$$
$$y = -\frac{16}{3}$$

The solution is $\left(\frac{17}{6}, -\frac{16}{3}\right)$.

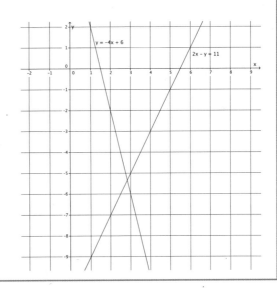

Problem Set Sample Solutions

Determine the solution, if it exists, for each system of linear equations. Verify your solution on the coordinate plane.

1. $\begin{cases} \frac{1}{2}x + 5 = y \\ 2x + y = 1 \end{cases}$

$2x + \frac{1}{2}x + 5 = 1$

$\frac{5}{2}x + 5 = 1$

$\frac{5}{2}x = -4$

$x = -\frac{8}{5}$

$2\left(-\frac{8}{5}\right) + y = 1$

$-\frac{16}{5} + y = 1$

$y = \frac{21}{5}$

The solution is $\left(-\frac{8}{5}, \frac{21}{5}\right).$

2. $\begin{cases} 9x + 2y = 9 \\ -3x + y = 2 \end{cases}$

$3(-3x + y = 2)$

$-9x + 3y = 6$

$\begin{cases} 9x + 2y = 9 \\ -9x + 3y = 6 \end{cases}$

$9x + 2y - 9x + 3y = 15$

$5y = 15$

$y = 3$

$-3x + 3 = 2$

$-3x = -1$

$x = \frac{1}{3}$

The solution is $\left(\frac{1}{3}, 3\right).$

3. $\begin{cases} y = 2x - 2 \\ 2y = 4x - 4 \end{cases}$

    These equations define the same line. Therefore, this system will have infinitely many solutions.

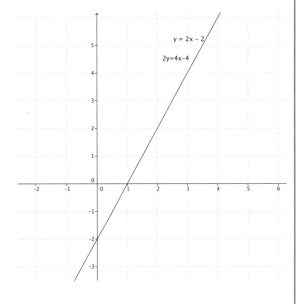

4. $\begin{cases} 8x + 5y = 19 \\ -8x + y = -1 \end{cases}$

    $$8x + 5y - 8x + y = 19 - 1$$
    $$5y + y = 18$$
    $$6y = 18$$
    $$y = 3$$

    $$8x + 5(3) = 19$$
    $$8x + 15 = 19$$
    $$8x = 4$$
    $$x = \frac{1}{2}$$

    The solution is $\left(\frac{1}{2}, 3\right)$.

5. $\begin{cases} x + 3 = y \\ 3x + 4y = 7 \end{cases}$

$$3x + 4(x + 3) = 7$$

$$3x + 4x + 12 = 7$$

$$7x + 12 = 7$$

$$7x = -5$$

$$x = -\frac{5}{7}$$

$$-\frac{5}{7} + 3 = y$$

$$\frac{16}{7} = y$$

The solution is $\left(-\frac{5}{7}, \frac{16}{7}\right)$.

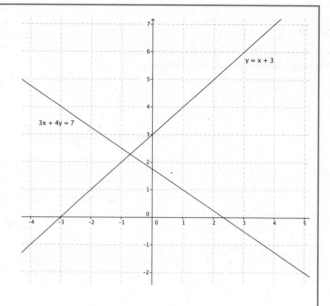

6. $\begin{cases} y = 3x + 2 \\ 4y = 12 + 12x \end{cases}$

The equations graph as distinct lines. The slopes of these two equations are the same, which means they graph as parallel lines. Therefore, this system will have no solutions.

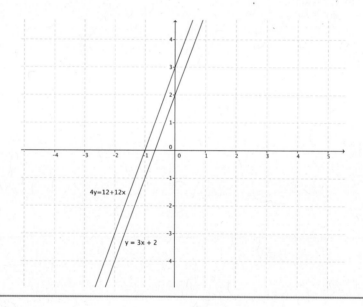

7. $\begin{cases} 4x - 3y = 16 \\ -2x + 4y = -2 \end{cases}$

$2(-2x + 4y = -2)$

$-4x + 8y = -4$

$\begin{cases} 4x - 3y = 16 \\ -4x + 8y = -4 \end{cases}$

$4x - 3y - 4x + 8y = 16 - 4$

$-3y + 8y = 12$

$5y = 12$

$y = \dfrac{12}{5}$

$4x - 3\left(\dfrac{12}{5}\right) = 16$

$4x - \dfrac{36}{5} = 16$

$4x = \dfrac{116}{5}$

$x = \dfrac{29}{5}$

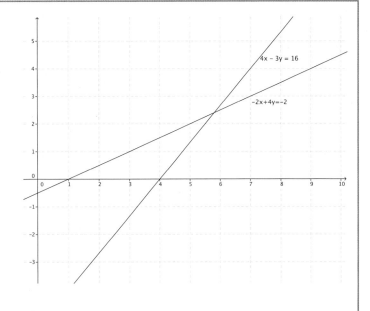

The solution is $\left(\dfrac{29}{5}, \dfrac{12}{5}\right)$.

8. $\begin{cases} 2x + 2y = 4 \\ 12 - 3x = 3y \end{cases}$

The equations graph as distinct lines. The slopes of these two equations are the same, which means they graph as parallel lines. Therefore, this system will have no solutions.

9. $\begin{cases} y = -2x + 6 \\ 3y = x - 3 \end{cases}$

$$3(y = -2x + 6)$$
$$3y = -6x + 18$$
$$\begin{cases} 3y = -6x + 18 \\ 3y = x - 3 \end{cases}$$
$$-6x + 18 = x - 3$$
$$18 = 7x - 3$$
$$21 = 7x$$
$$\frac{21}{7} = x$$
$$x = 3$$

$$y = -2(3) + 6$$
$$y = -6 + 6$$
$$y = 0$$

The solution is $(3, 0)$.

10. $\begin{cases} y = 5x - 1 \\ 10x = 2y + 2 \end{cases}$

These equations define the same line. Therefore, this system will have infinitely many solutions.

11. $\begin{cases} 3x - 5y = 17 \\ 6x + 5y = 10 \end{cases}$

$$3x - 5y + 6x + 5y = 17 + 10$$

$$9x = 27$$

$$x = 3$$

$$3(3) - 5y = 17$$

$$9 - 5y = 17$$

$$-5y = 8$$

$$y = -\frac{8}{5}$$

The solution is $\left(3, \frac{8}{5}\right)$.

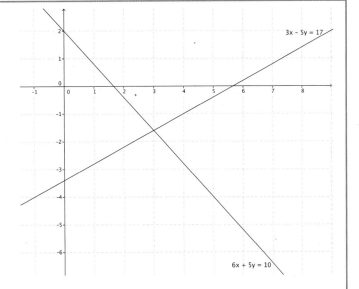

12. $\begin{cases} y = \frac{4}{3}x - 9 \\ y = x + 3 \end{cases}$

$$\frac{4}{3}x - 9 = x + 3$$

$$\frac{1}{3}x - 9 = 3$$

$$\frac{1}{3}x = 12$$

$$x = 36$$

$$y = 36 + 3$$

$$y = 39$$

The solution is $(36, 39)$.

13. $\begin{cases} 4x - 7y = 11 \\ x + 2y = 10 \end{cases}$

$$-4(x + 2y = 10)$$
$$-4x - 8y = -40$$
$$4x - 7y - 4x - 8y = 11 - 40$$
$$-15y = -29$$
$$y = \frac{29}{15}$$

$$x + 2\left(\frac{29}{15}\right) = 10$$

$$x + \frac{58}{15} = 10$$

$$x = \frac{92}{15}$$

The solution is $\left(\frac{92}{15}, \frac{29}{15}\right)$.

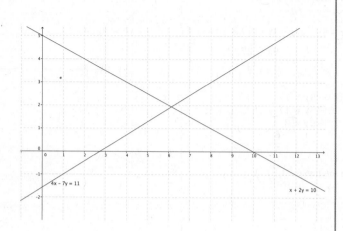

14. $\begin{cases} 21x + 14y = 7 \\ 12x + 8y = 16 \end{cases}$

The slopes of these two equations are the same and different y-intercepts, which means they graph as parallel lines. Therefore, this system will have no solution.

Lesson 29: Word Problems

Student Outcomes

- Students write word problems into systems of linear equations.
- Students solve systems of linear equations using elimination and substitution methods.

Lesson Notes

In this lesson, students will use many of the skills learned in this module. For example, they begin defining the variables as described in a word problem. Next, students must write a system of linear equations to represent the situation. Students will then have to decide which method for solving the system is most efficient. Finally, they solve the system and check to make sure their answer is correct. For each of the examples in the lesson, pose the questions and provide students time to answer them on their own. Then select students to share their thoughts and solutions with the class.

Classwork

Example 1 (5 minutes)

> **Example 1**
>
> The sum of two numbers is 361 and the difference between the two numbers is 173. What are the two numbers?

- Together we will read a word problem and work towards finding the solution.
- The sum of two numbers is 361 and the difference between the two numbers is 173. What are the two numbers?

Provide students time to work independently or in pairs to solve this problem. Have students share their solutions and explain how they arrived at their answers. Then show how the problem can be solved using a system of linear equations.

- What do we need to do first?
  - *We need to define our variables.*
- If we define our variables we can better represent the situation we have been given. What should the variables be for this problem?
  - *Let x represent one number and let y represent the other number.*
- Now that we know the numbers are x and y, what do we need to do now?
  - *We need to write equations to represent the information in the word problem.*
- Using x and y, write equations to represent the information we are provided.
  - *The sum of two numbers is 361 can be written as $x + y = 361$. The difference between the two numbers is 173 can be written as $x - y = 173$.*

- We have two equations to represent this problem. What is it called when we have more than one linear equation for a problem, and how is it represented symbolically?

  - *We have a system of linear equations:*

$$\begin{cases} x + y = 361 \\ x - y = 173 \end{cases}$$

- We know several methods for solving systems of linear equations. Which method do you think will be the most efficient and why?

  - *We should add the equations together to eliminate the variable y because we can do that in one step.*

- Solve the system: $\begin{cases} x + y = 361 \\ x - y = 173 \end{cases}$.

  - *Sample student work:*

$$\begin{cases} x + y = 361 \\ x - y = 173 \end{cases}$$
$$x + x + y - y = 361 + 173$$
$$2x = 534$$
$$x = 267$$

$$267 + y = 361$$
$$y = 94$$

  The solution is $(267, 94)$.

- Based on our work, we believe the two numbers are 267 and 94. Check to make sure your answer is correct by substituting the numbers in to both equations. If it makes a true statement, then we know we are correct. If it makes a false statement, then we need to go back and check our work.

  - *Sample student work:*

$$267 + 94 = 361$$
$$361 = 361$$

  and

$$267 - 94 = 173$$
$$173 = 173$$

- Now we are sure that the numbers are 267 and 94. Does it matter which number is x and which number is y?

  - *Not necessarily, but we need their difference to be positive, so x must be the larger of the two numbers to make sense of our equation $x - y = 173$.*

Example 2 (7 minutes)

Example 2

There are 356 Grade 8 students at Euclid's Middle School. Thirty-four more than four times the number of girls is equal to half the number of boys. How many boys are in Grade 8 at Euclid's Middle School? How many girls?

- Again we will work together to solve the following word problem.
- There are 356 Grade 8 students at Euclid's Middle School. Thirty-four more than four times the number of girls is equal to half the number of boys. How many boys are in Grade 8 at Euclid's Middle School? How many girls? What do we need to do first?
  - □ *We need to define our variables.*
- If we define our variables we can better represent the situation we have been given. What should the variables be for this problem?
  - □ *Let x represent the number of girls and let y represent the number of boys.*

Whichever way students define the variables, ask them if it could be done the opposite way. For example, if the students respond as stated above, ask them if we could let x represent the number of boys and y represent the number of girls. They should say that at this stage it doesn't matter if x represents girls or boys, but once the variable is defined, it does matter.

- Now that we know that x is the number of girls and y is the number of boys, what do we need to do now?
  - □ *We need to write equations to represent the information in the word problem.*
- Using x and y, write equations to represent the information we are provided.
  - □ *There are 356 Grade 8 students can be represented as $x + y = 356$. Thirty-four more than four times the number of girls is equal to half the number of boys can be represented as $4x + 34 = \frac{1}{2}y$.*
- We have two equations to represent this problem. What is it called when we have more than one linear equation for a problem, and how is it represented symbolically?
  - □ *We have a system of linear equations:*
  $$\begin{cases} x + y = 356 \\ 4x + 34 = \frac{1}{2}y \end{cases}$$
- We know several methods for solving systems of linear equations. Which method do you think will be the most efficient and why?
  - □ *Answers will vary. There is no obvious "most efficient" method. Accept any reasonable responses as long as they are justified.*
- Solve the system: $\begin{cases} x + y = 356 \\ 4x + 34 = \frac{1}{2}y \end{cases}$.
  - □ *Sample student work:*
  $$\begin{cases} x + y = 356 \\ 4x + 34 = \frac{1}{2}y \end{cases}$$
  $$2\left(4x + 34 = \frac{1}{2}y\right)$$
  $$8x + 68 = y$$
  $$\begin{cases} x + y = 356 \\ 8x + 68 = y \end{cases}$$

$$x + 8x + 68 = 356$$
$$9x + 68 = 356$$
$$9x = 288$$
$$x = 32$$

$$32 + y = 356$$
$$y = 324$$

The solution is $(32, 324)$.

- What does the solution mean in context?

  □ *Since we let x represent the number of girls and y represent the number of boys, it means that there are 32 girls and 324 boys at Euclid's Middle School in Grade 8.*

- Based on our work, we believe there are 32 girls and 324 boys. How can we be sure we are correct?

  □ *We need to substitute the values into both equations of the system to see if it makes a true statement. Then*

$$32 + 324 = 356$$
$$356 = 356$$

and

$$4(32) + 34 = \frac{1}{2}(324)$$
$$128 + 34 = 162$$
$$162 = 162$$

Example 3 (5 minutes)

Example 3

A family member has some five-dollar bills and one-dollar bills in their wallet. Altogether she has 18 bills and a total of $62. How many of each bill does she have?

- Again we will work together to solve the following word problem.

- A family member has some five-dollar bills and one-dollar bills in their wallet. Altogether she has 18 bills and a total of $62. How many of each bill does she have? What do we do first?

  □ *We need to define our variables.*

- If we define our variables we can better represent the situation we have been given. What should the variables be for this problem?

  □ *Let x represent the number of $5 bills and let y represent the number of $1 bills.*

Again, whichever way students define the variables, ask them if it could be done the opposite way.

- Now that we know that x is the number of $5 bills and y is the number of $1 bills, what do we need to do now?

  □ *We need to write equations to represent the information in the word problem.*

Lesson 29:	Word Problems
Date:	11/8/13

444

- Using x and y, write equations to represent the information we are provided.

  - *Altogether she has 18 bills and a total of $62 must be represented with two equations. The first being $x + y = 18$ to represent the total of 18 bills and the second being $5x + y = 62$ to represent the total amount of money she has.*

- We have two equations to represent this problem. What is it called when we have more than one linear equation for a problem, and how is it represented symbolically?

  - *We have a system of linear equations:*

  $$\begin{cases} x + y = 18 \\ 5x + y = 62 \end{cases}$$

- We know several methods for solving systems of linear equations. Which method do you think will be the most efficient and why?

  - *Answers will vary. Students will either say they could multiply one of the equations by -1, then they would be able to eliminate the variable y when they add the equations together. Other students may say it would be easiest to solve for y in the first equation and then substitute the value of y into the second equation. After they have justified their method, allow them to solve the system in any manner they choose.*

- Solve the system: $\begin{cases} x + y = 18 \\ 5x + y = 62 \end{cases}$.

  - *Sample student work:*

  $$\begin{cases} x + y = 18 \\ 5x + y = 62 \end{cases}$$

  $$x + y = 18$$
  $$y = -x + 18$$

  $$\begin{cases} y = -x + 18 \\ 5x + y = 62 \end{cases}$$

  $$5x + (-x) + 18 = 62$$
  $$4x + 18 = 62$$
  $$4x = 44$$
  $$x = 11$$

  $$11 + y = 18$$
  $$y = 7$$

  The solution is $(11, 7)$.

- What does the solution mean in context?

  - *Since we let x represent the number of $5 bills and y represent the number of $1 bills, it means that our family member has 11 $5 bills, and 7 $1 bills.*

- The next step is to check our work.

  - *It is obvious that $11 + 7 = 18$, so we know our family member has 18 bills. It makes more sense to check our work again the actual value of those 18 bills in this case. Now we check the second equation*

  $$5(11) + 1(7) = 62$$
  $$55 + 7 = 62$$
  $$62 = 62$$

Lesson 29:	Word Problems
Date:	11/8/13

445

Example 4 (9 minutes)

> **Example 4**
>
> A friend bought 2 boxes of pencils and 8 notebooks for school and it cost him $11. He went back to the store the same day to buy school supplies for his younger brother. He spent $11.25 on 3 boxes of pencils and 5 notebooks. How much would 7 notebooks cost?

- Again we will work together to solve the following word problem.
- A friend bought 2 boxes of pencils and 8 notebooks for school and it cost him $11. He went back to the store the same day to buy school supplies for his younger brother. He spent $11.25 on 3 boxes of pencils and 5 notebooks. How much would 7 notebooks cost? What do we do first?
  - *We need to define our variables.*
- If we define our variables we can better represent the situation we have been given. What should the variables be for this problem?
  - *Let x represent the cost of a box of pencils and let y represent the cost of a notebook.*

Again, whichever way students define the variables, ask them if it could be done the opposite way.

- Now that we know that x is the cost of a box of pencils and y is the cost of a notebook, what do we need to do now?
  - *We need to write equations to represent the information in the word problem.*

- Using x and y, write equations to represent the information we are provided.
  - *A friend bought 2 boxes of pencils and 8 notebooks for school and it cost him $11 is represented by the equation $2x + 8y = 11$.. He spent $11.25 on 3 boxes of pencils and 5 notebooks is represented by the equation $3x + 5y = 11.25$.*

- We have two equations to represent this problem. What is it called when we have more than one linear equation for a problem, and how is it represented symbolically?
  - *We have a system of linear equations:*
$$\begin{cases} 2x + 8y = 11 \\ 3x + 5y = 11.25 \end{cases}$$

- We know several methods for solving systems of linear equations. Which method do you think will be the most efficient and why?
  - *Answers will vary. Ask several students how what they believe the most efficient method is and have them share with the class a brief description of their plan. For example, a student may decide to multiply the first equation by 3 and the second equation by -2 to eliminate x from the system after adding the equations together. After several students have shared their plan, allow students to solve in any manner they choose.*

- Solve the system: $\begin{cases} 2x + 8y = 11 \\ 3x + 5y = 11.25 \end{cases}$.

  - *Sample student work:*

$$\begin{cases} 2x + 8y = 11 \\ 3x + 5y = 11.25 \end{cases}$$
$$3(2x + 8y = 11)$$
$$6x + 24y = 33$$
$$-2(3x + 5y = 11.25)$$
$$-6x - 10y = -22.50$$

$$\begin{cases} 6x + 24y = 33 \\ -6x - 10y = -22.50 \end{cases}$$

$$6x + 24y - 6x - 10y = 33 - 22.50$$
$$24y - 10y = 10.50$$
$$14y = 10.50$$
$$y = \frac{10.50}{14}$$
$$y = 0.75$$

$$2x + 8(0.75) = 11$$
$$2x + 6 = 11$$
$$2x = 5$$
$$x = 2.50$$

The solution is $(2.50, 0.75)$.

- What does the solution mean in context?

  - *It means that a box of pencils costs* $2.50 *and a notebook costs* $0.75.

- Before we answer the question that this word problem asked, check to make sure the solution is correct.

  - *Sample student work:*

$$2(2.50) + 8(0.75) = 11$$
$$5 + 6 = 11$$
$$11 = 11$$

  and

$$3(2.50) + 5(0.75) = 11.25$$
$$7.50 + 3.75 = 11.25$$
$$11.25 = 11.25$$

- Now that we know we have the correct costs for the box of pencils and notebooks we can answer the original question: How much would 7 notebooks cost?

  - *The cost of 7 notebooks is* $7(0.75) = 5.25$. *Therefore, 7 notebooks cost* $7.25.

- Keep in mind that some word problems require us to solve the system in order to answer a specific question, like this example about the cost of 7 notebooks. Other problems may just require the solution to the system to answer the word problem, like the first example about the two numbers and their sums and difference. It is always a good practice to reread the word problem to make sure you know what you are being asked to do.

Lesson 29:	Word Problems
Date:	11/8/13

Exercises 1–3 (9 minutes)

Students complete Exercises 1–3 independently or in pairs.

Exercises

1. A farm raises cows and chickens. The farmer has a total of 42 animals. One day he counts the legs of all of his animals and realizes he has a total of 114. How many cows does the farmer have? How many chickens?

    Let x represent the number of cows and y represent the number of chickens. Then,

    $$\begin{cases} x + y = 42 \\ 4x + 2y = 114 \end{cases}$$

    $$-2(x + y = 42)$$

    $$-2x - 2y = -84$$

    $$\begin{cases} -2x - 2y = -84 \\ 4x + 2y = 114 \end{cases}$$

    $$-2x - 2y + 4x + 2y = -84 + 114$$

    $$-2x + 4x = 30$$

    $$2x = 30$$

    $$x = 15$$

    $$15 + y = 42$$

    $$y = 27$$

    The solution is $(15, 27)$.

    $$4(15) + 2(27) = 114$$

    $$60 + 54 = 114$$

    $$114 = 114$$

    The farmer has 15 cows and 27 chickens.

2. The length of a rectangle is 4 times the width. The perimeter of the rectangle is 45 inches. What is the area of the rectangle?

    Let x represent the length and y represent the width. Then,

    $$\begin{cases} x = 4y \\ 2x + 2y = 45 \end{cases}$$

    $$2(4y) + 2y = 45$$

    $$8y + 2y = 45$$

    $$10y = 45$$

    $$y = 4.5$$

    $$x = 4(4.5)$$

    $$x = 18$$

    The solution is $(18, 4.5)$.

    $$2(18) + 2(4.5) = 45$$

    $$36 + 9 = 45$$

    $$45 = 45$$

    The area of the rectangle is $18 \times 4.5 = 81 \ in^2$.

Lesson 29:   Word Problems
Date: 11/8/13

3. The sum of the measures of angles x and y is $127°$. If the measure of $\angle x$ is $34°$ more than half the measure of $\angle y$, what is the measure of each angle?

Let x represent the measure of $\angle x$ and y represent the measure of $\angle y$. Then,

$$\begin{cases} x + y = 127 \\ x = 34 + \dfrac{1}{2}y \end{cases}$$

$$34 + \frac{1}{2}y + y = 127$$

$$34 + \frac{3}{2}y = 127$$

$$\frac{3}{2}y = 93$$

$$y = 62$$

$$x + 62 = 127$$

$$x = 65$$

The solution is $(65, 62)$.

$$65 = 34 + \frac{1}{2}(62)$$

$$65 = 34 + 31$$

$$65 = 65$$

The measure of $\angle x = 65°$ and the measure of $\angle y = 62°$.

Closing (5 minutes)

Summarize, or ask students to summarize, the main points from the lesson:

- We know how to write information from word problems into a system of linear equations.
- We can solve systems of linear equations using the elimination and substitution methods.
- When we solve a system we must clearly define the variables we intend to use, consider which method for solving the system would be most efficient, check our answer and think about what it means in context. Finally, we should check to make sure we have answered the question posed in the problem.

Exit Ticket (5 minutes)

Lesson 29:	Word Problems
Date:	11/8/13

449

Name _____   Date _____

Lesson 29: Word Problems

Exit Ticket

1. Small boxes contain DVDs and large boxes contain one gaming machine. Three boxes of gaming machines and a box of DVDs weigh 48 pounds. Three boxes of gaming machines and five boxes of DVDs weigh 72 pounds. How much does each box weigh?

2. A language arts test is worth 100 points. There are a total of 26 questions. There are spelling word questions that are worth 2 points each and vocabulary word questions worth 5 points each. How many of each type of question is there?

Exit Ticket Sample Solutions

1. Small boxes contain DVDs and large boxes contain one gaming machine. Three boxes of gaming machines and a box of DVDs weigh 48 pounds. Three boxes of gaming machines and five boxes of DVDs weigh 72 pounds. How much does each box weigh?

    Let x represent the weight of the gaming machine box and let y represent the weight of the DVD box. Then,

    $$\begin{cases} 3x + y = 48 \\ 3x + 5y = 72 \end{cases}$$

    $$-1(3x + y = 48)$$

    $$-3x - y = -48$$

    $$\begin{cases} -3x - y = -48 \\ 3x + 5y = 72 \end{cases}$$

    $$3x - 3x + 5y - y = 72 - 48$$

    $$4y = 24$$

    $$y = 6$$

    $$3x + 6 = 48$$

    $$3x = 42$$

    $$x = 14$$

    The solution is $(14, 6)$

    $$3(14) + 6 = 48$$

    $$48 = 48$$

    The box with one gaming machine weighs 14 pounds and the box containing DVDs weighs 6 pounds.

2. A language arts test is worth 100 points. There are a total of 26 questions. There are spelling word questions that are worth 2 points each and vocabulary word questions worth 5 points each. How many of each type of question is there?

    Let x represent the number of spelling word questions and let y represent the number of vocabulary word questions. Then,

    $$\begin{cases} x + y = 26 \\ 2x + 5y = 100 \end{cases}$$

    $$-2(x + y = 26)$$

    $$-2x - 2y = -52$$

    $$\begin{cases} -2x - 2y = -52 \\ 2x + 5y = 100 \end{cases}$$

    $$2x - 2x + 5y - 2y = 100 - 52$$

    $$3y = 48$$

    $$y = 16$$

    $$x + 16 = 26$$

    $$x = 10$$

    The solution is $(10, 16)$

    $$10 + 16 = 26$$

    $$26 = 26$$

    There are 10 spelling word questions and 16 vocabulary word questions.

Lesson 29:	Word Problems
Date:	11/8/13

Problem Set Sample Solutions

1. Two numbers have a sum of $1,212$ and a difference of 518. What are the two numbers?

    Let x represent one number and y represent the other number. Then,

    $$\begin{cases} x + y = 1212 \\ x - y = 518 \end{cases}$$

    $$x + y + x - y = 1212 - 518$$
    $$2x = 694$$
    $$x = 347$$

    $$347 + y = 1212$$
    $$y = 865$$

    The solution is $(347, 865)$.

    $$347 + 865 = 1212$$
    $$1212 = 1212$$

    The two numbers are 347 and 865.

2. The sum of the ages of two brothers is 46. The younger brother is 10 more than a third of the older brothers age. How old is the younger brother?

    Let x represent the age of the younger brother and y represent the age of the older brother. Then,

    $$\begin{cases} x + y = 46 \\ x = 10 + \dfrac{1}{3}y \end{cases}$$

    $$10 + \frac{1}{3}y + y = 46$$
    $$10 + \frac{4}{3}y = 46$$
    $$\frac{4}{3}y = 36$$
    $$y = 27$$

    $$x + 27 = 46$$
    $$x = 19$$

    The solution is $(19, 27)$.

    $$19 = 10 + \frac{1}{3}(27)$$
    $$19 = 10 + 9$$
    $$19 = 19$$

    The younger brother is 19 years old.

Lesson 29:   Word Problems
Date: 11/8/13

452

3. One angle measures 54 more than 3 times another angle. The angles are supplementary. What are their measures?

Let x represent the measure of one angle and y represent the measure of the other angle. Then,

$$\begin{cases} x = 3y + 54 \\ x + y = 180 \end{cases}$$

$$3y + 54 + y = 180$$
$$4y + 54 = 180$$
$$4y = 126$$
$$y = 31.5$$

$$x = 3(31.5) + 54$$
$$x = 94.5 + 54$$
$$x = 148.5$$

The solution is $(31.5, 148.5)$.

$$148.5 + 31.5 = 180$$
$$180 = 180$$

One angle measures $148.5°$ and the other measures $31.5°$.

4. Some friends went to the local movie theatre and bought four buckets of large popcorn and six boxes of candy. The total for the snacks was 46.50. The last time you were at the theatre you bought a large popcorn and a box of candy and the total was 9.75. How much would 2 large buckets of popcorn and 3 boxes of candy cost?

Let x represent the cost of a large bucket of popcorn and y represent the cost of a box of candy. Then,

$$\begin{cases} 4x + 6y = 46.50 \\ x + y = 9.75 \end{cases}$$

$$-4(x + y = 9.75)$$
$$-4x - 4y = -39$$

$$\begin{cases} 4x + 6y = 46.50 \\ -4x - 4y = -39 \end{cases}$$

$$4x + 6y - 4x - 4y = 46.50 - 39$$
$$6y - 4y = 7.50$$
$$2y = 7.50$$
$$y = 3.75$$

$$x + 3.75 = 9.75$$
$$x = 6$$

The solution is $(6, 3.75)$.

$$4(6) + 6(3.75) = 46.50$$
$$24 + 22.50 = 46.50$$
$$46.50 = 46.50$$

Two large buckets of popcorn and three boxes of candy will cost $2(6) + 3(3.75) = 12 + 11.25 = 23.25$ dollars.

5. You have 59 total coins for a total of 12.05. You only have quarters and dimes. How many of each coin do you have?

Let x represent the number of quarters and y represent the number of dimes. Then,

$$\begin{cases} x + y = 59 \\ 0.25x + 0.1y = 12.05 \end{cases}$$

$$-4(0.25x + 0.1y = 12.05)$$

$$-x - 0.4y = -48.20$$

$$\begin{cases} x + y = 59 \\ -x - 0.4y = -48.20 \end{cases}$$

$$x + y - x - 0.4y = 59 - 48.20$$

$$y - 0.4y = 10.80$$

$$0.6y = 10.80$$

$$y = \frac{10.80}{0.6}$$

$$y = 18$$

$$x + 18 = 59$$

$$x = 41$$

The solution is $(41, 18)$.

$$0.25(41) + 0.1(18) = 12.05$$

$$10.25 + 1.80 = 12.05$$

$$12.05 = 12.05$$

I have 41 quarters and 18 dimes.

6. A piece of string is 112 inches long. Isabel wants to cut it into 2 pieces so that one piece is three times as long as the other. How long is each piece?

Let x represent one piece and y represent the other, then

$$\begin{cases} x + y = 112 \\ 3y = x \end{cases}$$

$$3y + y = 112$$

$$4y = 112$$

$$y = 28$$

$$x + 28 = 112$$

$$x = 84$$

The solution is $(84, 28)$.

$$84 + 28 = 112$$

$$112 = 112$$

One piece should be 84 inches long and the other should be 28 inches long.

Lesson 30: Conversion between Celsius and Fahrenheit

Student Outcomes

- Students learn a real-world application of linear equations with respect to the conversion of temperatures from Celsius to Fahrenheit and Fahrenheit to Celsius.

Classwork

Discussion (20 minutes)

- There are two methods for measuring temperature: (a) Fahrenheit, which assigns the number 32 to the temperature of water freezing, and the number 212 to the temperature of water boiling; and (b) Celsius, which assigns the numbers 0 and 100, respectively, to the same temperatures. These numbers will be denoted by $32°F$, $212°F$, $0°C$, $100°C$, respectively.

- Our goal is to address the following two questions:

> (1) If t is a number, what is the degree in Fahrenheit that corresponds to $t°C$?
>
> (2) If t is a number, what is the degree in Fahrenheit that corresponds to $(-t)°C$?

- Instead of trying to answer these questions directly, let's try something simpler. With this in mind, can we find out what degree in Fahrenheit corresponds to $1°C$? Explain.

- We can use the following diagram to organize our thinking:

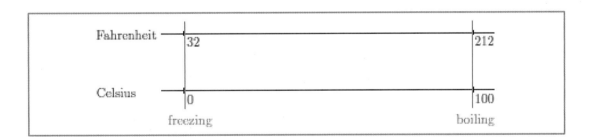

- At this point, the only information we have is that $0°C = 32°F$ and $100°C = 212°F$. We want to figure out what degree of Fahrenheit corresponds to $1°C$. Where on the diagram would $1°C$ be located? Be specific.

Provide students time to talk to their partners about a plan and then have them share. Ask them to make conjectures about what degree in Fahrenheit corresponds to $1°C$, have them explain their rationale for the numbers they chose. Consider recording the information and have the class vote on which answer they think is closest to correct.

> □ *We need to divide the Celsius number line from 0 to 100, into 100 equal parts. The first division to the right of zero will be the location of $1°C$.*

Now that we know where to locate $1°C$ on the lower number line, we need to figure out what number it corresponds to on the upper number line, representing Fahrenheit. Like we did with Celsius, we divide the number line from 32 to 212 into 100 equal parts. The number line from 32 to 212 is actually a length of 180 units $(212 - 32 = 180)$. Now, how would we determine the precise number in Fahrenheit that corresponds to $1°C$?

Provide students time to talk to their partners and compute the answer.

- *We need to take the length* 180 *and divide it into* 100 *equal parts. That is,*

$$\frac{180}{100} = \frac{9}{5} = 1\frac{4}{5} = 1.8.$$

- If we look at a magnified version of the number line with this division, we have:

- Based on your computation, what number falls at the intersection of the Fahrenheit number line and the red line that corresponds to $1°C$? Explain.

  - *Since we know that each division on the Fahrenheit number line has a length of* 1.8, *then when we start from* 32 *and add* 1.8 *we get* 33.8. *Therefore* $1°C$ *is equal to* $33.8°F$.

Revisit the conjecture made at the beginning of the activity and note which student came closest to guessing $33.8°F$. Ask the student to explain how they arrived at such a close answer.

- Eventually, we want to revisit the original two questions. But first, let's look at a few more concrete questions. What is $37°C$ in Fahrenheit? Explain.

Provide students time to talk to their partners about how to answer the question. Ask students to share their ideas and explain their thinking.

  - *Since the unit length on the Celsius scale is equal to the unit length on the Fahrenheit scale, then* $37°C$ *means we need to multiply* (37×1.8) *to determine the corresponding location on the Fahrenheit scale. But, because* 0 *on the Celsius scale is* 32 *on the Fahrenheit scale, we will need to add* 32 *to our answer. In other words,* $37°C = (32 + 37 \times 1.8)°F = (32 + 66.6)°F = 98.6°F$.

Exercises 1–5 (8 minutes)

Have students work in pairs or small groups to determine the corresponding Fahrenheit temperature for each given Celsius temperature. The goal is for students to be consistent in their use of repeated reasoning to lead them to the general equation for the conversion between Celsius and Fahrenheit.

Exercises 1–5

Determine the corresponding Fahrenheit temperate for the given Celsius temperatures in Exercises 1–5.

1. How many degrees Fahrenheit is $25°C$?

   $$25°C = (32 + 25 \times 1.8)°F = (32 + 45)°F = 77°F.$$

2. How many degrees Fahrenheit is $42°C$?

   $$42°C = (32 + 42 \times 1.8)°F = (32 + 75.6)°F = 107.6°F.$$

3. How many degrees Fahrenheit is $94°C$?

   $$94°C = (32 + 94 \times 1.8)°F = (32 + 169.2)°F = 201.2°F.$$

4. How many degrees Fahrenheit is $63°C$?

   $$63°C = (32 + 63 \times 1.8)°F = (32 + 113.4)°F = 145.4°F.$$

5. How many degrees Fahrenheit is $t°C$?

   $$t°C = (32 + 1.8t)°F$$

Discussion (10 minutes)

Have students share their answers from Exercise 5. Select several students to explain how they derived the equation to convert between Celsius and Fahrenheit. Close that part of the discussion by letting them know that they answered Question 1 that was posed at the beginning of the lesson:

> (1) If t is a number, what is the degree in Fahrenheit that corresponds to $t°C$?

The following discussion will answer question (2):

> (2) If t is a number, what is the degree in Fahrenheit that corresponds to $(-t)°C$?

- Now that Question 1 has been answered, let's beginning thinking about Question 2. Where on the number line would we find a negative Celsius temperature?
  - *A negative Celsius temperature will be to the left of zero on the number line.*

- Again, we will start simply. How can we determine the Fahrenheit temperature that corresponds to $-1°C$?

Provide students time to think, confirm with a partner, and then share with the class.

  - *We know that each unit on the Celsius scale is equal to $1.8°F$. Then $(-1)°C$ will equal $(32 - 1.8)°F = 30.2°F$.*

- How many degrees Fahrenheit corresponds to $(-15)°C$?

Provide students time to think, confirm with a partner, and then share with the class.

  - $(-15)°C = (32 - 15 \times 1.8)°F = (32 - 27)°F = 5°F.$

- How many degrees Fahrenheit corresponds to $(-36)°C$?

Provide students time to think, confirm with a partner, and then share with the class.

  - $(-36)°C = (32 - 36 \times 1.8)°F = (32 - 64.8)°F = -32.8°F.$

- How many degrees Fahrenheit corresponds to $(-t)°C$?

Provide students time to think, confirm with a partner, and then share with the class.

  - $(-t)°C = (32 - 1.8t)°F$

- Each of the previous four temperatures was negative. Then $(32 - 1.8t)°F$ can be rewritten as $\big(32 + 1.8(-t)\big)°F$. Where the second equation looks a lot like the one we wrote for $t°C$, i.e., $t°C = (32 + 1.8t)°F$. Are they the same equation? In other words, given any number t, positive or negative, would the result be the correct answer? We already know that the equation works for positive Celsius temperatures, so now let's focus on negative Celsius temperatures. Use $t°C = (32 + 1.8t)°F$ where $t = -15$. We expect the same answer as before: $(-15)°C = (32 - 15 \times 1.8)°F = (32 - 27)°F = 5°F$. Show that it is true.

  - $(-15)°C = \big(32 + 1.8(-15)\big)°F = \big(32 + (-27)\big) = 5°F.$

- Therefore, the equation $t°C = (32 + 1.8t)°F$ will work for any t.

- On a coordinate plane, if we let x be the given temperature and y be the temperature in Celsius, then we have the equation $y = x$. That is, there is no change in temperature. But, when we let x be the given temperature and y be the temperature in Fahrenheit, we have the equation $y = 32 + 1.8x$.

- Will these lines intersect? Explain?
  - *Yes. They have different slopes so at some point they will intersect.*

- What will that point of intersection represent?
  - *It represents the solution to the system* $\begin{cases} y = x \\ y = 1.8x + 32 \end{cases}$. *That point will be when the given temperature in Celsius is the same in Celsius, $y = x$, and when the given temperature in Celsius is the same temperature in Fahrenheit, $y = 1.8x + 32$.*

- Solve the system of equations algebraically to determine at what number $t°C = t°F$.
  - *Sample student work:*

$$\begin{cases} y = x \\ y = 1.8x + 32 \end{cases}$$

$$x = 1.8x + 32$$
$$-0.8x = 32$$
$$x = -40$$

At -40 degrees, the temperatures will be equal in both units. In other words, at -40 degrees Celcius, the temperature in Fahrenheit will also be -40 degrees.

Closing (3 minutes)

Summarize, or ask students to summarize, the main points from the lesson:

- We know how to use a linear equation in a real-world situation like converting between Celsius and Fahrenheit.
- We can use the computations we make for specific numbers to help us determine a general linear equation for a situation.

Exit Ticket (4 minutes)

Name _____   Date _____

Lesson 30: Conversion between Celsius and Fahrenheit

Exit Ticket

Use the equation developed in class to answer the following questions:

1. How many degrees Fahrenheit is $11°C$?

2. How many degrees Fahrenheit is $-3°C$?

3. Graph the equation developed in class and use it to confirm your results from Questions 1 and 2.

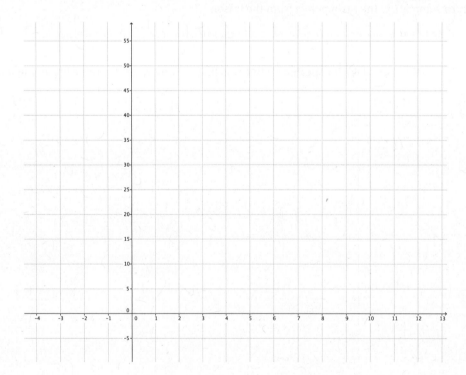

Use the equation developed in class to answer the following questions:

1. **How many degrees Fahrenheit is $11°C$?**

    $$11°C = (32 + 11 \times 1.8)°F$$
    $$11°C = (32 + 19.8)°F$$
    $$11°C = 51.8°F.$$

2. **How many degrees Fahrenheit is $-3°C$?**

    $$-3°C = (32 + (-3) \times 1.8)°F$$
    $$-3°C = (32 - 5.4)°F$$
    $$-3°C = 26.6°F.$$

3. **Graph the equation developed in class and use it to confirm your results from Questions 1 and 2.**

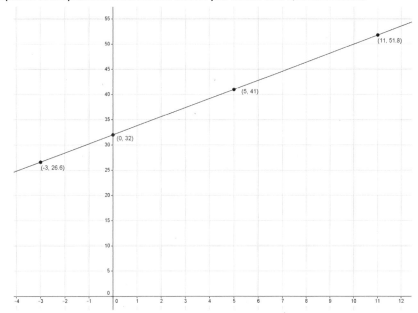

When I graph the equation developed in class, $t°C = (32 + 1.8t)°F$, the results from questions 1 and 2 are on the line; therefore, confirming they are solutions to the equation.

Problem Set Sample Solutions

1. Does the equation, $t°C = (32 + 1.8t)°F$, work for any rational number t? Check that is does with $t = 8\frac{2}{3}$ and $t = -8\frac{2}{3}$.

$$\left(8\frac{2}{3}\right)°C = \left(32 + 8\frac{2}{3} \times 1.8\right)°F = (32 + 15.6)°F = 47.6°F$$

$$\left(-8\frac{2}{3}\right)°C = \left(32 + \left(-8\frac{2}{3}\right) \times 1.8\right)°F = (32 - 15.6)°F = 16.4°F$$

2. Knowing that $t°C = \left(32 + \frac{9}{5}t\right)°F$ for any rational t, show that for any rational number d, $d°F = \left(\frac{5}{9}(d - 32)\right)°C$.

Since $d°F$ can be found by $\left(32 + \frac{9}{5}t\right)$, then $d = \left(32 + \frac{9}{5}t\right)$, and $d°F = t°C$. Substituting $d = \left(32 + \frac{9}{5}t\right)$ into $d°F$ we get:

$$d°F = \left(32 + \frac{9}{5}t\right)°F$$

$$d = 32 + \frac{9}{5}t$$

$$d - 32 = \frac{9}{5}t$$

$$\frac{5}{9}(d - 32) = t$$

Now that we know $t = \frac{5}{9}(d - 32)$, then $d°F = \left(\frac{5}{9}(d - 32)\right)°C$.

3. Drake was trying to write an equation to help him predict the cost of his monthly phone bill. He is charged $35 just for having a phone, and his only additional expense comes from the number of texts that he sends. He is charged $0.05 for each text. Help Drake out by completing parts (a)–(f).

   a. How much was his phone bill in July when he sent 750 texts?

   $$35 + 750(0.05) = 35 + 37.5 = 72.5$$

   His bill in July was $72.50.

   b. How much was his phone bill in August when he sent 823 texts?

   $$35 + 823(0.05) = 35 + 41.15 = 76.15$$

   His bill in August was $76.15.

   c. How much was his phone bill in September when he sent 579 texts?

   $$35 + 579(0.05) = 35 + 28.95 = 63.95$$

   His bill in September was $63.95.

   d. Let y represent the total cost of Drake's phone bill. Write an equation that represents the total cost of his phone bill in October if he sends t texts.

   $$y = 35 + t(0.05)$$

Lesson 30:   Conversion between Celsius and Fahrenheit
Date: 11/8/13

462

e.   Another phone plan charges $20 for having a phone and $0.10 per text. Let y represent the total cost of the phone bill for sending t texts. Write an equation to represent his total bill.

$$y = 20 + t(0.10)$$

f.   Write your equations in parts (d) and (e) as a system of linear equations and solve. Interpret the meaning of the solution in terms of the phone bill.

$$\begin{cases} y = 35 + t(0.05) \\ y = 20 + t(0.10) \end{cases}$$

$$35 + (0.05)t = 20 + (0.10)t$$
$$15 + (0.05)t = (0.10)t$$
$$15 = 0.05t$$
$$300 = t$$

$$y = 20 + 300(0.10)$$
$$y = 50$$

The solution is $(300, 50),$ *meaning that when Drake sends* 300 *texts, the cost of his bill will be* 50 *using his current phone plan or the new one.*

Optional Topic E:

Pythagorean Theorem

8.G.B.7, 8.EE.C.8

Focus Standard:	8.G.B.7	Apply the Pythagorean Theorem to determine unknown side lengths in right triangles in real-world and mathematical problems in two and three dimensions.
	8.EE.C.8	Analyze and solve pairs of simultaneous linear equations.
		a. Understand that solutions to a system of two linear equations in two variables correspond to points of intersection of their graphs, because points of intersection satisfy both equations simultaneously.
		b. Solve systems of two linear equations in two variables algebraically, and estimate solutions by graphing the equations. Solve simple cases by inspection. *For example, 3x + 2y = 5 and 3x + 2y = 6 have no solution because 3x + 2y cannot simultaneously be 5 and 6.*
		c. Solve real-world and mathematical problems leading to two linear equations in two variables. *For example, given coordinates for two pairs of points, determine whether the line through the first pair of points intersects the line through the second pair.*
Instructional Days:	1	
Lesson 31:	System of Equations Leading to Pythagorean Triples (S)[1]	

Lesson 31 shows students how to apply what they learned about systems of linear equations to find a Pythagorean triple (**8.G.B.7**, **8.EE.C.8b**). The Babylonian method of generating Pythagorean triples, described in Lesson 31, uses a system of linear equations.

---

[1] Lesson Structure Key: **P**-Problem Set Lesson, **M**-Modeling Cycle Lesson, **E**-Exploration Lesson, **S**-Socratic Lesson

Lesson 31: System of Equations Leading to Pythagorean Triples

Student Outcomes

- Students know that a Pythagorean triple can be obtained by multiplying any known triple by a common whole number. Students use this method to generate Pythagorean triples.
- Students use a system of equations to find three numbers, a, b, and c, so that $a^2 + b^2 = c^2$.

Lesson Notes

This lesson is optional as it includes content related to the Pythagorean Theorem. The purpose of this lesson is to demonstrate an application of systems of linear equations to other content in the curriculum. Though Pythagorean triples are not part of the standard for the grade, it is an interesting topic and should be shared with students if time permits.

Classwork

Discussion (10 minutes)

- A New York publicist, George Arthur Plimpton, bought a clay tablet from an archaeological dealer for $10 in 1922. This tablet was donated to Columbia University in 1936 and became known by its catalog number, Plimpton 322. What made this tablet so special was not just that it was 4,000 years old, but that it showed a method for finding Pythagorean triples. It was excavated near old Babylonia (which is now Iraq).

- Any three numbers, a, b, c, that satisfy $a^2 + b^2 = c^2$ are considered a triple, but when the three numbers are positive integers, then they are known as *Pythagorean triples*. It is worth mentioning that one of the Pythagorean triples found on the tablet was 12709, 13500, 18541.

- An easy-to-remember Pythagorean Triple is 3, 4, 5. (Quickly verify for students that 3, 4, 5 is a triple). To generate another Pythagorean triple, we need only to multiply each of the numbers 3, 4, 5 by the same whole number. For example, the numbers 3, 4, 5 when each is multiplied by 2, the result is the triple 6, 8, 10. (Again, quickly verify that 6, 8, 10 is a triple). Let's think about why this is true in a geometric context.

  Shown below are the two right triangles:

 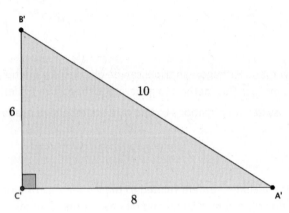

- Discuss with your partners how the method for finding Pythagorean triples can be explained mathematically.

  □ *Triangle △ A'B'C' can be obtained by dilating △ ABC by a scale factor of 2. Each triangle has a right angle with corresponding sides that are equal in ratio to the same constant, 2. That is how we know that these triangles are similar. The method for finding Pythagorean triples can be directly tied to our understanding of dilation and similarity. Each triple is just a set of numbers that represent a dilation of △ ABC by a whole-number scale factor.*

- Of course, we can also find triples by using a scale factor $0 < r < 1$, but since it produces a set of numbers that are not whole numbers, they are not considered to be Pythagorean triples. For example, if $r = \frac{1}{10}$, then a triple using side lengths 3, 4, 5 is 0.3, 0.4, 0.5.

Exercises 1–3 (5 minutes)

Students complete Exercises 1–3 independently. Allow students to use a calculator to verify that they are identifying triples.

Exercises 1–3

1. **Identify two Pythagorean triples using the known triple 3, 4, 5 (other than 6, 8, 10).**

    Answers will vary. Accept any triple that is a whole number multiple of 3, 4, 5.

2. **Identify two Pythagorean triples using the known triple 5, 12, 13.**

    Answers will vary. Accept any triple that is a whole number multiple of 5, 12, 13.

3. **Identify two triples using either 3, 4, 5 or 5, 12, 13.**

    Answers will vary.

Discussion (10 minutes)

- Pythagorean triples can also be explained algebraically. For example, assume a, b, c represent a triple. Let m be a positive integer. Then by the Pythagorean Theorem, $a^2 + b^2 = c^2$:

$$(ma)^2 + (mb)^2 = m^2a^2 + m^2b^2 \qquad \text{By the second law of exponents}$$
$$= m^2(a^2 + b^2) \qquad \text{By the Distributive Property}$$
$$= m^2c^2 \qquad \text{By substitution } (a^2 + b^2 = c^2)$$
$$= (mc)^2$$

  Our learning of systems of linear equations leads us to another method for finding Pythagorean triples, and it is actually the method that was discovered on the tablet Plimpton 322.

- Consider the system of linear equations:

$$\begin{cases} x + y = \dfrac{t}{s} \\ x - y = \dfrac{s}{t} \end{cases}$$

  where s and t are positive integers and $t > s$. Incredibly, the solution to this system results in a Pythagorean triple. When the solution is written as fractions with the same denominator, $\left(\dfrac{c}{b}, \dfrac{a}{b}\right)$ for example, the numbers a, b, c are a Pythagorean triple.

- To make this simpler, let's replace s and t with 1 and 2, respectively. Then we have:

$$\begin{cases} x + y = \dfrac{2}{1} \\ x - y = \dfrac{1}{2} \end{cases}$$

- Which method should we use to solve this system? Explain.

  □ *We should add the equations together to eliminate the variable y.*

- By the elimination method we have:

$$x + y + x - y = 2 + \frac{1}{2}$$
$$2x = \frac{5}{2}$$
$$x = \frac{5}{4}$$

  Now, we can substitute x into one of the equations to find y:

$$\frac{5}{4} + y = 2$$
$$y = 2 - \frac{5}{4}$$
$$y = \frac{3}{4}$$

  Then, the solution to the system is $\left(\dfrac{5}{4}, \dfrac{3}{4}\right)$. Since the solution, when written as fractions with the same denominator, $\left(\dfrac{c}{b}, \dfrac{a}{b}\right)$ for example, represents the Pythagorean triple, a, b, c, then our solution yields the triple 3, 4, 5.

Lesson 31:	System of Equations Leading to Pythagorean Triples
Date:	11/8/13

467

The remaining time can be used to complete Exercises 4–7 where students practice finding triples using the system of linear equations just described, or with the discussion below which shows the solution to the general system (without using concrete numbers for s and t).

Exercises 4–7 (10 minutes)

These exercises are to be completed in place of the discussion below. Have students complete Exercises 4–7 independently.

Exercises 4–7

Use the system $\begin{cases} x + y = \dfrac{t}{s} \\ x - y = \dfrac{s}{t} \end{cases}$ to find Pythagorean triples for the given values of s and t. Recall that the solution, in the form of $\left(\dfrac{c}{b}, \dfrac{a}{b}\right)$ is the triple, a, b, c.

4. $s = 4$, $t = 5$

$$\begin{cases} x + y = \dfrac{5}{4} \\ x - y = \dfrac{4}{5} \end{cases}$$

$$x + y + x - y = \frac{5}{4} + \frac{4}{5} \qquad\qquad \frac{41}{40} + y = \frac{5}{4}$$

$$2x = \frac{5}{4} + \frac{4}{5} \qquad\qquad y = \frac{5}{4} - \frac{41}{40}$$

$$2x = \frac{41}{20} \qquad\qquad y = \frac{9}{40}$$

$$x = \frac{41}{40}$$

Then the solution is $\left(\dfrac{41}{40}, \dfrac{9}{40}\right)$ and the triple is $9, 40, 41$.

5. $s = 7$, $t = 10$

$$\begin{cases} x + y = \dfrac{10}{7} \\ x - y = \dfrac{7}{10} \end{cases}$$

$$x + y + x - y = \frac{10}{7} + \frac{7}{10} \qquad\qquad \frac{149}{140} + y = \frac{10}{7}$$

$$2x = \frac{149}{70} \qquad\qquad y = \frac{10}{7} - \frac{149}{140}$$

$$x = \frac{149}{140} \qquad\qquad y = \frac{51}{140}$$

Then the solution is $\left(\dfrac{149}{140}, \dfrac{51}{140}\right)$ and the triple is $51, 140, 149$.

Lesson 31:	System of Equations Leading to Pythagorean Triples
Date:	11/8/13

468

6. $s = 1,\ t = 4$

$$\begin{cases} x + y = \dfrac{4}{1} \\ x - y = \dfrac{1}{4} \end{cases}$$

$$x + y + x - y = 4 + \frac{1}{4}$$

$$2x = \frac{17}{4}$$

$$x = \frac{17}{8}$$

$$\frac{17}{8} + y = \frac{4}{1}$$

$$y = 4 - \frac{17}{8}$$

$$y = \frac{15}{8}$$

Then the solution is $\left(\dfrac{17}{8}, \dfrac{15}{8}\right)$ *and the triple is* 15, 8, 17.

7. Use a calculator to verify that you found a Pythagorean triple in each of the Exercises 4–6. Show your work below.

    For the triple $9, 40, 41$:

    $$9^2 + 40^2 = 41^2$$
    $$81 + 1,600 = 1,681$$
    $$1,681 = 1,681$$

    For the triple $51, 140, 149$:

    $$51^2 + 140^2 = 149^2$$
    $$2601 + 19,600 = 22,201$$
    $$22,201 = 22,201$$

    For the triple $15, 8, 17$:

    $$15^2 + 8^2 = 17^2$$
    $$225 + 64 = 289$$
    $$289 = 289$$

Discussion (10 minutes)

This discussion is optional and replaces Exercises 4–7 above.

- Now we solve the system generally.

$$\begin{cases} x + y = \dfrac{t}{s} \\ x - y = \dfrac{s}{t} \end{cases}$$

- Which method should we use to solve this system? Explain.
    - *We should add the equations together to eliminate the variable y.*

Lesson 31:   System of Equations Leading to Pythagorean Triples
Date: 11/8/13

▪ By the elimination method we have:

$$x + y + x - y = \frac{t}{s} + \frac{s}{t}$$

$$2x = \frac{t}{s} + \frac{s}{t}$$

To add the fractions we will need the denominators to be the same. So, we use what we know about equivalent fractions, and multiply the first fraction by $\frac{t}{t}$ and the second fraction by $\frac{s}{s}$:

$$2x = \frac{t}{s}\left(\frac{t}{t}\right) + \frac{s}{t}\left(\frac{s}{s}\right)$$

$$2x = \frac{t^2}{st} + \frac{s^2}{st}$$

$$2x = \frac{t^2 + s^2}{st}$$

Now, we multiply both sides of the equation by $\frac{1}{2}$:

$$\frac{1}{2}(2x) = \frac{1}{2}\left(\frac{t^2 + s^2}{st}\right)$$

$$x = \frac{t^2 + s^2}{2st}$$

Now that we have a value for x we can solve for y as usual, but it is simpler to go back to the system:

$$\begin{cases} x + y = \dfrac{t}{s} \\ x - y = \dfrac{s}{t} \end{cases}$$

Is equivalent to the system:

$$\begin{cases} x = \dfrac{t}{s} - y \\ x = \dfrac{s}{t} + y \end{cases}$$

$$\frac{t}{s} - y = \frac{s}{t} + y$$

$$\frac{t}{s} = \frac{s}{t} + 2y$$

$$\frac{t}{s} - \frac{s}{t} = 2y$$

Which is very similar to what we have done before when we solved for x. Therefore,

$$y = \frac{t^2 - s^2}{2st}$$

The solution to the system is $\left(\frac{t^2+s^2}{2st}, \frac{t^2-s^2}{2st}\right)$. Since the solution, when written as fractions with the same denominator, such as $\left(\frac{c}{b}, \frac{a}{b}\right)$ for example, represent the Pythagorean triple, a, b, c, then our solution yields the triple $t^2 - s^2, 2st, t^2 + s^2$.

Closing (5 minutes)

Summarize, or ask students to summarize, the main points from the lesson:

- We know how to find an infinite number of Pythagorean triples: multiply a known triple by a whole number.
- We know that if the numbers a, b, c are not whole numbers they can still be considered a triple, just not a Pythagorean triple.
- We know how to use a system of linear equations, just like the Babylonians did 4,000 years ago, to find Pythagorean triples.

> **Lesson Summary**
>
> A Pythagorean triple is a set of three positive integers that satisfies the equation $a^2 + b^2 = c^2$.
>
> An infinite number of Pythagorean triples can be found by multiplying the numbers of a known triple by a whole number. For example, $3, 4, 5$ is a Pythagorean triple. Multiply each number by 7, then you have $21, 28, 35$ which is also a Pythagorean triple.
>
> The system of linear equations, $\begin{cases} x + y = \dfrac{t}{s} \\ x - y = \dfrac{s}{t} \end{cases}$ can be used to find Pythagorean triples, just like the Babylonians did 4,000 years ago.

Exit Ticket (5 minutes)

Name _____   Date _____

Lesson 31: System of Equations Leading to Pythagorean Triples

Exit Ticket

Use a calculator to complete problems 1–3.

1. Is 7, 20, 21 a Pythagorean triple? Is $1, \frac{15}{8}, \frac{17}{8}$ a Pythagorean triple? Explain.

2. Identify two Pythagorean triples using the known triple $9, 40, 41$.

3. Use the system $\begin{cases} x + y = \dfrac{t}{s} \\ x - y = \dfrac{s}{t} \end{cases}$ to find Pythagorean triples for the given values of $s = 2$ and $t = 3$. Recall that the

    solution, in the form of $\left(\frac{c}{b}, \frac{a}{b} \right)$, is the triple, a, b, c. Verify your results.

472

Exit Ticket Sample Solutions

Use a calculator to complete problems 1–3.

1. Is 7, 20, 21 a Pythagorean triple? Is $1, \frac{15}{8}, \frac{17}{8}$ a Pythagorean triple? Explain.

   The set of numbers 7, 20, 21 is not a Pythagorean triple because $7^2 + 20^2 \neq 21^2$.

   The set of numbers $1, \frac{15}{8}, \frac{17}{8}$ is not a Pythagorean triple because the numbers $\frac{15}{8}$ and $\frac{17}{8}$ are not whole numbers.

   But, they are a triple because $1^2 + \left(\frac{15}{8}\right)^2 = \left(\frac{17}{8}\right)^2$.

2. Identify two Pythagorean triples using the known triple $9, 40, 41$.

   Answers will vary. Accept any triple that is a whole number multiple of $9, 40, 41$.

3. Use the system $\begin{cases} x + y = \dfrac{t}{s} \\ x - y = \dfrac{s}{t} \end{cases}$ to find Pythagorean triples for the given values of $s = 2$ and $t = 3$. Recall that the solution, in the form of $\left(\dfrac{c}{b}, \dfrac{a}{b}\right)$, is the triple, a, b, c. Verify your results.

$$\begin{cases} x + y = \dfrac{3}{2} \\ x - y = \dfrac{2}{3} \end{cases}$$

$$x + y + x - y = \frac{3}{2} + \frac{2}{3} \qquad\qquad \frac{13}{12} + y = \frac{3}{2}$$
$$2x = \frac{13}{6} \qquad\qquad y = \frac{3}{2} - \frac{13}{12}$$
$$x = \frac{13}{12} \qquad\qquad y = \frac{5}{12}$$

Then the solution is $\left(\dfrac{13}{12}, \dfrac{5}{12}\right)$ and the triple is 5, 12, 13.

$$5^2 + 12^2 = 13^2$$
$$25 + 144 = 169$$
$$169 = 169$$

Problem Set Sample Solutions

Students practice finding triples using both methods discussed in this lesson.

1. Explain in terms of similar triangles why it is that when you multiply the known Pythagorean triple 3, 4, 5 by 12, it generates a Pythagorean triple.

    The triangle with lengths 3, 4, 5 is similar to the triangle with lengths 36, 48, 60. They are both right triangles whose corresponding side lengths are equal to the same constant:

    $$\frac{36}{3} = \frac{48}{4} = \frac{60}{5} = 12.$$

    Therefore, the triangles are similar. Thus, we can say that there is a dilation from some center with scale factor $r = 12$ that makes the triangles congruent.

2. Identify three Pythagorean triples using the known triple 8, 15, 17.

    Answers will vary. Accept any triple that is a whole number multiple of 8, 15, 17.

3. Identify three triples (numbers that satisfy $a^2 + b^2 = c^2$, but a, b, c are not whole numbers) using the triple 8, 15, 17.

    Answers will vary. Accept any triple that is not a set of whole numbers.

    Use the system $\begin{cases} x + y = \frac{t}{s} \\ x - y = \frac{s}{t} \end{cases}$ to find Pythagorean triples for the given values of s and t. Recall that the solution, in the form of $\left(\frac{c}{b}, \frac{a}{b}\right)$, is the triple, a, b, c.

4. $s = 2$, $t = 9$

    $$\begin{cases} x + y = \frac{9}{2} \\ x - y = \frac{2}{9} \end{cases}$$

    $$x + y + x - y = \frac{9}{2} + \frac{2}{9}$$
    $$2x = \frac{85}{18}$$
    $$x = \frac{85}{36}$$

    $$\frac{85}{36} + y = \frac{9}{2}$$
    $$y = \frac{9}{2} - \frac{85}{36}$$
    $$y = \frac{77}{36}$$

    Then the solution is $\left(\frac{85}{36}, \frac{77}{36}\right)$ and the triple is 77, 36, 85.

5. $s = 6$, $t = 7$

$$\begin{cases} x + y = \dfrac{7}{6} \\ x - y = \dfrac{6}{7} \end{cases}$$

$$x + y + x - y = \frac{7}{6} + \frac{6}{7}$$
$$2x = \frac{85}{42}$$
$$x = \frac{85}{84}$$

$$\frac{85}{84} + y = \frac{7}{6}$$
$$y = \frac{7}{6} - \frac{85}{84}$$
$$y = \frac{13}{84}$$

Then the solution is $\left(\dfrac{85}{84}, \dfrac{13}{84}\right)$ *and the triple is* $13, 84, 85$.

6. $s = 3$, $t = 4$

$$\begin{cases} x + y = \dfrac{4}{3} \\ x - y = \dfrac{3}{4} \end{cases}$$

$$x + y + x - y = \frac{4}{3} + \frac{3}{4}$$
$$2x = \frac{25}{12}$$
$$x = \frac{25}{24}$$

$$\frac{25}{24} + y = \frac{4}{3}$$
$$y = \frac{4}{3} - \frac{25}{24}$$
$$y = \frac{7}{24}$$

Then the solution is $\left(\dfrac{25}{24}, \dfrac{7}{24}\right)$ *and the triple is* $7, 24, 25$.

7. Use a calculator to verify that you found a Pythagorean triple in each of the problems 4–6. Show your work below.

For the triple $77, 36, 85$:
$$77^2 + 36^2 = 85^2$$
$$5929 + 1,296 = 7,225$$
$$7,225 = 7,225$$

For the triple $13, 84, 85$:
$$13^2 + 84^2 = 85^2$$
$$169 + 7,056 = 7,225$$
$$7,225 = 7,225$$

For the triple $7, 24, 25$:
$$7^2 + 24^2 = 25^2$$
$$49 + 576 = 625$$
$$625 = 625$$

Name _____   Date _____

1. Use the graph below to answer parts (a)–(c).

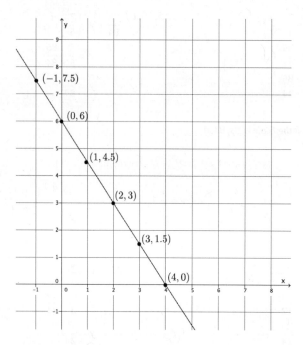

a. Use any pair of points to calculate the slope of the line.

b. Use a different pair of points to calculate the slope of the line.

c. Explain why the slopes you calculated in parts (a) and (b) are equal.

2. Jeremy rides his bike at a rate of 12 miles per hour. Below is a table that represents the number of hours and miles Kevin rides. Assume both bikers ride at a constant rate.

Time in hours (x)	Distance in miles (y)
1.5	17.25
2	23
3.5	40.25
4	46

a.   Which biker rides at a greater speed? Explain your reasoning.

b.   Write an equation for a third biker, Lauren, who rides twice as fast as Kevin. Use y to represent the number of miles Lauren travels in x hours. Explain your reasoning.

c.   Create a graph of the equation in part (b).

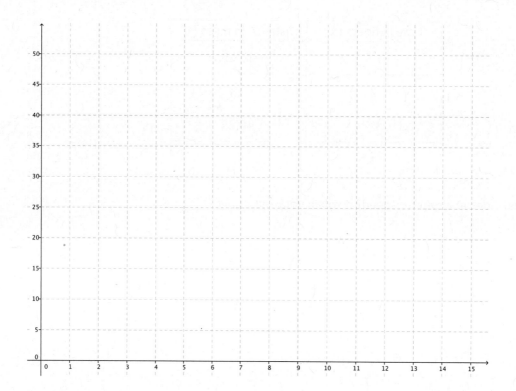

d.   Calculate the slope of the line in part (c) and interpret its meaning in this situation.

3. The cost of five protractors is $14.95 at Store A. The graph below compares the cost of protractors at Store A with the cost at Store B.

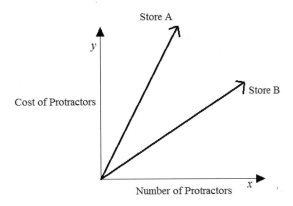

Estimate the cost of one protractor at Store B. Use evidence from the graph to justify your answer.

4. Given the equation, $3x + 9y = -8$, write a second linear equation to create a system that:

   a. Has exactly one solution. Explain your reasoning.

   b. Has no solution. Explain your reasoning.

   c. Has infinitely many solutions. Explain your reasoning.

   d. Interpret the meaning of the solution, if it exists, in the context of the graph of the following system of equations.

   $$\begin{cases} -5x + 2y = 10 \\ 10x - 4y = -20 \end{cases}$$

5. Students sold 275 tickets for a fundraiser at school. Some tickets are for children and cost $3, while the rest are adult tickets that cost $5. If the total value of all tickets sold was $1,025, how many of each type of ticket was sold?

6. a. Determine the equation of the line connecting the points $(0, -1)$ and $(2,3)$.

    b. Will the line described by the equation in (a) intersect the line passing through the points $(-2,4)$ and $(-3,3)$? Explain why or why not.

7.   Line l_1 and line l_2 are shown on the graph below. Use the graph to answer parts (a)–(d).

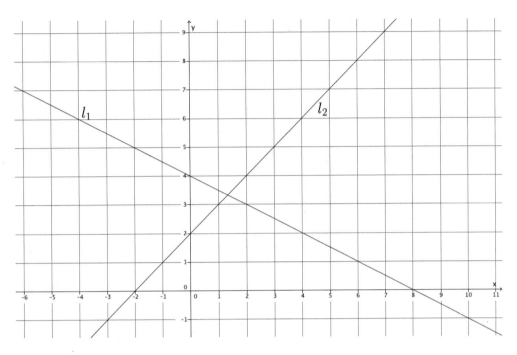

a.   What is the y-intercept of l_1?

b.   What is the y-intercept of l_2?

c.   Write a system of linear equations representing lines l_1 and l_2.

d.   Use the graph to estimate the solution to the system.

e.   Solve the system of linear equations algebraically.

f.   Show that your solution from part (e) satisfies both equations.

A Progression Toward Mastery

Assessment Task Item		STEP 1 Missing or incorrect answer and little evidence of reasoning or application of mathematics to solve the problem.	STEP 2 Missing or incorrect answer but evidence of some reasoning or application of mathematics to solve the problem.	STEP 3 A correct answer with some evidence of reasoning or application of mathematics to solve the problem, OR an incorrect answer with substantial evidence of solid reasoning or application of mathematics to solve the problem.	STEP 4 A correct answer supported by substantial evidence of solid reasoning or application of mathematics to solve the problem.
1	a–b 8.EE.B.5	Student made no attempt to find the slope in part (a) and/or part (b).	Student computed the slope in parts (a) and (b), but made computational errors leading to slopes that were not equal. Student may have used the same two points for both parts (a) and (b).	Student computed slope, both times, but may have forgotten to include the negative sign, or made another simple computational error. Student found the slopes in both parts (a) and (b) to be equal.	Student correctly computed the slope, both times, and found $m = -\frac{3}{2}$ (or an equivalent fraction to $-\frac{3}{2}$). Student found the slopes in both parts (a) and (b) to be equal.
	c 8.EE.B.6	Student made no attempt to answer the question.	Student stated that the slopes in parts (a) and (b) were not equal.	Student made a weak argument by stating that the slopes are equal because the fractions are equal, or that the fractions representing the slope are equivalent.	Student made a convincing argument and referenced similar triangles to explain why the slopes between any two points on a line are equal.
2	a 8.EE.B.5	Student made no attempt to answer the question or wrote "Kevin" or "Jeremy" with no evidence of an application of mathematics to solve the problem.	Student wrote an incorrect answer but showed some evidence of reasoning in their explanation.	Student wrote the correct answer. Students' explanation lacked precision or was incorrect. For example, student may have written that Jeremy travels a farther distance in 2 hours, instead of referencing the rates of each biker.	Student wrote the correct answer. Student provided a strong mathematical explanation as to which biker rides at a greater speed by referencing a graph (slopes of each line where one slope is steeper) or a numerical comparison of their rates.

	b–d 8.EE.B.5	Student made little or no attempt to complete parts (b)–(d). Student may have plotted points on the graph with no relevance to the problem.	Student wrote an incorrect equation in part (b) and/or graphed the equation incorrectly and/or calculated the slope incorrectly. Student did not connect the slope of the line to Lauren's rate.	Student may have correctly identified the equation, graphed, and calculated slope and identified it as Lauren's rate but may not have explained their reasoning in part (b). OR Student may have made a mistake in writing the equation for part (b) which led to an incorrect graph and slope in parts (c)–(d).	Student correctly wrote the equation, $y = 23x$ in part (b) or an equivalent equation. Student explained "twice as fast" in terms of distance traveled for a given time interval compared to the data for Kevin given in the table. Student correctly graphed the situation in (c) and correctly identified the slope of the line, 23, as the rate that Lauren rides for part (d).
3	8.EE.B.5	Student made no attempt to answer the question OR wrote a dollar amount with no explanation.	Student may or may not have correctly calculated the unit rate of protractors for Store A. Student wrote an estimate for Store B, but did not justify their estimate using evidence from the graph.	Student used the information provided about Store A to determine the unit rate of protractors buy may have made a computation error leading to a poor estimate. Student may or may not have used evidence from the graph to justify their estimate or made a weak connection between their estimate and the graph.	Student used the information provided about Store A to determine the unit rate of protractors and referenced the unit rate at Store A in the justification of their estimate. Student wrote an estimate that made sense (e.g., less than Store A, about half as much) and used evidence from the graph in their justification (e.g., comparison of slopes, size of angles).
4	a–c 8.EE.C.7a 8.EE.C.8	Student made no attempt to answer any parts of (a)–(c) OR just rewrote the given equation as an answer.	Student answered at least one part of (a)–(c) correctly. Student may have left two parts blank. Student may or may not have explained their reasoning.	Student answered at least two parts of (a)–(c) correctly. Student may have left one part blank. Student explained their reasoning in at least two parts of (a)–(c) noting the characteristics required to achieve the desired number of solutions.	Student provided a correct equation and explanation for each of the parts of (a)–(c). Specifically, for part (a) an equation that represents a distinct line from the given equation will have a slope different than $-\frac{1}{3}$, for part (b) an equation that represents a line parallel to the given equation will have the same slope, and for part (c) an equation that represents the same line as the given equation whose graphs coincide.

Module 4:   Linear Equations
Date: 11/8/13

485

	d 8.EE.C.8	Student made little or no attempt to answer the question. Student did not provide a mathematical explanation or apply any mathematical reasoning to support their answer.	Student gave an incorrect answer. Student may have said that the point of intersection of the lines is the solution to the system, or that there is no solution because the lines are parallel.	Student may have tried to find the solution algebraically. Student stated that there are infinitely many solutions to the system, but may not have referenced what the graph would look like (i.e., each equation produced the same line on the graph). Student supplied weak mathematical reasoning to support their answer.	Student correctly stated that the graphs of the equations produce the same line. Student explained that one equation can be obtained by the other by multiplying the first equation by -2, or the second equation by $-\frac{1}{2}$. OR Student explained that both lines had the same slope of $\frac{5}{2}$ and the same y-intercept of $(0,5)$. Student supplied strong mathematical reasoning to support their answer.
5	8.EE.C.8	Student made little or no attempt to write and solve a system of linear equations.	Student may have written an incorrect system of equations to represent the situation. Student may or may not have defined their variables. Student may have used another strategy to determine the numbers of tickets of each type were sold. There is some evidence of mathematical reasoning.	Student correctly wrote a system of linear equations to represent the situation, but made a computational error leading to an incorrect solution OR student correctly wrote and solved a system but did not define their variables.	Student correctly wrote and solved a system of linear equations to solve the problem. Student defined the variables used in the system. Student stated clearly that 175 children's tickets and 100 adult's tickets were sold.
6	**a** 8.EE.C.8	Student made little or no attempt to write the equation.	Student incorrectly computed the slope of the line as something other than 2. Student did not write the correct equation of the line.	Student used the points to correctly determine the slope of the line as 2, but may have written an incorrect equation.	Student used the points to determine the slope of the line, then wrote the equation of the line passing through those two points as $y = 2x - 1$ or equivalent.
	b 8.EE.C.8	Student made little or no attempt to answer the question. OR Student responded with "yes" or "no" only.	Student incorrectly computed the slope of the line as something other than 1 and may or may not have drew an incorrect conclusion about whether or not the lines would intersect.	Student used the points to correctly determine the slope of the line as 1, but made an incorrect conclusion about whether or not the lines would intersect. OR Student made a computational error for the slope and drew the	Students used the points to determine the slope as 1 AND correctly concluded that the lines will intersect because the slopes are different.

				wrong conclusion about the lines. <u>OR</u> Student said the lines would intersect, but did not provide an explanation.	
7	**a–b** **8.EE.C.8**	Student left both parts (a) and (b) blank. <u>OR</u> Student identified coordinates that do not fall on either the x or y axis.	Student identified one of the two y-intercepts, but may have inversed the coordinates. Student may have left one of (a) or (b) blank.	Student identified the y-intercepts of l_1 and l_2, but may have inversed the coordinates, i.e., $(4,0)$ and $(2,0)$, or identified the slope of l_1 as $(0,2)$, and l_2 as $(0,4)$.	Student correctly identified the y-intercepts of l_1 and l_2, $(0,4)$ and $(0,2)$, respectively.
	c–d **8.EE.C.8**	Student left the item blank. <u>OR</u> Student only wrote one equation that may or may not have represented one of the lines on the graph. Student may or may not have written an estimate or wrote and estimate where the x-value was not between 1 and 2 and the y-value was not between 3 and 4.	Student wrote two equations to represent the system but the equations did not represent the lines on the graph. Student may or may not have written an estimate or wrote and estimate where the x-value was not between 1 and 2 and the y-value was not between 3 and 4.	Student wrote a system of equations but one of the equations may have been written incorrectly. Student wrote an estimate where the x-value was between 1 and 2 and the y-value was between 3 and 4.	Student correctly wrote the system as $\begin{cases} x-y=-2 \\ x+2y=8 \end{cases}$ or a system equivalent to this given one. Student wrote an estimate where the x-value was between 1 and 2 and the y-value was between 3 and 4.
	e–f **8.EE.C.8**	Student was unable to solve the system algebraically.	Student solved the system algebraically, but made serious computational errors leading to an incorrect solution. Student was unable to complete part (f) or may have realized their error and did not correct it.	Student solved the system, but may have made a computational error leading to an incorrect x or y coordinate. Student verified their solution in part (f). Student may have made a computational error leading them to believe their solution was correct.	Student correctly solved the system and identified the solution as $\left(\frac{4}{3}, \frac{10}{3}\right)$. Student verified their solution in part (f).

Name _____   Date _____

1. Use the graph below to answer parts (a–c).

a. Use any pair of points to calculate the slope of the line.

$$m = \frac{6-3}{0-2} = \frac{3}{-2} = -\frac{3}{2}$$

b. Use a different pair of points to calculate the slope of the line.

$$m = \frac{6-0}{0-4} = \frac{6}{-4} = -\frac{3}{2}$$

c. Explain why the slopes you calculated in parts (a) and (b) are equal.

THE SLOPES ARE EQUAL BECAUSE THE SLOPE TRIANGLES ARE SIMILAR, $\triangle ABC \sim \triangle AB'C'$. EACH TRIANGLE HAS A 90° ANGLE AT $\angle ABC$ & $\angle AB'C'$, RESPECTIVELY. THEY ARE 90° BECAUSE THEY ARE AT THE INTERSECTION OF THE GRID LINES. BOTH TRIANGLES SHARE $\angle BAC$. BY THE AA CRITERION $\triangle ABC \sim \triangle AB'C'$ WHICH MEANS THEIR CORRESPONDING SIDES ARE EQUAL IN RATIO. SPECIFICALLY, $\frac{AB'}{AB} = \frac{AC'}{AC}$ WHICH IS THE SAME AS $\frac{AB'}{AC'} = \frac{AB}{AC}$ WHERE $\frac{AB'}{AC'}$ IS THE SLOPE IN (b) AND $\frac{AB}{AC}$ IS THE SLOPE IN (a).

2. Jeremy rides his bike at a rate of 12 miles per hour. Below is a table that represents the number of hours and miles Kevin rides. Assume both bikers ride at a constant rate.

Time in hours (x)	Distance in miles (y)
1.5	17.25
2	23
3.5	40.25
4	46

a. Which biker rides at a greater speed? Explain.

LET y BE THE DISTANCE TRAVELED AND x BE THE NUMBER OF HOURS.
THEN FOR JEREMY, $\frac{y}{x} = \frac{12}{1} \Rightarrow y = 12x$.

FOR KEVIN, $\frac{46-23}{4-2} = \frac{23}{2} = 11.5$, THEN $y = 11.5x$

WHEN YOU COMPARE THEIR RATES, $12 > 11.5$, THEREFORE JEREMY RIDES AT A GREATER SPEED.

GRAPHICALLY:

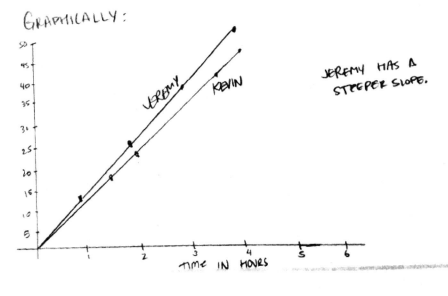

JEREMY HAS A STEEPER SLOPE.

b.   Write an equation for a third biker, Lauren, who rides twice as fast as Kevin. Use y to represent the number of miles Lauren travels in x hours. Explain your reasoning.

"TWICE AS FAST" MEANS LAUREN GOES TWICE THE DISTANCE IN THE SAME TIME. THEN IN 2 HOURS SHE RIDES 46 MILES AND 8 HOURS, 92 MILES. IF y IS TOTAL DISTANCE IN x HOURS,

$$y = \frac{46}{2}x$$

$$y = 23x$$

c.   Create a graph of the equation in part (b).

d.   Calculate the slope of the line in part (c) and interpret its meaning in this situation.

$$m = \frac{46-23}{2-1} = \frac{23}{1}$$

THE SLOPE IS THE RATE THAT LAUREN RIDES, 23 MILES PER HOUR.

3. The cost of five protractors is $14.95 at Store A. The graph below compares the cost of protractors at Store A with the cost at Store B.

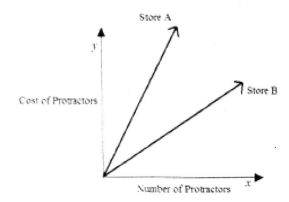

Estimate the cost of one protractor at Store B. Use evidence from the graph to justify your answer.

$$\begin{array}{r} 299 \\ 5\overline{)1495} \\ \underline{10} \\ 49 \\ \underline{45} \\ 45 \end{array}$$

THE COST OF PROTRACTORS AT STORE B IS PROBABLY ABOUT $1.50. STORE A CHARGES $2.99 PER PROTRACTOR AND IT LOOKS LIKE THE SLOPE FOR STORE B IS ABOUT HALF OF THE SLOPE FOR STORE A.

✱ ANSWERS WILL VARY

4. Given the equation, $3x + 9y = -8$, write a second linear equation to create a system that:

a. Has exactly one solution. Explain your reasoning.

$4x + 9y = -10$ THIS EQUATION HAS A SLOPE DIFFERENT FROM $3x + 9y = -8$ SO THE GRAPHS OF THIS EQUATIONS WILL INTERSECT.

b. Has no solution. Explain your reasoning.

$x + 3y = 10$ THIS EQUATION HAS THE SAME SLOPE AS $3x + 9y = -8$, AND NO COMMON POINTS (SOLUTIONS) THEREFORE THE GRAPHS OF THE EQUATIONS ARE PARALLEL LINES

c. Has infinitely many solutions. Explain your reasoning.

$6x + 18y = -16$ THIS EQUATION DEFINES THE SAME LINE AS $3x + 9y = -8$ AND THE GRAPHS OF THE EQUATIONS WILL COINCIDE.

d. Interpret the meaning of the solution, if it exists, in the context of the graph of the following system of equations.

$$\begin{cases} -5x + 2y = 10 \\ 10x - 4y = -20 \end{cases}$$ $m = \frac{5}{2}$ $(0,5)$ $m = \frac{5}{2}$ $(0,5)$

THIS SYSTEM WILL HAVE INFINITELY MANY SOLUTIONS BECAUSE THE GRAPHS OF THESE LINEAR EQUATIONS ARE THE SAME LINE. EACH EQUATION HAS A SLOPE OF $m = \frac{5}{2}$ AND A Y-INTERCEPT AT $(0,5)$. THERE EXISTS ONLY ONE LINE THROUGH A POINT AND A GIVEN SLOPE. THEREFORE THIS SYSTEM GRAPHS AS THE SAME LINE AND HAS INFINITELY MANY SOLUTIONS.

5. Students sold 275 tickets for a fundraiser at school. Some tickets are for children and cost $3, while the rest are adult tickets that cost $5. If the total value of all tickets sold was $1,025, how many of each type of ticket was sold?

LET x BE THE # OF KIDS TICKETS

LET y BE THE # OF ADULTS TICKETS

$$\begin{cases} x+y=275 \\ 3x+5y=1025 \end{cases}$$

$$3x+5y=1025$$
$$-3x-3y=-825$$

$$2y=200$$
$$y=100$$

$$x+100=275$$
$$x=175$$

$$(175,100)$$

175 CHILDREN'S TICKETS AND 100 ADULTS TICKETS WERE SOLD.

6.

  a.   Determine the equation of the line connecting the points $(0, -1)$ and $(2,3)$.

$$m = \frac{3-(-1)}{2-0} = \frac{4}{2} = 2$$

$$y = 2x - 1$$

  b.   Will the line described by the equation in (a) intersect the line passing through the points $(-2,4)$ and $(-3,3)$? Explain why or why not.

$$m = \frac{4-3}{-2-(-3)} = \frac{1}{1}$$

YES, THE LINES WILL INTERSECT BECAUSE THEY HAVE DIFFERENT SLOPES. THEY WILL EVENTUALLY INTERSECT.

7. Line l_1 and line l_2 are shown on the graph below. Use the graph to answer parts (a–d).

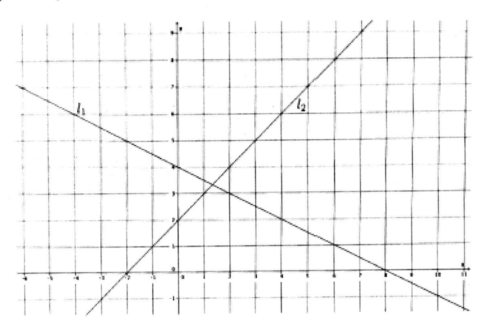

a. What is the y-intercept of l_1?

$(0, 4)$

b. What is the y-intercept of l_2?

$(0, 2)$

c. Write a system of linear equations representing lines l_1 and l_2.

$l_1 : \ y = -\frac{1}{2}x + 4$ $\begin{cases} y = -\frac{1}{2}x + 4 \\ y = x + 2 \end{cases}$

$l_2 : \ y = x + 2$

d. Use the graph to estimate the solution to the system.

$(1.2, 3.3)$

e. Solve the system of linear equations algebraically.

$\begin{cases} y = -\frac{1}{2}x + 4 \\ y = x + 2 \end{cases}$ $-\frac{1}{2}x + 4 = x + 2$ $y = \frac{4}{3} + 2$

$4 = \frac{3}{2}x + 2$ $= \frac{10}{3}$

$2 = \frac{3}{2}x$

$\frac{4}{3} = x$ $\left(\frac{4}{3}, \frac{10}{3}\right)$

f. Show that your solution from part (e) satisfies both equations.

$\frac{10}{3} = -\frac{1}{2}\left(\frac{4}{3}\right) + 4$ $\frac{10}{3} = \frac{4}{3} + 2$

$\frac{10}{3} = -\frac{2}{3} + 4$ $\frac{10}{3} = \frac{10}{3}$

$\frac{10}{3} = \frac{10}{3}$

Student Materials

Lesson 1: Writing Equations Using Symbols

Classwork

Exercises

Write each of the following statements using symbolic language.

1. The sum of four consecutive even integers is −28.

2. A number is four times larger than the square of half the number.

3. Steven has some money. If he spends nine dollars, then he will have $\frac{3}{5}$ of the amount he started with.

4. The sum of a number squared and three less than twice the number is 129.

5. Miriam read a book with an unknown number of pages. The first week she read five less than $\frac{1}{3}$ of the pages. The second week she read 171 pages and finished the book. Write an equation that represents the total number of pages in the book.

Lesson Summary

Begin all word problems by defining your variables. State clearly what you want each symbol to represent.

Written mathematical statements can be represented as more than one correct symbolic statement.

Break complicated problems into smaller parts or try working them with simpler numbers.

Problem Set

Write each of the following statements using symbolic language.

1. Bruce bought two books. One book costs four dollars more than three times the other. Together, the two books cost him $72.

2. Janet is three years older than her sister Julie. Janet's brother is eight years younger than their sister Julie. The sum of all of their ages is 55.

3. The sum of three consecutive integers is 1,623.

4. One number is six more than another number. The sum of their squares is 90.

5. When you add 18 to $\frac{1}{4}$ of a number, you get the number itself.

6. When a fraction of 12 is taken away from 17, what remains exceeds one-third of seventeen by six.

7. The sum of two consecutive even integers divided by four is 189.5.

8. Subtract seven more than twice a number from the square of one-third of the number to get zero.

9. The sum of three consecutive integers is 42. Let x be the middle of the three integers. Transcribe the statement accordingly.

Lesson 2: Linear and Non-Linear Expressions in x

Classwork

Exercises

Write each of the following statements in Exercises 1–12 as a mathematical expression. State whether or not the expression is linear or non-linear. If it is non-linear, then explain why.

1. The sum of a number and four times the number.

2. The product of five and a number.

3. Multiply six and the reciprocal of the quotient of a number and seven.

4. Twice a number subtracted from four times a number, added to 15.

5. The square of the sum of six and a number.

6. The cube of a positive number divided by the square of the same positive number.

7. The sum of four consecutive numbers.

8. Four subtracted from the reciprocal of a number.

9. Half of the product of a number multiplied by itself, three times.

10. The sum that shows how many pages Maria read if she read 45 pages of a book yesterday and $\frac{2}{3}$ of the remaining pages today.

11. An admission fee of $10 plus an additional $2 per game.

12. Five more than four times a number, then twice that sum.

> **Lesson Summary**
>
> Linear expressions are sums of constants and products of constants and x raised to a power of 0 or 1. For example, $4 + 3x$, $7x + x - 15$, and $\frac{1}{2}x + 7 - 2$ are all linear expressions in x.
>
> Non-linear expressions are also sums of constants and products of constants and a x raised to a power that is not 0 or 1. For example, $2x^2 - 9$, $-6x^{-3} + 8 + x$, and $\frac{1}{x} + 8$ are all non-linear expressions in x.

Problem Set

Write each of the following statements as a mathematic expression. State whether the expression is linear or non-linear. If it is non-linear, then explain why.

1. A number decreased by three squared.

2. The quotient of two and a number, subtracted from seventeen.

3. The sum of thirteen and twice a number.

4. 5.2 more than the product of seven and a number.

5. The sum that represents tickets sold if 35 tickets were sold Monday, half of the remaining tickets were sold on Tuesday, and 14 tickets were sold on Wednesday.

6. The product of 19 and a number, subtracted from the reciprocal of the number cubed.

7. The product of 15 and number, multiplied by itself four times.

8. A number increased by five, divided by two.

9. Eight times the result of subtracting three from a number.

10. The sum of twice a number and four times a number subtracted from the number squared.

11. One-third of the result of three times a number that is increased by 12.

12. Five times the sum of one-half and a number.

13. Three-fourths of a number multiplied by seven.

14. The sum of a number and negative three, multiplied by the number.

15. The square of the difference between a number and 10.

Lesson 3: Linear Equations in x

Exercises

1. Is the equation true when $x = -3$; in other words, is -3 a solution to the equation: $6x + 5 = 5x + 8 + 2x$? Explain.

2. Does $x = 12$ satisfy the equation: $16 - \frac{1}{2}x = \frac{3}{4}x + 1$? Explain.

3. Chad solved the equation $24x + 4 + 2x = 3(10x - 1)$ and is claiming that $x = 2$ makes the equation true. Is Chad correct? Explain.

4. Lisa solved the equation $x + 6 = 8 + 7x$ and claimed that the solution is: $x = -\frac{1}{3}$.   Is she correct? Explain.

5. Angel transformed the following equation from $6x + 4 - x = 2(x + 1)$ to $10 = 2(x + 1)$. He then stated that the solution to the equation is $x = 4$. Is he correct? Explain.

6. Claire was able to verify that $x = 3$ was a solution to her teacher's linear equation, but the equation got erased from the board. What might the equation have been? Identify as many equations as you can with a solution of $x = 3$.

7. Does an equation always have a solution? Could you come up with an equation that does not have a solution?

Lesson Summary

Equations are statements about equality. If the expression on the left side of the equal sign has the same value as the expression on the right side of the equal sign, then you have a true equation.

A solution to a linear equation in x is a number, such that when all instances of x are replaced with the number, the left side will equal the right side. For example, $x = 2$ is a solution to $3x + 4 = x + 8$ because the left side of the equation is

$$3x + 4 = 3(2) + 4$$
$$= 6 + 4$$
$$= 10$$

and the right side of the equation is

$$x + 8 = 2 + 8$$
$$= 10$$

Since $10 = 10$, then $x = 2$ is a solution to the linear equation $3x + 4 = x + 8$.

Problem Set

1. Given that $2x + 7 = 27$ and $3x + 1 = 28$, does $2x + 7 = 3x + 1$? Explain.

2. Is -5 a solution to the equation: $6x + 5 = 5x + 8 + 2x$? Explain.

3. Does $x = 1.6$ satisfy the equation: $6 - 4x = -\frac{x}{4}$? Explain.

4. Use the linear equation $3(x + 1) = 3x + 3$ to answer parts (a)–(d).
    a. Does $x = 5$ satisfy the equation above? Explain.
    b. Is $x = -8$ a solution the equation above? Explain.
    c. Is $x = \frac{1}{2}$ a solution the equation above? Explain.
    d. What interesting fact about the equation $3(x + 1) = 3x + 3$ is illuminated by the answers to parts (a), (b), and (c)? Why do you think this is true?

Lesson 4: Solving a Linear Equation

Classwork

Exercises

For each problem, show your work, and check that your solution is correct.

1. Solve the linear equation: $x + x + 2 + x + 4 + x + 6 = -28$. State the property that justifies your first step and why you chose it.

2. Solve the linear equation: $2(3x + 2) = 2x - 1 + x$. State the property that justifies your first step and why you chose it.

3. Solve the linear equation: $x - 9 = \frac{3}{5}x$. State the property that justifies your first step and why you chose it.

4. Solve the linear equation: $29 - 3x = 5x + 5$. State the property that justifies your first step and why you chose it.

5. Solve the linear equation: $\frac{1}{3}x - 5 + 171 = x$. State the property that justifies your first step and why you chose it.

Lesson Summary

The properties of equality, shown below, are used to transform equations into simpler forms. If A, B, C are rational numbers, then

- If $A = B$, then $A + C = B + C$ Addition Property of Equality
- If $A = B$, then $A - C = B - C$ Subtraction Property of Equality
- If $A = B$, then $A \cdot C = B \cdot C$ Multiplication Property of Equality
- If $A = B$, then $\dfrac{A}{C} = \dfrac{B}{C}$, where C is not equal to zero   Division Property of Equality

To solve an equation, transform the equation until you get to the form of x equal to a constant ($x = 5$, for example).

Problem Set

For each problem, show your work and check that your solution is correct.

1. Solve the linear equation: $x + 4 + 3x = 72$. State the property that justifies your first step and why you chose it.

2. Solve the linear equation: $x + 3 + x - 8 + x = 55$. State the property that justifies your first step and why you chose it.

3. Solve the linear equation: $\dfrac{1}{2}x + 10 = -\dfrac{1}{4}x + 54$. State the property that justifies your first step and why you chose it.

4. Solve the linear equation: $\dfrac{1}{4}x + 18 = x$. State the property that justifies your first step and why you chose it.

5. Solve the linear equation: $17 - x = \dfrac{1}{3} \cdot 15 + 6$. State the property that justifies your first step and why you chose it.

6. Solve the linear equation: $\dfrac{x+x+2}{4} = 189.5$. State the property that justifies your first step and why you chose it.

7. Alysha solved the linear equation: $2x - 3 - 9x = 14 + x - 1$. Her work is shown below. When she checked her answer, the left side of the equation did not equal the right side. Find and explain Alysha's error, and then solve the equation correctly.

$$2x - 3 - 9x = 14 + x - 1$$
$$-6x - 3 = 13 + 2x$$
$$-6x - 3 + 3 = 13 + 3 + 2x$$
$$-6x = 16 + 2x$$
$$-6x + 2x = 16$$
$$-4x = 16$$
$$\frac{-4}{-4}x = \frac{16}{-4}$$
$$x = -4$$

Lesson 4:   Solving a Linear Equation
Date: 11/7/13

Lesson 5: Writing and Solving Linear Equations

Example 1

One angle is five less than three times the size of another angle. Together they have a sum of 143°. What are the sizes of each angle?

Example 2

Given a right triangle, find the size of the angles if one angle is ten more than four times the other angle and the third angle is the right angle.

Exercises

For each of the following problems, write an equation and solve.

1. A pair of congruent angles are described as follows: the measure of one angle is three more than twice a number and the other angle's measure is 54.5 less than three times the number. Determine the size of the angles.

2. The measure of one angle is described as twelve more than four times a number. Its supplement is twice as large. Find the measure of each angle.

3. A triangle has angles described as follows: the first angle is four more than seven times a number, another angle is four less than the first and the third angle is twice as large as the first. What are the sizes of each of the angles?

4. One angle measures nine more than six times a number. A sequence of rigid motions maps the angle onto another angle that is described as being thirty less than nine times the number. What is the measure of the angles?

5. A right triangle is described as having an angle of size "six less than negative two times a number," another angle that is "three less than negative one-fourth the number", and a right angle. What are the measures of the angles?

6. One angle is one less than six times the size of another. The two angles are complementary angles. Find the size of each angle.

Problem Set

For each of the following problems, write an equation and solve.

1. The measure of one angle is thirteen less than five times the measure of another angle. The sum of the measures of the two angles is $140°$. Determine the measures of each of the angles.

2. An angle measures seventeen more than three times a number. Its supplement is three more than seven times the number. What is the measure of each angle?

3. The angles of a triangle are described as follows: $\angle A$ is the largest angle, its measure is twice the measure of $\angle B$. The measure of $\angle C$ is 2 less than half the measure of $\angle B$. Find the measures of the three angles.

4. A pair of corresponding angles are described as follows: the measure of one angle is five less than seven times a number and the measure of the other angle is eight more than seven times the number. Are the angles congruent? Why or why not?

5. The measure of one angle is eleven more than four times a number. Another angle is twice the first angle's measure. The sum of the measures of the angles is $195°$. What is the measure of each angle?

6. Three angles are described as follows: $\angle B$ is half the size of $\angle A$. The measure of $\angle C$ is equal to one less than 2 times the measure of $\angle B$. The sum of $\angle A$ and $\angle B$ is 114. Can the three angles form a triangle? Why or why not?

Lesson 6: Solutions of a Linear Equation

Exercises

Find the value of x that makes the equation true.

1. $17 - 5(2x - 9) = -(-6x + 10) + 4$

2. $-(x - 7) + \frac{5}{3} = 2(x + 9)$

3. $\dfrac{4}{9} + 4(x - 1) = \dfrac{28}{9} - (x - 7x) + 1$

4. $5(3x + 4) - 2x = 7x - 3(-2x + 11)$

5. $7x - (3x + 5) - 8 = \frac{1}{2}(8x + 20) - 7x + 5$

6. Write at least three equations that have no solution.

Lesson Summary

The distributive property is used to expand expressions. For example, the expression $2(3x - 10)$ is rewritten as $6x - 20$ after the distributive property is applied.

The distributive property is used to simply expressions. For example, the expression $7x + 11x$ is rewritten as $(7 + 11)x$ and $18x$ after the distributive property is applied.

The distributive property is applied only to terms within a group:

$$4(3x + 5) - 2 = 12x + 20 - 2$$

Notice that the term -2 is not part of the group and therefore not multiplied by 4.

When an equation is transformed into an untrue sentence, like $5 \neq 11$, we say the equation has <u>no solution</u>.

Problem Set

Transform the equation if necessary, then solve it to find the value of x that makes the equation true.

1. $x - (9x - 10) + 11 = 12x + 3\left(-2x + \frac{1}{3}\right)$

2. $7x + 8\left(x + \frac{1}{4}\right) = 3(6x - 9) - 8$

3. $-4x - 2(8x + 1) = -(-2x - 10)$

4. $11(x + 10) = 132$

5. $37x + \frac{1}{2} - \left(x + \frac{1}{4}\right) = 9(4x - 7) + 5$

6. $3(2x - 14) + x = 15 - (-9x - 5)$

7. $8(2x + 9) = 56$

Lesson 7: Classification of Solutions

Exercises

Solve each of the following equations for x.

1. $7x - 3 = 5x + 5$

2. $7x - 3 = 7x + 5$

3. $7x - 3 = -3 + 7x$

Give a brief explanation as to what kind of solution(s) you expect the following linear equations to have. Transform the equation into a simpler form if necessary.

4. $11x - 2x + 15 = 8 + 7 + 9x$

5. $3(x - 14) + 1 = -4x + 5$

6. $-3x + 32 - 7x = -2(5x + 10)$

7. $\frac{1}{2}(8x + 26) = 13 + 4x$

8.   Write two equations that have no solutions.

9.   Write two equations that have one unique solution each.

10. Write two equations that have infinitely many solutions.

Lesson Summary

There are three classifications of solutions to linear equations: one solution (unique solution), no solution, or infinitely many solutions.

Equations with no solution will, after being simplified, have coefficients of x that are the same on both sides of the equal sign and constants that are different. For example, $x + b = x + c$, where b, c are constants that are not equal. A numeric example is $8x + 5 = 8x - 3$.

Equations with infinitely many solutions will, after being simplified, have coefficients of x and constants that are the same on both sides of the equal sign. For example, $x + a = x + a$, where a is a constant. A numeric example is $6x + 1 = 1 + 6x$.

Problem Set

1. Give a brief explanation as to what kind of solution(s) you expect the linear equation to have:
   $18x + \dfrac{1}{2} = 6(3x + 25)$. Transform the equation into a simpler form if necessary.

2. Give a brief explanation as to what kind of solution(s) you expect the linear equation to have:
   $8 - 9x = 15x + 7 + 3x$. Transform the equation into a simpler form if necessary.

3. Give a brief explanation as to what kind of solution(s) you expect the linear equation to have:
   $5(x + 9) = 5x + 45$. Transform the equation into a simpler form if necessary.

4. Give three examples of equations where the solution will be unique, that is, only one solution is possible.

5. Solve one of the equations you wrote in problem 4 and explain why it is the only solution.

6. Give three examples of equations where there will be no solution.

7. Attempt to solve one of the equations you wrote in problem 6 and explain why it has no solution.

8. Give three examples of equations where there will be infinitely many solutions.

9. Attempt to solve one of the equations you wrote in problem 8 and explain why it has infinitely many solutions.

Lesson 8: Linear Equations in Disguise

Example 3

Can this equation be solved?

$$\frac{6+x}{7x+\frac{2}{3}} = \frac{3}{8}$$

Example 4

Can this equation be solved?

$$\frac{7}{3x+9} = \frac{1}{8}$$

Example 5

In the diagram below, $\triangle ABC \sim \triangle A'B'C'$. Using what we know about similar triangles, we can determine the value of x.

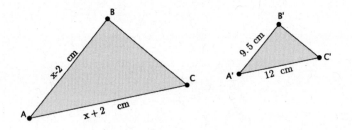

Exercises

Solve the following equations of rational expressions, if possible.

1. $\dfrac{2x+1}{9} = \dfrac{1-x}{6}$

2.　$\dfrac{5+2x}{3x-1} = \dfrac{6}{7}$

3.　$\dfrac{x+9}{12} = \dfrac{-2x-\frac{1}{2}}{3}$

4.　$\dfrac{8}{3-4x} = \dfrac{5}{2x+\frac{1}{4}}$

Lesson Summary

Proportions are linear equations in disguise and are solved the same way we normally solve proportions.

When multiplying a fraction with more than one term in the numerator and/or denominator by a number, put the expressions with more than one term in parentheses so you remember to use the distributive property when transforming the equation. For example:

$$\frac{x+4}{2x-5} = \frac{3}{5}$$
$$5(x+4) = 3(2x-5)$$

The equation $5(x+4) = 3(2x-5)$ is now clearly a linear equation and can be solved using the properties of equality.

Problem Set

Solve the following equations of rational expressions, if possible. If it cannot be solved, explain why.

1. $\dfrac{5}{6x-2} = \dfrac{-1}{x+1}$

2. $\dfrac{4-x}{8} = \dfrac{7x-1}{3}$

3. $\dfrac{3x}{x+2} = \dfrac{5}{9}$

4. $\dfrac{\frac{1}{2}x+6}{3} = \dfrac{x-3}{2}$

5. $\dfrac{7-2x}{6} = \dfrac{x-5}{1}$

6. $\dfrac{2x+5}{2} = \dfrac{3x-2}{6}$

7. $\dfrac{6x+1}{3} = \dfrac{9-x}{7}$

8. $\dfrac{\frac{1}{3}x-8}{12} = \dfrac{-2-x}{15}$

9. $\dfrac{3-x}{1-x} = \dfrac{3}{2}$

10. In the diagram below, $\triangle ABC \sim \triangle A'B'C'$. Determine the lengths of AC and BC.

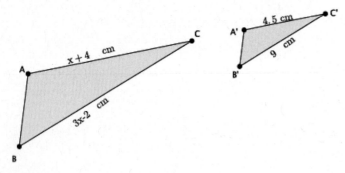

Lesson 9: An Application of Linear Equations

Exercises 1–2

1. Write the equation for the fifteenth step.

2. How many people would see the photo after fifteen steps? Use a calculator if needed.

Exercises 3–11

3. Marvin paid an entrance fee of $5 plus an additional $1.25 per game at a local arcade. Altogether he spent $26.25. Write and solve an equation to determine how many games Marvin played.

4. The sum of four consecutive numbers is -26. What are the numbers?

5. A book has x pages. How many pages are in the book if Maria read 45 pages of a book Monday, $\frac{1}{2}$ the book Tuesday, and the remaining 72 pages Wednesday?

6. A number increased by 5 and divided by 2 is equal to 75.

| Lesson 9: | An Application of Linear Equations |
| Date: | 11/7/13 |

7. The sum of thirteen and twice a number is seven less than six times a number. What is the number?

8. The width of a rectangle is 7 less than twice the length. If the perimeter of the rectangle is 43.6 inches, what is the area of the rectangle?

9. Two hundred and fifty tickets are available for sale for a school dance. On Monday 35 tickets were sold. An equal number of tickets were sold each day for the next 5 days. How many tickets were sold on one of those 5 days?

10. Shonna skateboarded for some number of minutes on Monday. On Tuesday, she skateboarded for twice as many minutes as she did on Monday, and on Wednesday, she skateboarded for half the sum of minutes from Monday and Tuesday. Altogether she skateboarded for a total of 3 hours. How many minutes did she skateboard each day?

11. In the diagram below, $\triangle ABC \sim \triangle A'B'C'$. Determine the length of AC and BC.

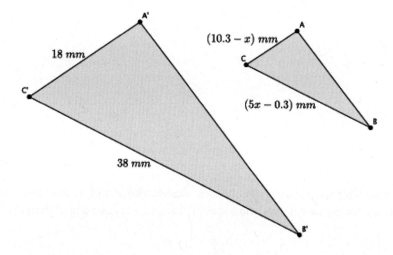

Problem Set

1. You forward an e-card you found online to three of your friends. They liked it so much that they forwarded it on to four of their friends, who then forwarded it on to four of their friends, and so on. The number of people who saw the e-card is shown below. Let S_1 represent the number of people who saw the e-card after one step, let S_2 represent the number of people who saw the e-card after two steps, and so on.

$$S_1 = 3$$
$$S_2 = 3 + 3 \cdot 4$$
$$S_3 = 3 + 3 \cdot 4 + 3 \cdot 4^2$$
$$S_4 = 3 + 3 \cdot 4 + 3 \cdot 4^2 + 3 \cdot 4^3$$

   a. Find the pattern in the equations.

   b. Assuming the trend continues, how many people will have seen the e-card after 10 steps?

   c. How many people will have seen the e-card after n steps?

For each of the following questions, write an equation and solve to find each answer.

2. Lisa has a certain amount of money. She spent 39 dollars and has $\frac{3}{4}$ of the original amount left. How much money did she have originally?

3. The length of a rectangle is 4 more than 3 times the width. If the perimeter of the rectangle is 18.4 cm, what is the area of the rectangle?

4. Eight times the result of subtracting 3 from a number is equal to the number increased by 25.

5. Three consecutive odd integers have a sum of 3. What are the numbers?

6. Each month Liz pays $35 to her phone company just to use the phone. Each text she sends costs her an additional $0.05. In March her phone bill was $72.60. In April her phone bill was $65.85. How many texts did she send each month?

7. Claudia is reading a book that has 360 pages. She has already read some of the book last week. She plans to read 46 pages today. When she does, she will be $\frac{4}{5}$ of the way through the book. How many pages did she read last week?

	Lesson 9:	An Application of Linear Equations
	Date:	11/7/13

S.32

8. In the diagram below, $\triangle ABC \sim \triangle A'B'C'$. Determine the measure of $\angle A$.

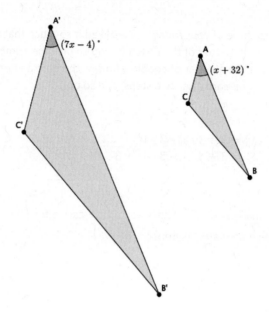

9. In the diagram below, $\triangle ABC \sim \triangle A'B'C'$. Determine the measure of $\angle A$.

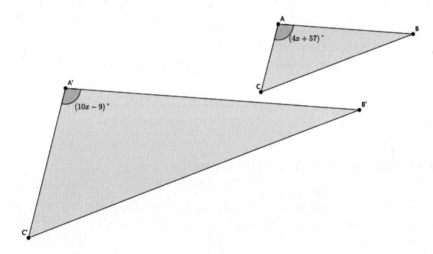

Lesson 10: A Critical Look at Proportional Relationships

Classwork

Example 1

Paul walks 2 miles in 25 minutes. How many miles can Paul walk in 137.5 minutes?

Time (in minutes)	Distance (in miles)
25	2

Exercises

1. Wesley walks at a constant speed from his house to school 1.5 miles away. It took him 25 minutes to get to school.

    a.   What fraction represents his constant speed, C?

    b.   You want to know how many miles he has walked after 15 minutes. Let y represent the distance he traveled after 15 minutes of walking at the given constant speed.   Write a fraction that represents the constant speed, C in terms of y.

    c.   Write the fractions from parts (a) and (b) as a proportion and solve to find out many miles Wesley walked after 15 minutes.

    d.   Let y be the distance in miles that Wesley traveled after x minutes. Write a linear equation in two variables that represents how many miles Wesley walked after x minutes.

2. Stefanie drove at a constant speed from her apartment to her friend's house 20 miles away. It took her 45 minutes to reach her destination.

    a.   What fraction represents her constant speed, C?

    b.   What fraction represents constant speed, C, if it takes her x number of minutes to get half-way to her friend's house?

c.   Write a proportion using the fractions from parts (a) and (b) to determine how many minutes it takes her to get to the half-way point.

d.   Write a two variable equation to represent how many miles Stefanie can drive over any time interval.

3.   The equation that represents how many miles, y, Dave travels after x hours is $y = 50x + 15$. Use the equation to complete the table below.

x (hours)	Linear equation in y: $y = 50x + 15$	y (miles)
1	$y = 50(1) + 15$	65
2		
3		
3.5		
4.1		

> **Lesson Summary**
>
> Average speed is found by taking the total distance traveled in a given time interval, divided by the time interval.
>
> If y is the total distance traveled in a given time interval x, then $\dfrac{y}{x}$ is the average speed.
>
> If we assume the same average speed over any time interval, then we have constant speed, which can then be used to express a linear equation in two variables relating distance and time.
>
> If $\dfrac{y}{x} = C$, where C is a constant, then you have constant speed.

Problem Set

1. Eman walks from the store to her friend's house, 2 miles away. It takes her 35 minutes.
    a. What fraction represents her constant speed, C?
    b. Write the fraction that represents her constant speed, C, if she walks y miles in 10 minutes.
    c. Write a proportion using the fractions from parts (a) and (b) to determine how many miles she walks after 10 minutes. Round your answer to the hundredths place.
    d. Write a two-variable equation to represent how many miles Eman can walk over any time interval.

2. Erika drives from school to soccer practice 1.3 miles away. It takes her 7 minutes.
    a. What fraction represents her constant speed, C?
    b. What fraction represents her constant speed, C, if it takes her x minutes to drive exactly 1 mile?
    c. Write a proportion using the fractions from parts (a) and (b) to determine how much time it takes her to drive exactly 1 mile. Round your answer to the tenths place.
    d. Write a two-variable equation to represent how many miles Erika can drive over any time interval.

3. Darla drives at a constant speed of 45 miles per hour.
    a. If she drives for y miles and it takes her x hours, write the two variable equation to represent the number of miles Darla can drive in x hours.
    b. Darla plans to drive to the market 14 miles from her house, then to the post office 3 miles from the market, and then return home, which is 15 miles from the post office. Assuming she drives at a constant speed the entire time, how long will it take her to get back home after running her errands? Round your answer to the hundredths place.

4. Aaron walks from his sister's house to his cousin's house, a distance of 4 miles, in 80 minutes. How far does he walk in 30 minutes?

5.   Carlos walks 4 miles every night for exercise. It takes him exactly 63 minutes to finish his walk.

    a.   Assuming he walks at a constant rate, write an equation that represents how many miles, y, Carlos can walk in x minutes.

    b.   Use your equation from part (a) to complete the table below. Use a calculator and round all values to the hundredths place.

x (minutes)	Linear equation in y:	y (miles)
15		
30		
40		
60		
75		

Lesson 11: Constant Rate

Classwork

Example 1

Pauline mows a lawn at a constant rate. Suppose she mows a 35 square foot lawn in 2.5 minutes. What area, in square feet, can she mow in 10 minutes? t minutes?

t (time in minutes)	Linear equation:	y (area in square feet)

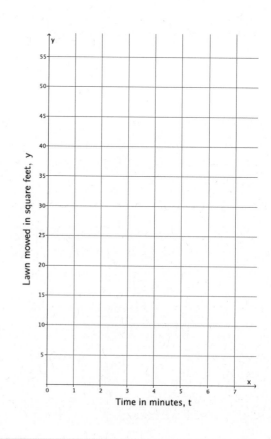

Example 2

Water flows at a constant rate out of a faucet. Suppose the volume of water that comes out in three minutes is 10.5 gallons. How many gallons of water comes out of the faucet in t minutes?

t (time in minutes)	Linear equation:	V (in gallons)
0		
1		
2		
3		
4		

Lesson 11:	Constant Rate
Date:	10/31/13

S.40

Exercises

1. Jesus types at a constant rate. He can type a full page of text in $3\frac{1}{2}$ minutes. We want to know how many pages, p, Jesus can type after t minutes.

    a. Write the linear equation in two variables that represents the number of pages Jesus types in any given time interval.

    b. Complete the table below. Use a calculator and round answers to the tenths place.

t (time in minutes)	Linear equation:	p (pages typed)
0		
5		
10		
15		
20		

    c. Graph the data on a coordinate plane.

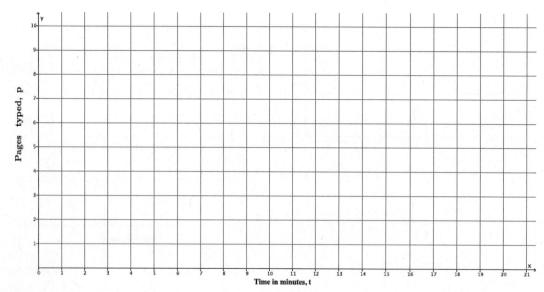

d.   About how long would it take Jesus to type a 5-page paper? Explain.

2.   Emily paints at a constant rate. She can paint 32 square feet in five minutes. What area, A, can she paint in t minutes?

a.   Write the linear equation in two variables that represents the number of square feet Emily can paint in any given time interval.

b.   Complete the table below. Use a calculator and round answers to the tenths place.

t (time in minutes)	Linear equation:	A (area painted in square feet)
0		
1		
2		
3		
4		

c.   Graph the data on a coordinate plane.

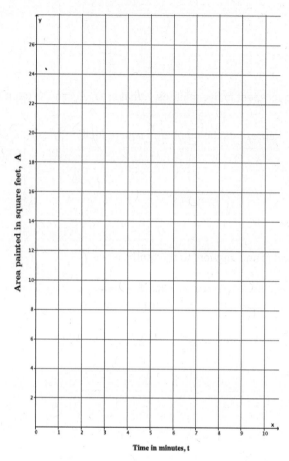

d.   About how many square feet can Emily paint in $2\frac{1}{2}$ minutes? Explain.

3.   Joseph walks at a constant speed. He walked to the store, one-half mile away, in 6 minutes. How many miles, m, can he walk in t minutes?

  a.   Write the linear equation in two variables that represents the number of miles Joseph can walk in any given time interval, t.

b.   Complete the table below. Use a calculator and round answers to the tenths place.

t (time in minutes)	Linear equation:	m (distance in miles)
0		
30		
60		
90		
120		

c.   Graph the data on a coordinate plane.

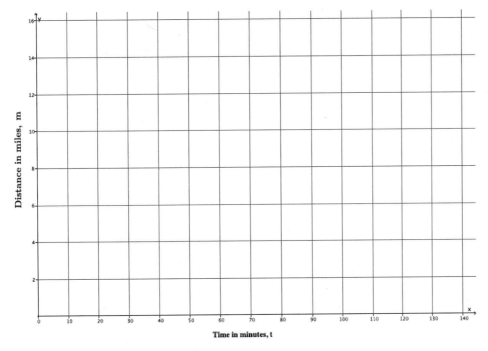

d.   Joseph's friend lives 4 miles away from him. About how long would it take Joseph to walk to his friend's house? Explain.

Lesson Summary

When constant rate is stated for a given problem, you can express the situation as a two variable equation. The equation can be used to complete a table of values that can then be graphed on a coordinate plane.

Problem Set

1. A train travels at a constant rate of 45 miles per hour.
   a. What is the distance, d, in miles, that the train travels in t hours?
   b. How many miles will it have traveled in 2.5 hours?

2. Water is leaking from a faucet at a constant rate of $\frac{1}{3}$ gallons per minute.
   a. What is the amount of water, w, that is leaked from the faucet after t minutes?
   b. How much water is leaked after an hour?

3. A car can be assembled on an assembly line in 6 hours. Assume that the cars are assembled at a constant rate.
   a. How many cars, y, can be assembled in t hours?
   b. How many cars can be assembled in a week?

4. A copy machine makes copies at a constant rate. The machine can make 80 copies in $2\frac{1}{2}$ minutes.
   a. Write an equation to represent the number of copies, n, that can be made over any time interval, t.
   b. Complete the table below.

t (time in minutes)	Linear equation:	n (number of copies)
0		
0.25		
0.5		
0.75		
1		

---

c.   Graph the data on a coordinate plane.

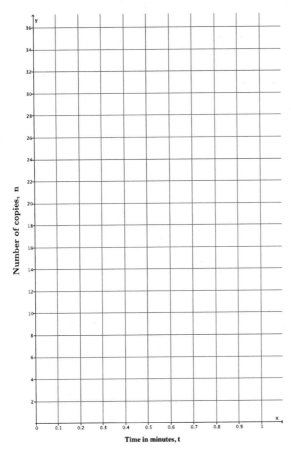

d.   The copy machine runs for 20 seconds, then jams. About how many copies were made before the jam occurred? Explain.

5.   Connor runs at a constant rate. It takes him 34 minutes to run four miles.

a.   Write the linear equation in two variables that represents the number of miles Connor can run in any given time interval, t.

b.   Complete the table below. Use a calculator and round answers to the tenths place.

t (time in minutes)	Linear equation:	m (distance in miles)
0		
15		
30		
45		
60		

c. Graph the data on a coordinate plane.

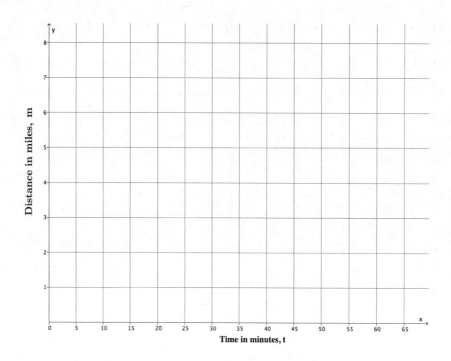

d. Connor ran for 40 minutes before tripping and spraining his ankle. About how many miles did he run before he had to stop?   Explain.

Lesson 12: Linear Equations in Two Variables

Opening Exercise

Emily tells you that she scored 32 points in a basketball game with only two- and three-point baskets (no free throws). How many of each type of basket did she score? Use the table below to organize your work.

Number of Two-pointers	Number of Three-pointers

Let x be the number of two-pointers and y be the number of three-pointers that Emily scored. Write an equation to represent the situation.

Exercises

1. Find five solutions for the linear equation $x + y = 3$, and plot the solutions as points on a coordinate plane.

x	Linear equation: $x + y = 3$	y

2. Find five solutions for the linear equation $2x - y = 10$, and plot the solutions as points on a coordinate plane.

x	Linear equation: $2x - y = 10$	y

3. Find five solutions for the linear equation $x + 5y = 21$, and plot the solutions as points on a coordinate plane.

x	Linear equation: $x + 5y = 21$	y

4. Consider the linear equation $\frac{2}{5}x + y = 11$.

    a. Will you choose to fix values for x or y? Explain.

    b. Are there specific numbers that would make your computational work easier? Explain.

c. Find five solutions to the linear equation $\frac{2}{5}x + y = 11$, and plot the solutions as points on a coordinate plane.

x	Linear equation: $\frac{2}{5}x + y = 11$	y

5. At the store you see that you can buy a bag of candy for $2 and a drink for $1. Assume you have a total of $35 to spend. You are feeling generous and want to buy some snacks for you and your friends.

a. Write an equation in standard form to represent the number of bags of candy, x, and the number of drinks, y, you can buy with $35.

b. Find five solutions to the linear equation, and plot the solutions as points on a coordinate plane.

x	Linear equation:	y

Lesson Summary

A two-variable linear equation in the form $ax + by = c$ is said to be in *standard form*.

A solution to a linear equation in two variables is the ordered pair (x, y) that makes the given equation true. Solutions can be found by fixing a number for x and solving for y or fixing a number for y and solving for x.

Problem Set

1. Consider the linear equation $x - \dfrac{3}{2}y = -2$.

   a. Will you choose to fix values for x or y? Explain.

   b. Are there specific numbers that would make your computational work easier? Explain.

   c. Find five solutions to the linear equation $x - \dfrac{3}{2}y = -2$ and plot the solutions as points on a coordinate plane.

x	Linear equation: $x - \dfrac{3}{2}y = -2$	y

2. Find five solutions for the linear equation $\dfrac{1}{3}x + y = 12$, and plot the solutions as points on a coordinate plane.

3. Find five solutions for the linear equation $-x + \dfrac{3}{4}y = -6$, and plot the solutions as points on a coordinate plane.

4. Find five solutions for the linear equation $2x + y = 5$, and plot the solutions as points on a coordinate plane.

5. Find five solutions for the linear equation $3x - 5y = 15$, and plot the solutions as points on a coordinate plane.

Lesson 13: The Graph of a Linear Equation in Two Variables

Classwork

Exercises

1. Find at least 10 solutions to the linear equation $3x + y = -8$ and plot the points on a coordinate plane.

x	Linear Equation: $3x + y = -8$	y

What shape is the graph of the linear equation taking?

2.   Find at least 10 solutions to the linear equation $x - 5y = 11$ and plot the points on a coordinate plane.

x	Linear Equation: $x - 5y = 11$	y

What shape is the graph of the linear equation taking?

3. Compare the solutions you found in Exercise 1 with a partner. Add their solutions to your graph.

    Is the prediction you made about the shape of the graph still true? Explain.

4. Compare the solutions you found in Exercise 2 with a partner. Add their solutions to your graph.

    Is the prediction you made about the shape of the graph still true? Explain.

5. Joey predicts that the graph of $-x + 2y = 3$ will look like the graph shown below. Do you agree? Explain why or why not.

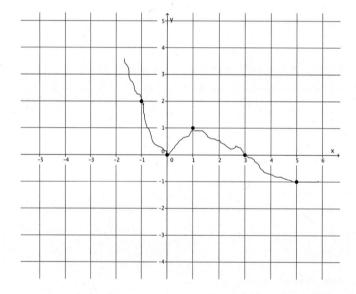

6. We have looked at some equations that appear to be lines. Can you write an equation that has solutions that do not form a line? Try to come up with one, and prove your assertion on the coordinate plane.

Problem Set

1. Find at least 10 solutions to the linear equation $\frac{1}{2}x + y = 5$ and plot the points on a coordinate plane.

   What shape is the graph of the linear equation taking?

2. Can the following be a graph of the equation $x - y = 0$? Explain.

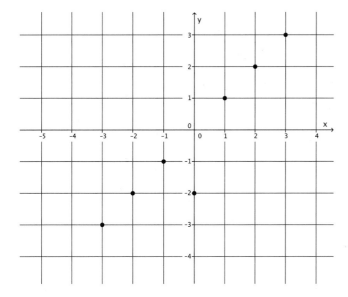

3.   Can the following be a graph of the equation $x + 2y = 2$? Explain.

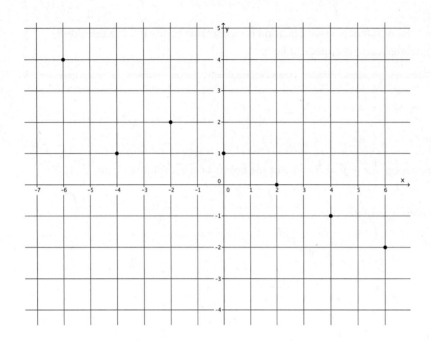

4.   Can the following be a graph of the equation $x - y = 7$? Explain.

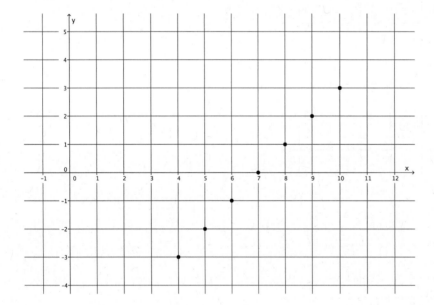

5. Can the following be a graph of the equation $x + y = 2$? Explain.

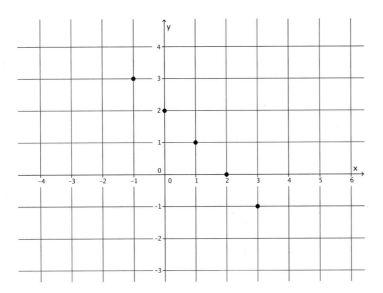

6. Can the following be a graph of the equation $2x - y = 9$? Explain.

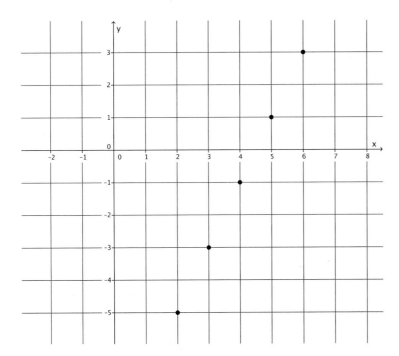

7.   Can the following be a graph of the equation $x - y = 1$? Explain.

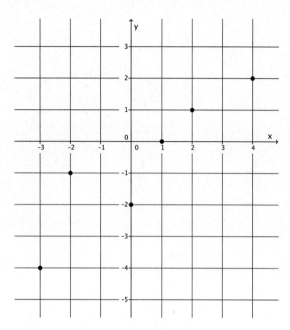

Lesson 14: The Graph of a Linear Equation—Horizontal and Vertical Lines

Classwork

Exercises

1. Find at least 4 solutions to graph the linear equation $1x + 2y = 5$.
2. Find at least 4 solutions to graph the linear equation $1x + 0y = 5$.
3. What was different about the equations in Exercises 1 and 2? What effect did this change have on the graph?

4. Graph the linear equation $x = -2$.
5. Graph the linear equation $x = 3$.
6. What will the graph of $x = 0$ look like?

7. Find at least 4 solutions to graph the linear equation $2x + 1y = 2$.
8. Find at least 4 solutions to graph the linear equation $0x + 1y = 2$.
9. What was different about the equations in Exercises 7 and 8? What effect did this change have on the graph?

10. Graph the linear equation $y = -2$.
11. Graph the linear equation $y = 3$.
12. What will the graph of $y = 0$ look like?

Lesson 14:   The Graph of a Linear Equation—Horizontal and Vertical Lines
Date: 11/1/13

Lesson Summary

A linear equation in standard form, $ax + by = c$, where $a = 1$ and $b = 0$, is the graph of the equation $x = c$. The graph of $x = c$ is the vertical line passing through the point $(c, 0)$.

A linear equation in standard form, $ax + by = c$, where $a = 0$ and $b = 1$, is the graph of the equation $y = c$. The graph of $y = c$ is the horizontal line passing through the point $(0, c)$.

Problem Set

1. Graph the two variable linear equation $ax + by = c$ when $a = 0$, $y = 1$, and $c = -4$.

2. Graph the two variable linear equation $ax + by = c$ when $a = 1$, $y = 0$, and $c = 9$.

3. Graph the linear equation $y = 7$.

4. Graph the linear equation $x = 1$.

5. Explain why the graph of a linear equation in the form of $y = c$ is the horizontal line, parallel to the x-axis passing through the point $(0, c)$.

6. Explain why there is only one line with the equation $y = c$ that passes through the point $(0, c)$.

Lesson 15: The Slope of a Non-Vertical Line

Opening Exercise

Example	
Graph A	Graph B

a.   Which graph is steeper?

b.   Write directions that explain how to move from one point on the graph to the other for each of Graph A and Graph B.

c.   Write the directions from part (b) as ratios, and then compare the ratios. How does this relate to which graph was steeper in part (a)?

Pair 1:

Graph A

Graph B

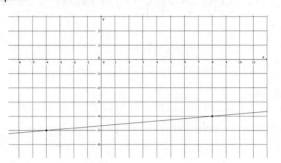

a.   Which graph is steeper?

b.   Write directions that explain how to move from one point on the graph to the other for each of Graph A and Graph B.

c.   Write the directions from part (b) as ratios, and then compare the ratios. How does this relate to which graph was steeper in part (a)?

Pair 2:

Graph A

Graph B

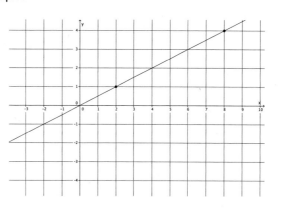

a.   Which graph is steeper?

b.   Write directions that explain how to move from one point on the graph to the other for each of Graph A and
     Graph B.

c.   Write the directions from part (b) as ratios, and then compare the ratios. How does this relate to which graph
     was steeper in part (a)?

Pair 3:

Graph A

Graph B

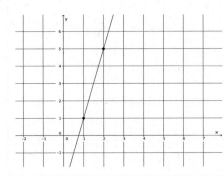

a.   Which graph is steeper?

b.   Write directions that explain how to move from one point on the graph to the other for each of Graph A and Graph B.

c.   Write the directions from part (b) as ratios, and then compare the ratios. How does this relate to which graph was steeper in part (a)?

Pair 4:	
Graph A	Graph B
	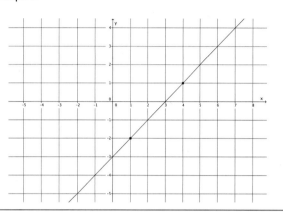

a.   Which graph is steeper?

b.   Write directions that explain how to move from one point on the graph to the other for each of Graph A and Graph B.

c.   Write the directions from part (b) as ratios, and then compare the ratios. How does this relate to which graph was steeper in part (a)?

Exercises

Use your transparency to find the slope of each line if needed.

1. What is the slope of this non-vertical line?

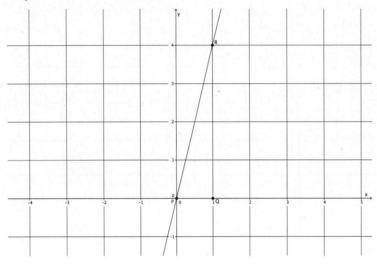

2. What is the slope of this non-vertical line?

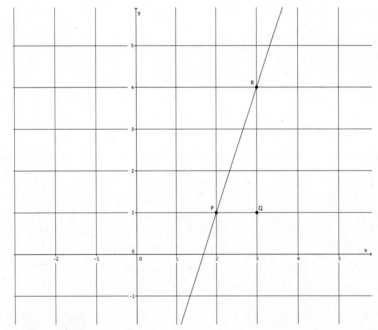

3. Which of the lines in Exercises 1 and 2 is steeper? Compare the slopes of each of the lines. Is there a relationship between steepness and slope?

COMMON
CORE™

Lesson 15:   The Slope of a Non-Vertical Line
Date: 11/7/13

Lesson 15   8•4

S.67

4.   What is the slope of this non-vertical line?

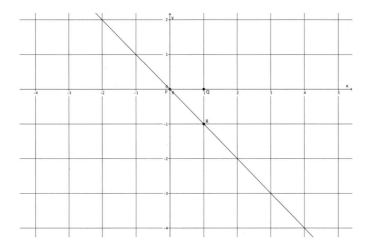

5.   What is the slope of this non-vertical line?

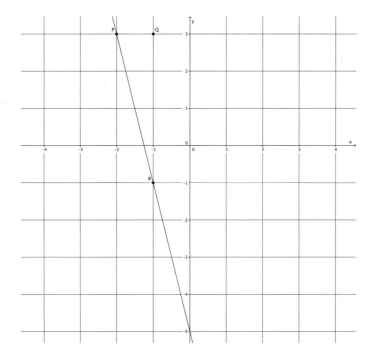

6.   What is the slope of this non-vertical line?

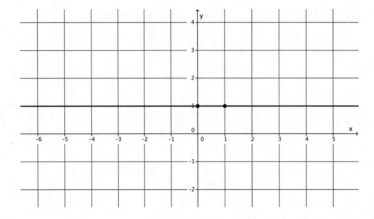

Lesson Summary

Slope is a number that describes the steepness of a line. Slope is represented by the symbol   .

Lines that are left-to-right inclining have a positive slope, as shown below.

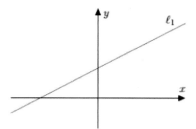

Lines that are left-to-right declining have a negative slope, as shown below.

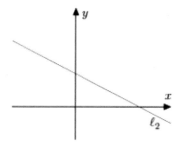

Determine the slope of a line when the horizontal distance between points is fixed at 1 by translating point Q to the origin of the graph, and then identifying the y-coordinate of point R.

The slope of the line shown below is 2, so $m = 2$, because point R is at 2 on the y-axis.

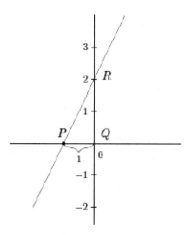

Problem Set

1. Does the graph of the line shown below have a positive or negative slope? Explain.

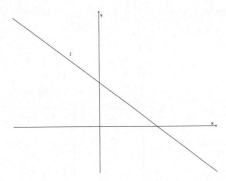

2. Does the graph of the line shown below have a positive or negative slope? Explain.

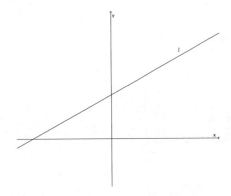

3. What is the slope of this non-vertical line? Use your transparency if needed.

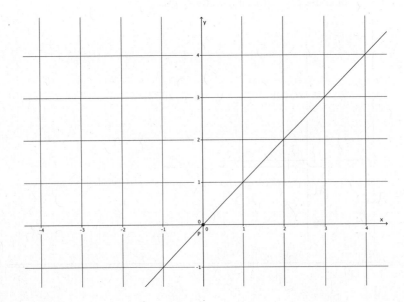

4.   What is the slope of this non-vertical line? Use your transparency if needed.

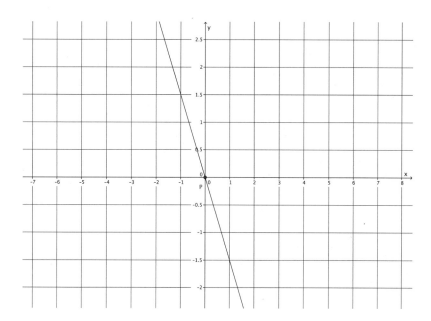

5.   What is the slope of this non-vertical line? Use your transparency if needed.

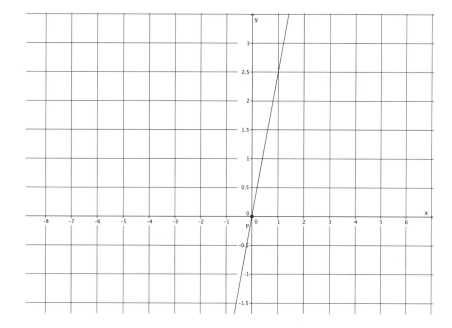

6. What is the slope of this non-vertical line? Use your transparency if needed.

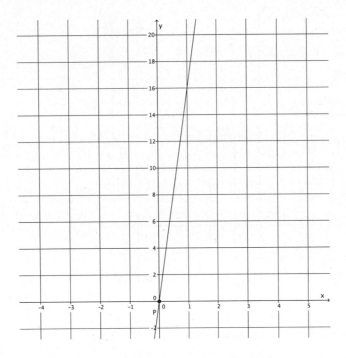

7. What is the slope of this non-vertical line? Use your transparency if needed.

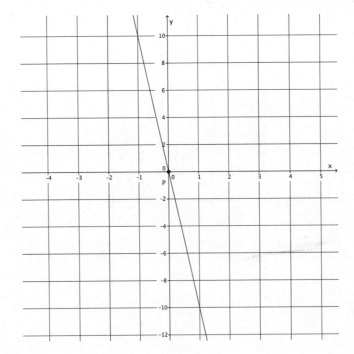

8.   What is the slope of this non-vertical line? Use your transparency if needed.

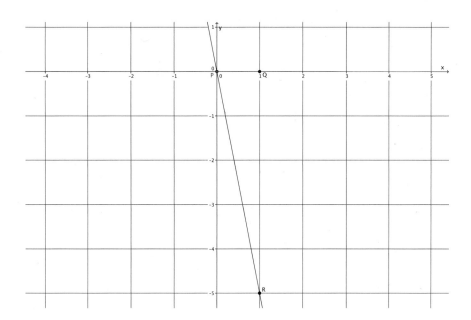

9.   What is the slope of this non-vertical line? Use your transparency if needed.

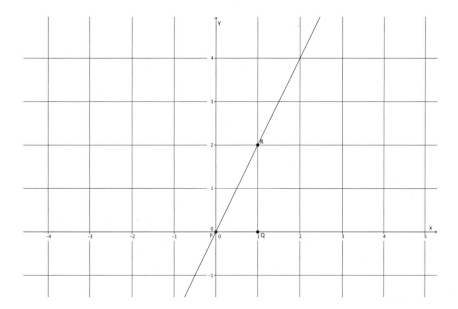

10. What is the slope of this non-vertical line? Use your transparency if needed.

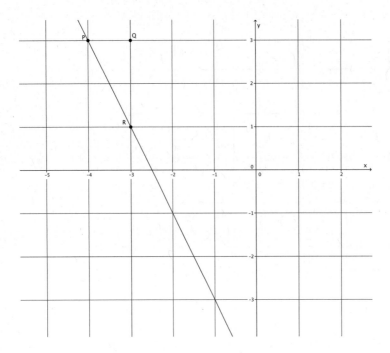

11. What is the slope of this non-vertical line? Use your transparency if needed.

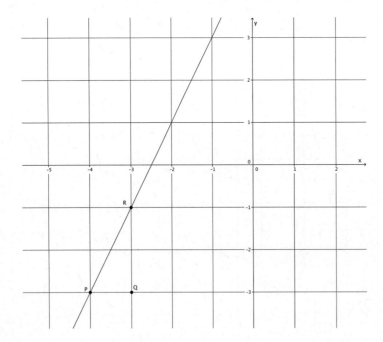

12. What is the slope of this non-vertical line? Use your transparency if needed.

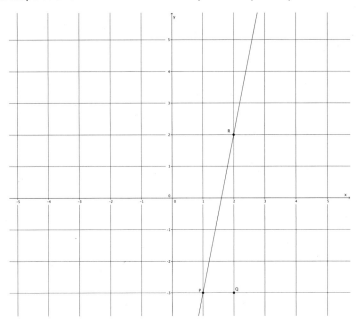

13. What is the slope of this non-vertical line? Use your transparency if needed.

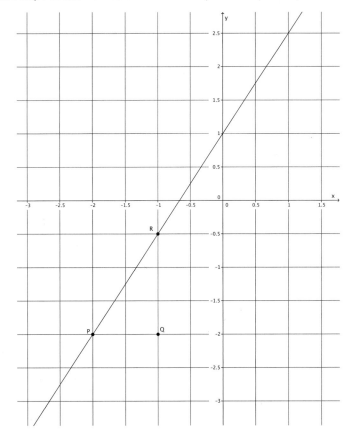

14. What is the slope of this non-vertical line? Use your transparency if needed.

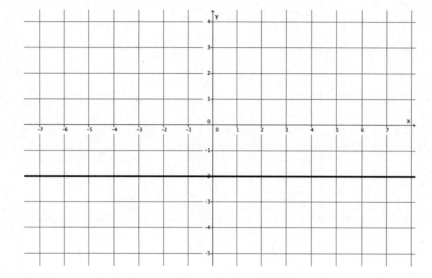

In Lesson 11, you did the work below involving constant rate problems. Use the table and the graphs provided to answer the questions that follow.

15. Suppose the volume of water that comes out in three minutes is 10.5 gallons.

t (time in minutes)	Linear equation: $V = \dfrac{10.5}{3} t$	V (in gallons)
0	$V = \dfrac{10.5}{3}(0)$	0
1	$V = \dfrac{10.5}{3}(1)$	$\dfrac{10.5}{3} = 3.5$
2	$V = \dfrac{10.5}{3}(2)$	$\dfrac{21}{3} = 7$
3	$V = \dfrac{10.5}{3}(3)$	$\dfrac{31.5}{3} = 10.5$
4	$V = \dfrac{10.5}{3}(4)$	$\dfrac{42}{3} = 14$

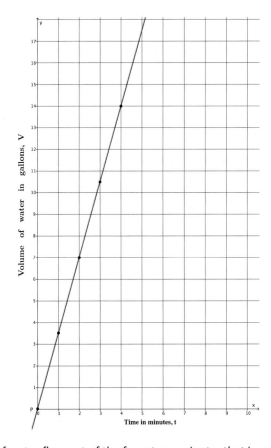

a. How many gallons of water flow out of the faucet per minute, that is, what is the unit rate of water flow?

b. Assume that the graph of the situation is a line, as shown in the graph. What is the slope of the line?

Lesson 15:	The Slope of a Non-Vertical Line
Date:	11/7/13

S.78

16. Emily paints at a constant rate. She can paint 32 square feet in five minutes.

t (time in minutes)	Linear equation: $A = \dfrac{32}{5}t$	A (area painted in square feet)
0	$A = \dfrac{32}{5}(0)$	0
1	$A = \dfrac{32}{5}(1)$	$\dfrac{32}{5} = 6.4$
2	$A = \dfrac{32}{5}(2)$	$\dfrac{64}{5} = 12.8$
3	$A = \dfrac{32}{5}(3)$	$\dfrac{96}{5} = 19.2$
4	$A = \dfrac{32}{5}(4)$	$\dfrac{128}{5} = 25.6$

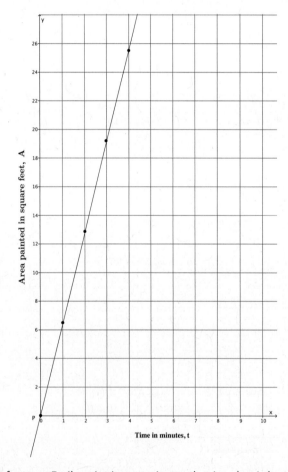

Time in minutes, t

a. How many square feet can Emily paint in one minute; that is, what is her unit rate of painting?

b. Assume that the graph of the situation is a line, as shown in the graph. What is the slope of the line?

17. A copy machine makes copies at a constant rate. The machine can make 80 copies in $2\frac{1}{2}$ minutes.

t (time in minutes)	Linear equation: $n = 32t$	n (number of copies)
0	$n = 32(0)$	0
0.25	$n = 32(0.25)$	8
0.5	$n = 32(0.5)$	16
0.75	$n = 32(0.75)$	24
1	$n = 32(1)$	32

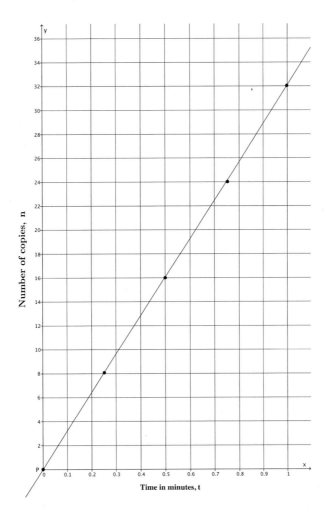

a. How many copies can the machine make each minute; that is, what is the unit rate of the copy machine?

b. Assume that the graph of the situation is a line, as shown in the graph. What is the slope of the line?

Lesson 16: The Computation of the Slope of a Non-Vertical Line

Example 1

Using what you learned in the last lesson, determine the slope of the line with the following graph:

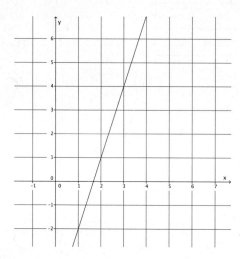

Example 2

Using what you learned in the last lesson, determine the slope of the line with the following graph:

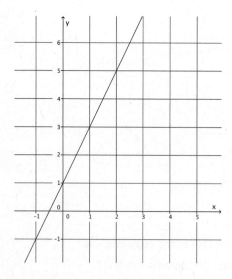

Example 3

What is different about this line compared to the last two examples?

Exercise

Let's investigate concretely to see if the claim that we can find slope between any two points is true.

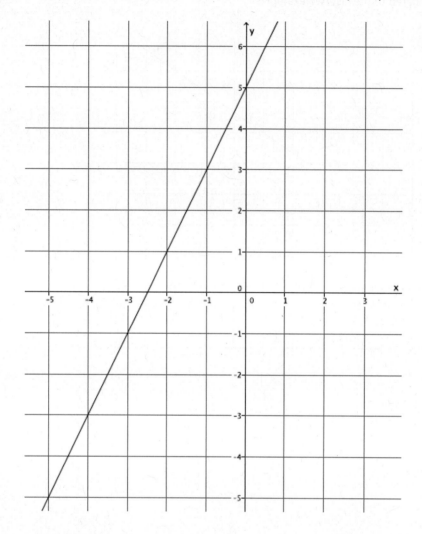

a.   Select any two points on the line to label as P and R.

b.   Identify the coordinates of points P and R.

c.   Find the slope of the line using as many different points as you can. Identify your points and show your work below.

The slope of a line can be calculated using *any* two points on the same line because the slope triangles formed are similar and corresponding sides will be equal in ratio.

The formula to calculate slope between points $P = (p_1, p_2)$ and $R = (r_1, r_2)$ is

$$m = \frac{p_2 - r_2}{p_1 - r_1}$$

The numerator in the formula is referred to as the difference in y-values and the denominator as the difference in x-values.

Problem Set

1. Calculate the slope of the line using two different pairs of points.

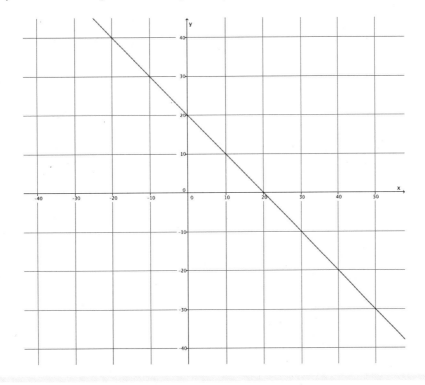

2. Calculate the slope of the line using two different pairs of points.

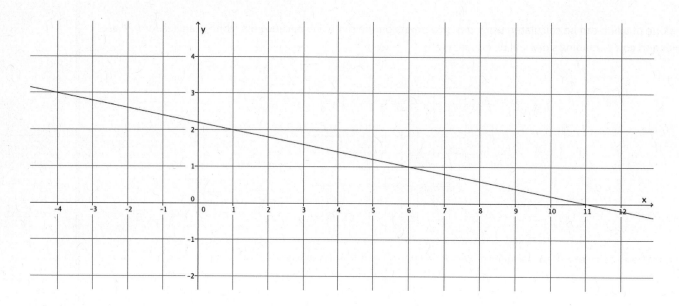

3. Calculate the slope of the line using two different pairs of points.

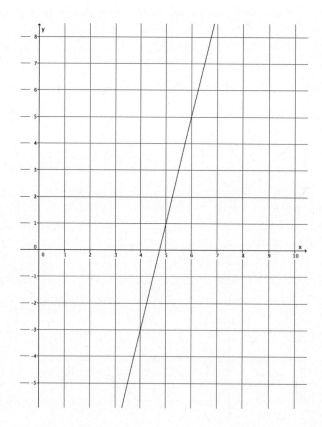

4. Calculate the slope of the line using two different pairs of points.

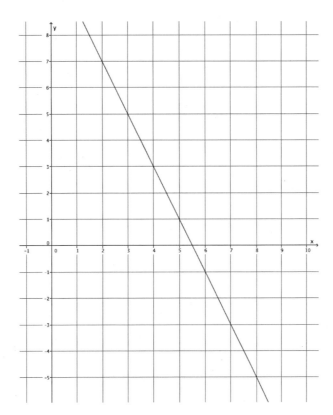

5. Calculate the slope of the line using two different pairs of points.

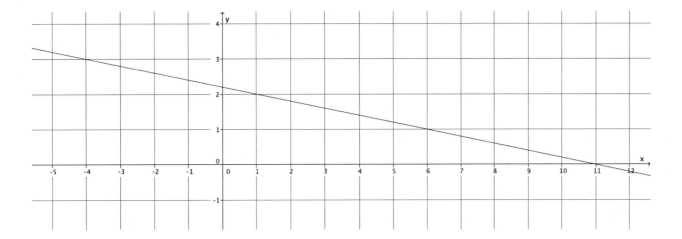

6.　Calculate the slope of the line using two different pairs of points.

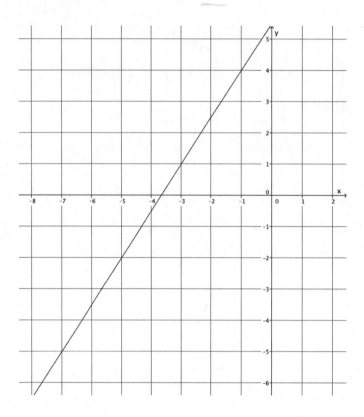

a.　Select any two points on the line to compute the slope.

b.　Select two different points on the line to calculate the slope.

c.　What do you notice about your answers in parts (a) and (b)?　Explain.

7. Calculate the slope of the line in the graph below.

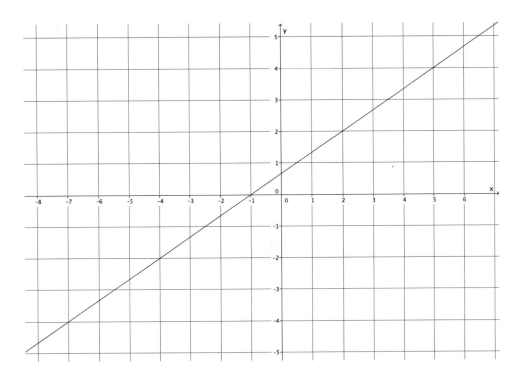

8. Your teacher tells you that a line goes through the points $\left(-6, \frac{1}{2}\right)$ and $(-4, 3)$. Calculate the slope of this line.

    Do you think the slope will be the same if the order of the points is reversed? Verify by calculating the slope and explain your result.

9. Use the graph below to complete parts (a)–(c).

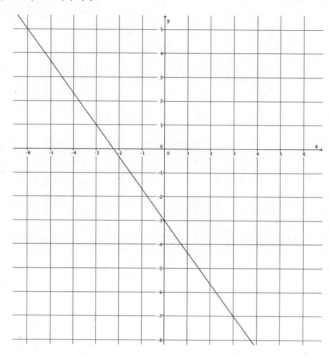

   a.   Select any two points on the line to calculate the slope.

   b.   Compute the slope again, this time reversing the order of the coordinates.

   c.   What do you notice about the slopes you computed in parts (a) and (b)?

   d.   Why do you think $m = \dfrac{(p_2 - r_2)}{(p_1 - r_1)} = \dfrac{(r_2 - p_2)}{(r_1 - p_1)}$?

10. Each of the lines in the lesson was non-vertical. Consider the slope of a non-vertical line, $x = 2$. Select two points on the line to calculate slope. Based on your answer, why do you think the topic of slope focuses only on non-vertical lines?

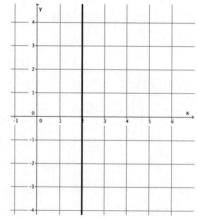

11. Challenge: A certain line has a slope of $\dfrac{1}{2}$. Name two points that may be on the line.

Lesson 17: The Line Joining Two Distinct Points of the Graph $y = mx + b$ has slope m

Classwork

Exercises

1. Find at least three solutions to the equation $y = 2x$, and graph the solutions as points on the coordinate plane. Connect the points to make a line. Find the slope of the line.

2. Find at least three solutions to the equation $y = 3x - 1$, and graph the solutions as points on the coordinate plane. Connect the points to make a line. Find the slope of the line.

3. Find at least three solutions to the equation $y = 3x + 1$, and graph the solutions as points on the coordinate plane. Connect the points to make a line. Find the slope of the line.

Lesson 17:	The Line Joining Two Distinct Points of the Graph $y = mx + b$ has Slope m	S.90
Date:	11/8/13	

© 2013 Common Core, Inc. All rights reserved. **commoncore.org**

4. The graph of the equation $y = 7x - 3$ has what slope?

5. The graph of the equation $y = -\frac{3}{4}x - 3$ has what slope?

6. You have $20 in savings at the bank. Each week, you add $2 to your savings. Let y represent the total amount of money you have saved at the end of x weeks. Write an equation to represent this situation and identify the slope of the equation. What does that number represent?

7. A friend is training for a marathon. She can run 4 miles in 28 minutes. Assume she runs at a constant rate. Write an equation to represent the total distance, y, your friend can run in x minutes. Identify the slope of the equation. What does that number represent?

8. Four boxes of pencils cost $5. Write an equation that represents the total cost, y, for x boxes of pencils. What is the slope of the equation? What does that number represent?

9. Solve the following equation for y: $9x - 3y = 15$, then identify the slope of the line.

10. Solve the following equation for y: $5x + 9y = 6$, then identify the slope of the line.

11. Solve the following equation for y: $ax + by = c$, then identify the slope of the line.

Lesson Summary

The line joining two distinct points of the graph of the linear equation $y = mx + b$ has slope m.

The m of $y = mx + b$ is the number that describes the slope. For example, in the equation $y = -2x + 4$, the slope of the graph of the line is -2.

Problem Set

1. Solve the following equation for y: $-4x + 8y = 24$.

   a. Based on your transformed equation, what is the slope of the linear equation $-4x + 8y = 24$?

   b. Complete the table to find solutions to the linear equation.

x	Transformed linear equation:	y

   c. Graph the points on the coordinate plane.

   d. Find the slope between any two points.

   e. The slope you found in part (d) should be equal to the slope you noted in part (a). If so, connect the points to make the line that is the graph of an equation of the form $y = mx + b$ that has slope m.

   f. Note the location (ordered pair) that describes where the line intersects the y-axis.

2. Solve the following equation for y: $9x + 3y = 21$.

   a. Based on your transformed equation, what is the slope of the linear equation $9x + 3y = 21$?

   b. Complete the table to find solutions to the linear equation.

x	Transformed linear equation:	y

   c. Graph the points on the coordinate plane.

   d. Find the slope between any two points.

   e. The slope you found in part (d) should be equal to the slope you noted in part (a). If so, connect the points to make the line that is the graph of an equation of the form $y = mx + b$ that has slope m.

   f. Note the location (ordered pair) that describes where the line intersects the y-axis.

3. Solve the following equation for y: $2x + 3y = -6$.

   a. Based on your transformed equation, what is the slope of the linear equation $2x + 3y = -6$?

   b. Complete the table to find solutions to the linear equation.

x	Transformed linear equation:	y

   c. Graph the points on the coordinate plane.

   d. Find the slope between any two points.

   e. The slope you found in part (d) should be equal to the slope you noted in part (a). If so, connect the points to make the line that is the graph of an equation of the form $y = mx + b$ that has slope m.

   f. Note the location (ordered pair) that describes where the line intersects the y-axis.

4. Solve the following equation for y: $5x - y = 4$.

a. Based on your transformed equation, what is the slope of the linear equation $5x - y = 4$?

b. Complete the table to find solutions to the linear equation.

x	Transformed linear equation:	y

c. Graph the points on the coordinate plane.

d. Find the slope between any two points.

e. The slope you found in part (d) should be equal to the slope you noted in part (a). If so, connect the points to make the line that is the graph of an equation of the form $y = mx + b$ that has slope m.

f. Note the location (ordered pair) that describes where the line intersects the y-axis.

COMMON CORE™

Lesson 17:   The Line Joining Two Distinct Points of the Graph $y = mx + b$ has
              Slope m
Date: 11/8/13

© 2013 Common Core, Inc. All rights reserved. commoncore.org

S.95

Lesson 18: There is Only One Line Passing Through a Given Point

with a Given Slope

Classwork

Opening Exercise

Examine each of the graphs and their equations below. Identify the coordinates of the point where the line intersects the y-axis. Describe the relationship between the point and the equation $y = mx + b$.

a. $y = \frac{1}{2}x + 3$

b. $y = -3x + 7$

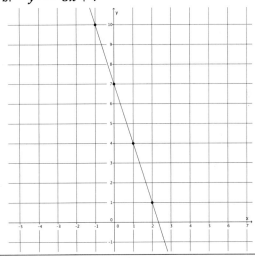

c. $y = -\frac{2}{3}x - 2$

d. $y = 5x - 4$

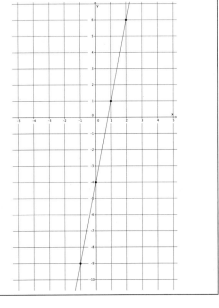

Opening Exercise

Example 1

Graph the equation $y = \frac{2}{3}x + 1$. Name the slope and y-intercept.

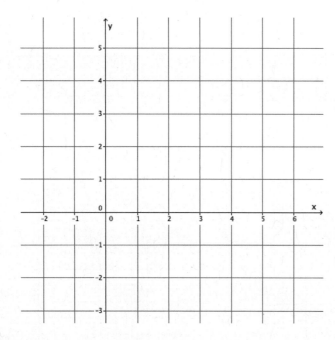

Example 2

Graph the equation $y = -\frac{3}{4}x - 2$. Name the slope and y-intercept.

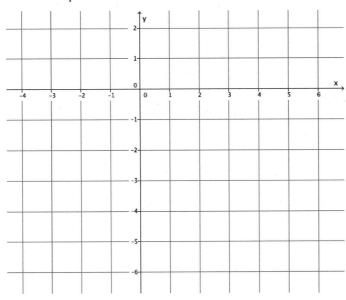

Exercises

1. Graph the equation $y = \frac{5}{2}x - 4$.

   a. Name the slope and the y-intercept.

   b. Graph the known point, then use the slope to find a second point before drawing the line.

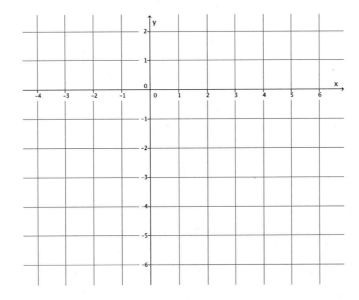

COMMON CORE™

Lesson 18:	There is Only One Line Passing Through a Given Point with a Given Slope
Date:	11/8/13

2. Graph the equation $y = -3x + 6$.

    a. Name the slope and the y-intercept.

    b. Graph the known point, then use the slope to find a second point before drawing the line.

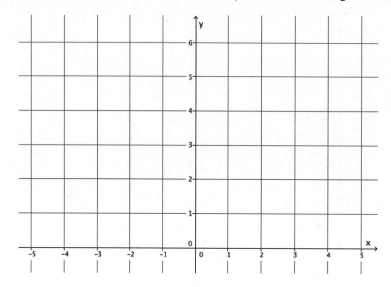

3. The equation $y = 1x + 0$ can be simplified to $y = x$. Graph the equation $y = x$.

    a. Name the slope and the y-intercept.

    b. Graph the known point, then use the slope to find a second point before drawing the line.

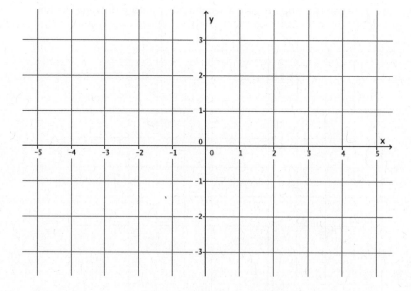

4. Graph the point $(0, 2)$.

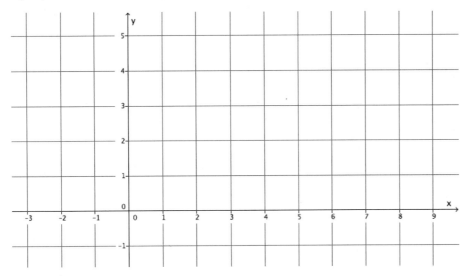

a. Find another point on the graph using the slope, $m = \frac{2}{7}$.

b. Connect the points to make the line.

c. Draw a different line that goes through the point $(0, 2)$ with slope $m = \frac{2}{7}$. What do you notice?

5. A bank put $10 into a savings account when you opened the account. Eight weeks later you have a total of $24. Assume you saved the same amount every week.

a. If y is the total amount of money in the savings account and x represents the number of weeks, write an equation in the form $y = mx + b$ that describes the situation.

b. Identify the slope and the y-intercept. What do these numbers represent?

c.   Graph the equation on a coordinate plane.

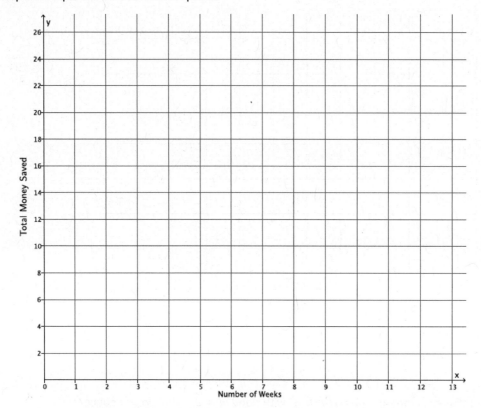

d.   Could any other line represent this situation? For example, could a line through point $(0,10)$ with slope $\frac{7}{5}$ represent the amount of money you save each week? Explain.

6. A group of friends are on a road trip. So far they have driven 120 miles. They continue their trip and drive at a constant rate of 50 miles per hour.

    a. Let y represent the total distance traveled in x hours. Write an equation to represent the total number of miles driven in x hours.

    b. Identify the slope and the y-intercept. What do these numbers represent?

    c. Graph the equation on a coordinate plane.

    d. Could any other line represent this situation? For example, could a line through point $(0, 120)$ with slope 75 represent the total distance the friends drive? Explain.

> ### Lesson Summary
>
> The equation $y = mx + b$ is in slope-intercept form. The number m represents the slope of the graph and the point $(0, b)$ is the location where the graph of the line intersects the y-axis.
>
> To graph a line from the slope-intercept form of a linear equation, begin with the known point, $(0, b)$, then use the slope to find a second point. Connect the points to graph the equation.
>
> There is only one line passing through a given point with a given slope.

Problem Set

Graph each equation on a separate pair of x and y axes.

1. Graph the equation $y = \frac{4}{5}x - 5$.

    a.   Name the slope and the y-intercept.

    b.   Graph the known point, and then use the slope to find a second point before drawing the line.

2. Graph the equation $y = x + 3$.

    a.   Name the slope and the y-intercept.

    b.   Graph the known point, and then use the slope to find a second point before drawing the line.

3. Graph the equation $y = -\frac{4}{3}x + 4$.

    a.   Name the slope and the y-intercept.

    b.   Graph the known point, and then use the slope to find a second point before drawing the line.

4. Graph the equation $y = \frac{5}{2}x$.

    a.   Name the slope and the y-intercept.

    b.   Graph the known point, and then use the slope to find a second point before drawing the line.

5. Graph the equation $y = 2x - 6$.

    a.   Name the slope and the y-intercept.

    b.   Graph the known point, and then use the slope to find a second point before drawing the line.

6. Graph the equation $y = -5x + 9$.

    a.   Name the slope and the y-intercept.

    b.   Graph the known point, and then use the slope to find a second point before drawing the line.

Lesson 18:	There is Only One Line Passing Through a Given Point with a Given Slope
Date:	11/8/13

S.103

7. Graph the equation $y = \frac{1}{3}x + 1$.

    a. Name the slope and the y-intercept.

    b. Graph the known point, and then use the slope to find a second point before drawing the line.

8. Graph the equation $5x + 4y = 8$. (Hint: transform the equation so that it is of the form $y = mx + b$.)

    a. Name the slope and the y-intercept.

    b. Graph the known point, and then use the slope to find a second point before drawing the line.

9. Graph the equation $-2x + 5y = 30$.

    a. Name the slope and the y-intercept.

    b. Graph the known point, and then use the slope to find a second point before drawing the line.

10. Let l and l' be two lines with the same slope m passing through the same point P. Show that there is only one line with a slope m, where $m < 0$, passing through the given point P. Draw a diagram if needed.

Lesson 19: The Graph of a Linear Equation in Two Variables is a Line

Classwork

Exercises

Theorem: The graph of a linear equation $y = mx + b$ is a non-vertical line with slope m and passing through $(0, b)$, where b is a constant.

1. Prove the theorem by completing parts (a)–(c). Given two distinct points, P and Q, on the graph of $y = mx + b$ and let l be the line passing through P and Q. You must show:

   (1) any point on the graph of $y = mx + b$ is on line l, and

   (2) any point on the line l is on the graph of $y = mx + b$.

   a. Proof of (1): Let R be any point on the graph of $y = mx + k$. Show that R is on l. Begin by assuming it is not. Assume the graph looks like the diagram below where R is on l'.

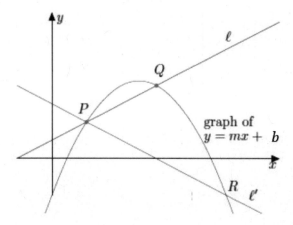

   What is the slope of line l?

   What is the slope of line l'?

   What can you conclude about lines l and l'? Explain.

b.   Proof of (2): Let S be any point on line l, as shown.

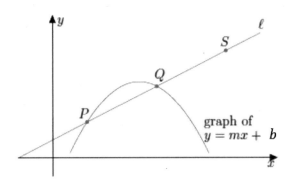

Show that S is a solution to $y = mx + b$. Hint: Use the point $(0, b)$.

c.   Now that you have shown that any point on the graph of $y = mx + b$ is on line l (part (a)), and any point on line l is on the graph of $y = mx + b$ (part (b)), what can you conclude about the graphs of linear equations?

2. Use $x = 4$ and $x = -4$ to find two solutions to the equation $x + 2y = 6$. Plot the solutions as points on the coordinate plane and connect the points to make a line.

    a. Identify two other points on the line with integer coordinates. Verify that they are solutions to the equation $x + 2y = 6$.

    b. When $x = 1$, what is the value of y? Does this solution appear to be a point on the line?

    c. When $x = -3$, what is the value of y? Does this solution appear to be a point on the line?

    d. Is the point $(3, 2)$ on the line?

    e. Is the point $(3, 2)$ a solution to the linear equation $x + 2y = 6$?

3. Use $x = 4$ and $x = 1$ to find two solutions to the equation $3x - y = 9$. Plot the solutions as points on the coordinate plane and connect the points to make a line.

    a. Identify two other points on the line with integer coordinates. Verify that they are solutions to the equation $3x - y = 9$.

    b. When $x = 4.5$, what is the value of y? Does this solution appear to be a point on the line?

c.   When $x = \frac{1}{2}$, what is the value of y? Does this solution appear to be a point on the line?

d.   Is the point $(2, 4)$ on the line?

e.   Is the point $(2, 4)$ a solution to the linear equation $3x - y = 9$?

4.   Use $x = 3$ and $x = -3$ to find two solutions to the equation $2x + 3y = 12$. Plot the solutions as points on the coordinate plane and connect the points to make a line.

   a.   Identify two other points on the line with integer coordinates. Verify that they are solutions to the equation $2x + 3y = 12$.

   b.   When $x = 2$, what is the value of y? Does this solution appear to be a point on the line?

   c.   When $x = -2$, what is the value of y? Does this solution appear to be a point on the line?

   d.   Is the point $(8, -3)$ on the line?

   e.   Is the point $(8, -3)$ a solution to the linear equation $2x + 3y = 12$?

5. Use $x = 4$ and $x = -4$ to find two solutions to the equation $x - 2y = 8$. Plot the solutions as points on the coordinate plane and connect the points to make a line.

    a. Identify two other points on the line with integer coordinates. Verify that they are solutions to the equation $x - 2y = 8$.

    b. When $x = 7$, what is the value of y? Does this solution appear to be a point on the line?

    c. When $x = -3$, what is the value of y? Does this solution appear to be a point on the line?

    d. Is the point $(-2, -3)$ on the line?

    e. Is the point $(-2, -3)$ a solution to the linear equation $x - 2y = 8$?

6. Based on your work in Exercises 2–5, what conclusions can you draw about the points on a line and solutions to a linear equation?

7. Based on your work in Exercises 2–5, will a point that is not a solution to a linear equation be a point on the graph of a linear equation? Explain.

8. Based on your work in Exercises 2–5, what conclusions can you draw about the graph of a linear equation?

Lesson 19: The Graph of a Linear Equation in Two Variables is a Line
Date: 11/8/13

S.109

9. Graph the equation $-3x + 8y = 24$ using intercepts.

10. Graph the equation $x - 6y = 15$ using intercepts.

11. Graph the equation $4x + 3y = 21$ using intercepts.

Lesson Summary

The graph of a linear equation is a line. A linear equation can be graphed using two-points: the x-intercept and the y-intercept.

Example:

Graph the equation: $2x + 3y = 9$.

Replace x with zero and solve for y to determine the y-intercept:

$$2(0) + 3y = 9$$
$$3y = 9$$
$$y = 3$$

The y-intercept is at $(0, 3)$.

Replace y with zero and solve for x to determine the x-intercept:

$$2x + 3(0) = 9$$
$$2x = 9$$
$$x = \frac{9}{2}$$

The x-intercept is at $\left(\frac{9}{2}, 0\right)$.

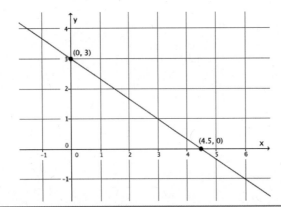

Problem Set

Graph each of the equations in the Problem Set on a different pair of x and y axes.

1. Graph the equation: $y = -6x + 12$.

2. Graph the equation: $9x + 3y = 18$.

3. Graph the equation: $y = 4x + 2$.

4. Graph the equation: $y = -\frac{5}{7}x + 4$.

5. Graph the equation: $\frac{3}{4}x + y = 8$.

6. Graph the equation: $2x - 4y = 12$.

7. Graph the equation: $y = 3$. What is the slope of the graph of this line?

8. Graph the equation: $x = -4$. What is the slope of the graph of this line?

9. Is the graph of $4x + 5y = \frac{3}{7}$ a line? Explain.

10. Is the graph of $6x^2 - 2y = 7$ a line? Explain.

Lesson 20: Every Line is a Graph of a Linear Equation

Classwork

Opening Exercise

Graph 1

Graph 2

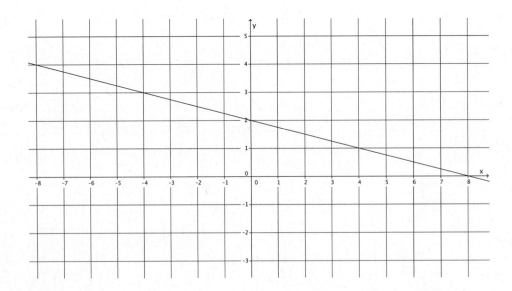

Exercises

1. Write the equation that represents the
    line shown.

    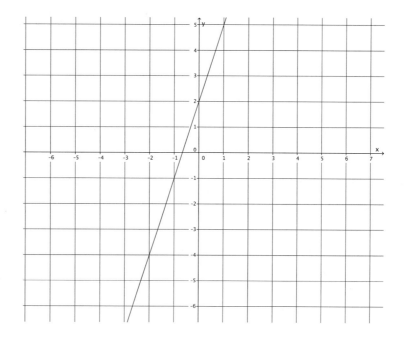

    Use the properties of equality to change
    the equation from slope intercept form,
    $y = mx + b,$ to standard form,
    $ax + by = c$, where a, b, and c are
    integers and a is not negative.

2. Write the equation that represents the
    line shown.

    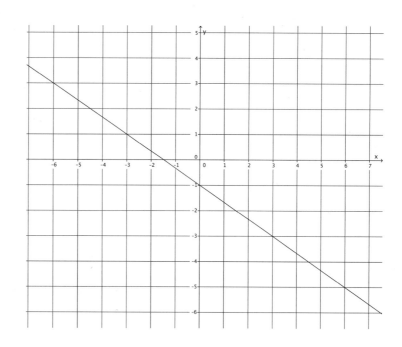

    Use the properties of equality to change
    the equation from slope intercept form,
    $y = mx + b,$ to standard form,
    $ax + by = c$, where a, b, and c are
    integers and a is not negative.

3. Write the equation that represents the line shown.

   Use the properties of equality to change the equation from slope intercept form, $y = mx + b$, to standard form, $ax + by = c$, where a, b, and c are integers and a is not negative.

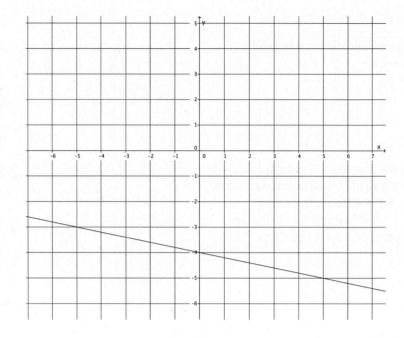

4. Write the equation that represents the line shown.

   Use the properties of equality to change the equation from slope intercept form, $y = mx + b$, to standard form, $ax + by = c$, where a, b, and c are integers and a is not negative.

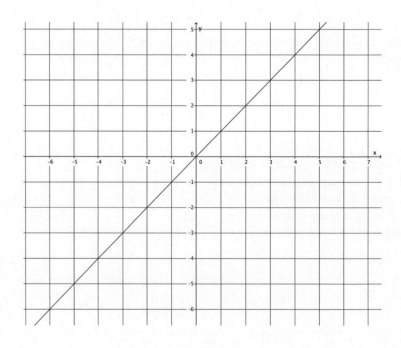

5. Write the equation that represents the line shown.

    Use the properties of equality to change the equation from slope intercept form, $y = mx + b$, to standard form, $ax + by = c$, where a, b, and c are integers and a is not negative.

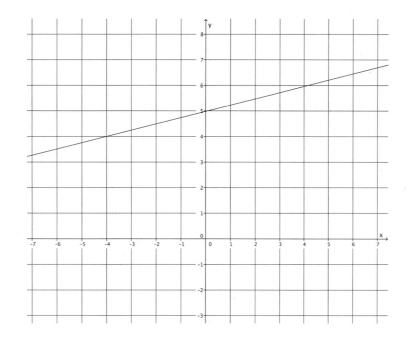

6. Write the equation that represents the line shown.

    Use the properties of equality to change the equation from slope intercept form, $y = mx + b$, to standard form, $ax + by = c$, where a, b, and c are integers and a is not negative.

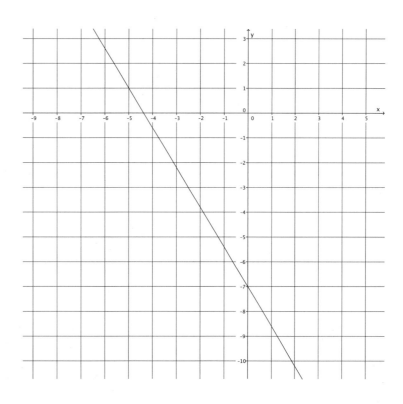

Lesson Summary

Write the equation of a line by determining the y-intercept, $(0, b)$ and the slope, m, and replacing the numbers b and m into the equation $y = mx + b$.

Example:

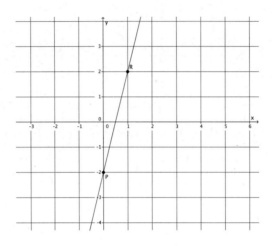

The y-intercept of this graph is $(0, -2)$.

The slope of this graph is $m = \dfrac{4}{1} = 4$.

The equation that represents the graph of this line is $y = 4x - 2$.

Problem Set

1. Write the equation that represents the line shown.

    Use the properties of equality to change the equation from slope intercept form, $y = mx + b$, to standard form, $ax + by = c$, where a, b, and c are integers and a is not negative.

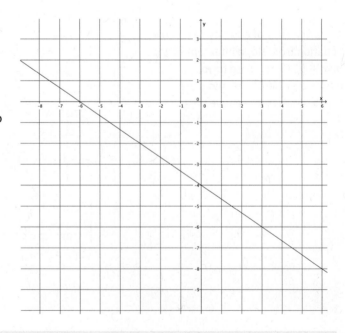

2. Write the equation that represents the line shown.

    Use the properties of equality to change the
    equation from slope intercept form, $y = mx + b$, to
    standard form, $ax + by = c$, where a, b, and c are
    integers and a is not negative.

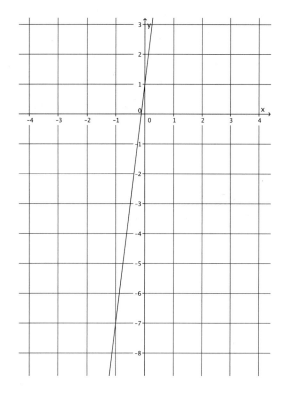

3. Write the equation that represents the line shown.

    Use the properties of equality to change the
    equation from slope intercept form, $y = mx + b$, to
    standard form, $ax + by = c$, where a, b, and c are
    integers and a is not negative.

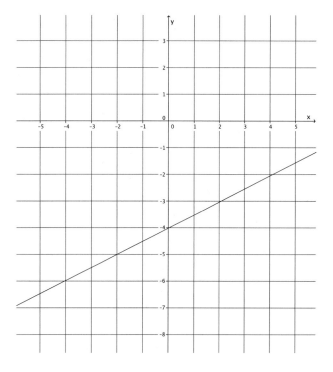

4. Write the equation that represents the line shown.

    Use the properties of equality to change the
    equation from slope intercept form, $y = mx + b$, to
    standard form, $ax + by = c$, where a, b, and c are
    integers and a is not negative.

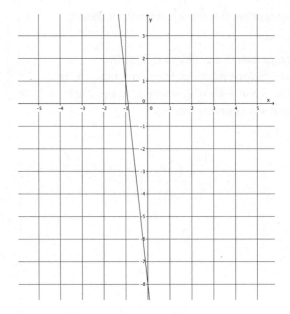

5. Write the equation that represents the line shown.

    Use the properties of equality to change the
    equation from slope intercept form, $y = mx + b$, to
    standard form, $ax + by = c$, where a, b, and c are
    integers and a is not negative.

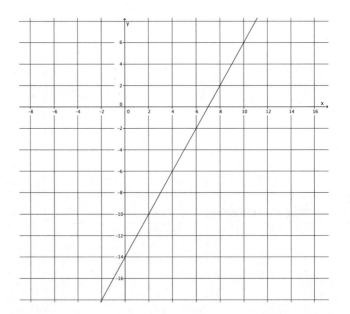

6. Write the equation that represents the line shown.

    Use the properties of equality to change the
    equation from slope intercept form, $y = mx + b$, to
    standard form, $ax + by = c$, where a, b, and c are
    integers and a is not negative.

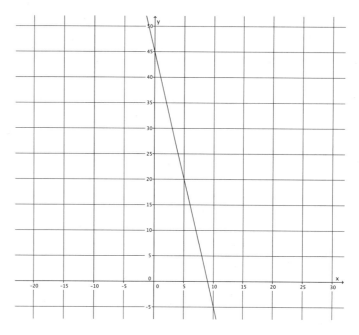

Lesson 21: Some Facts about Graphs of Linear Equations in Two Variables

Classwork

Example 1

Let a line l be given in the coordinate plane. What linear equation is the graph of line?

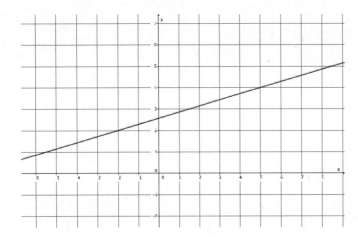

Example 2

Let a line l be given in the coordinate plane. What linear equation is the graph of line?

Example 3

Let a line l be given in the coordinate plane. What linear equation is the graph of line?

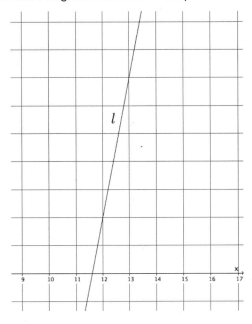

Example 4

Let a line l be given in the coordinate plane. What linear equation is the graph of line?

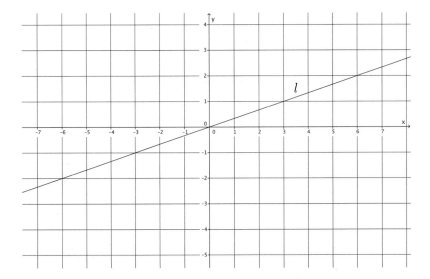

Exercises

1. Write the equation for the line l shown in the graph.

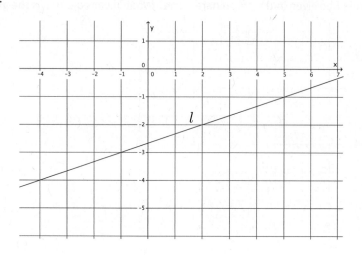

2. Write the equation for the line l shown in the graph.

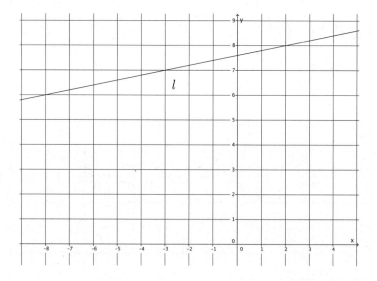

3. Determine the equation of the line that goes through points $(-4, 5)$ and $(2, 3)$.

4. Write the equation for the line l shown in the graph.

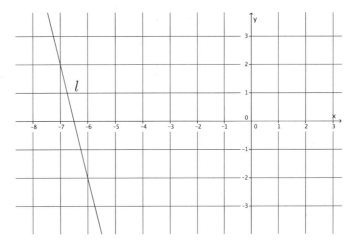

5. A line goes through the point $(8, 3)$ and has slope $m = 4$. Write the equation that represents the line.

Lesson Summary

Let (x_1, y_1) and (x_2, y_2) be the coordinates of two distinct points on the graph of a line l. We find the slope of the line by:

$$m = \frac{y_2 - y_1}{x_2 - x_1}$$

Where this version of the slope formula, using coordinates of x and y instead of p and r, is a commonly accepted version.

As soon as you multiply the slope by the denominator of the fraction above you get the following equation:

$$m(x_2 - x_1) = y_2 - y_1$$

This form of an equation is referred to as the point-slope form of a linear equation.

Given a known (x, y), then the equation is written as

$$m(x - x_1) = (y - y_1)$$

The following is slope-intercept form of a line:

$$y = mx + b$$

In this equation, m is slope and $(0, b)$ is the y-intercept.

To write the equation of a line you must have two points, one point and slope, or a graph of the line.

Problem Set

1. Write the equation for the line l shown in the graph.

2.   Write the equation for the line l shown in the graph.

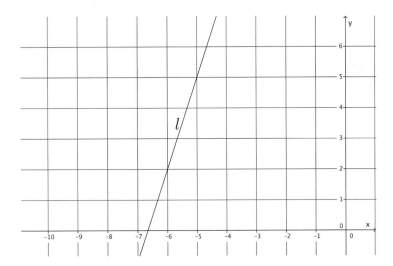

3.   Write the equation for the line l shown in the graph.

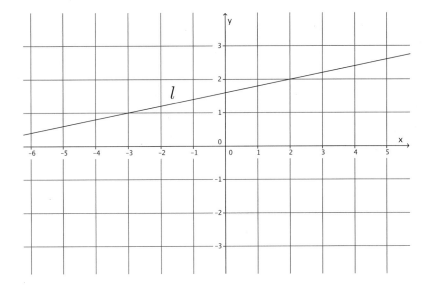

4. Triangle △ ABC is made up line segments formed from the intersection of lines L_{AB}, L_{BC}, and L_{AC}. Write the equations that represents the lines that make up the triangle.

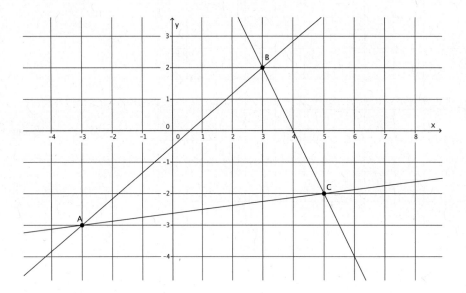

5. Write the equation for the line that goes through point $(-10, 8)$ with slope $m = 6$.

6. Write the equation for the line that goes through point $(12, 15)$ with slope $m = -2$.

7. Write the equation for the line that goes through point $(1, 1)$ with slope $m = -9$.

8. Determine the equation of the line that goes through points $(1, 1)$ and $(3, 7)$.

Lesson 22: Constant Rates Revisited

Exercises

1. Peter paints a wall at a constant rate of 2 square-feet per minute. Assume he paints an area y, in square feet after x minutes.

   a. Express this situation as a linear equation in two variables.

   b. Graph the linear equation.

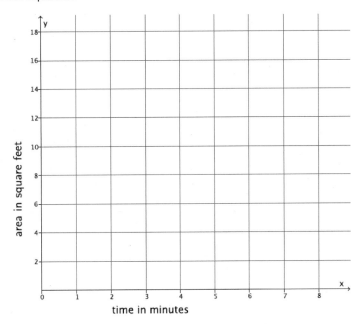

   c. Using the graph or the equation, determine the total area he paints after 8 minutes, $1\frac{1}{2}$ hours, and 2 hours. Note that the units are in minutes and *hours*.

2. The graph below represents Nathan's constant rate of walking.

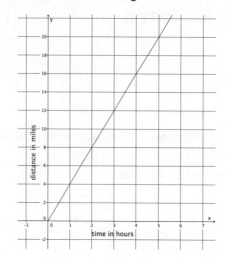

a. Nicole just finished a 5 mile walkathon. It took her 1.4 hours. Assume she walks at a constant rate. Let y represent the distance Nicole walks in x hours. Describe Nicole's walking at a constant rate as a linear equation in two variables.

b. Who walks at a greater speed? Explain.

3. a. Susan can type 4 pages of text in 10 minutes. Assuming she types at a constant rate, write the linear equation that represents the situation.

b. The table of values below represents the number of pages that Anne can type, y, in x minutes. Assume she types at a constant rate.

Minutes (x)	Pages Typed (y)
3	2
5	$\dfrac{10}{3}$
8	$\dfrac{16}{3}$
10	$\dfrac{20}{3}$

Who types faster? Explain.

4. a. Phil can build 3 birdhouses in 5 days. Assuming he builds birdhouses at a constant rate, write the linear equation that represents the situation.

    b. The graph represents Karl's constant rate of building the same kind of birdhouses. Who builds birdhouses faster? Explain.

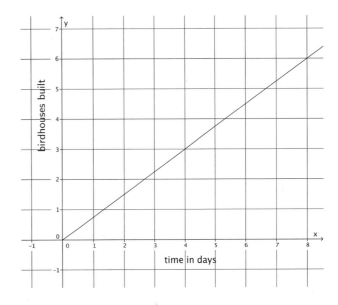

5. Explain your general strategy for comparing proportional relationships.

Lesson Summary

Problems involving constant rate can be expressed as linear equations in two variables.

When given information about two proportional relationships, determine which is less or greater by comparing their slopes (rates of change).

Problem Set

1. a. Train A can travel a distance of 500 miles in 8 hours. Assuming the train travels at a constant rate, write the linear equation that represents the situation.

    b. The graph represents the constant rate of travel for Train B.

    Which train is faster? Explain.

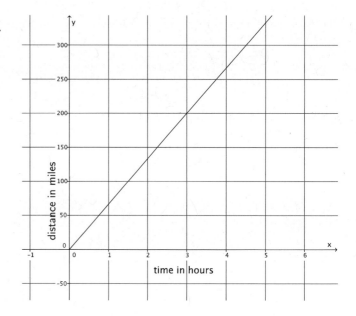

2. a. Natalie can paint 40 square feet in 9 minutes. Assuming she paints at a constant rate, write the linear equation that represents the situation.

    b. The table of values below represents Steven's constant rate of painting.

Minutes (x)	Area Painted (y)
3	10
5	$\dfrac{50}{3}$
6	20
8	$\dfrac{80}{3}$

    Who paints faster? Explain.

3. a. Bianca can run 5 miles in 41 minutes. Assuming she runs at a constant rate, write the linear equation that represents the situation.

    b. The graph below represents Cynthia's constant rate of running.

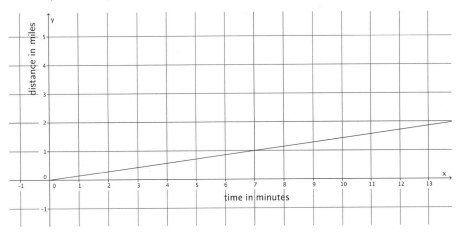

    Who runs faster? Explain.

4. a. Geoff can mow an entire lawn of 450 square feet in 30 minutes. Assuming he mows at a constant rate, write the linear equation that represents the situation.

    b. The graph represents Mark's constant rate of mowing a lawn.

    Who mows faster? Explain.

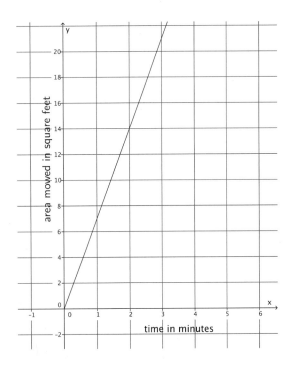

5.   a.   Juan can walk to school, a distance of 0.75 miles in 8 minutes. Assuming he walks at a constant rate, write the linear equation that represents the situation.

     b.   The graph below represents Lena's constant rate of walking.

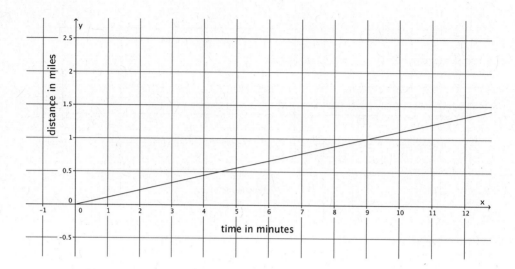

     Who walks faster? Explain.

COMMON
CORE™
Lesson 22:   Constant Rates Revisited
Date: 11/5/13

S.133

© 2013 Common Core, Inc. All rights reserved. commoncore.org

Lesson 23: The Defining Equation of a Line

Exploratory Challenge/Exercises 1–3

1. Graph the equation $9x + 3y = 18$ using intercepts. Then answer parts (a)–(f) that follow.

   a. Graph the equation $y = -3x + 6$ on the same coordinate plane.

   b. What do you notice about the graphs of $9x + 3y = 18$ and $y = -3x + 6$? Why do you think this is so?

   c. Rewrite $y = -3x + 6$ in standard form.

   d. Identify the constants, a, b, c of the equation in standard form from part (c).

   e. Identify the constants of the equation $9x + 3y = 18$. Note them as a', b', and c'.

   f. What do you notice about $\dfrac{a'}{a}$, $\dfrac{b'}{b}$, and $\dfrac{c'}{c}$?

---

2. Graph the equation $y = \frac{1}{2}x + 3$ using the y-intercept and the slope. Then answer parts (a)–(f) that follow.

   a.   Graph the equation $4x - 8y = -24$ using intercepts on the same coordinate plane.

   b.   What do you notice about the graphs of $y = \frac{1}{2}x + 3$ and $4x - 8y = -24$? Why do you think this is so?

   c.   Rewrite $y = \frac{1}{2}x + 3$ in standard form.

   d.   Identify the constants, a, b, c of the equation in standard form from part (c).

   e.   Identify the constants of the equation $-4x - 8y = -24$. Note them as a', b', and c'.

   f.   What do you notice about $\dfrac{a'}{a}$, $\dfrac{b'}{b}$, and $\dfrac{c'}{c}$?

3. The equations $y = \frac{2}{3}x - 4$ and $6x - 9y = 36$ graph as the same line.

   a. Rewrite $y = \frac{2}{3}x - 4$ in standard form.

   b. Identify the constants, a, b, c, of the equation in standard form from part (a).

   c. Identify the constants of the equation $6x - 9y = 36$. Note them as a', b', and c'.

   d. What do you notice about $\dfrac{a'}{a}, \dfrac{b'}{b}$, and $\dfrac{c'}{c}$?

   e. You should have noticed that each fraction was equal to the same constant. Multiply that constant by the standard form of the equation from part (a). What do you notice?

Exercises 4–8

4. Write three equations that would graph as the same line as the equation $3x + 2y = 7$.

5.   Write three equations that would graph as the same line as the equation $x - 9y = \frac{3}{4}$.

6.   Write three equations that would graph as the same line as the equation $-9x + 5y = -4$.

7.   Write at least two equations in the form $ax + by = c$ that would graph as the line shown below

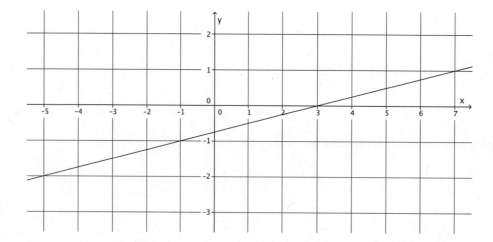

8.   Write at least two equations in the form $ax + by = c$ that would graph as the line shown below.

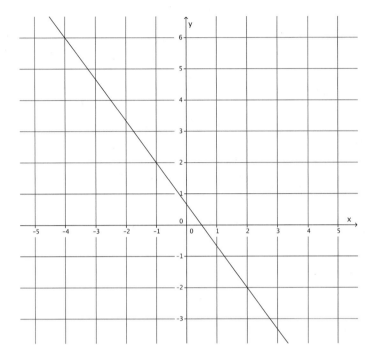

Lesson Summary

Two equations that graph as the same line are said to define the same line. Two equations that define the same line are the same equation, just in different forms. The equations may look different (different constants, different coefficients, or different forms).

When two equations are written in standard form, $ax + by = c$ and $a'x + b'y = c'$, they define the same line when $\dfrac{a'}{a} = \dfrac{b'}{b} = \dfrac{c'}{c}$ is true.

Problem Set

1. Do the equations $x + y = -2$ and $3x + 3y = -6$ define the same line? Explain.

2. Do the equations $y = -\dfrac{5}{4}x + 2$ and $10x + 8y = 16$ define the same line? Explain.

3. Write an equation that would define the same line as $7x - 2y = 5$.

4. Challenge: Show that if the two lines given by $ax + by = c$ and $a'x + b'y = c'$ are the same when $b = 0$ (vertical lines), then there exists a non-zero number s, so that $a' = sa$, $b' = sb$, and $c' = sc$.

5. Challenge: Show that if the two lines given by $ax + by = c$ and $a'x + b'y = c'$ are the same when $a = 0$ (horizontal lines), then there exists a non-zero number s, so that $a' = sa$, $b' = sb$, and $c' = sc$.

Lesson 24: Introduction to Simultaneous Linear Equations

Classwork

Opening Exercise

1. Derek scored 30 points in the basketball game he played and not once did he go to the free throw line. That means that Derek scored two point shots and three point shots. List as many combinations of two and three pointers as you can that would total 30 points.

Number of Two-Pointers	Number of Three-Pointers

Write an equation to describe the data.

2. Derek tells you that the number of two-point shots that he made is five more than the number of three-point shots. How many combinations can you come up with that fit this scenario? (Don't worry about the total number of points.)

Number of Two-Pointers	Number of Three-Pointers

Write an equation to describe the data.

3. Which pair of numbers from your table in Exercise 2 would show Derek's actual score of 30 points?

Exercises

4. Efrain and Fernie are on a road trip. Each of them drives at a constant speed. Efrain is a safe driver and travels 45 miles per hour for the entire trip. Fernie is not such a safe driver. He drives 70 miles per hour throughout the trip. Fernie and Efrain left from the same location, but Efrain left at 8:00 a.m. and Fernie left at 11:00 a.m. Assuming they take the same route, will Fernie ever catch up to Efrain? If so, approximately when?

   a. Write the linear equation that represents Efrain's constant speed. Make sure to include in your equation the extra time that Efrain was able to travel.

   b. Write the linear equation that represents Fernie's constant speed.

   c. Write the system of linear equations that represents this situation.

   d. Sketch the graph.

   e. Will Fernie ever catch up to Efrain? If so, approximately when?

   f. At approximately what point do the graphs of the lines intersect?

5.   Jessica and Karl run at constant speeds. Jessica can run 3 miles in 15 minutes. Karl can run 2 miles in 8 minutes. They decide to race each other. As soon as the race begins Karl realizes that he did not tie his shoes properly and takes 1 minute to fix them.

     a.   Write the linear equation that represents Jessica's constant speed. Make sure to include in your equation the extra time that Jessica was able to run.

     b.   Write the linear equation that represents Karl's constant speed.

     c.   Write the system of linear equations that represents this situation.

     d.   Sketch the graph.

e. Use the graph to answer the questions below.

    i. If Jessica and Karl raced for 2 miles. Who would win? Explain.

    ii. If the winner of the race was the person who got to a distance of $\frac{1}{2}$ mile first, who would the winner be? Explain.

    iii. At approximately what point would Jessica and Karl be tied? Explain.

Lesson Summary

Simultaneous linear equations, or a system of linear equations, is when two or more linear equations are involved in the same problem. Simultaneous linear equations are graphed on the same coordinate plane.

The solution to a system of linear equations is the set of all points that make the equations of the system true. If given two equations in the system, the solution(s) must make both equations true.

Systems of linear equations are identified by the notation used, for example: $\begin{cases} y = \frac{1}{8}x + \frac{5}{2} \\ y = \frac{4}{25}x \end{cases}$

Problem Set

1. Jeremy and Gerardo run at constant speeds. Jeremy can run 1 mile in 8 minutes and Gerardo can run 3 miles in 33 minutes. Jeremy started running 10 minutes after Gerardo. Assuming they run the same path, when will Jeremy catch up to Gerardo?

   a. Write the linear equation that represents Jeremy's constant speed.

   b. Write the linear equation that represents Gerardo's constant speed. Make sure to include in your equation the extra time that Gerardo was able to run.

   c. Write the system of linear equations that represents this situation.

   d. Sketch the graph.

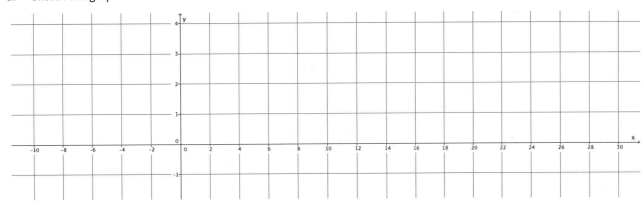

   e. Will Jeremy ever catch up to Gerardo? If so, approximately when?

   f. At approximately what point do the graphs of the lines intersect?

---

2. Two cars drive from town A to town B at constant speeds. The blue car travels 25 miles per hour and the red car travels 60 miles per hour. The blue car leaves at 9:30 a.m. and the red car leaves at noon. The distance between the two towns is 150 miles. Who will get there first? Write and graph the system of linear equations that represents this situation.

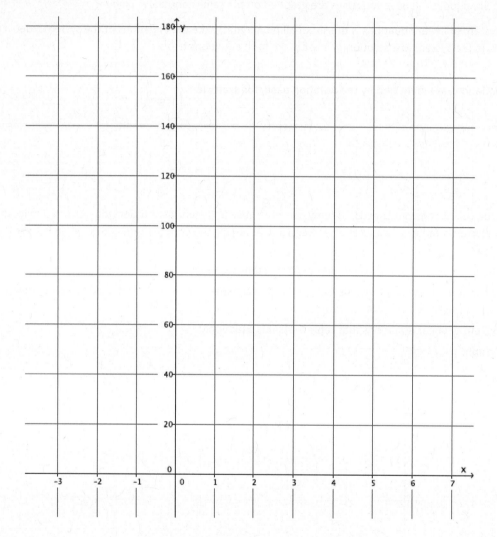

a. At approximately what point do the graphs of the lines intersect?

Lesson 25: Geometric Interpretation of the Solutions of a Linear System

Classwork

Exercises

1. Graph the linear system on a coordinate plane: $\begin{cases} 2y + x = 12 \\ y = \dfrac{5}{6}x - 2 \end{cases}$.

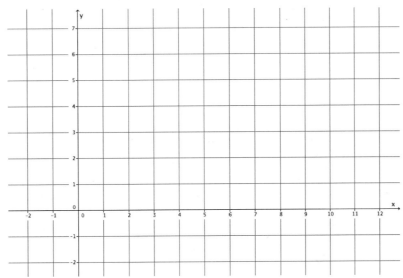

a. Name the ordered pair where the graphs of the two linear equations intersect.

b. Verify that the ordered pair named in (a) is a solution to $2y + x = 12$.

c. Verify that the ordered pair named in (a) is a solution to $y = \dfrac{5}{6}x - 2$.

d. Could the point $(4, 4)$ be a solution to the system of linear equations? That is, would $(4, 4)$ make both equations true? Why or why not?

COMMON CORE™	**Lesson 25:** Geometric Interpretation of the Solutions of a Linear System **Date:** 11/6/13

S.146

2. Graph the linear system on a coordinate plane: $\begin{cases} x + y = -2 \\ y = 4x + 3 \end{cases}$.

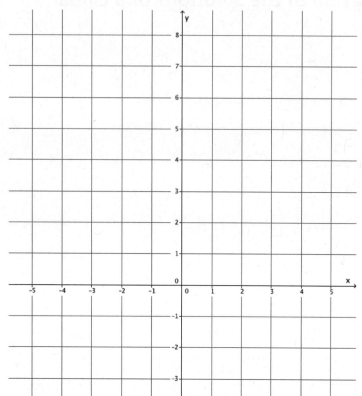

a. Name the ordered pair where the graphs of the two linear equations intersect.

b. Verify that the ordered pair named in (a) is a solution to $x + y = -2$.

c. Verify that the ordered pair named in (a) is a solution to $y = 4x + 3$.

d. Could the point $(-4, 2)$ be a solution to the system of linear equations? That is, would $(-4, 2)$ make both equations true? Why or why not?

3. Graph the linear system on a coordinate plane: $\begin{cases} 3x + y = -3 \\ -2x + y = 2 \end{cases}$.

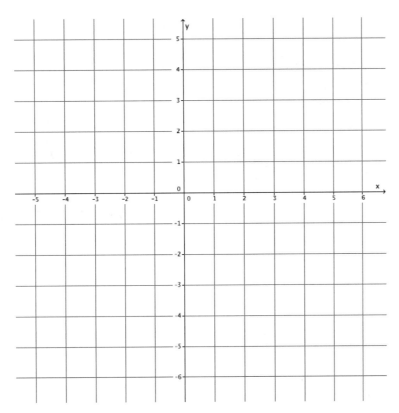

a. Name the ordered pair where the graphs of the two linear equations intersect.

b. Verify that the ordered pair named in (a) is a solution to $3x + y = -3$.

c. Verify that the ordered pair named in (a) is a solution to $-2x + y = 2$.

d. Could the point $(1, 4)$ be a solution to the system of linear equations? That is, would $(1, 4)$ make both equations true? Why or why not?

4. Graph the linear system on a coordinate plane: $\begin{cases} 2x - 3y = 18 \\ 2x + y = 2 \end{cases}$.

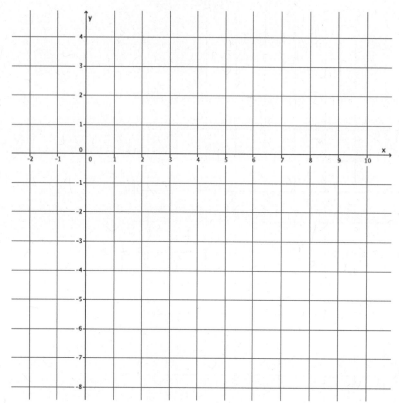

a. Name the ordered pair where the graphs of the two linear equations intersect.

b. Verify that the ordered pair named in (a) is a solution to $2x - 3y = 18$.

c. Verify that the ordered pair named in (a) is a solution to $2x + y = 2$.

d. Could the point $(3, -1)$ be a solution to the system of linear equations? That is, would $(3, -1)$ make both equations true? Why or why not?

5. Graph the linear system on a coordinate plane: $\begin{cases} y - x = 3 \\ y = -4x - 2 \end{cases}$.

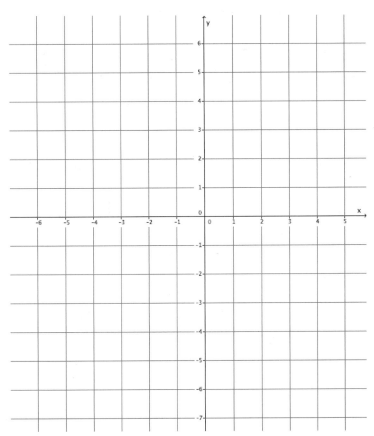

a. Name the ordered pair where the graphs of the two linear equations intersect.

b. Verify that the ordered pair named in (a) is a solution to $y - x = 3$.

c. Verify that the ordered pair named in (a) is a solution to $y = -4x - 2$.

d. Could the point $(-2, 6)$ be a solution to the system of linear equations? That is, would $(-2, 6)$ make both equations true? Why or why not?

6. Write two different systems of equations with $(1, -2)$ as the solution.

Lesson Summary

When a system of linear equations is graphed, the point of intersection of the lines of the graph represents the solution to the system. Two distinct lines intersect at most at one point. The coordinates of that point (x, y) represent values that make both equations of the system true.

Example: The system $\begin{cases} x + y = 3 \\ x - y = 5 \end{cases}$ graphs as shown below.

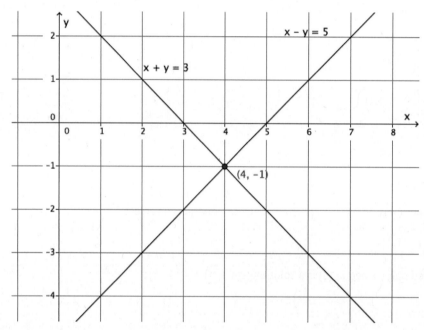

The graphs of the lines intersect at $(4, -1)$. That means the equations in the system are true when $x = 4$ and $y = -1$:

$$x + y = 3$$
$$4 + (-1) = 3$$
$$3 = 3$$

$$x - y = 5$$
$$4 - (-1) = 5$$
$$5 = 5$$

Problem Set

1. Graph the linear system on a coordinate plane: $\begin{cases} y = \frac{1}{3}x + 1 \\ y = -3x + 11 \end{cases}$.

   a. Name the ordered pair where the graphs of the two linear equations intersect.

   b. Verify that the ordered pair named in (a) is a solution to $y = \frac{1}{3}x + 1$.

   c. Verify that the ordered pair named in (a) is a solution to $y = -3x + 11$.

2. Graph the linear system on a coordinate plane: $\begin{cases} y = \frac{1}{2}x + 4 \\ x + 4y = 4 \end{cases}$.

   a. Name the ordered pair where the graphs of the two linear equations intersect.

   b. Verify that the ordered pair named in (a) is a solution to $y = \frac{1}{2}x + 4$.

   c. Verify that the ordered pair named in (a) is a solution to $x + 4y = 4$.

3. Graph the linear system on a coordinate plane: $\begin{cases} y = 2 \\ x + 2y = 10 \end{cases}$.

   a. Name the ordered pair where the graphs of the two linear equations intersect.

   b. Verify that the ordered pair named in (a) is a solution to $y = 2$.

   c. Verify that the ordered pair named in (a) is a solution to $x + 2y = 10$.

4. Graph the linear system on a coordinate plane: $\begin{cases} -2x + 3y = 18 \\ 2x + 3y = 6 \end{cases}$.

   a. Name the ordered pair where the graphs of the two linear equations intersect.

   b. Verify that the ordered pair named in (a) is a solution to $-2x + 3y = 18$.

   c. Verify that the ordered pair named in (a) is a solution to $2x + 3y = 6$.

5. Graph the linear system on a coordinate plane: $\begin{cases} x + 2y = 2 \\ y = \frac{2}{3}x - 6 \end{cases}$.

   a. Name the ordered pair where the graphs of the two linear equations intersect.

   b. Verify that the ordered pair named in (a) is a solution to $x + 2y = 2$.

   c. Verify that the ordered pair named in (a) is a solution to $y = \frac{2}{3}x - 6$.

6. Without graphing, name the ordered pair where the graphs of the two linear equations intersect.

$$\begin{cases} x = 2 \\ y = -3 \end{cases}$$

Lesson 25:	Geometric Interpretation of the Solutions of a Linear System	**S.152**
Date:	11/6/13	

Lesson 26: Characterization of Parallel Lines

Exercises

1. Graph the system: $\begin{cases} y = \dfrac{2}{3}x + 4 \\ y = \dfrac{4}{6}x - 3 \end{cases}$.

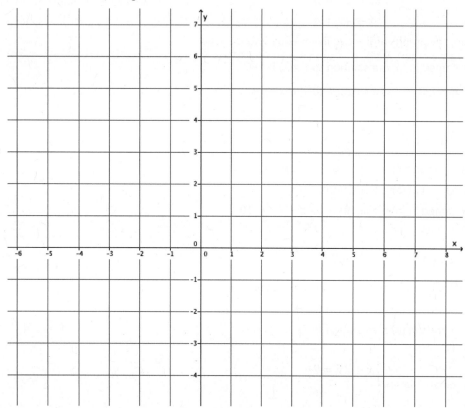

a. Identify the slope of each equation. What do you notice?

b. Identify the y-intercept of each equation. Are the y-intercepts the same or different?

---

2.   Graph the system: $\begin{cases} y = -\dfrac{5}{4}x + 7 \\ y = -\dfrac{5}{4}x + 2 \end{cases}$.

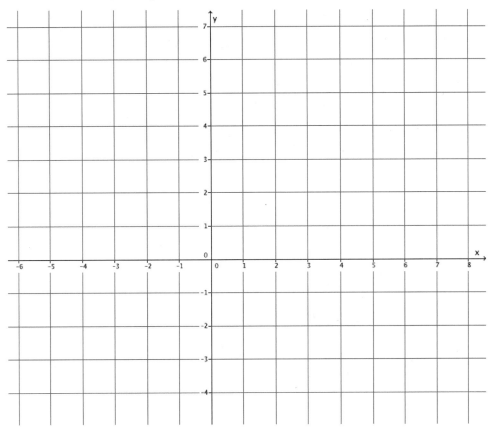

a.   Identify the slope of each equation. What do you notice?

b.   Identify the y-intercept of each equation. Are the y-intercepts the same or different?

Lesson 26:   Characterization of Parallel Lines
             Date: 11/6/13

3. Graph the system: $\begin{cases} y = 2x - 5 \\ y = 2x - 1 \end{cases}$.

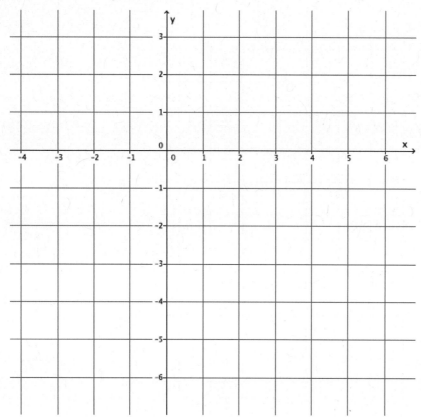

a. Identify the slope of each equation. What do you notice?

b. Identify the y-intercept of each equation. Are the y-intercepts the same or different?

4. Write a system of equations that has no solution.

5. Write a system of equations that has $(2, 1)$ as a solution.

6. How can you tell if a system of equations has a solution or not?

7. Does the system of linear equations shown below have a solution? Explain.
$$\begin{cases} 6x - 2y = 5 \\ 4x - 3y = 5 \end{cases}$$

8. Does the system of linear equations shown below have a solution? Explain.
$$\begin{cases} -2x + 8y = 14 \\ \quad x = 4y + 1 \end{cases}$$

9. Does the system of linear equations shown below have a solution? Explain.

$$\begin{cases} 12x + 3y = -2 \\ 4x + y = 7 \end{cases}$$

10. Genny babysits for two different families. One family pays her $6 each hour and a bonus of $20 at the end of the night. The other family pays her $3 every half hour and a bonus of $25 dollars at the end of the night. Write and solve the system of equations that represents this situation. At what number of hours do the two families pay the same for babysitting service from Genny?

Problem Set

1. Does the system of linear equations shown below have a solution? Explain.

$$\begin{cases} 2x + 5y = 9 \\ -4x - 10y = 4 \end{cases}$$

2. Does the system of linear equations shown below have a solution? Explain.

$$\begin{cases} \dfrac{3}{4}x - 3 = y \\ 4x - 3y = 5 \end{cases}$$

3. Does the system of linear equations shown below have a solution? Explain.

$$\begin{cases} x + 7y = 8 \\ 7x - y = -2 \end{cases}$$

4. Does the system of linear equations shown below have a solution? Explain.

$$\begin{cases} y = 5x + 12 \\ 10x - 2y = 1 \end{cases}$$

5. Does the system of linear equations shown below have a solution? Explain.

$$\begin{cases} y = \dfrac{5}{3}x + 15 \\ 5x - 3y = 6 \end{cases}$$

6. Given the graph of a system of linear equations below, is there a solution to the system that we cannot see on this portion of the coordinate plane? That is, will the lines intersect somewhere on the plane not represented in the picture? Explain.

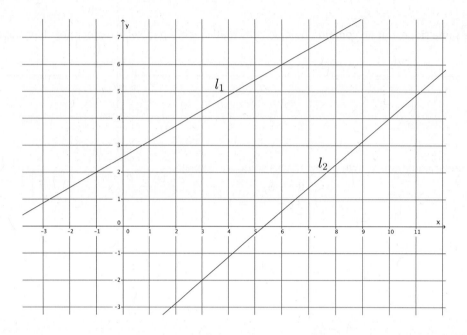

7. Given the graph of a system of linear equations below, is there a solution to the system that we cannot see on this portion of the coordinate plane? That is, will the lines intersect somewhere on the plane not represented in the picture? Explain.

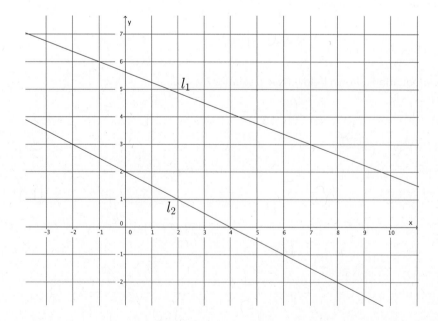

8. Given the graph of a system of linear equations below, is there a solution to the system that we cannot see on this portion of the coordinate plane? That is, will the lines intersect somewhere on the plane not represented in the picture? Explain.

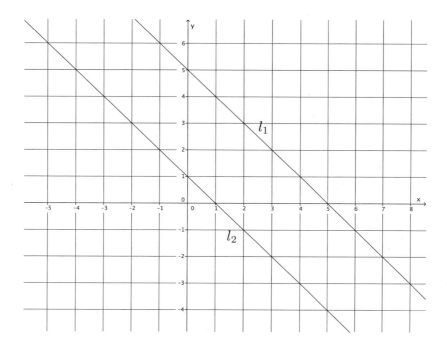

9. Given the graph of a system of linear equations below, is there a solution to the system that we cannot see on this portion of the coordinate plane? That is, will the lines intersect somewhere on the plane not represented in the picture? Explain.

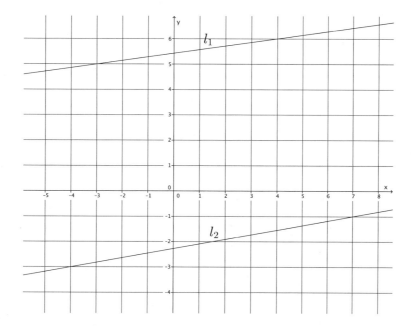

10. Given the graph of a system of linear equations below, is there a solution to the system that we cannot see on this portion of the coordinate plane? That is, will the lines intersect somewhere on the plane not represented in the picture? Explain.

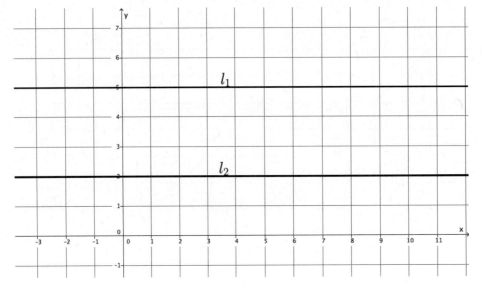

Lesson 27: Nature of Solutions of a System of Linear Equations

Exercise

Determine the nature of the solution to each system of linear equations.

1. $\begin{cases} 3x + 4y = 5 \\ y = -\dfrac{3}{4}x + 1 \end{cases}$

2. $\begin{cases} 7x + 2y = -4 \\ x - y = 5 \end{cases}$

3. $\begin{cases} 9x + 6y = 3 \\ 3x + 2y = 1 \end{cases}$

Determine the nature of the solution to each system of linear equations. If the system has a solution, find it algebraically; then, verify that your solution is correct by graphing.

4. $\begin{cases} 3x + 3y = -21 \\ x + y = -7 \end{cases}$

5. $\begin{cases} y = \frac{3}{2}x - 1 \\ 3y = x + 2 \end{cases}$

6. $\begin{cases} x = 12y - 4 \\ x = 9y + 7 \end{cases}$

7. Write a system of equations with $(4, -5)$ as its solution.

Lesson Summary

A system of linear equations can have a unique solution, no solutions, or infinitely many solutions.

Systems with a unique solution will be comprised of linear equations that have different slopes that graph as distinct lines, intersecting at only one point.

Systems with no solution will be comprised of linear equations that have the same slope that graph as parallel lines (no intersection).

Systems with infinitely many solutions will be comprised of linear equations that have the same slope and y-intercept that graph as the same line. When equations graph as the same line, every solution to one equation will also be a solution to the other equation.

A system of linear equations can be solved using a substitution method. That is, if two expressions are equal to the same value, then they can be written equal to one another.

Example:

$$\begin{cases} y = 5x - 8 \\ y = 6x + 3 \end{cases}$$

Since both equations in the system are equal to y, we can write the equation, $5x - 8 = 6x + 3$, and use it to solve for x and then the system.

Example:

$$\begin{cases} 3x = 4y + 2 \\ x = y + 5 \end{cases}$$

In this example, you can multiply each term of the equation $x = y + 5$ by 3 to produce the equivalent equation $3x = 3y + 15$. Now, as is the previous example, since both equations equal $3x$ we can write $4y + 2 = 3y + 15$, and use this equation to solve for y and then the system.

Problem Set

Determine the nature of the solution to each system of linear equations. If the system has a solution, find it algebraically; then, verify that your solution is correct by graphing.

1. $\begin{cases} y = \frac{3}{7}x - 8 \\ 3x - 7y = 1 \end{cases}$

2. $\begin{cases} 2x - 5 = y \\ -3x - 1 = 2y \end{cases}$

3. $\begin{cases} x = 6y + 7 \\ x = 10y + 2 \end{cases}$

COMMON CORE™

Lesson 27:   Nature of Solutions of a System of Linear Equations
Date: 11/6/13

S.165

4. $\begin{cases} 5y = \dfrac{15}{4}x + 25 \\ y = \dfrac{3}{4}x + 5 \end{cases}$

5. $\begin{cases} x + 9 = y \\ x = 4y - 6 \end{cases}$

6. $\begin{cases} 3y = 5x - 15 \\ 3y = 13x - 2 \end{cases}$

7. $\begin{cases} 6x - 7y = \dfrac{1}{2} \\ 12x - 14y = 1 \end{cases}$

8. $\begin{cases} 5x - 2y = 6 \\ -10x + 4y = -14 \end{cases}$

9. $\begin{cases} y = \dfrac{3}{2}x - 6 \\ 2y = 7 - 4x \end{cases}$

10. $\begin{cases} 7x - 10 = y \\ y = 5x + 12 \end{cases}$

11. Write a system of linear equations with $(-3, 9)$ as its solution.

Lesson 28: Another Computational Method of Solving a Linear System

Classwork

Example 1

Use what you noticed about adding equivalent expressions to solve the following system by elimination:

$$\begin{cases} 6x - 5y = 21 \\ 2x + 5y = -5 \end{cases}$$

Example 2

Solve the following system by elimination:

$$\begin{cases} -2x + 7y = 5 \\ 4x - 2y = 14 \end{cases}$$

Example 3

Solve the following system by elimination:

$$\begin{cases} 7x - 5y = -2 \\ 3x - 3y = 7 \end{cases}$$

Exercises

Each of the following systems has a solution. Determine the solution to the system by eliminating one of the variables. Verify the solution using the graph of the system.

1. $\begin{cases} 6x - 7y = -10 \\ 3x + 7y = -8 \end{cases}$

2. $\begin{cases} x - 4y = 7 \\ 5x + 9y = 6 \end{cases}$

3. $\begin{cases} 2x - 3y = -5 \\ 3x + 5y = 1 \end{cases}$

COMMON CORE

Lesson 28:   Another Computational Method of Solving a Linear System
Date: 11/8/13

S.169

Lesson Summary

Systems of linear equations can be solved by eliminating one of the variables from the system. One way to eliminate a variable is by setting both equations equal to the same variable, then writing the expressions equal to one another.

Example: Solve the system $\begin{cases} y = 3x - 4 \\ y = 2x + 1 \end{cases}$

Since both equation of the system are equal to y, then we can write and solve the equation:

$$3x - 4 = 2x + 1$$

Another way to eliminate a variable is by multiplying each term of an equation by the same constant to make an equivalent equation. Then use the equivalent equation to eliminate one of the variables and solve the system.

Example: Solve the system $\begin{cases} 2x + y = 8 \\ x + y = 10 \end{cases}$

Multiply the second equation by -2 to eliminate the x:

$$-2(x + y = 10)$$
$$-2x - 2y = -20$$

Now we have the system $\begin{cases} 2x + y = 8 \\ -2x - 2y = -20 \end{cases}$

When the equations are added together, the x is eliminated:

$$2x + y - 2x - 2y = 8 + (-20)$$
$$y - 2y = 8 + (-20)$$

Once a solution has been found, verify the solution graphically or by substitution.

Problem Set

Determine the solution, if it exists, for each system of linear equations. Verify your solution on the coordinate plane.

1. $\begin{cases} \frac{1}{2}x + 5 = y \\ 2x + y = 1 \end{cases}$

2. $\begin{cases} 9x + 2y = 9 \\ -3x + y = 2 \end{cases}$

3. $\begin{cases} y = 2x - 2 \\ 2y = 4x - 4 \end{cases}$

4. $\begin{cases} 8x + 5y = 19 \\ -8x + y = -1 \end{cases}$

5. $\begin{cases} x + 3 = y \\ 3x + 4y = 7 \end{cases}$

6. $\begin{cases} y = 3x + 2 \\ 4y = 12 + 12x \end{cases}$

7. $\begin{cases} 4x - 3y = 16 \\ -2x + 4y = -2 \end{cases}$

8. $\begin{cases} 2x + 2y = 4 \\ 12 - 3x = 3y \end{cases}$

9. $\begin{cases} y = -2x + 6 \\ 3y = x - 3 \end{cases}$

10. $\begin{cases} y = 5x - 1 \\ 10x = 2y + 2 \end{cases}$

11. $\begin{cases} 3x - 5y = 17 \\ 6x + 5y = 10 \end{cases}$

12. $\begin{cases} y = \frac{4}{3}x - 9 \\ y = x + 3 \end{cases}$

13. $\begin{cases} 4x - 7y = 11 \\ x + 2y = 10 \end{cases}$

14. $\begin{cases} 21x + 14y = 7 \\ 12x + 8y = 16 \end{cases}$

Lesson 29: Word Problems

Example 1

The sum of two numbers is 361 and the difference between the two numbers is 173. What are the two numbers?

Example 2

There are 356 Grade 8 students at Euclid's Middle School. Thirty-four more than four times the number of girls is equal to half the number of boys. How many boys are in Grade 8 at Euclid's Middle School? How many girls?

Example 3

A family member has some five-dollar bills and one-dollar bills in their wallet. Altogether she has 18 bills and a total of $62. How many of each bill does she have?

Example 4

A friend bought 2 boxes of pencils and 8 notebooks for school and it cost him $11. He went back to the store the same day to buy school supplies for his younger brother. He spent $11.25 on 3 boxes of pencils and 5 notebooks. How much would 7 notebooks cost?

Exercises

1. A farm raises cows and chickens. The farmer has a total of 42 animals. One day he counts the legs of all of his animals and realizes he has a total of 114. How many cows does the farmer have? How many chickens?

2. The length of a rectangle is 4 times the width. The perimeter of the rectangle is 45 inches. What is the area of the rectangle?

3. The sum of the measures of angles x and y is 127°. If the measure of $\angle x$ is 34° more than half the measure of $\angle y$, what is the measure of each angle?

Problem Set

1. Two numbers have a sum of 1,212 and a difference of 518. What are the two numbers?

2. The sum of the ages of two brothers is 46. The younger brother is 10 more than a third of the older brothers age. How old is the younger brother?

3. One angle measures 54 more than 3 times another angle. The angles are supplementary. What are their measures?

4. Some friends went to the local movie theatre and bought four buckets of large popcorn and six boxes of candy. The total for the snacks was $46.50. The last time you were at the theatre you bought a large popcorn and a box of candy and the total was $9.75. How much would 2 large buckets of popcorn and 3 boxes of candy cost?

5. You have 59 total coins for a total of $12.05. You only have quarters and dimes. How many of each coin do you have?

6. A piece of string is 112 inches long. Isabel wants to cut it into 2 pieces so that one piece is three times as long as the other. How long is each piece?

Lesson 30: Conversion Between Celsius and Fahrenheit

Classwork

(1)   If t is a number, what is the degree in Fahrenheit that corresponds to $t°C$?

(2)   If t is a number, what is the degree in Fahrenheit that corresponds to $(-t)°C$?

Exercises

Determine the corresponding Fahrenheit temperate for the given Celsius temperatures in Exercises 1–5.

1. How many degrees Fahrenheit is $25°C$?

2. How many degrees Fahrenheit is $42°C$?

3. How many degrees Fahrenheit is $94°C$?

4. How many degrees Fahrenheit is $63°C$?

5. How many degrees Fahrenheit is $t°C$?

Problem Set

1. Does the equation, $t°C = (32 + 1.8t)°F$, work for any rational number t? Check that is does with $t = 8\frac{2}{3}$ and $t = -8\frac{2}{3}$.

2. Knowing that $t°C = \left(32 + \frac{9}{5}t\right)°F$ for any rational t, show that for any rational number d, $d°F = \left(\frac{5}{9}(d - 32)\right)°C$.

3. Drake was trying to write an equation to help him predict the cost of his monthly phone bill. He is charged \$35 just for having a phone, and his only additional expense comes from the number of texts that he sends. He is charged \$0.05 for each text. Help Drake out by completing parts (a)–(f).

   a. How much was his phone bill in July when he sent 750 texts?

   b. How much was his phone bill in August when he sent 823 texts?

   c. How much was his phone bill in September when he sent 579 texts?

   d. Let y represent the total cost of Drake's phone bill. Write an equation that represents the total cost of his phone bill in October if he sends t texts.

   e. Another phone plan charges \$20 for having a phone and \$0.10 per text. Let y represent the total cost of the phone bill for sending t texts. Write an equation to represent his total bill.

   f. Write your equations in parts (d) and (e) as a system of linear equations and solve. Interpret the meaning of the solution in terms of the phone bill.

Copy Ready Materials

Name _____   Date_____

Lesson 1: Writing Equations Using Symbols

Exit Ticket

Write each of the following statements using symbolic language.

1. When you square five times a number you get three more than the number.

2. Monica had some cookies. She gave seven to her sister. Then, she divided the remainder in half, and she still had five cookies.

Name _____   Date_____

Lesson 2: Linear and Non-Linear Expressions in x

Exit Ticket

Write each of the following statements as a mathematic expression. State whether the expression is a linear or non-linear expression in x.

1.   Seven subtracted from five times a number, then the difference added to nine times a number.

2.   Three times a number subtracted from the product of fifteen and the reciprocal of a number.

3.   Half of the sum of two and a number multiplied by itself three times.

Name _____   Date_____

Lesson 3: Linear Equations in x

Exit Ticket

1. Is 8 a solution to $\frac{1}{2}x + 9 = 13$? Explain.

2. Write three different equations that have $x = 5$ as a solution.

3. Is -3 a solution to the equation $3x - 5 = 4 + 2x$? Explain.

Name _____   Date_____

Lesson 4: Solving a Linear Equation

Exit Ticket

1. Guess a number for x that would make the equation true. Check your solution.

$$5x - 2 = 8$$

2. Use the properties of equality to solve the equation: $7x - 4 + x = 12$. State which property justifies your first step and why you chose it. Check your solution.

3. Use the properties of equality to solve the equation: $3x + 2 - x = 11x + 9$. State which property justifies your first step and why you chose it. Check your solution.

Name _____   Date _____

Lesson 5: Writing and Solving Linear Equations

Exit Ticket

For each of the following problems, write an equation and solve.

1. Given a right triangle, find the measures of all the angles if one angle is a right angle and the measure of the second angle is six less than seven times the measure of the third angle.

2. In a triangle, the measure of the first angle is six times a number. The measure of the second angle is nine less than the first angle. The measure of the third angle is three times the number more than the measure of the first angle. Determine the measures of each of the angles.

Name _____   Date _____

Lesson 6: Solutions of a Linear Equation

Exit Ticket

Transform the equation if necessary, then solve to find the value of x that makes the equation true.

1. $5x - (x + 3) = \frac{1}{3}(9x + 18) - 5$

2. $5(3x + 9) - 2x = 15x - 2(x - 5)$

Name _____   Date _____

Lesson 7: Classification of Solutions

Exit Ticket

Give a brief explanation as to what kind of solution(s) you expect the following linear equations to have. Transform the equation into a simpler form if necessary.

1. $3(6x + 8) = 24 + 18x$

2. $12(x + 8) = 11x - 5$

3. $5x - 8 = 11 - 7x + 12x$

COMMON CORE

Lesson 7:   Classification of Solutions
Date: 11/8/13

Lesson 7   8•4

© 2013 Common Core, Inc. All rights reserved. **commoncore.org**

Name _____   Date _____

Lesson 8: Linear Equations in Disguise

Exit Ticket

Solve the following equations for x.

1. $\dfrac{5x-8}{3} = \dfrac{11x-9}{5}$

2. $\dfrac{x+11}{7} = \dfrac{2x+1}{-8}$

3. $\dfrac{-x-2}{-4} = \dfrac{3x+6}{2}$

Name _____   Date _____

Lesson 9: An Application of Linear Equations

Exit Ticket

1. Rewrite the equation that would represent the fifth step of the Facebook problem:

$$S_5 = 7 + 7 \cdot 5 + 7 \cdot 5^2 + 7 \cdot 5^3 + 7 \cdot 5^4$$

2. The sum of four consecutive integers is 74. Write an equation and solve to find the numbers?

Name _____   Date _____

Lesson 10: A Critical Look at Proportional Relationships

Exit Ticket

1. Alex skateboards at a constant speed from his house to school 3.8 miles away. It takes him 18 minutes.

    a. What fraction represents his constant speed, C?

    b. After school, Alex skateboards at the same constant speed to his friend's house. It takes him 10 minutes.
        Write the fraction that represents constant speed, C, if he travels a distance of y.

    c. Write the fractions from part (a) and (b) as a proportion, and solve to find out how many miles Alex's friend's
        house is from school. Round your answer to the tenths place.

Name _____   Date _____

Lesson 11: Constant Rate

Exit Ticket

1. Vicky reads at a constant rate. She can read 5 pages in 9 minutes. We want to know how many pages, p, Vicky can read after t minutes.

    a. Write a linear equation in two variables that represents the number of pages Vicky reads in any given time interval.

    b. Complete the table below. Use a calculator and round answers to the tenths place.

(time in minutes)	Linear equation:	(pages read)
0		
20		
40		
60		

    c. About how long would it take Vicky to read 25 pages? Explain.

Lesson 11:	Constant Rate
Date:	11/8/13

Name _____   Date _____

Lesson 12: Linear Equations in Two Variables

Exit Ticket

1. Is the point $(1, 3)$ a solution to the linear equation $5x - 9y = 32$? Explain.

2. Find three solutions for the linear equation $4x - 3y = 1$, and plot the solutions as points on a coordinate plane.

x	Linear equation: $4x - 3y = 1$	y

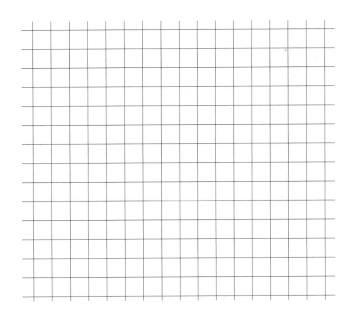

Name _____   Date _____

Lesson 13: The Graph of a Linear Equation in Two Variables

Exit Ticket

1. Ethan found solutions to the linear equation $3x - y = 8$ and graphed them. What shape is the graph of the linear equation taking?

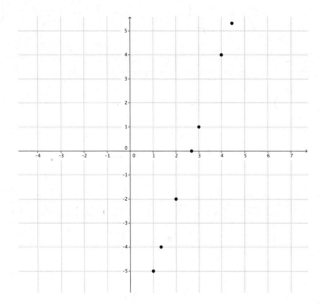

2. Could the following be the graph of $-x + 2y = 5$?

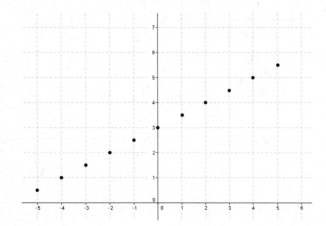

Name _____   Date _____

Lesson 14: Graph of a Linear Equation—Horizontal and Vertical Lines

Exit Ticket

1. Graph the linear equation $ax + by = c$ where $a = 0$, $b = 1$, and $c = 1.5$.

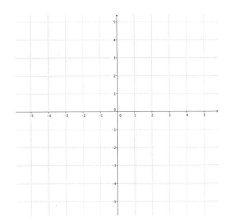

2. Graph the linear equation $ax + by = c$, where $a = 1$, $b = 0$, and $c = -\dfrac{5}{2}$.

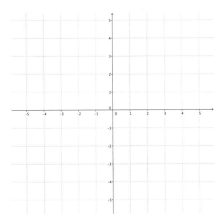

3. What linear equation represents the graph of the line that coincides with the x-axis?

4. What linear equation represents the graph of the line that coincides with the y-axis?

Name _____ Date _____

1. Write and solve each of the following linear equations.

   a. Ofelia has a certain amount of money. If she spends \$12, then she has $\frac{1}{5}$ of the original amount left. How much money did Ofelia have originally?

   b. Three consecutive integers have a sum of 234. What are the three integers?

   c. Gil is reading a book that has 276 pages. He has already read some of it last week. He plans to read 20 pages tomorrow. By then, he will be $\frac{2}{3}$ of the way through the book. How many pages did Gil read last week?

Module 4:	Linear Equations
Date:	11/8/13

2. a. Without solving, identify which of the following equations has a unique solution, no solution, or infinitely many solutions.

$$3x + 5 = -2$$

$$6(x - 11) = 15 - 4x$$

$$12x + 9 = 8x + 1 + 4x$$

$$2(x - 3) = 10x - 6 - 8x$$

$$5x + 6 = 5x - 4$$

b. Solve the following equation for a number x. Verify that your solution is correct.

$$-15 = 8x + 1$$

c. Solve the following equation for a number x. Verify that your solution is correct.

$$7(2x + 5) = 4x - 9 - x$$

3. a. Parker paid $4.50 for three pounds of gummy candy. Assuming each pound of gummy candy costs the same amount, complete the table of values representing the cost of gummy candy in pounds.

Gummy Candy in pounds (x)	1	2	3	4	5	6	7	8	9
Cost (y)			$4.50						

b. Graph the data on the coordinate plane.

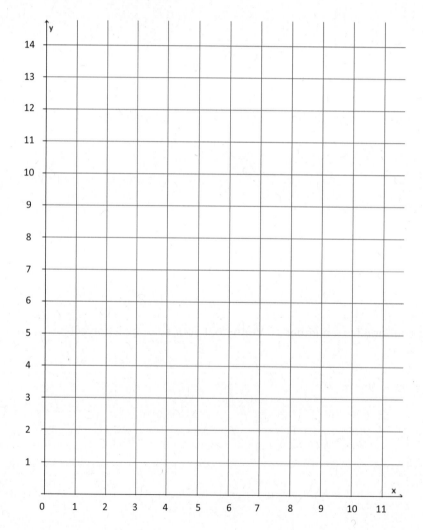

c.   On the same day, Parker's friend Peggy was charged $5 for $1\frac{1}{2}$ lb. of gummy candy. Explain in terms of the graph why this must be a mistake.

Name _____   Date _____

Lesson 15: The Slope of a Non-Vertical Line

Exit Ticket

1. What is the slope of this non-vertical line? Use your transparency if needed.

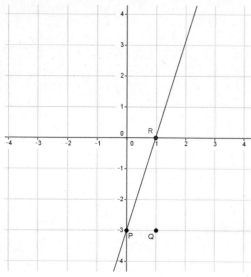

2. What is the slope of this non-vertical line? Use your transparency if needed.

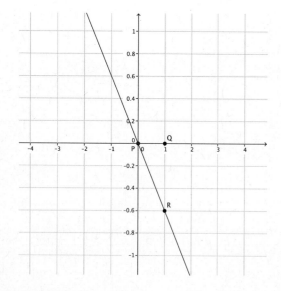

Name _____   Date _____

Lesson 16: The Computation of the Slope of a Non-Vertical Line

Exit Ticket

1.   Find the rate of change of the line by completing parts (a) and (b).

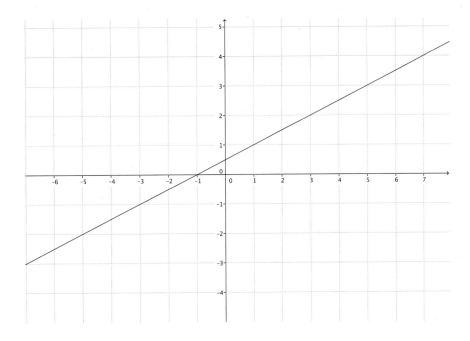

    a.   Select any two points on the line to label as P and R. Name their coordinates.

    b.   Compute the rate of change of the line.

Name _____   Date _____

Lesson 17: The Line Joining Two Distinct Points of the Graph $y = mx + b$ has Slope m

Exit Ticket

1. Solve the following equation for y: $35x - 7y = 49$.

2. What is the slope of the equation in problem 1?

3. Show, using similar triangles, why the graph of an equation of the form $y = mx$ is a line with slope m.

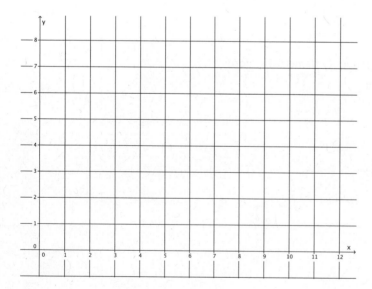

Name _____   Date _____

Lesson 18: There is Only One Line Passing Through a Given Point with a Given Slope

Exit Ticket

Mrs. Hodson said that the graphs of the equations below are incorrect. Find the student's errors and correctly graph the equations.

1. Student graph of $y = \frac{1}{2}x + 4$. 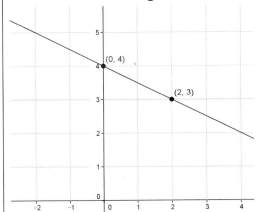	Error: Correct graph of equation: 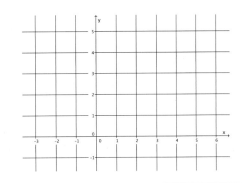
2. Student graph of $y = -\frac{3}{5}x - 1$. 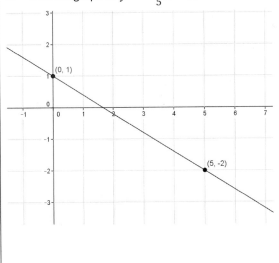	Error: Correct graph of equation: 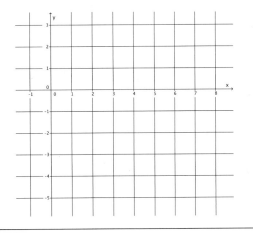

Name _____ Date _____

Lesson 19: The Graph of a Linear Equation in Two Variables is a Line

Exit Ticket

1. Graph the equation $y = \frac{5}{4}x - 10$ using the y-intercept and slope.

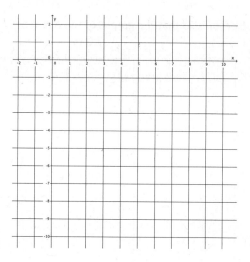

2. Graph the equation $5x - 4y = 40$ using intercepts.

3. What can you conclude about the equations $y = \frac{5}{4}x - 10$ and $5x - 4y = 40$?

Name _____   Date _____

Lesson 20: Every Line is a Graph of a Linear Equation

Exit Ticket

1. Write an equation in slope intercept form that represents the line shown.

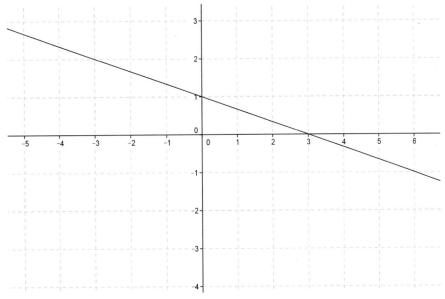

2. Use the properties of equality to change the equation you wrote for problem 1 from slope intercept form, $y = mx + b$, to standard form, $ax + by = c$, where a, b, and c are integers and a is not negative.

3.   Write an equation in slope intercept form that represents the line shown.

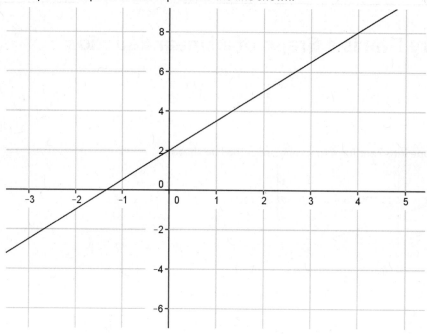

4.   Use the properties of equality to change the equation you wrote for problem 3 from slope intercept form, $y = mx + b$, to standard form, $ax + by = c$, where a, b, and c are integers and a is not negative.

Name _____   Date _____

Lesson 21: Some Facts about Graphs of Linear Equations in Two Variables

1.   Write the equation for the line l shown in the graph below.

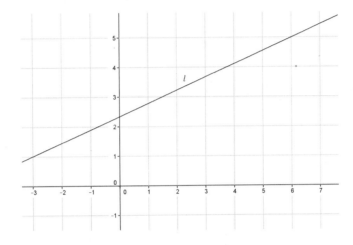

2.   A line goes through the point $(5, -7)$ and has slope $m = -3$. Write the equation that represents the line.

Name _____   Date _____

Lesson 22: Constant Rates Revisited

Exit Ticket

1.   Water flows out of Pipe A at a constant rate. Pipe A can fill 3 buckets of the same size in 14 minutes.
   a.   Write a linear equation that represents the situation.

The graph below represents the rate at which Pipe B can fill the same sized buckets.

   b.   Which pipe fills buckets faster? Explain.

Name _____   Date _____

Lesson 23: The Defining Equation of a Line

Exit Ticket

1. Do the equations $-16x + 12y = 33$ and $-4x + 3y = 8$ graph as the same line? Why or why not?

2. Given the equation $3x - y = 11$, write another equation that will graph as the same line. Explain why.

Name _____   Date _____

Lesson 24: Introduction to Simultaneous Equations

Exit Ticket

1. Darnell and Hector ride their bikes at constant speeds. Darnell leaves Hector's house to bike home. He can bike the 8 miles in 32 minutes. Five minutes after Darnell leaves, Hector realizes that Darnell left his phone. Hector rides to catch up. He can ride to Darnell's house in 24 minutes. Assuming they bike the same path, will Hector catch up to Darnell before he gets home?

    a. Write the linear equation that represents Darnell's constant speed.

    b. Write the linear equation that represents Hector's constant speed. Make sure to take into account that Hector left after Darnell.

    c. Write the system of linear equations that represents this situation.

d.   Sketch the graph.

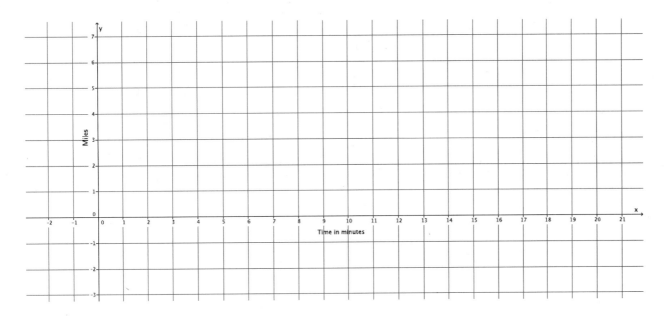

e.   Will Hector catch up to Darnell before he gets home? If so, approximately when?

f.   At approximately what point do the graphs of the lines intersect?

Name _____   Date _____

Lesson 25: Geometric Interpretation of the Solutions of a Linear System

Exit Ticket

1. Graph the linear system on a coordinate plane: $\begin{cases} 2x - y = -1 \\ y = 5x - 5 \end{cases}$.

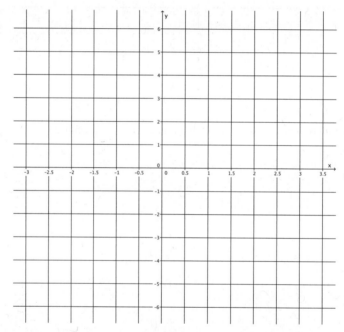

a.   Name the ordered pair where the graphs of the two linear equations intersect.

b.   Verify that the ordered pair named in (a) is a solution to $2x - y = -1$.

c.   Verify that the ordered pair named in (a) is a solution to $y = 5x - 5$.

Name _____ Date _____

Lesson 26: Characterization of Parallel Lines

Does each system of linear equations have a solution? Explain your answer.

1. $\begin{cases} y = \frac{5}{4}x - 3 \\ y + 2 = \frac{5}{4}x \end{cases}$

2. $\begin{cases} y = \frac{2}{3}x - 5 \\ 4x - 8y = 11 \end{cases}$

3. $\begin{cases} \frac{1}{3}x + y = 8 \\ x + 3y = 12 \end{cases}$

Name _____   Date _____

Lesson 27: Nature of Solutions of a System of Linear Equations

Exit Ticket

Determine the nature of the solution to each system of linear equations. If the system has a solution, then find it without graphing.

1. $\begin{cases} y = \frac{1}{2}x + \frac{5}{2} \\ x - 2y = 7 \end{cases}$

2. $\begin{cases} y = \frac{2}{3}x + 4 \\ 2y + \frac{1}{2}x = 2 \end{cases}$

3. $\begin{cases} y = 3x - 2 \\ -3x + y = -2 \end{cases}$

Name _____ Date _____

Lesson 28: Another Computational Method of Solving a Linear System

Exit Ticket

Determine the solution, if it exists, for each system of linear equations. Verify your solution on the coordinate plane.

1. $\begin{cases} y = 3x - 5 \\ y = -3x + 7 \end{cases}$

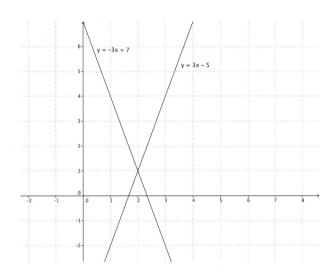

2. $\begin{cases} y = -4x + 6 \\ 2x - y = 11 \end{cases}$

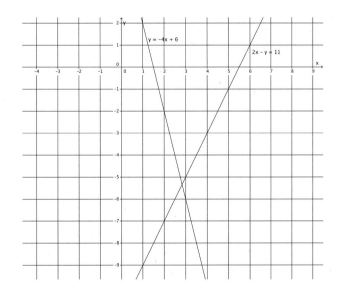

Name _____   Date _____

Lesson 29: Word Problems

Exit Ticket

1. Small boxes contain DVDs and large boxes contain one gaming machine. Three boxes of gaming machines and a box of DVDs weigh 48 pounds. Three boxes of gaming machines and five boxes of DVDs weigh 72 pounds. How much does each box weigh?

2. A language arts test is worth 100 points. There are a total of 26 questions. There are spelling word questions that are worth 2 points each and vocabulary word questions worth 5 points each. How many of each type of question is there?

Name _____   Date _____

Lesson 30: Conversion between Celsius and Fahrenheit

Exit Ticket

Use the equation developed in class to answer the following questions:

1. How many degrees Fahrenheit is $11°C$?

2. How many degrees Fahrenheit is $-3°C$?

3. Graph the equation developed in class and use it to confirm your results from Questions 1 and 2.

Name _____   Date _____

Lesson 31: System of Equations Leading to Pythagorean Triples

Exit Ticket

Use a calculator to complete problems 1–3.

1.   Is 7, 20, 21 a Pythagorean triple? Is $1, \dfrac{15}{8}, \dfrac{17}{8}$ a Pythagorean triple? Explain.

2.   Identify two Pythagorean triples using the known triple 9, 40, 41.

3.   Use the system $\begin{cases} x + y = \dfrac{t}{s} \\ x - y = \dfrac{s}{t} \end{cases}$ to find Pythagorean triples for the given values of $s = 2$ and $t = 3$. Recall that the

solution, in the form of $\left(\dfrac{c}{b}, \dfrac{a}{b} \right)$, is the triple, a, b, c. Verify your results.

Name _____ Date _____

1. Use the graph below to answer parts (a)–(c).

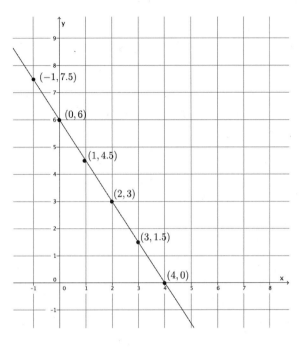

a. Use any pair of points to calculate the slope of the line.

b. Use a different pair of points to calculate the slope of the line.

c. Explain why the slopes you calculated in parts (a) and (b) are equal.

2. Jeremy rides his bike at a rate of 12 miles per hour. Below is a table that represents the number of hours and miles Kevin rides. Assume both bikers ride at a constant rate.

Time in hours (x)	Distance in miles (y)
1.5	17.25
2	23
3.5	40.25
4	46

a. Which biker rides at a greater speed? Explain your reasoning.

b. Write an equation for a third biker, Lauren, who rides twice as fast as Kevin. Use y to represent the number of miles Lauren travels in x hours. Explain your reasoning.

c.   Create a graph of the equation in part (b).

d.   Calculate the slope of the line in part (c) and interpret its meaning in this situation.

3. The cost of five protractors is $14.95 at Store A. The graph below compares the cost of protractors at Store A with the cost at Store B.

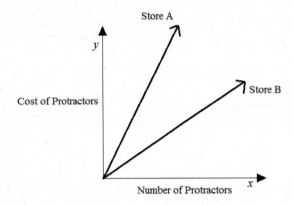

Estimate the cost of one protractor at Store B. Use evidence from the graph to justify your answer.

4. Given the equation, $3x + 9y = -8$, write a second linear equation to create a system that:

    a. Has exactly one solution. Explain your reasoning.

    b. Has no solution. Explain your reasoning.

    c. Has infinitely many solutions. Explain your reasoning.

    d. Interpret the meaning of the solution, if it exists, in the context of the graph of the following system of equations.

$$\begin{cases} -5x + 2y = 10 \\ 10x - 4y = -20 \end{cases}$$

5. Students sold 275 tickets for a fundraiser at school. Some tickets are for children and cost $3, while the rest are adult tickets that cost $5. If the total value of all tickets sold was $1,025, how many of each type of ticket was sold?

6. a. Determine the equation of the line connecting the points $(0, -1)$ and $(2,3)$.

    b. Will the line described by the equation in (a) intersect the line passing through the points $(-2,4)$ and $(-3,3)$? Explain why or why not.

7. Line l_1 and line l_2 are shown on the graph below. Use the graph to answer parts (a)–(d).

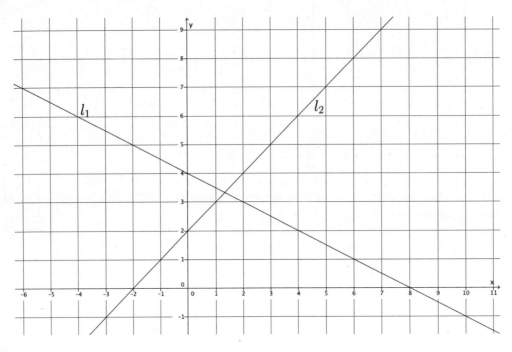

a. What is the y-intercept of l_1?

b. What is the y-intercept of l_2?

c. Write a system of linear equations representing lines l_1 and l_2.

d. Use the graph to estimate the solution to the system.

e. Solve the system of linear equations algebraically.

f. Show that your solution from part (e) satisfies both equations.

Module 4:   Linear Equations
Date: 11/8/13